Pitt Latin American Series

D1608109

THE MEANING OF
Freedom

ECONOMICS, POLITICS, AND CULTURE AFTER SLAVERY

Frank McGlynn and Seymour Drescher, Editors

University of Pittsburgh Press
Pittsburgh and London

Published by the University of Pittsburgh Press, Pittsburgh, Pa., 15260
Copyright © 1992, University of Pittsburgh Press

Eurospan, London
Manufactured in the United States of America

LIBRARY OF CONGRESS CATALOGING-IN-PUBLICATION DATA

The meaning of freedom : economics, politics, and culture after
slavery / Frank McGlynn and Seymour Drescher, editors.
     p.   cm. — (Pitt Latin American series)
    Includes bibliographical references.
    ISBN 0-8229-3695-X
    1. Freedmen.   2. Afro-Americans—History—1863–1867.   3. Blacks—
Caribbean Area—History—19th century.   4. Slaves—United States—
Emancipation.   5. Slaves—Caribbean Area—Emancipation.
I. McGlynn, Frank. (Frank S.)   II. Drescher, Seymour.   III. Series.
E185.2.M43   1992
973'.0496—dc20   91-26606
                                              CIP

A CIP catalogue record for this book is available from the British Library.

7   ISBN 0-8229-5479-6 (PBK)

CONTENTS

PREFACE

Credit and gratitude is extended to all who generously gave of their insights and efforts in the furthering of scientific research. This collection of essays is the outcome of an international conference on the dynamics of postslavery societies in the New World. The meeting was held at the University of Pittsburgh at the Greensburg and Pittsburgh campuses on 25–27 August 1988, under the direction of Frank McGlynn and coordinated by Gerry Enlow. Our first gesture of gratitude goes to Ms. Enlow, who besides being a model of efficiency and planning was a source of morale and good humor and, as all participants attest, proved to be a supportive friend.

In addition to the contributors to the present volume, the editors are deeply indebted to the other participants and commentators at the multidisciplinary conference: George Reid Andrews, Richard Blackett, Rosemary Brana-Shute, Dennis Brutus, Sidney Chaloub, Lambros Comitas, Robert W. Fogel, Elizabeth Fox-Genovese, Larry Glasco, William Green, Gad Heuman, Thomas Holt, Herbert Klein, Magnus Morner, David Nicholls, Nell Painter, Robert L. Paquette, Rebecca Scott, I. K. Sundiata, Arthur Tuden, Rollo Turner, Emilia Viotti da Costa, and James Walvin. Four commentators generously expanded their initial remarks into full essays: Pieter Emmer, Stanley Engerman, Sidney Mintz, and Raymond Smith.

We are grateful for the support of the following departments at the University of Pittsburgh: anthropology, black community, education, research and development, and history; the Center for Latin American Studies and the University Center for International Studies; the Office of Research; the president of the Greensburg campus; and the Rockefeller Foundation's Bellagio Study Center. Generous support was also provided by the Wenner-Gren Foundation for Anthropological Research, the Pennsylvania Ethnic Heritage Center, and the Research Institute for the Study of Man. The Pittsburgh Center for Social History cosponsored and supported the entire project.

We should like to add a special note of thanks to Provost Donald Henderson, whose support and encouragement of this project never

waned. Thanks are also extended to Burkhart Holzner, director for the
Center for International Studies of the University of Pittsburgh, whose
advice and encouragement was always timely and decisive, and to Associate Provost James Hunter, who was always there when needed.

The Greensburg campus of the university earned the appreciation
of all the participants by hosting the conference with such high standards of hospitality. Dr. George Chambers, Greensburg campus president, supported this project from its inception, backed by Dr. Guy
Rossetti, dean of administration, and his staff.

THE MEANING OF
Freedom

SEYMOUR DRESCHER AND
FRANK MCGLYNN

Introduction

The growth of an Atlantic slave system was one of the most distinctive characteristics of Western development during the three centuries following Columbus's voyages. By the end of the eighteenth century, every European state bordering the Atlantic and many further eastward had attempted to secure a foothold on the African coast or in the Americas. At this peak of dynamic growth and seemingly unbounded potential, a remarkable reversal began. In one society after another, the Atlantic slave trade and the institution of chattel slavery were constricted and destroyed. The process was uneven and contradictory, punctuated by legal closures and revolutionary upheavals in some areas and by unprecedented expansion in others. In the 1780s, some of the northern states of the United States began to abolish or dismantle the slave system. The same decade witnessed the launching of the first mass abolitionist movement against the African slave trade in England and the founding of antislavery societies in the United States and France.

Three generations were required to finally close down the entire transatlantic slave trade. Slave emancipation in the plantation zone of the Americas began in 1791 with a mass slave uprising in St. Domingue and ended with the passage of Brazil's Golden Law almost a century later, in 1888. This extraordinary dismantling of one of the most vigorous elements of the capitalist world economy has been a focus of enormous curiosity for almost two centuries, and scholarly interest in the dynamics of Atlantic slavery and its abolition has never been stronger. During the past decade the centenaries of the abolition process have occasioned frequent commemorative conferences. The year 1988 alone was a triple anniversary: the bicentenary of British popular abolitionism, the sesquicentenary of the termination of the British colonial apprenticeship system, and the centenary of slave emancipation in Brazil. Universities from Brazil to the United States sponsored conferences on the African slave trade and on emancipation and its aftermath in the New World.

A noteworthy aspect of most of these conferences was the increasing attention devoted by scholars, not to the process of abolition itself, but to the more prosaic theme of postemancipation development. This development was already noted earlier in the decade. In 1983 an international conference was held at Kingston-upon-Hull, England, to mark the one-hundred-fiftieth anniversary of the British Slave Emancipation Act of 1833. The keynote speaker drew attention to the extraordinary contrast between the focus of the sesquicentennial commemoration and that of the centennial events in the same city fifty years earlier (Drescher 1985).

In 1933, historians, in a celebratory mood, had focused almost exclusively upon abolition as an epic struggle of metropolitan saints and heroes. The colonial slaves themselves entered the story only at the moment of liberation, as they gathered on the West Indian hilltops at the dawn of emancipation day to receive the first rays of liberty from the east (Great Britain). The slaves entered and exited from the scene at the moment of apotheosis. At the 1983 conference, these British saints and their metropolitan epic had virtually vanished from view. Scholars were less inclined to leave the scene of action at the moment of redemption. The 1983 program focused on abolition and its aftermath, an aftermath extending into the present.

Five years later, the 1988 commemorations in Brazil, the West Indies, and the United States were organized along similar postslavery themes. This volume of essays is the outcome of one of these conferences, held at the University of Pittsburgh in August 1988. The conference attempted to take advantage of the rising scholarly interest to stimulate comparative and long-range reflections on New World postemancipation societies. It was our hope that a comparative and interdisciplinary perspective would stimulate an investigation of both general trends and historical peculiarities in societies united by the tradition of plantation slavery and abolition.

Although the conference papers nominally focused upon the politics and economics of freedom as molded by the dynamics of race, class, and culture, some dominant issues emerged as papers were subjected to formal commentaries and free-ranging discussion. A number of the essays in this volume are elaborations by commentators of remarks that seemed to crystalize important underlying questions of perspective generated by the original papers. These questions address the nature and impact of slave emancipation over both the short and long term. How revolutionary was the abolition of slavery? Did the transformation of legal status conceal deeper continuities in the plantation societies of the Americas? Did emancipation differentially enlarge or constrain opportunities for the major social groups in each society and for the plantation zone as a whole? Did a common peculiar economic, political, and racial configuration of the plantation slave zones tend to lead them to a peculiar postemancipation pattern of development? Were there dramatic differences in short- and long-term development? Were there alternative and even radically different possible opportunities for economic or political development, aborted by structures of internal political power and external colonial constraints?

I

The economic historians whose essays open this volume differ about the degree to which fundamental change occurred with emancipation, and about whether one or another kind of revolutionary action might have altered the long-term socioeconomic development of societies after slavery came to an end. All seem to agree, however, that despite or even because of the legal transformation, there were very considerable constraints placed upon long-term economic development and material standards of living in postslavery societies compared to Europe or the northern United States. Pieter Emmer's opening essay begins with a note of profound skepticism about postemancipation development, which reverberates through the collection. His perspective is grounded in recent historiographical analyses of slavery and abolition that emphasize that the relative productivity, economic rationality, viability, and international competitiveness of plantation slavery were as clear during the century of abolition as they had been in the centuries preceding it. By contrast, Emmer notes, postemancipation economies were often less competitive than they had been under slavery or under systems that temporarily retained slavery and the slave trade. Postslavery plantation societies faced stagnating output, declining attractiveness to European capital, and a diminished role in the expansion of western capitalism. Some areas slowly sank into insignificance relative to their preemancipation positions.

Insofar as freedom enabled former slaves to place new limits and higher costs on the mode of production, it also constrained their own potential economic betterment. From the perspective of European governments, the plantation economies were transformed from areas of profitable investment to impoverished burdens on the metropolis. These

economies converged more toward the "third world" tropical economies than the developed world of Euro-America, with correspondingly
low standards of living. In terms of peasant aspirations (peasantization),
the more radical the economic and political revolution that accompanied
the legal revolution (e.g., in Haiti), the more bleak was the long-term
economic outcome.

In contrast, and in world historical perspective, the long-term outcome of slave emancipation for Europe was minimal. The end of colonial slavery did not significantly retard economic growth or rising living
standards for the European metropolitan population as a whole. In the
plantation Americas, the effect was more profound and enduring. Planters were more concerned with the new economic requirements of the
production of staples, Emmer concludes, than with racial preferences
or political goals. For the planter, freedom meant a new set of constraints, which forced him to experiment with new forms of contractual
relations and new sources of labor.

Emmer's chapter also implicitly argues against the possibility of a
radically different economic outcome, given the political and ideological framework of Europe and the West in general during the nineteenth
century. The dominant metropolitan zone (industrializing Europe and
the northern United States) were unwilling to consider more than the
most cautious welfare initiatives for their own metropolitan poor and
working classes. It is hardly likely that any industrial society would have
long expended more resources on its staple periphery than on its own
masses at home. That the plantation zones were of declining economic
interest to Europe was a further motive for disinterest in overseas welfare systems for colonial populations. In the long run, even the free
peasant proprietors of the circum-Caribbean and their descendants were
dependent upon the success of the plantation sector. Paradoxically, expansion of the plantation system would have produced higher economic
growth and a higher long-term standard of living, notwithstanding that
this may have been the inverse of the aspirations of the freed. Hence,
Emmer's insistence that the meaning of freedom be viewed in constant
relation to the price of freedom.

In the next essay, Stanley Engerman continues the discussion of the
economic implications of emancipation for the meaning of freedom. Beginning with one premise very similar to Emmer's, he stresses the need
to understand the outcome of emancipation in terms of the dynamism
and competitiveness of slavery before and during the age of abolition.

Engerman emphasizes that the changes created by the emancipation of the labor force were not those desired by the planters and placed considerable inhibitions on planters' behavior after slavery. By providing a total or partial escape from some of the harshest and most disliked features of a gang labor system that had engulfed all ages and both sexes of the plantations, emancipation made manifest many conflicts in the values and aspirations of ex-masters and ex-slaves. It did not provide for the new free-labor harmony envisioned by metropolitan abolitionists.

The general outcome of these new conflicts was usually economic decline or stagnation, sometimes brief, sometimes permanent. There were major shifts to new labor forces or to new organizations of staple production involving less intensive or less supervised labor. Engerman stresses systematic variation within the trend as much as the general pattern. These variations usually reflected land-labor ratios in local areas at the time of liberation. The land-labor model of the meaning of freedom plays an important role in a number of other essays as well. In general, there was more continuity of labor, and even rising postemancipation output, in the most densely populated Caribbean islands. Brazil also achieved an easy transition by immediate access to a new immigrant labor population. In the United States, the Cotton South came to rely increasingly upon white farmers. In general, due to changes in the world labor market, the later emancipation occurred, the greater were the alternatives to coerced African labor and the easier the retention of staple production for export.

Engerman, like Emmer, discusses the impact of emancipation for the freed and for their descendants. Since his economic model presumes the invaluable good of free choice, he begins with the premise that, by definition, the expansion of the ex-slaves' choices about consumption, leisure, culture, and employers constituted a clear welfare gain. Some short-term welfare gains might later promote long-term constraints on both economic growth and the standard of living, even if the expansion of choice was in itself an irrevocable gain. In terms of the meaning of freedom, this secular perspective implies increasing difficulties for plantation production in the face of ex-slave priorities and limitations on the long-term growth of welfare for both slaves and masters. As for the possibility of alternative outcomes, Engerman, like Emmer, offers a comparison with later nineteenth-century Euro-America to show that certain developments, such as those limiting material welfare and subjection to the world market, were not the fate of ex-slaves alone. In secular terms, the Caribbean plantation zones converged with tropical Afro-Asia in economic underdevelopment. But, Engerman cautions, the longer the period after slavery allowed for comparison, the more difficult it becomes for scholars to sort out the competing causal weights of colonial rule, racism, cultural choices, and family patterns.

Jay Mandle pursues the central issue of economic constriction in a narrower geographic range and by a more precisely defined measure. While Emmer and Engerman draw attention to constraints of the world market upon plantation societies as a whole, Mandle affirms that the planters of the U.S. South in particular were remarkably successful in accomplishing the transition to freedom while maintaining both their economic and political positions. A similar premise is the point of departure for a number of other contributors to this collection. For Mandle, the major weapon in the hands of the southern planters was racial division and antipathy. From this came what Mandle calls the economic entrapment of emancipated Afro-Americans. This is illustrated by their lack of mobility out of the southern agricultural sector for two generations after the Civil War.

If Mandle's evaluation of the impact of emancipation for the southern ex-slave is no less pessimistic than Emmer's, his causal nexus is quite different. Mandle posits not the international market, demography, or the priorities of the ex-slaves, but political and racial repression by the ruling class. Mandle does not pursue his subject comparatively, but one might, for example, compare his equation regarding lack of geographical mobility and deterioration with Emmer's passing observation about the detrimental effects of long-distance mobility on Caribbean family cohesion. Engerman's closing observations on the relative rates of economic success for the descendants of southern slaves compared with those of other areas in the Americas also points to another potential comparison: the relative weight of other variables in assessing the impact of racism in the meaning of freedom.

Gavin Wright, like Mandle, concentrates his analysis primarily on the postbellum South, with a brief excursus toward the end of his essay into comparative perspectives. For Wright, the peculiarities of the South were more significant in accounting for the outcome of southern emancipation than was the common institutional background of plantation slavery in the Americas. A peculiar population mix (predominantly free and white) and the political supremacy of the northern-dominated Union indicates for Wright considerable economic and political constraints upon the power of the planter class. Wright gives far more weight than Mandle to the dictates of the international market on the cotton planters. The long-term decline in the price of cotton and the impossibility of either forcing a return to gang labor or of establishing a full wage labor system resulted in the emergence of a sharecropping system. That mode of organization was a rational economic outcome, given the constraints of law and political regime on planters and ex-slaves alike.

Wright's general analysis of the postemancipation outcome, while stressing the unique aspects of southern development, is consistent with Emmer's conclusion that the postslavery organization of production was dictated to a great extent by the international market system and the new, if limited, bargaining power of labor, both beyond the control of any planter group. Wright, however, is more emphatic about the significance of race, not in determining the new forms of production, but in the development of political rule in the South after Reconstruction. Racial attitudes allowed for a differential degradation of the Afro-American political and welfare position by the end of the century, independent of the heritage of slavery and liberation. The result was an ex-slave population closer to its Caribbean counterparts than to the white population of its own region.

It was racism, not general economic constraints, that allowed white southerners to anticipate the convergence of their race, rather than of their region, with northern and western European patterns, while simultaneously explaining the backwardness of their section of the country in terms of an inherent flaw in the most downtrodden segment of its population. Race became the cause and the rationale for southern difference. Wright finds a comparison with South Africa to be a heuristically appropriate analogy of this process. One might also consider whether the racial explanation of deterioration was not also widely used by Europeans to explain the failures of colonial emancipation. Brazil offered a parallel example of a partial shift to white labor for staple production following emancipation, a labor import policy exclusively favoring Europeans, the progressive marginalization of the ex-slave labor force, and racial explanations for lags vis-à-vis Europe. Racial differentiation in the distribution of political power generally remained characteristic of most of the Caribbean into the twentieth century.

The theme of constraints which emerges powerfully in these first four essays by economic historians, is inevitably expressed in relation to access to land and economic mobility. Mandle follows a long tradition in making the absence of land redistribution in the South a key to its postbellum history. Wright is somewhat more cautious about making "forty acres and a mule" the pivot of postbellum economic history and the potential mechanism of convergence with the Euro-American metropolis.

The chapters by Mandle and Wright both emphasize racial constraints as determinant of the differential fates of whites and blacks in post-emancipation plantation societies. That is also the salient concern of the chapters by O. Nigel Bolland, Jean Besson, and Michel-Rolph Trouillot. As with Mandle on the South, Bolland's essay on the British Caribbean takes the successful continuity of the old ruling class as its point of departure. Emancipation in the British West Indies came without the far-reaching social revolution that occurred in Haiti. Bolland examines the role of the state in maintaining that dominant position through a variety of policies: subsidized immigration, control of the justice and criminal systems, fiscal and tax allocations, and proprietary encumbrances upon the reconstituted peasantry after emancipation and apprenticeship. These were at least partial solutions to planter concerns with the land-labor ratio and peasant resistance to the regimen of plantation labor (the backward-bending labor supply curve).

This process reproduced the class continuities of hegemony and subordination of masters and slaves in the new regime. Like its predecessor, the postslavery British Caribbean was essentially a bipolar society with status, power, color, and culture reinforcing each other to maintain the old antagonistic dualism in a struggle over land, labor, and cultural autonomy. Like Engerman, Bolland takes note of the variations in the slaves' struggles to impose their own meanings of freedom on the process of emancipation, especially in outlying colonial areas such as the Bahamas and Belize. Everywhere, however, freedom meant the reproduction of the class struggle within the nexus of a new legal status for the freed.

Where Emmer, Engerman, and to a lesser extent, Wright place the shape of freedom within the frame of reference of the world market, Bolland concentrates on the meaning of freedom as the outcome of a ubiquitous class struggle, with cultural as well as political dimensions. On one side were ranged the planters and their metropolitan allies. Their ideological allegiance was to the "bourgeois" notion of freedom, stressing competitive individualism, efficient production in response to world market requirements, and a capitalist ethic. On the other side, the freed retained a solidaristic communal ethic akin to the moral economy of traditional peasantries elsewhere.

The development of what Emmer's essay refers to as *peasantization* is the main concern of Jean Besson's chapter on freedom and community in the British West Indies after emancipation. For Besson (as for most of the contributors), continuity (in this case, of community formation) is central to understanding the meaning of freedom. For Besson's subjects, freedom meant new possibilities for long-nurtured aspirations to independence. They sought to take maximum advantage of the land-labor ratio at the time of emancipation to obtain outright possession of the means of subsistence or to gain increased choice and bargaining power within the organization of plantation labor. Major insights into the peasant interpretation of liberation may be found in one very novel postemancipation peasant formation. New "free villages" proliferated beyond the boundaries of the plantations. Like Bolland, Besson envisions the meaning of freedom to lie within a secular conflict between groups and values, extending into alternative patterns of kinship, customs, and land tenure. For Besson, as for Bolland, the aspirations of the freed were determined more by class conflict and ruling class action than by economic growth or the impersonal world market. In terms of possible alternative outcomes, a more radical displacement of the ruling elite, or at least a more radical reallocation of the landholding class than actually occurred (analogous to the hoped-for effects of forty acres and a mule after the U.S. Civil War), would have fundamentally expanded freedom and altered its meaning for the ex-slaves. The possibilities of a radically divergent development seem clearer for Besson than for Emmer and Engerman.

Michel-Rolph Trouillot's chapter is, at least implicitly, a two-case comparative test of one aspect of the "revolutionary alternative" hypothesis. Trouillot examines the political development of the free people of color following slave emancipation in British-ruled Dominica and in French-ruled St. Domingue/Haiti. Because of the ruling class displacement, the shift to peasantization, and the achievement of autonomy from direct metropolitan control, the case of Haitian emancipation is usually deemed the most revolutionary in the history of slavery. Indeed, by such measures and by many others, the St. Domingue/Haiti revolution of 1791–1804 was the most violent upheaval in the age of the French Revolution.

By contrast, Dominican emancipation, half a century later, was but one of nineteen simultaneous emancipations in the British slave colonies legally transformed by imperial power. It was part of the largest, the most peaceful, and the most tightly controlled slave emancipation in the circum-Caribbean during the first half of the nineteenth century.

The displacement of the white planter class in Dominica was also gradual and nonrevolutionary.

Trouillot's two cases are examples of the decline of plantation agriculture and the expansion of peasantization after slavery. The fact that these outcomes were so similar in dramatically different political circumstances poses an interesting heuristic problem for those who place great emphasis on the significance of radical revolutionary transformation in the evolution of postemancipation societies.

Trouillot's point of departure is the continuity of color-class stratification so central to the essays of Mandle and Bolland. Trouillot, however, gives the story a different twist by following the fate of the intermediate free colored class in Caribbean societies after emancipation. In Trouillot's essay, the state in Haiti and Dominica was not merely a well-controlled mechanism for insuring the continuity of either planter rule or the plantation system. It became, in itself, a principle source of income, status, power, and security for a new ruling class in the postplantation economy. In a compromise with peasantization, this new elite reconstituted itself within the state.

In this respect the similarities of outcomes are far more interesting than the mode of emancipation, the degree of political independence, or the continuity of the plantation system in a racially bipolar milieu. For the free colored class, the relation between the meaning and the price of freedom seems to have been, in Trouillot's terms, largely a matter of political opportunity and affordable economic inconvenience. One might look for similar politico-economic compromises elsewhere, even where the plantation system remained viable and where the white planter class retained more wealth and power. The presence of third groups—Asians and free coloreds in the Caribbean, Europeans in Brazil, and indigenous white farmers in the United States—may have represented analogous crucial ingredients in the meaning of freedom to former masters and former slaves, alike.

Trouillot's essay poses heuristic problems for those who hypothesize that more radical political revolutions, in areas that did not experience them, would have had dramatically different socioeconomic outcomes. Does the example of the Haitian revolution imply that postemancipation peasant societies would have achieved long-term outcomes of class structure, cultural values, or economic systems much different and more desirable than those achieved in areas where the old master class was peacefully displaced?

II

There is almost universal agreement among the contributors to this volume that sharp differences in values between masters and slaves were characteristic of plantation society and that these differences persisted and sometimes sharpened after emancipation. Even those who are most emphatic about the persistence of severe economic and political constrictions on the freed population indicate that the realms of family, religion, and community seemed to offer greater room for autonomy and self-expression after emancipation.

Diane Austin-Broos follows the long-term impact of legal emancipation on the reconceptualization of the moral order in Jamaica. In relation to the other essays, she makes three important points. First, in the Jamaican case, the bipolar model of Afro-Caribbean or black culture versus European or white culture seems inadequate to describe the meaning of freedom in religious terms. Regarding religion, the continuity model must be dramatically revised. Jamaican religion after emancipation was not the continuation of a struggle for separate African survival in a European-dominated Christianity. Austin-Broos rejects the concept of Christianity as a white hegemonic religion against which African survivals and revivals asserted themselves as the representative religion of the ex-slave community. In religion, as in law, emancipation was a watershed. The appropriation of Christianity by the newly freed was accelerated; the missionary influence reached its apogee.

However, consistent with an extensive European historiographical tradition, Austin-Broos emphasizes the lower-class appropriation of fundamentally oppositional and radical messages within the Judeo-Christian tradition itself. Although the missionaries formulated one modern variant (English nonconformist) of an oppositional message to the planter elite, the subsequent story of Jamaican religion involves fundamental deviations from, and rejections of, the moral order of early Victorian religious dissent. Austin-Broos traces a succession of mass religious movements attuned to the changing environment of Jamaica's working classes and responsive to gender as well as to class consciousness. Jamaica was obviously fertile sociological soil for the reinvention of God. The moral order was contested not only at the major boundary lines of color but within the ex-slave communities themselves. The resulting picture is one of fragmentation, volatility, and local variation. In religious terms, Austin-Broos concludes, slave emancipation did not bring freedom to all Jamaicans, but it permitted a wider and more subtle struggle.

What did freedom mean when, in Austin-Broos's terms, the struggle first began in earnest on the morrow of emancipation? Sidney Mintz, like her, focuses on emancipation as a turning point, asking readers to liberate themselves from structural and long-term frames of reference. He asks us to consider a hypothetical outcome based on the ex-slave's meaning of freedom and avoiding the constraints of hindsight. Mintz is cognizant of and does not dissent from the prevailing view that the history of plantation societies after slavery makes for sober reading, with its picture of continuing constraints. If anything, Mintz emphasizes that contemporaries underestimated the harshness of postemancipation labor systems. But he feels that a focus on such constraints makes it more difficult to contemplate alternative histories or to grasp the aspirations of the slaves at the moment of liberation.

Mintz speculatively proposes what he regards as a countercontext to the developmental model that prevails not only among our initial essayists but among more radical scholars working within the powerful assumptions of Marxian or progressive models of development. Mintz proposes to evoke, as a point of departure, the world of possibilities grounded in slave aspirations at the dawn of liberation. As the traditional diplomatic historian George Kennan puts it: "History is not what happened. History is what it felt like to be there when it happened," a far different issue (Marshall 1970).

This is, perhaps, not unlike the image projected by the historians of the centennial of British emancipation discussed at the beginning of this introduction. Mintz's proposal, however, offers two crucial differences from the centennialists. It is not the hopes of the metropolitan abolitionists, nor those of the British colonial office, but the hopes of the slaves that interest Mintz. Unlike Kennan's diplomats, whose daily hopes and fears have been recorded in an unbroken flow through the in- and out-trays of ministerial archives, Mintz's historical actors are not accessible to us, he emphasizes, through a ceaseless paper trail. We have no interviews of ex-slaves recorded on the day of liberation.

Mintz's thought experiment requires something more than recapturing sentiments and perceptions. He asks us to imagine a wholly different history, based on the presumption that the newly freed had been, not just allowed, but "helped to become what *they* aspired to." This intentionally counterfactual suggestion fruitfully stimulates the comparative perspective. It again raises issues that Emmer and others have addressed concerning the situation of other groups at the moment of liberation and afterward. To fully imagine Mintz's counterfactual history, one has to reimagine not only the position of the planter classes and colonial offices, but that of the metropolitan masses—working class, lower middle class, and the elite.

What would have been necessary for all classes to reach agreement that the newly freed West Indians should not only be allowed, but "helped to become what *they* aspired to"? Among the potential British "helpers" we would have to consider the agricultural poor, urban workers and shopkeepers, and women of all classes for whom the bill for helping the freed might have seemed even less bearable in the "hungry forties" than the twenty million pounds expended as compensation to slaveholders in the 1830s. The request for aid would probably have fared even more poorly in the France of 1848. A Republican National Assembly, ready to risk the bloodiest working class uprising in the century by closing down the national workshops of Paris in June 1848, would certainly have hesitated to offer abroad what they were refusing at home.

In other words, this bold thought experiment requires that the aspirations of the rest of the West be incorporated into the hypothesis. It forces us to recall, with Emmer and Engerman, that in the mid–nineteenth century many European workers lacked the right to vote, had few opportunities for education, and enjoyed limited religious tolerance. Sometimes they faced material standards of living at least as bad as those of the newly emancipated and lived in a political and ideological world in which the very idea of a welfare state was still well beyond the horizon.[1] To achieve the aspirations of the emancipated would have considerably increased the price of freedom for European societies and altered the meaning of freedom in the metropolis as well. At what point would averting "westernization" for nonwestern folk have retarded westernization for western folk? Mintz might well reply that speculation about the aspirations of the ex-slave remains as imperative as speculation about everyone else's.

Mintz's haunting question underlines a persistent tension between two frames of reference in this collection, despite a broad range of empirical agreement. Interpretations of the meaning of freedom will be affected by fundamental views of the driving forces of history and basic notions of human interaction. One conceptual framework implies that economic development is fundamental to a world of expanding choices, which is one meaning of freedom. In the nineteenth century it was constraints on development, including ex-slave actions, that helped to determine the price of freedom in the plantation Americas. The second conceptual framework found in this collection, while it theoretically recognizes the dependency of material and cultural well-being on some economically determined outer limit, begins with the persistently unequal distributions of wealth, power, and values in postemancipation societies.

In acknowledging that emancipation held out abolitionist promises and unleashed ex-slave aspirations that were not fulfilled in the two centuries after 1788, we come face to face with what Raymond Smith refers to as the stubborn cultural residue of racism. For Smith, the fundamental distortion that altered the meaning of freedom from the moment of freedom was that gap between the egalitarian ideology of emancipation and the continuity and persistence of a hierarchical order in the plantation societies. As indicated in the chapters by Wright, Bolland, and Mandle, the tension was handled and mediated through racially defined antagonisms. To this extent, emancipation was illusory, and Smith's opening citation from Carlyle is not inconsistent with Emmer's skeptical opening French proverb on the nature of change in general. However, for Smith, as for Mandle, Bolland, and Besson, the source of the deception rested less in the inexorable pressures of the international market for staples than in the old hierarchies of power and culture, which reemerged after emancipation. To maintain that specific hierarchical system in the face of the subversive emancipatory ideology, the dominant elite had recourse to the residue of racism that characterized all of the plantation Americas.

Smith does not illustrate his point through case studies or comparative analysis but concentrates on a theoretical analysis of the relation of class domination to the concept of race. Since *race* is a social construct, elaborated over time, the emergence and function of socioracial ideologies is of major theoretical interest. Its articulation from above — from the dominant cultural group — is as noteworthy as the creation of varied religious ideologies of liberation from below. One could hardly identify a more potent cultural barrier to the fulfillment of slave hopes than this persistent ideological fact.

Peter Kolchin's concluding essay on the interpretation of the postbellum era in the South addresses the general historiographic sense of disappointment in all plantation societies after slavery. He concludes that this sense of tragedy is a subtle but persistent inheritance of the original actors in the drama of Reconstruction and its aftermath. Alternatively, Kolchin proposes a retroactive lowering of expectations about the outcome of emancipation on the basis of a comparative sense of shattered illusions, so characteristic of other massive social transformations. In one sense, Kolchin's strategy for ferreting out the meaning of freedom elaborates one of Engerman's and Mintz's insistent points. Any attempt to evaluate the results of emancipation confronts us with the single primary fact that every liberation was final and created the possibility of a new pattern of development. Historians who confront the problem of evaluation in analogous events, such as the Great French Revolution, generally conclude that the upheaval produced, at a minimum, a new legal and institutional relationship that was the prerequisite of eventual modernization.

Emmer proposes that emancipation in plantation societies represents a type of revolution that did little to further subsequent modernization — in the western sense. Kolchin argues that U.S. emancipation was unique among those in the plantation Americas in having occurred in the context of a larger democratizing trend within the society. The immediate extension of universal adult male suffrage to the ex-slaves represented a singular extension of the meaning of freedom. Although the St. Domingue revolution also occurred within the larger setting of the Great French Revolution, there was certainly no integration of the ex-slave population into a liberal democratic France. On the contrary, the Haitian armies that achieved final separation from France broke with a Bonapartist dictatorship that had rejected institutionalized democracy for its own citizens as well.

Further comparative analysis might include later emancipations within Kolchin's concept of emancipations in a democratizing context. One might consider, for example, the relation of British slave emancipation to the enormous expansion of popular mobilization in Britain and the West Indies between 1828 and 1833 and to the passage of the Great Reform Act in 1832. The ending of France's second slave system in 1848 is even closer to Kolchin's model. In 1848 French ex-slaves became the first in the plantation Americas to vote, under a system of universal male suffrage, for representatives to the National Assembly of the French Republic. They were also the first group of Afro-Americans to lose that right with the overthrow of that republic by a second Bonaparte in 1851. Thus, French ex-slaves went through a full cycle of democratization and political constraint well before the beginning of a similar experiment in the postbellum South. Since the old French colonies, like the states of the South, have remained part of a larger nonplantation society, the American experience might usefully be compared with other regions in which the descendants of slaves have remained a minority.

III

The contributors to this volume are roughly divided between economic or social historians and social anthropologists, which provides for a salutory mix of perspectives and emphases. Nonetheless, the differing viewpoints suggest a need to deal creatively with the theoretical and methodological tensions in an attempt to provide an explanatory bridge between local and global histories.

In the most ambitious attempt by an anthropologist to bring ethnography and history together on this bridge, Eric Wolf sums up the new global era that was the century of emancipation in this manner:

Capitalist accumulation thus continues to engender new working classes in widely dispersed areas of the world. It recruits these working classes from a wide variety of social and cultural backgrounds, and inserts them into variable political and economic hierarchies. The new working classes change these hierarchies by their presence, and are themselves changed by the forces to which they are exposed. On one level, the diffusion of the capitalist mode creates everywhere a wider unity through the constant reconstitution of its characteristic capital–labor relationship. On another level, it also creates diversity, accentuating social opposition and segmentation even as it unifies. Within an ever more integrated world, we witness the growth of ever more diverse proletarian diasporas. (1982:383)

The participants understood that the comparative study of the economic, political, and social consequences of emancipation remains in its infancy. As was true for slavery studies, a comparative view of the postemancipation era can broaden our perspectives and introduce new questions and concepts. Certainly the value of a conference of this nature is measured in large part by the stimulation provided for both basic research and theory.

Wolf's statement raises two questions, which constantly bedevil the comparative approach in history: (1) Of what sense is one history equally the history of other cases? and (2) Is that history the only one that can be written of these cases? The chapters in this volume are to be read with these issues in mind as they lead us to additional considerations of comparison.

The slave system was a social system that could not be overturned overnight, however profitable or unprofitable it may have been. With the coming of emancipation, slavery could no longer be regarded as an economic alternative. Freedom for black slaves had implications for the whole social order of the traditional plantation regime. The state was in a position to insist on some measure of contractual conditions in production and to formalize the institutional framework under which freedom became a legal reality. The state, whether national or colonial, attempted to promote the general conditions required for a labor market economy.

Trouillot neatly captures the paradox of this moment in his comparison of Haiti and Dominica. The mulatto ascendency in Dominica was no less a colonial elite than its white equivalents, elsewhere, and was no less determined to dominate black labor. But its political success was inimical to imperial values and to the Crown colony administration. Although several contributors question the ability or even the willingness of the state to positively intervene in behalf of the welfare of the ex-slaves, this needs to be read against the class dynamics of the Haitian revolution and the experience of the European class struggles.

Yet the political language of class and race in nineteenth-century Britain, France, the U.S. north, and the Brazilian south were not identical. Nor were the political languages static. They have their own distinct morphologies.

"We fell under the leadership of those who would compromise with truth in the past in order to make peace in the present and guide policy in the future" (DuBois 1935:727). "Truth, we are told, will prevail, and freedom we know is truth" (Sewell 1862:323). The truths spoken by DuBois and Sewell about the American South and the West Indies may suggest a tragic reading of the role of the state as the guarantor of promised freedom, but they still require close examinations of the institutions during the transformation and of the many voices and truths used to express and repress these institutions.

What were the tactics, adaptations, and modes of resistance used by the ex-slaves and bound laborers in response to the varying conditions and promises of freedom? The planters saw everything that was once theirs about to be taken from them — manpower, money, power, prosperity, and history. By combining franchise restrictions, legislative fraud, collusion, and the fear of the masses, the planter class strove to keep the newly freed subservient. Where the plantation survived, the state's fear of revolt and the plantocracy's confusion and labor disorganization were codified in new canons of law and order. For the black peasant and indentured plantation worker, any degree of collusion between the state and the landed oligarchy presented a more or less formidable hurdle.

Under what conditions could the nonelite mount strategies and mobilize to defend and expand their rights as they contended with both official and extralegal forms of social control? What were the opportunities, the successes, and failures in attempts to maintain client-master relations through credit, confidence, and loyalty? The weighing of these factors might provide further comparative instances of the way in which freedom struggles have defined freedom.

How are the largely rural populations of the plantation zone to be conceptualized? The answer to this question may be framed by stressing the following factors: (1) the degree of the involvement of the local economy in the international market, (2) the strength of the state and of its political components in imposing labor and land controls, and (3) the nature of the alternatives open to the freed as landless laborers, petty commodity producers, and ancillary producers for the market as subsistence cultivators. Freedom fundamentally changed the relationships among people, labor, and land. The variations in land-labor relationships in the plantation zone of the New World led to the development of numerous characterizations of the rural inhabitants. They have been variously labeled as fictive, marginal, and reconstituted peasants, or neither full peasants nor proletarians. Previous typologies tied to local experiences of emancipation often have not been adequately integrated into the dynamics of the global political economy of the era.

Fruitful classification and comparison involve consideration of labor use and family budget strategies, information availability, and sensitivity to the continuous tension between aversion to drudgery and social goals. Primary communities of peasants and proletarians had to accommodate or create new types of budgetary constraints on the wage nexus and on a more socialized economy. New modes of interfamily and intrafamily cooperation were necessary. There were new opportunities for patronage and clientism, for kinship loyalties and factional hostilities.

It is at this point that microhistorical and critical anthropology enters the analysis. As Austin-Broos, Besson, Smith, and Mintz show, in this enterprise culture becomes neither anonymous nor consensual. The cultural concepts of person, class, ethnicity, or gender do not exist in a vacuum. As several of the contributors indicate, culture is expressed through recognizing its political moment.

All of these issues are inseparable from the persistence of racism. Comparative history and anthropology have much to suggest about the ambiguous and pervasive role of racism in the modern world. Its meaning in different social settings remains elusive. To what extent does race constitute a single ideological construct? Why do definitions of blacks and other culturally determined color shadings differ so markedly in postemancipation societies? How are the concepts of race and class to be weighted, and what are the changing components?

The global processes set in motion by emancipation remain living traditions and daily practices. We need to understand the traditions and practices that peoples once constructed if we are to recount precisely how they made or failed to make their own history.

IV

The collection as a whole testifies to far more general agreement upon the trends, continuities, and connections between economic, political, and cultural outcomes than one might imagine from the debates over the evaluation and interpretation of the meaning of freedom. Much of the divergence arises from predispositions to assign greater or lesser weight to contradictory aspects of very complex interactions and outcomes. Other, perhaps related, differences arise out of general theories of social change and the ideas, institutions, or material forces inherited by postemancipation societies.

Some fundamental substantive points of agreement seem to be characteristic of the collection as a whole. Emancipation was a profound legal transformation and a successful step toward the elimination of chattel slavery throughout the world. Adjustments to the world market, attempts to constrain political power or economic mobility, and the struggle for cultural redefinition all had to be conducted within the context of that irreversible fact.

Second, the outcome of emancipation in the perspective of the twenty-first century evokes a sense of disappointment tinged with resignation or bitterness. Only by a retrospective revolution of falling expectations, or by returning to the zero hour of freedom, can one avoid confronting the comparative dreariness of the history of the plantation Americas in the century or so after their slave emancipations. With few exceptions, the conditions of the ex-slaves converged more toward the relatively impoverished levels of the Afro-Asian tropics than those of the old North Atlantic world or of the new Pacific Rim. Between these two simple but disparate facts lie all of the complexities, variations, constraints, and aspirations that find voice or echo in this volume.

NOTE

1. On the standards of living of British manual laborers and West Indian slaves at the time of slave emancipation, see Ward (1988:261–63, 286–88).

REFERENCES

DuBois, W. E. B. 1935. *Black Reconstruction.* New York: Harcourt Brace.

Drescher, Seymour. 1985. The Historical Context of British Abolition. In *Abolition and Its Aftermath: The Historical Context, 1790–1916,* edited by David Richardson, 3–24. London: Frank Cass.

Marshall, John. 1970. The Castle's Keep: The Villa Serbelloni in History. Typescript. Villa Serbelloni.

Sewell, William G. 1862. *Ordeal of Free Labor.* London: Sampson, Low.

Ward, J. R. 1988. *British West Indian Slavery, 1750–1834: The Process of Amelioration.* Oxford: Oxford University Press.

Wolf, Eric. 1982. *Europe and the People Without History.* Berkeley and Los Angeles: University of California Press.

PIETER C. EMMER

The Price of Freedom
The Constraints of Change in Postemancipation America

There is a very discouraging French proverb that says that "the more things change, the more things stay the same." In discussing the effects of emancipation, this skepticism provides a useful antidote to the high-strung expectations of the abolitionists of the time. These expectations were part of a very persistent myth that drastic socioeconomic changes could be achieved by altering a law, a regime, or a government.

Two hundred years ago, many revolutionaries in France hoped to increase the general prosperity of their country by attacking the rigid social hierarchy while leaving alone the rigidity of the economic structure. Many French resources were subsequently expended in experimenting with new forms of government and in fending off the opponents of these experiments, both at home and abroad. The result was considerable economic stagnation. France definitely lost out to Britain in the neck-and-neck race for economic primacy.[1]

Another example of a process aimed at reforming the society in order to increase economic growth is the process of decolonization after World War II. By breaking their colonial links, the undeveloped or under-developed countries in Asia and Africa were expected to be able finally to follow the path of sustained economic growth that Europe and North America had walked in the past. In reality, the act of decolonization by itself did not change the economic position of the newly independent countries, and in some cases decolonization actually slowed economic growth or even reversed it, because the scarce factors of production were diverted to building a new governmental elite or used in creating an army or in experimenting with a different division of land.

This is not to say that all revolutions and decolonizations were necessarily expensive. The Glorious Revolution in England, the Revolt of the Netherlands, and the decolonization of the United States do not seem to have negatively affected the economic development of these

23

countries. All these examples, however, do warn us of the fact that words such as *revolution* and *decolonization* are usually intended to give the impression of drastic changes, thus hiding the much more important reality of structural continuities. Returning to eighteenth-century France, it seems safe to conclude that the revolution finally cemented the gap between British and French economic development, which had already been visible before 1789. In the same vein, it can be said that the post–World War II wave of decolonizations only directed world opinion toward the difficulties of economic growth in nonindustrialized countries; the process of decolonization itself did not alter the rate of such growth. Similarly, the Dutch revolt and the English and American revolutions hardly changed the prospects for economic development that existed in those countries before 1568, 1689, and 1776.

With these reflections in mind, the words *emancipation* and *abolition* should be regarded with the utmost suspicion. These words describe a change in the legal status of the work force in plantation America; they do not necessarily imply a change in the national and international economic and social ramifications of the societies geared to the exportation of tropical cash crops. The abolitionists, however, rarely paid attention to the limitations to obtaining social and economic changes within plantation America. Abolitionism in the United Kingdom and in parts of the United States had grown into a mass movement, and the dynamics of such a mass movement left little room for a nuanced debate about the possibilities of change in the plantation societies after emancipation.

Abolitionist public opinion simply wanted slavery to be stamped out, like alcoholism and corporal punishment. A society without these evils could only be a better one for all who lived in it. When the abolitionists talked about the postemancipation society in the tropical parts of the New World, they believed that the ex-slaves would either continue to work on the plantations or become yeomen-farmers. Emancipation was expected to boost the agricultural economies of the previous slave societies. Both ex-slaves and planters would be able to increase their incomes. The freedmen would finally be paid a wage allowing them to buy more than the bare necessities of life, which they had been allotted as slaves. Planters would have to pay these wages, but they surely would be more than compensated for this expenditure by the higher productivity of free labor as compared to that of slave labor (Engerman and Eltis 1980:275–80; Eltis 1987:20).

The planters warned that with emancipation ex-slaves would become displaced Africans, idlers who could not be induced to supply regular labor. They contended that only slavery provided the means to force slaves to work regularly and that the system itself did not necessarily force these ex-Africans to work harder or to live more poorly than agricultural laborers in Europe. As long as free land was available, the majority of the freedmen would certainly rather squat than provide regular labor on the plantations (Lewis 1983:106).

These two sets of arguments clearly indicate that a common appreciation of the future of agriculture in plantation America was impossible to achieve. For outsiders, the unique features of the capitalist plantation production of coffee, cotton, and sugar were indeed difficult to envision. The very idea that farmhands would turn into squatters was not easily conceived by the abolitionists in western Europe. Equally, they could not be made to understand that in producing many of the tropical cash crops there was an inherent need to have a regular and available supply of labor, which—as a consequence of these prerequisites—had to live on the plantations, especially those producing sugar. In the days before the introduction of complicated, mechanized production lines, a similar absolute necessity for such a regular and readily available labor supply could be found aboard sailing ships, which lost their seaworthiness once too many of the crew jumped ship or died.[2]

The abolitionists expected important changes to occur as a result of emancipation, while the planters hoped for a large degree of continuity. Both agreed that agriculture would remain the principal economic activity and that the only comparative economic advantage of plantation America in the world economy, the production of tropical cash crops, should be retained (Eltis 1982:201).

In what way did slave emancipation actually affect the various parties involved? In order to see whether change or continuity prevailed, we will first look at the groups and institutions that used slave labor or profited from it: the governments, the trading companies, and the investors in the metropole, as well as the colonial governments and the planters. Then we will turn to a discussion of the changes and continuities that occurred when the slaves were freed.

Emancipation and the Course of European Expansion

Within the expansion of Europe before 1800, plantation America held a special position. The region's economic ties with Europe were unlike those of the white settlements in North and South America, and they were equally different from those of the various trading establishments in Asia and Africa. The plantation colonies needed a disproportionally large share of Europe's overseas investments and consumer goods, while in return the area produced a disproportionally large amount of the bulk products for a popular market in Europe and North America: sugar, coffee, and cotton.[3]

Strangely, the ending of American plantation slavery did not change the course of European expansion after 1800. There are no indications that the geographic and economic course of nineteenth-century imperialism was in any way influenced by the disappearance of forced labor in the "darlings of the empire" of old and in spite of the attempts made at establishing cash crop production in other parts of the various colonial empires outside plantation America.

As far as Africa is concerned, some authors have indeed suggested that European penetration into Africa was prompted in part by the ending of the slave trade and by the consequences of slave emancipation in the Americas. Some actually point to the connections between the European attempts at stopping the illegal slave trade and Europe's subsequent occupation of some of the slave-exporting areas on the coast of West Africa. However, it should be remembered that, before the Europeans started to colonize Africa, it was already known that the transfer of New World plantation agriculture was impossible; all such attempts had failed. In the 1880s when the real scramble for Africa started, slave emancipation in the Americas no longer was an issue for the metropolitan governments. By that time, it had become obvious that plantation America would always remain the most important production area of coffee, sugarcane, and cotton.[4]

As far as Latin America is concerned, it seems possible to argue that the wave of decolonizations after 1800 did not affect Europe's growing economic influence in that part of the world. In fact, it could be said that Europe's demand for cash crops actually stalled the emancipation of the Brazilian and Cuban slaves. Europe's informal influence in nineteenth-century Latin America, however, did not lead to the creation of new slave societies (Donghi 1985:341–42).

Asia provides us with a more interesting case, since its production of sugar and coffee increased considerably at exactly the period when slave emancipation in the Americas was being executed. However, there is no proof that European expansion in Asia was in any way connected with the search for an alternative plantation region. The Asian production of sugar and coffee for export came in the wake of European penetration, not vice versa (Fieldhouse 1973:92–103).

In India sugar production was widespread, but most of that sugar was consumed locally. Attempts by the East India Company to increase production in order to export sugar to England failed. The only period in which Indian sugar was exported to Europe can be dated between 1836, when the sugar duties within the British empire were equalized, and 1846, when the sugar duties were abolished. In those years, several private entrepreneurs in India started to produce sugar, using techniques and expertise acquired in the West Indies. The short period of Indian sugar exports is an indication of the fact that sugar production by Indian peasants in combination with central mills owned by colonists could at best compete with only the marginal sugar plantations in the British West Indies. After the subsidy on British-grown sugar had been withdrawn, Indian sugar production could not compete with the production in plantation America at large (Deerr 1949:56–57).

The only exception to this rule was nineteenth-century Java. The Dutch colonial administration had imposed a system of forced cropping (the so-called cultivation system) on the rural population of Java in order to defray the increasing costs of the Dutch colonial administration. The results were far beyond the boldest expectations; after 1830 Java obtained a steady lead in sugar production in comparison to the Dutch West Indies, and during the second half of the nineteenth century the island produced as much sugar as several large British sugar colonies in the Caribbean taken together. However, this success was only possible by excluding the free labor market. Until 1900 the Javanese laborers in the cane—whether communal or private—were not paid a market price (Elson 1984:122–23). Similar observations can be made about the production of sugar in Queensland, Natal, Fiji, and Hawaii, and about beet sugar in Europe itself, which were all flourishing toward the end of the nineteenth century. In every single case, protection in the consumer market or nonmarket wages fostered the growth of these sugar industries. In spite of the fact that the impact of the whip of the market was softened in these cases, labor management on the plantations in the new sugar regions also instituted a regime by which the laborers worked in gangs and lived on the estates. Only the cultivation of sugar beets in Europe was organized differently.[5]

In summing up this section, it seems important to stress again that the course of nineteenth-century European expansion in Africa and Asia was not caused by slave emancipation and a drive to obtain new planta-tion colonies. The relative physical and organizational advantages of plantation America in the production of cotton, coffee, and sugar could not be approached elsewhere, even after the price of labor in America had increased considerably. Production of sugar and coffee in Asia and Africa for export overseas was feasible only in case labor could be sub-sidized or forced to work below market prices or in case the consumer market was protected.

There also existed metropolitan trading firms with strong commer-cial interests in plantation America. Were they affected by emancipa-tion? Again, there seems little reason to assume that they were. A study of the Liverpool slave trade has shown that the abolition of that trade could easily be compensated by opportunities in the long-distance trade, which were opening up right after abolition (Drescher 1977:75).

Last but not least, the international capital market should be men-tioned. Again, it seems possible to conclude that slave emancipation caused certain changes in the pattern of overseas investment, but it did not significantly reduce opportunities for such investment in general. As far as the investors in the New World plantations were concerned, the payment of compensation money to the slave owners enabled many metropolitan investors to take their money elsewhere. Opportunities for investment at home and abroad abounded after the 1830s, and the re-duced investment opportunities in plantation America were more than made good by the growth of overseas investment elsewhere. It seems likely that emancipation considerably lowered plantation America on the scale of international investment opportunities. Slave emancipation might well have led to disinvestment, and in any case it certainly helped to speed up a development by which plantation America as an area re-ceiving international investments came to resemble tropical Africa and Asia rather than the colonies of white settlement.[6]

Emancipation and the
Ruling Elite of Plantation America

It seems obvious that the impact of slave emancipation in plantation America was most profound on the lives of the ex-slaves and on the administrative practices of local governments. Plantation management also had to cope with changes in the labor supply, but these seem minor in comparison to the dramatic changes in the personal freedom of the liberated slaves and in comparison to the explosive increase in the demand for governmental services faced by the various local public authorities. The abolitionist movement had always stressed the fact that plantation managers who resisted change could put the whole process of emancipation into jeopardy. Thus local governments were expected to intervene in case the employers continued to behave as slave owners (Green 1976:65–95).

The plantation managers were not at liberty to change the production techniques of raising coffee, cotton, and sugar; consequently, after emancipation they were forced to retain many of the labor management techniques that had been used during the slavery period. The profitable production of coffee, tobacco, cotton, and sugarcane required a strict regimentation of labor. Certainly, the plantation managers tried to profit as much as possible from the new industrial technology of the nineteenth century. But these innovations were limited to that part of the production process that started once the cane, the coffee beans, and the cotton had been cut or picked. On sugar plantations, the new technology was aimed at increasing the amount of sucrose through the use of more effective cane crushers and new refining equipment. In addition, it was possible to save on labor by installing railways for the transportation of freshly cut cane from the fields to the factories and for connecting the plantation with the seaports. Unfortunately, the heavy field labor of planting and cutting cane could not be mechanized at the time, and even mechanized preparation of the soil was difficult to achieve; steam ploughs were not successful in the Caribbean, not even in the lowlands of Guiana (Green 1976:240–48). The possibility of mechanizing fieldwork in the production of coffee and cotton was even more limited than in producing sugar.[7]

Whatever the possibilities of change in the fields and in the factories of the plantations, the introduction of new technology occurred over a long period, starting well before the 1830s; emancipation only accelerated the speed of change. Nevertheless, the obstacles to reducing the heavy physical exertion in fieldwork were far more obvious than the blessings of the new technology. In view of that, it was understandable that many freedmen were disappointed in plantation management because the demand for heavy physical labor had not been reduced. It is also understandable that many abolitionists confused the unyielding attitudes of the plantation management with a racist nostalgia for a return to slavery among the majority of the planters. Actually, nowhere in plantation America did any action among the planters occur to re-instate slavery once it had been abolished.

However, there is no evidence to support the contention that planta-tion managers deviated from their prime task of producing for a profit by paying a price for their nostalgia and racist convictions. It is true that, over time, labor conditions on the plantations changed. Many of these changes — such as asking rent for housing and for the use of gar-den plots, stopping free medical care, and ending payments in kind to the young, the old, and the sick, who did not actually provide labor — were only bringing labor conditions in plantation America in line with those prevalent in industrializing Europe and North America. Even the hiring of seasonal labor in order to quickly increase the labor force on the plantation during the harvest had its counterpart in many European farm areas (Hall 1959:157–58).

Nevertheless, the abolitionists blamed the racism of both plantation ownership and management for preventing freedmen from obtaining jobs and work schedules that were different from those during slavery. The planters were also blamed for their unwillingness to increase wages as well as for evicting those freedmen from their plantations who no longer provided regular labor. However, there is little doubt that the same abolitionists would also have blamed the planters had they in-creased their expenditure on nonproductive labor and thus allowed the competitiveness of their plantations to decrease, creating massive un-employment in the region (Curtin 1975:109, 121).

In reality, the changing economy of plantation agriculture did result in several changes in the management of plantation labor. In order to combat rising labor costs, the number of temporary jobs on Caribbean plantations was increased considerably, allowing for the extensive use of jobbing gangs (Ward 1988:252). In contrast to the production of sugar, the cultivation of cotton enabled the introduction of sharecropping. In the U.S. South, this adaptation was made (Engerman 1982:213). The continued growth of the plantations made it profitable to change the ratio between labor paid on a weekly basis and labor paid on a task basis in favor of the latter wage system. Such changes allowed the strong and healthy laborers to earn more than before, but they took a toll on those who were not so strong.

All of these innovations were dictated by the changing business eco-nomics of plantation agriculture. It makes little sense to ascribe the changes and continuities in postemancipation plantation management simply to racism, in a world where racism was the rule, not the excep-

tion. The most interesting question is whether the economy of plantation America could have developed differently without racism. There
is no evidence to support the idea that it would have been different, at
least not in the history of the Caribbean. On the contrary, before abolition the increased pressures to minimize labor costs on the plantation
had already forced the planters in the Dutch and British Caribbean to
abandon their tradition of giving the higher ranking jobs by preference
to mulatto slaves. After emancipation, plantation owners also had to
give up their preference for hiring exclusively expatriate Europeans to
fill the highest management positions. Increasingly, mulattoes and blacks
were employed as managers and assistant managers (Ward 1988:219;
Curtin 1975:43).

In accepting the economic and technical constraints within the private sector in postemancipation America, one assumes that there ought
to have been some room for innovative change in the public sector.
In theory this assumption is justified, especially since the various local governments could at least have made an effort to make up for
the persisting continuities in the private sector. Local government
could have attempted forcibly to stamp out the remnants of slavery
through a variety of actions: by imposing new labor conditions, strictly
supervising the planters, dispensing equal justice, offering public education, public housing, and public medical care, and safeguarding the
missionary activities of the various Christian churches and societies.
To achieve all these aims the various local administrative and judicial
bodies would have had to be enlarged and staffed by new personnel coming from outside plantation America and imbued with the abolitionist
ideology.

These theoretical assumptions about local governments as agents of
postemancipation change do not reflect reality. First of all, the resources
to finance a dramatic increase in administrative and legal staff in order
to execute all these new public tasks could simply not be found. Even
allowing for subsidies to plantation America coming from the metropolitan governments, it was not realistic to expect the mother country
to finance a level of public service that continually would have exceeded
such expenditure at home. It is a strange paradox that many metropolitan abolitionists crying for state intervention in the ex-slaveholding areas
seemed to have been blind to the consequences of the state's noninter-
vention at home. Nowhere in the metropole was there equal justice,
regardless of social class. During the first half of the nineteenth century,
state intervention in education was still very limited, as it was in the

imposition and the supervision of labor laws. The same applied to state-supplied public housing and medical care.

The public sector could only play a limited part in changing the underlying socioeconomic realities of plantation America. The prevalent ideology about the general role of government in society and the practical limits of government spending did not permit the various governments in the American plantation areas to carry out a restructuring of the postslavery society single-handedly. It also should be kept in mind that the links between the private and public elite were quite close in plantation America, as they were in many other societies at the time. Local planters occupied positions of authority in administration, the judiciary, and the army. Only in Haiti and in the U.S. South were such positions lost due to the fact that slave emancipation had been achieved after a war in which the established plantation elite had been defeated.[8]

In many ex-slaveholding areas, the state intervention that materialized after emancipation closely resembled the level of state intervention already existing during the last decades of slavery. A good example of this is provided by the Dutch colony of Surinam, where since the early 1850s the colonial government officially accepted complaints by slaves against their masters and instituted minimum food rations as well as the compulsory distribution of household utensils and clothing. The judicial powers of the slave owners had also been curtailed, and severe corporal punishment — more than twenty lashes — could be administered only by a public servant. Plantations had to comply, at least on paper, with minimum standards set for slave housing and medical care. In order to encourage the propagation of Christianity, the colonial government in Surinam published yearly surveys of those plantations where missionary activities were allowed (Boogaart and Emmer 1977:205–25; Siwpersad 1979:240–43).

After emancipation, the local governments carried on in the same vein. In Surinam special circuit judges were appointed to allow the ex-slaves better access to justice. New labor laws were published, which set minimum wages according to the type of work performed. Attending school was made compulsory. Public hospital capacity and public welfare payments were increased to compensate for the reduction of medical care and for the stoppage of free food rations and free clothing for the ex-slave young, sick, and elderly.

It seems clear, therefore, that the financial and ideological constraints on the role of government at the time of emancipation made for continuity and precluded a dramatic increase in the provision of social and judicial services in plantation America, which could have made the freed-men's position in society really different from that held during slavery. In comparison to the level of government intervention in society in general, however, governmental attempts to influence labor and living conditions of the freedmen in postslavery America were considerable (Green 1976:353–79; Donald 1978:179–90).

Emancipation and the Freedmen of Plantation America

In envisioning a slaveless society, the abolitionists had not only far-flung expectations about the role of government but also about the future social and economic position of the liberated slaves. They expected that after emancipation the ex-slaves would be able to choose the means of making a living according to their own decisions, either as independent farmers or as employees. Exercising their freedom of movement, the ex-slaves would have access to public services. As consumers, they would increase the demand for food and other consumer goods, thus creating more opportunities for local industries and for the sale of more goods imported from the metropole. And—last but not least—the ex-slaves were expected to convert en masse to Christianity and to embrace Western norms and values (Hind 1987).

It is certain that most of these expectations held by the metropolitan abolitionists were not shared by the ex-slaves. From what we know about the insurrections and strikes by slaves in the decades preceding abolition and from the behavior of freedmen during the first years following emancipation, it is clear that (1) freedom of movement was very important to the former slaves, (2) the freedmen were keen on changing the mix between undertaking self-employed economic activities and taking up employment as plantation laborers to include more self-employment, and (3) the freedmen considered receiving wages as a reward for labor to be very important (Foner 1983:8–38).

Yet another set of expectations about the future of the postemancipation societies in the Americas was to be found among managers and owners of plantations. Their views were usually rather pessimistic as they envisioned a general decline in plantation agriculture due to the ex-slaves' reversion to barbarism. In using the word *barbarism,* the planters sought primarily to express their fears that the ex-slaves would not be interested in maximizing their monetary incomes but, instead, would be content to earn just enough to satisfy their limited needs. In Europe, the money needed for sheer physical survival usually required a full week's work by virtually all members of a proletarian family, but in plantation America, the labor of just one member of a freedman's family for only a few days per week would suffice, thus causing a considerable decline in the regular supply of the available labor force (Foner 1983:40–41; Lobdell 1988:198).

In spite of the differences between these various expectations, all parties assumed that the future lives of the freedmen would be drastically different from their lives as slaves. Few observers imagined there would be substantial continuity between the last decades of slavery and the first decades of freedom.

First of all, if the freedmen remained at home their employment opportunities were usually rather limited. As has been pointed out before, most economic activities in plantation America revolved around agriculture, and this did not change because of slave emancipation. In order to enjoy continued economic growth, plantation America had to continue producing goods that were in high demand in the outside world: tropical cash crops. The competitive production of these crops virtually excluded opportunities for small-scale export agriculture. The small-scale farming of food crops for the internal market at higher than plantation incomes was possible for only a limited number of freedmen (Klein and Engerman 1985:255–69).

The abolitionists did not seem to have taken account of these important limitations in the freedmen's opportunities to exercise a completely free choice in a plantation society. Some ex-slaves, however, had been able to make a realistic evaluation of squatting as an alternative to plantation labor. In eighteenth-century Surinam and Jamaica, groups of maroons regularly attacked the plantations and encouraged the slaves there to flee and join them in their forest communities. In spite of the obvious chance to obtain their freedom, many slaves preferred to remain on the plantation, seemingly aware of the precarious living conditions of the various maroon groups in the interior of the colony. It is true that after emancipation the military harassment of the runaway slaves was halted, and maroon life subsequently became more sedentary and comfortable. After the ending of hostilities, some maroons started to specialize in the production, transport, and sale of wood to the plantations. However, these activities failed to create substantial opportunities to obtain a regular increase in income among the communities of runaway slaves (Kappler 1983:136; Hoogbergen 1983:109). At no time and at no place could the plantation slaves and freedmen have seen or experienced that the maroon economy provided at least as regular a personal income as plantation labor did. Thus in choosing to move into the interior after abolition, the ex-slaves must have continued to be aware of the fact that they were cutting their ties with the most reliable employment sector in the economy. In plantation America, small-scale farming provided the ex-slaves with no more than a subsistence income, comparable to that of a Third World peasant today, substantially lower than the income of a small European or North American yeoman-farmer.[9]

Indeed, the freedmen seemed to have realized that they could not sever the links with the plantations completely. In the first decade after emancipation, with the ending of apprenticeship, only the ex-slave women and children withdrew more or less completely from offering labor to the plantations. The male freedmen gradually stopped supplying regular labor, though many continued to work as part of jobbing gangs for a contracted period of time in order to do a particular job. The ex-slaves did this in spite of the fact that the wages increased in many areas before the introduction of Asian immigrant labor and in spite of the fact that their concerted action would have made it possible to increase wages and to improve conditions even more in view of the expensive alternatives of obtaining labor elsewhere. The reluctance of the plantation managers to increase wages out of fear of thereby obtaining even less labor seems to have been a reaction to the freedmen's defiance of the laws of supply and demand (Green 1976:196–99; Adamson 1972: 119–21, 165–66; Engerman 1982:200–01).

What explains the noncapitalist behavior of the ex-slaves and their backward-bending labor supply curve? It has been argued that life on the plantations enabled slaves to prepare themselves for the market economy that came into existence after abolition. For example, slaves were able to cultivate their own garden plots. It has been pointed out that the private production of the slaves far exceeded their consumption of food, that they marketed much of this produce outside the plantations, and they they derived considerable amounts of money from this. All this would appear to demonstrate that slaves were capable of running their own enterprises, of regulating their own time, and of applying their agricultural skills without the pressures of the plantation management (Mintz 1985:134–39).

Unfortunately, many of these explanations miss the essential point. There is no doubt that the slaves could work without the constant threat of the whip and possessed the capacity to grow and to sell foodstuffs. These phenomena by themselves do not constitute sufficient skills to compete in the market economy. Thus, doubt remains about whether

the slaves were positioned to grasp the intricacies of a market for agricultural produce and to work and cultivate according to the demands
of such a market. The plantation had not prepared the slaves for that.
Slave markets were not really part of the capitalist economy but were
the colorful proof of a "vent for surplus," since the slaves had their
basic necessities of life provided by the plantations. In fact, slavery had
shielded the slaves from the market economy in which the maximizing
of income constitutes the key element. This would explain why the economic behavior of the freedmen was much more a reaction to the plantation society than a careful calculation of economic opportunities.

The lack of a full exposure to the market would explain the peculiarities of the supply of rental labor by the ex-slaves on a market with
rapidly increasing rewards for such labor. In addition, this lacuna would
also explain why the ex-slaves did not really attempt to tap the next
best opportunity to obtain a regular income by developing an alternative, small-scale agricultural economy when working away from the
plantations. Research regarding the freedmen's attitude to this type of
agriculture and its economic profitability clearly reveals the freedmen's
disastrously inefficient division of land and inheritance of land, as well
as the voluntary nonuse and communal use of land, which resulted in
low yields and poor incomes.[10] By creating their "counterculture" and
by moving away from the plantations, many slaves paid a price in declining incomes in kind and reduced money, on average.[11]

What evidence do we have regarding the freedmen's economic attitudes? First, we will look into the availability of public welfare after
the ending of slavery. Then we will discuss the advantages and disad-
vantages of the new freedom of movement. Finally, attention will be
paid to the consequences of exchanging an income in kind for a monetary income.

It is surprising to note that the freedmen seemed not to worry that
the general availability of public welfare would take a long time to come
about and would involve a considerable amount of public expenditure.
Obviously, the services of the estate hospitals and of the visiting estate
doctors could not easily be replaced. Access to medical care after emancipation became even more difficult for those freedmen who had moved
to the sparsely populated hinterland of the plantation areas. Demographic
research will have to show whether this decline of medical care, as well
as a decline in income for the young, the old, and the sick, actually did
have detrimental effects on the mortality and fertility of the freedmen
(Green 1976:309–13; Sheridan 1985:337–42; Kiple and King 1981:187–90).

The freedom of the ex-slave to move around also looked better on paper than it turned out to be in actual practice. Obviously, the many years of slavery had built up a desperate desire among large numbers of freedmen to just move. The cohesion among the slaves turned out to be much weaker than had been expected. Some studies based on plantation records indicate that the slaves living on plantations had slowly created closeknit village communities, especially after the ending of the slave imports from Africa. This argument has also been used to explain why the slaves had always been opposed to moving to other plantations, in the case of two or more plantations combining under the same management in an attempt to reduce costs. The massive exodus after emancipation, however, seems to suggest that ex-slaves were not opposed to moving frequently and were obviously not afraid of cutting their ties with relatives and neighbors.

Within plantation regions, the possibilities for freedmen actually to profit from increased mobility were limited to moving either to another plantation in search of better paid employment or to cities and villages. Over time, some freedmen even migrated over much longer distances and took up temporary employment abroad. Did they move in the hope of obtaining a higher income, easier work, or more labor satisfaction by settling on unoccupied lands? Many of these movements—at least within the plantation region—did not coincide with an increase in income. In the Dutch Caribbean, ex-slaves started to move during the period of apprenticeship, when all plantations offered exactly the same wages to their apprentices. This seems to indicate that they did not move in response to market pressures but out of other considerations. The detrimental effects of the "disease to constantly move" were mentioned time and again by various observers. The internal and external migrations broke up families and reduced the possibilities of access to medical care and to schools for the children.[12]

The changeover from nonmonetary to monetary incomes also had some drawbacks, especially for those who could not unload the pressures of inflation on their employer. True, the monetization of society allowed the freedmen to tune their economic needs more precisely to their own wishes. In reality, however, the ability to buy other items than those provided during slavery was limited. In addition, the rapid monetization of the ex-slave societies caused price inflation, eroding the buying power of those who could not adjust their incomes. The children and elderly relatives of the freedmen no longer had an income in kind of their own, as had been the case before emancipation. Thus the

payment of wages allowed for greater economic and social differentiation in the postemancipation society than had been possible in the previous slave society. Those who could offer skilled labor and had few
dependents were able to increase their personal income, while the incomes of single women with young children, as well as of the aged, declined. Some observers, however, have given us a different impression
of the freedmen's buying power, indicating an increase in luxury imports into the former slave-holding areas right after emancipation. A
caveat is in order here. Some of these imports might in fact have been
paid for from savings accumulated during slavery but spent after emancipation, because only then did a sufficient number of retail shops become established.

It should also be remembered that the payment of wages linked the
freedmen to the market economy, with its changing prices. The changes
in consumer goods prices had previously been faced by the plantation
management. After the introduction of wages, however, the freedmen
were exposed to the ups and downs of the market for labor as well as
the market for consumer goods; many freedmen did not like these changes
or at least had not been prepared for them. Consequently, the rebellions and riots against the pressures within the slavery system were replaced by riots and rebellions against the vicissitudes of the market economy (Ward 1988:244).[13]

Finally, the freedmen's improved access to Western religion and culture should be mentioned. It is doubtful whether this aspect of emancipation was as highly valued by the ex-slaves as the abolitionists had
hoped for. In the U.S. South, where there were white majorities everywhere, readier access to Christian churches and schools could be an important means of obtaining more social prestige and better jobs. By contrast, in the Caribbean and in northeastern Brazil there was virtually
no employment available requiring a Western type of education. What
good was such education if it could not be used? In view of this, it is
not surprising that the missionaries, who had attributed the persistence
of non-Christian religious beliefs among the slaves to their own limited
access to plantations, continued to complain that the freedmen at times
openly showed that their religious and cultural preferences were Creole,
not Western (Green 1976:327–32; Ransom and Sutch 1977:23–31).

In concluding this essay on the meaning of freedom for ex-slaves,
it should be stressed again that the margins of change in plantation
America were extremely limited both for employers and employed, much

more so than in the diversified economies of western Europe and north-eastern America. Any move away from the plantation system was both costly and a step away from increased personal incomes and national economic growth. The creation of a counterculture by the freedmen brought them, on average, a decline in income, and the freedmen's use of their new freedom to move broke up established communities and families. The introduction of money could hardly have rapid beneficial effects in a plantation society after abolition; instead, it created decreases in the power to consume of the young, the old, and the sick.

Many of these phenomena also occurred in Europe and North America, when the securities of the ancien régime were exchanged for the uncertainties of an industrialized society. However, that transition turned out to have been the start of unrivalled economic growth, which pushed such transitional drawbacks into oblivion. In plantation America, on the other hand, the transition from slavery to freedom did not create new possibilities for economic growth. Instead, the outcome of emancipation adversely affected the only growth sector in the economy. The subsequent decline took decades to reverse, if it was reversed at all.

Conclusion

In reviewing the paragraphs dealing with the influence of slave emancipation on the course of nineteenth-century European political expansion overseas, it seems difficult to detect any important connection between these two phenomena. European expansion into Asia had already started before 1800, and the French and British penetration of Africa occurred long after abolition in the Americas. Similarly, while slave emancipation and the subsequent decline in international investment in plantation America might have increased the capital available for investment in Europe's new industrial enterprises and mines, in railways, and in land development companies in North and South America, slave emancipation itself did not cause any further internationalization of trade and monetary flows.

Turning to plantation America itself, a similar observation can be made. Emancipation speeded up the process by which the amount of investment from Europe came to resemble that in other nonsettlement areas. Emancipation did not change the management of plantations nor the role of government and justice. Emancipation itself did not give rise to innovations, it only increased the speed of their implementation. Emancipation did increase the range of options for settlement and employment for the ex-slaves, but hardly any of these new options allowed for a dramatic increase in their incomes.

In many ways, emancipation reduced plantation America to the economic situation that existed in most agricultural areas at the time outside of Europe and North America. Emancipation could not and did not elevate plantation America to the economic level of the colonies of white settlement, where the increasing opportunities for growth allowed some of these areas to surpass even European income levels. Only the plantations provided tropical America with a strong link to the investment and consumer markets of both North America and western Europe. On the other hand, the production of subsistence farming in northeastern Brazil, the Caribbean, and the U.S. South did not attract the interest of international investors or overseas consumers. The special agro-industrial export areas in the New World could not retain their productive capacity without the presence of a readily available labor force bound to these industries.

There were a few exceptions. First, the cotton plantations of the U.S. South have already been mentioned. Their cash crop could be grown on small plots without the costs of production rising to uncompetitive levels. For that reason, many southern ex-slaves took the opportunity to become producers of cotton as sharecroppers and thus managed to share in the profits from the special endowments of the Cotton South for some decades after emancipation.

In the densely populated areas in the Caribbean, the sugar planters could rely on the availability of local labor. The plantations in the areas concerned, Barbados and Antigua, were able to continue to profit from the international demand for sugar. Unfortunately, the ex-slaves were not able to increase their share in these profits because of the exceptionally large supply of labor, partly due to a unique natural increase of the population on these two islands. As a result, many Barbadian and Antiguan freedmen saw their incomes decline, some having to migrate overseas in order to escape unemployment. This would indicate that by migrating the Barbadians and Antiguans responded to the postemancipation changes as a capitalist proletariat, while the freedmen in Jamaica, Trinidad, and the Guyanas did not.

Brazil also retained its profitable link with the international commodity market by producing coffee on the new plantations in the south, worked by European immigrants. The ex-slaves from the old plantations in the *nordeste* should have moved to these new coffee areas, but they did not. Because of an imperfect labor market, the Brazilian freedmen remained in the north, where the declining plantation sector hardly allowed them any more leverage to obtain a greater share in the proceeds of these plantations than they used to have as slaves (Klein and Engerman 1985:250–67).[14]

This leaves us with the sparsely populated parts of the Caribbean. Here the key question is why the ex-slaves in those areas did not manage to use more of the international advantages of Caribbean sugar production to their own benefit. In most of the Caribbean, there was no danger of a rapid increase in the local supply of labor; on the eve of emancipation, the labor force in the region was still shrinking due to demographic decline. Admittedly, the huge sugar plantations of the Caribbean required difficult and hard work, and many plantations could be considered health hazards. However, during the last decades of slavery, abolitionist action had created labor laws for the plantations, which at the time were scarce anywhere. Some of these measures had been successful in reducing mortality among the plantation laborers. The flight from the plantations prevented the growth of capitalist labor relations as occurred in western Europe and North America at the time. There is reason to assume that the freedmen could have forced the plantation management to raise the general wage level to about or even somewhat beyond the costs of importing indentured laborers from British India and China.[15]

In the existing literature, the withdrawal of the freedmen from the plantation has been mainly ascribed to psychological reasons. Slavery's redistributive system of set wages in kind had not prepared the slaves for a market economy nor had the economic traditions the slaves had carried over from Africa. Even if we make allowances for the different legal settings for slaves and indentured laborers, it is surprising to see how the Chinese and Indian immigrants, alien to the Caribbean but coming from societies with market economies, did manage to use the Caribbean plantations to their advantage (Green 1976:285–86).

More research is needed to see what made the alternatives to plantation labor seem so advantageous to the freedmen. The possibility to obtain nothing more than a most basic income in kind from subsistence farming was perhaps not evident right away. Did the freedmen expect that over time their new agricultural pursuits would show potential for economic growth? Did the ex-slave women and children earn more by working their own small plots than by offering their labor on the plantations? In theory, the development of small-scale market agriculture would have been possible in the Caribbean, but in actual practice the absence of a Creole middle class of farmers in this sector of the economy, who could have improved agricultural techniques and who could have introduced new equipment, precluded the development of highly profitable, small-scale farming à la North America and western Europe.

Taking up employment elsewhere in the Caribbean was another alternative to obtaining an income outside the hated plantations at home, and many freedmen resorted to this in spite of the fact that many of these overseas jobs were also located at plantations. The financial benefits of the inter-Caribbean labor migration are not known, but these were not so substantial as to allow for a rise in living standards for those who stayed at home. The same applied for going into the forests in search of gold and rubber. In addition, the social costs of the alternatives to plantation labor should also be considered. It might well be that the long-distance labor migration in the Caribbean caused more harm to the cohesion of the freedmen's families than the plantations had caused to those of the slaves (Ward 1985:56–60).

We should return to the French proverb quoted at the beginning of this chapter. Emancipation could not possibly square the circle by providing higher incomes without regimented plantation labor, at least not in those parts of America where the business economics of cash crop production could not be organized in any other way than by using large-scale plantation agriculture. The decline of the plantations made the Caribbean and Brazil lose their position as the darlings of the New World. Instead, without export crops these regions had become the "cinderellas" of America, with a low potential for growth, a nonmarket-oriented peasantry, high unemployment, and a massive influx of migrant workers from Asia and Europe.[16]

It is fortunate that most Europen colonial powers did not use the declining economy of their Caribbean possessions as an argument to abandon them in the course of the nineteenth century. By retaining their presence in the Caribbean, the colonial powers were increasingly forced to subsidize the creation of a basic infrastructure of schools, roads, and medical services in the postslavery era. Only in Haiti did emancipation— again—mean real change, because it completely destroyed the colonial ties with France and thus the possibility ever to receive metropolitan subsidies. The postslavery type of freedom in Haiti and its complete break with the outside world, however, have never stimulated the staging of an encore anywhere else in plantation America.[17]

In Haiti, the successful slave revolt and the sudden drop in exports caused a dramatic decline in national and personal income. This analysis seems to have also been made by several of the ex-slave leaders during Haiti's early years of independence. In spite of the wholesale destruction of the plantations in that country, it is doubtful whether the leaders of the abolitionist party actually were in favor of the ending of plantation agriculture. Right after the most violent phase of the Haitian revolution had passed and the foreign troops had left, attempts were made to revive part of the plantation agriculture worked by *corvée* labor. However, the process of peasantization had progressed to such an extent that it could not be reversed. The country's new autarkic peasant economy soon yielded incomes, which were, and are, similar to the income levels in many other Third World areas. Other Caribbean plantation areas had at least been able to retain some of their exceptional export earnings after abolition. By contrast, Haiti lost its international earning capacity quickly and became a typical Third World country much earlier than its neighbors. That is why the French proverb, when applied to the Caribbean might be changed to say, the more things change, the more they become the same.

NOTES

My thanks to Seymour Drescher and Larry Yarak for their editorial assistance.

1. The dramatic costs of the French Revolution are calculated by Sédillot (1987).
2. The question whether the system of free labor could be exported from Europe to other parts of the world is discussed in Drescher (1986:241–44).
3. Figures on the relative economic importance of the West Indies within the British Empire are provided in Drescher (1977:16–25).
4. On the links between the suppression of the Atlantic slave trade and the European penetration into West Africa, see Fage (1978:332). On the physical difficulties in growing sugar in coastal West Africa, see Gemery and Hogendorn (1979: 429–49). On the resilience of plantation America in the production of sugar, tobacco, and cotton, see Davis (1979:124–25).
5. See Richardson (1984:257). On Queensland, see Galloway (1989:232). On Hawaii, see Beechert (1985:79–80). On the rise of beet sugar production, see Galloway (1989:132–33).
6. Fieldhouse (1973:97, 55–59) gives the geographical distribution of British, French, German, and U.S. overseas investments around 1900.
7. Innovations in the production of coffee were limited to the process of depulping after the beans had been harvested by hand (Stein 1985: 234–38). Techno-

logical improvements in cotton production were limited to ginning and compressing cotton after it had been picked by hand (Ransom and Sutch 1977:116).

8. On the financial limitations of local governments in the British Caribbean, see Green (1976:309–12). The place of abolitionism within a wider metropolitan movement pressing for reform is discussed by Harrison (1980:109–48).

9. On the resistance of plantation slaves to join the maroons in their difficult life in the jungle, see Hoogbergen (1985:403).

10. Jean Besson (1987:14–31) argues that the development of family land outside the plantations first of all had a symbolic value.

11. On the development of per capita incomes, see Klein and Engerman (1985: 261, 265). On the changing consumption pattern of the ex-slaves, see Ward (1988: 246–48).

12. After the abolition of the slave trade, it was impossible to increase the enslaved labor force except by buying slaves already employed elsewhere. See Boogaart and Emmer (1977:209). Surprisingly, Ward (1988:19) indicates that Jamaican planters hardly resorted to amalgamating groups of slaves. On the freedom to move, see Stein (1985:263); Ransom and Sutch (1977:44). For complaints by missionaries on the freedom to move, see Oostindie (1989:195–99).

13. The most violent opposition to the new market conditions for labor and consumer goods was the Morant Bay Rebellion, Jamaica, 1865. See Green (1976: 381–82).

14. On postemancipation migration within and out of the Caribbean, see Watts (1987:481–83). On Brazil see da Costa (1985:170) and da Costa (1988).

15. On the wages and strikes in the Caribbean, see Green (1976:198–99). The willingness of employers to spend more on labor was, of course, most obvious in the sparsely populated Caribbean (Moore 1987:37–39).

16. Admittedly, the cash crop production could not give the same growth rate to plantation America as was achieved in Europe and parts of North America (Ward 1985:63–65).

17. Unfortunately, there exists no survey of metropolitan subsidies to the Caribbean between 1830 and decolonization. For a general evaluation of government spending within the British Empire, see Davis and Huttenback (1986:306–18). There is no doubt that the French and Dutch also heavily subsidized government spending in their respective Caribbean possessions. See August (1985:40).

REFERENCES

Adamson, Alan H. 1972. *Sugar Without Slaves: The Political Economy of British Guiana, 1838–1904.* New Haven: Yale University Press.

August, Thomas G., 1985. *The Selling of Empire: British and French Imperialist Propaganda, 1890–1940.* Westport: Greenwood Press.

Beechert, Edward D. 1985. *Working in Hawaii: A Labor History.* Honolulu: University of Hawaii Press.

Besson, Jean. 1987. A Paradox in Caribbean Attitudes to Land. In *Land and Development in the Caribbean,* edited by Jean Besson and Janet Momsen, 13–45. London: Macmillan.

Boogaart, E. van den, and P. C. Emmer. 1977. Plantation Slavery in Surinam in the Last Decade before Emancipation: The Case of Catharina Sophia. In *Comparative Perspectives on Slavery in New World Plantation Societies*, edited by Vera Rubin and Arthur Tuden, 205–25. New York: The New York Academy of Sciences.

Curtin, Philip D. 1975. *Two Jamaicas: The Role of Ideas in a Tropical Colony, 1830–1865.* New York: Atheneum.

da Costa, Emilia Viotti. 1985. *The Brazilian Empire: Myths and Histories.* Chicago: The University of Chicago Press.

———. 1988. The Policy of Neglect or the Neglect of Policy. Paper prepared for the Conference on the Meaning of Freedom. University of Pittsburgh.

Davis, Lance, and Robert A. Huttenback. 1986. *Mammon and the Pursuit of Empire: The Political Economy of British Imperialism, 1860–1912.* Cambridge: Cambridge University Press.

Davis, Ralph. 1979. *The Industrial Revolution and British Overseas Trade.* Leicester: Leicester University Press.

Deerr, Noel. 1949. *The History of Sugar.* London: Chapman and Hall.

Donald, David Herbert. 1978. *Liberty and Union.* Lexington: D. C. Heath.

Donghi, Tulio Halperin. 1985. Economy and Society in Post-Independence Spanish America. In *The Cambridge History of Latin America* 3:299–345. Cambridge: Cambridge University Press.

Drescher, Seymour. 1977. *Econocide: British Slavery in the Era of Abolition.* Pittsburgh: University of Pittsburgh Press.

———. 1986. *Capitalism and Antislavery: British Mobilization in Comparative Perspective.* London: Macmillan.

Elson, R. E. 1984. *Javanese Peasants and the Colonial Sugar Industry: Impact and Change in an East Java Residence, 1830–1940.* Singapore: Oxford University Press.

Eltis, David. 1982. Abolitionist Perceptions of Society After Slavery. In *Slavery and British Society, 1776–1846,* edited by James Walvin. London: Macmillan.

———. 1987. *Economic Growth and the Ending of the Transatlantic Slave Trade.* New York: Oxford University Press.

Engerman, Stanley L. 1982. Economic Adjustments to Emancipation in the United States and British West Indies. *Journal of Interdisciplinary History* 13:191–220.

Engerman, Stanley L., and David Eltis. 1980. Economic Aspects of the Abolition Debate. In *Anti-Slavery, Religion, and Reform: Essays in Memory of Roger Anstey,* edited by Christine Bolt and Seymour Drescher, 275–80. Folkestone: Dawson.

Fage, J. D. 1978. *A History of Africa.* London: Hutchinson.

Fieldhouse, D. K. 1973. *Economics and Empire, 1830–1914.* London: Weidenfeld and Nicolson.

Foner, Eric. 1983. *Nothing But Freedom: Emancipation and Its Legacy.* Baton Rouge: Louisiana State University Press.

Galloway, J. H. 1989. *The Sugar Cane Industry: An Historical Geography from Its Origins to 1914.* Cambridge: Cambridge University Press.

Gemery, H. A., and Jan Hogendorn. 1979. Comparative Disadvantage: The Case of Sugar Cultivation in West Africa. *Journal of Interdisciplinary History* 9:429–49.

Green, William A. 1976. *British Slave Emancipation: The Sugar Colonies and the Great Experiment, 1830–1865.* Oxford: Oxford University Press.

Hall, Douglas. 1959. *Free Jamaica, 1838–1865: An Economic History.* New Haven: Yale University Press.

Harrison, Brian. 1980. A Genealogy of Reform in Modern Britain. In *Anti-Slavery, Religion, and Reform: Essays in Memory of Roger Anstey,* edited by Christine Bolt and Seymour Drescher, 109–48. Folkestone: Dawson.

Hind, Robert J. 1987. William Wilberforce and the Perceptions of the British People. *Historical Research: The Bulletin of the Institute of Historical Research* 60:321–35.

Hoogbergen, Wim S. M. 1983. Marronage en Marrons, 1760–1863: De niet-gepacificeerde Marrons van Suriname. In *Suriname, de schele onafhankelijkheid,* edited by Glenn Willemsen, 75–110. Amsterdam: De Arbeiderspers.

———. 1985. *De Boni-oorlogen, 1757–1860: Marronage en guerilla in Oost-Suriname.* Utrecht: Centrum voor Caraïbische Studies.

Kappler, A. 1983. *Zes jaren in Suriname, 1836–1842: Schetsen en taferelen.* Zutphen: Walberg Pers.

Kiple, Kenneth F., and Virginia Himmelsteib King. 1981. *Another Dimension to the Black Diaspora: Diet, Disease, and Racism.* Cambridge: Cambridge University Press.

Klein, Herbert S., and Stanley L. Engerman. 1985. The Transition from Slave to Free Labor: Notes on a Comparative Economic Model. In *Between Slavery and Free Labor: The Spanish-Speaking Caribbean in the Nineteenth Century,* edited by Manuel Moreno Fraginals, Frank Moya Pons, and Stanley L. Engerman, 255–69. Baltimore: Johns Hopkins University Press.

Lewis, Gordon K. 1983. *Main Currents in Caribbean Thought: The Historical Evolution of Caribbean Society in Its Ideological Aspects, 1492–1900.* Kingston: Heinemann.

Lobdell, Richard A. 1988. British Officials and the West Indian Peasantry, 1842–1938. In *Labour in the Caribbean: From Emancipation to Independence,* edited by Malcolm Cross and Gad Heuman, 195–207. London: Macmillan.

Mintz, Sidney W. 1985. From Plantations to Peasantries in the Caribbean. In *Caribbean Contours,* edited by Sidney W. Mintz and Sally Price, 127–53. Baltimore: Johns Hopkins University Press.

Moore, Brian L. 1987. *Race, Power, and Social Segmentation in Colonial Society: Guyana After Slavery, 1838–1891.* New York: Gordon and Breach.

Oostindie, Gert. 1989. *Roosenburg in Mon Bijou: Twee Surinamse Plantages, 1720–1870.* Dordrecht: Foris.

Ransom, Roger L., and Richard Sutch. 1977. *One Kind of Freedom: The Economic Consequences of Emancipation.* Cambridge: Cambridge University Press.

Richardson, Peter. 1984. The Natal Sugar Industry in the Nineteenth Century. In *Crisis and Change in the International Sugar Economy, 1860–1914,* edited by Bill Albert and Adrian Graves, 237–58. Norwich: ISC Press.

Sédillot, Réné. 1987. *Le coût de la Révolution française: Vérités et légendes.* Paris: Perrin.

Sheridan, Richard. 1985. *Doctors and Slaves: A Medical and Demographic History of Slavery in the British West Indies, 1680–1834.* Cambridge: Cambridge University Press.

Siwpersad, J. P. 1979. *De Nederlandse regering en de afschaffing van de Surinaamse slavernij, 1833–1863*. Groningen/Castricum: Bouma/Hagen.

Stein, Stanley J. 1985. *Vassouras: A Brazilian Coffee County, 1850–1900: The Roles of Planter and Slave in a Plantation Society*. Princeton: Princeton University Press.

Ward, J. R. 1985. *Poverty and Progress in the Caribbean, 1800–1960*. London: Macmillan.

——. 1988. *British West Indian Slavery, 1750–1834: The Process of Amelioration*. Oxford: Oxford University Press.

Watts, David. 1987. *The West Indies: Patterns of Development, Culture, and Environmental Change Since 1492*. Cambridge: Cambridge University Press.

STANLEY L. ENGERMAN

The Economic Response to Emancipation and Some Economic Aspects of the Meaning of Freedom

Frames of Reference for the Evaluation of Emancipation

Interest in the study of emancipation — and the meaning of freedom and its converse, the meaning of nonfreedom — is reflected in two central concerns of historians. For some, the study of emancipation and its consequences may offer insight into the beliefs and attitudes of slaves and masters prior to this dramatic change in the legal arrangements under which society operated. For others, emancipation and its aftermath present important historical issues in their own right. These two approaches are related. The two major issues to be examined include (1) the influence upon the outcomes of emancipation of the values and beliefs that were carried out of slavery by ex-slaves and free whites and planters, and (2) comparisons between the lives of slaves and ex-slaves after the legal change imposed by the end of slavery — a change that may or may not, however, have dramatically changed much else.

It is, of course, very difficult to provide any simple overarching interpretation of the meaning of emancipation. New World emancipations took place in a number of quite different societies, in which slavery had played quite distinct roles, and in which there were a wide variety of slave experiences.[1] There were also important differences in the process of emancipation and the circumstances in which the stage was set for postslavery behavior. Moreover, emancipation had differential impacts upon all aspects of human life. We must not assume that all the outcomes proceeded along parallel lines. Historical judgments also differ depending on whether we are asking about short-run changes in ex-slave standards of living, the long-term economic developments of society, political controls, social and cultural life, or demographic changes. Often what is regarded as a favorable outcome in one dimension implies an unfavorable outcome in another.

The analysis of emancipation is linked to the understanding of the study of slavery.[2] Patterns of behavior and belief developed over centuries cannot be expected to change overnight with the granting of freedom. As our views change of the nature of the slave economy, of the roles of slaves in these economies, and of the abilities of slaves to develop their own cultures, our views of emancipation should also be adjusted. The arguments that slave economies were expanding, that slave labor yielded high levels of output, and that slaves' religion and culture were stronger than earlier scholars had argued all point to a need to reconsider the short- and long-term consequences of the ending of slavery.

Thus, one key economic question historians and economic historians ask deals with the impact of the ex-slaves' value system interacting with (resisting?) basic economic constraints (whether imposed by local society or exogenously determined). How do values influence choices about ex-slaves' work and leisure, for example, or about market production versus self-sufficiency production (two quite distinct matters). A choice for either more leisure or more self-sufficiency, perhaps regarded as desirable goals in themselves, may have meant lowered long-term income. Thus less consumption, poorer health care, and prolonged debt—none of which are desirable goals—could have been the possible, if unintended, consequences of ex-slaves' freedom to make decisions about work patterns. These decisions are important to analyze because emancipation, and the resulting changes in legal controls over the labor force, intensified the conflicting values of ex-planters and ex-slaves and the need for these conflicts to be resolved within the new legal order.

The current focus of historical studies is on ex-slaves, with less concern given to planters and their circumstances. This concentration, however attractive politically, means that some important possible paths of economic growth within the postemancipation society are downplayed, if not ignored. More generally, too often emancipation is, to use the jargon, looked upon as a zero-sum game: if one group benefits, the other necessarily loses. Yet, as most cases of postemancipation societies abundantly illustrate, there are policy decisions that could benefit both parties, planters and ex-slaves, as well as policy decisions wherein all might lose. Thus it is necessary to look at both sides of the issue, both to see what could have happened and to analyze what actually occurred. The lack of success of one party did not have to mean a gain for the other, even if neither succeeded in what they attempted.

A final consideration at the start needs to be stressed. Short-term political and economic changes in one direction may generate unanticipated long-term developments in a quite different direction, whether due to the response of one party to the perceived gains of the other in the immediate aftermath of emancipation or to the long-run consequences of the earlier decisions. Over time, there will be some interaction with subsequent events, not necessarily directly related to slavery or emancipation. These, too, will influence the long-term outcomes.

Changing Concepts of the Preemancipation Economy and Society

In discussing emancipation, we are heavily influenced by our interpretations of the conditions existing under slavery. New World slavery can be understood historically as the legal control by one individual over another, who is held as property and who can be bought, sold, and moved at the owner's will. The status of slave was generally inherited. Slavery had long been in existence, in many parts of the world, as the extreme end of a spectrum of coerced labor and control over a population. During its long existence, however, there were no major attacks upon slavery as a system in the Western world before the last quarter of the eighteenth century. Earlier concerns were with the treatment of the enslaved or with the encouragement of manumissions, often conditional, for particular individuals, but these concerns did not question the existence of slavery itself. Then, during a period of about one hundred years in the Americas (and somewhat longer in Africa and Asia), slavery was limited and terminated (Miers and Roberts 1988). First the slave trade—whose ending was often expected, via a demographic effect, to weaken slavery—and then slavery itself were prohibited. In some cases the change was immediate, through military or legal action; in others it was achieved gradually, through periods of apprenticeship and restricted labor controls. These changes were achieved by metropolitan legislation for colonial areas or by domestic law (as a response to a civil war, revolution, or other political activity). The least common denominator indicating what emancipation meant was the withdrawal of a set of legal constraints that had existed to remove rights from the enslaved. Such redefined limits of control were a basic legal change more or less enforced by government and courts. It is important to emphasize that this basic meaning of emancipation, a legal change, did not necessarily entail any other important societal changes in the lives of ex-slaves or their ex-masters.

However, if the basic concept of slavery is its legal definition in contrast with the condition of free individuals, there are a number of nonlegal issues to consider when evaluating the impact of emancipation. Several recent interpretations concerning slavery have implications for the analysis and interpretation of emancipation. Much of this work is concerned with the depiction and analysis of the social and cultural life of the enslaved. It is clear that legal provisions (or their lack) do not necessarily define actual behavior. Despite the legal definition of slavery, slaves generated belief and behavior systems that combined, in an as yet uncertain combination, patterns drawn from Africa, Europe, and America.[3] Studies now indicate that the absence of legal terms favorable to slave family formation and maintenance did not preclude a strong sense of family, which the slaves carried forward after emancipation. And in areas of behavior where the law was basically silent, the slaves' influence upon the process and outcome of emancipation needs to be considered. Thus slave culture, religion, and work and family attitudes are not to be ignored when discussing the transition to freedom, and there is now more scholarly concern with continuities of belief systems and their interaction with other features of the postemancipation world. Slavery signified a sharp legal break, but its ending did not create so sharp a cultural break as many contemporary and earlier scholars have argued.

Similar points about nonlegal aspects of belief and behavior are also important in understanding white and nonslave society. One of the pervasive questions, given that by the time of emancipation in the New World all slaves were blacks or at least partially descended from involuntary migrants from Africa, concerns the role of racism and racial attitudes among whites and freed blacks. The interconnections of slavery and racism, and questions as to which were cause and which were effect, remain debated, and while the continued existence of racism and racial attitudes among whites around the time of emancipation is not to be doubted, its virulence did vary, and the policy dictates of a racial society point to rather diverse outcomes, as conditions vary. Laws can end slavery, but law alone cannot end racism.

In regard to economic questions, the major New World slave economies of the nineteenth century are no longer seen as stagnant, inefficient, and declining. Rather, these economies were frequently expanding, and that expansion was based primarily upon the production of staple crops on plantations, relying upon enslaved labor. Moreover, these slave economies had experienced growth for long periods and in competitive world markets. They had demonstrated considerable flexibility in regard to changing crop mix and geographic location in response to economic and political pressures. New World slave prices were rising through most of this period and, indeed, were at their peak a decade or two before emancipation. This understanding of the economic conditions of slave societies has led to a renewed debate concerning the politics of emancipation and the relative importance of economic and noneconomic facets (religious, secular, or humanitarian), within and without the slave areas, in the timing and the nature of the ending of slavery. Interpreting the consequences of emancipation requires an understanding of conditions at the end of the slave era and answers to such questions as how productive were plantations and how rapidly did these economies grow within the slave labor system.

Thus, while the ending of slavery entailed dramatic legal effects, other aspects of society did not change as dramatically, if at all. Such aspects include the locus of political, social, and economic power and policy in society; change and continuity in political leadership; the racial attitudes of the ruling classes (white or black) and the working classes (white or black); world economic conditions, including demand for plantation crops, tariffs and trade controls in consuming countries, and the existence of alternative sources of supply; production technology for agricultural crops and industries, including scale economies influencing the productivity of labor; and the climatic conditions impacting crop production. Similarly, attitudes and ideology, as seen in antislavery rhetoric and in the understanding of class factors, may carry over into the emancipation period.

Thus it is possible that the ideology of successful abolition movements actually limited economic choice when legal slavery was eliminated. Moreover, as freed slaves became part of the working and lower classes, upper- and middle-class beliefs regarding these classes influenced the social outcomes of emancipation. Not all aspects of white attitudes toward ex-slaves were the product of slavery or of the process of emancipation, as seen when the ex-slaves were regarded as one part of the working class. White beliefs that affected the outcome of emancipation were often generated with only limited attention to the peculiarities of the changing legal conditions of the ex-slaves. Concerns with local conditions and local working classes were therefore the basis of many of the rules under which emancipation evolved.

Economic Continuities and Changes

The basic economic fact of emancipation is that it caused dramatic changes in the profitability and efficiency of plantation production. With the shift to free labor, plantation crop output (and possibly total output) declined due to an exodus of ex-slaves from the plantation labor force. The planters' interest was to maintain the large-scale plantation. Attempts to keep ex-slaves on the plantation were usually unsuccessful, leading either to a long-term decline in plantation production or else, where it was still financially rewarding, the attraction of contract or bonded labor from elsewhere. The causes of their economic failure, given continuity in their political power and powers of coercion, remain under discussion, as does the incomplete use of power by remote ruling elites in dealing with the conflicting interests of the ex-masters, ex-slaves, and consumers. In any event, the decline of the plantation and the shift of the ex-slave labor force to small-scale production, at some possible cost to both planter elite and former slaves, represents one of the major, and seldom reversed, results of emancipation.

Economic adjustments varied dramatically among the societies in which emancipation occurred, depending upon crops produced and the overall ratio of labor to land. Even within a single polity with uniform laws and cultural patterns, results were diverse, as seen in the decline of plantation production upon emancipation, the quick recovery of this production, the mix of white and black labor in such recovery, and the location of crop production. These patterns reflected the differing optimum sizes of productive units under slavery and the feasibility of low-cost production with units of smaller sizes.

In the United States, for example, production declines were most severe and recovery slowest (if it occurred at all) on sugar and rice plantations, whose crops required the largest slave labor units. Indeed, the South Carolina rice industry effectively disappeared in the postemancipation era. And when the sugar industry in Louisiana recovered, it was on the basis of a dual sector — some large plantations with black labor and some small cane farms, generally with white owner-operators. For the major southern crop, cotton, and another staple, tobacco, the declines were less severe and the recoveries more rapid. Here, the optimum scale of a plantation was smaller than for sugar and rice, and the differences in efficiency between family farms and larger units were less pronounced. In cotton, plantation laborers did seek alternative arrangements. Family farms sharecropped by black labor were an important source of output in the expanding postbellum cotton sector, but much of the expansion in production came from white farmers who had been unable to compete with plantation gang labor in the antebellum era. These comparisons indicate the decisive role of scale in producing plantation crops, as well as the importance of alternative supplies of labor in permitting production to recover after emancipation and in leading to relocations of the ex-slave population.

The recovery of staple output and the adjustment of the labor force varied throughout the Americas by crop and population density. Most frequently, there were declines in plantation production, particularly of sugar, and an initial reduction of the plantation population. The planter class generally tried to maintain, for economic and other reasons, a large plantation sector. It did this by controlling the movements of freed laborers, both by new legal controls and by limiting laborers' access to land. The success of such policies was, as shall be shown, limited and not uniform across areas. Understanding these differences is important in analyzing the economic and political outcomes.

The plantation sector frequently resumed production under quite different circumstances than those under slavery. In sugar production, continuity and increased output characterized plantations in Barbados and Antigua, two islands of the British West Indies with extremely high population densities. Later, these islands were sources of labor for other places in the Caribbean. Several other British colonies, particularly British Guiana and Trinidad, rapidly expanded their plantation sectors and increased their sugar output, after several years of output decline. Since ex-slaves in these areas had largely left the plantations to live on small farms or in their own communities, the plantation revival depended upon a so-called new system of slavery, that is, indentured labor brought under contract from elsewhere in the world, most importantly India. But whereas British Guiana and Trinidad were thus able to resume the rapid expansion that characterized the late years of slavery, those areas in which growth was less rapid toward the end of slavery were not able to afford contract labor to replace the ex-slaves who left the plantations. In Jamaica, the largest of the British West Indian islands, the plantation sector declined, and sugar output did not return to preemancipation levels for a century. There, ex-slaves moved to small landholdings and produced different crops than that of the plantation. Initial attempts to attract European and Asian contract labor failed to have an important

impact upon the economy. The access to contract labor thus had quite
different outcomes, depending upon the underlying conditions in the
different areas, often reflecting the different conditions existing at the
end of the slave era.

In the major mid-nineteenth-century slave powers—the United States,
Cuba, and Brazil—the ending of slavery resulted in a quite different pattern of economic response from that in the British Caribbean. As noted,
in the United States, cotton, the principal slave-produced crop, suffered
an early decline in output. Yet cotton production recovered relatively
rapidly. The southern states remained the world's leading producer of
cotton, which actually represented a larger share of southern agricultural output in the postbellum than in the antebellum era. While most
ex-slaves remained in the cotton-producing sector, they now worked
on small farms, not plantations. White southerners also became heavily
involved in the production of cotton on small farms; they were drawn
from the reservoir of antebellum yeomen who had presumably been unable to compete with the slave plantation during its existence. In this
case, there was no need to attract additional agricultural labor from
overseas or from the northern states.

In Brazil, the rapidly expanding coffee sector declined briefly with
emancipation, but it soon recovered and continued to dominate world
markets. Yet, for the most part, ex-slaves had left coffee-producing plantations for inland rural areas or urban centers. The size of producing
units for coffee declined relative to that under slavery, and the primary
labor force was imported white labor, mostly immigrants from Italy
attracted by government subsidy. In northern Brazil, sugar output declined with emancipation. The ensuing recovery, with sales mainly in
Brazilian and not export markets, was based upon local labor, not immigrants, and involved the expansion of subsidized central mills. In both
Brazil and the United States, the end of slavery and the decline of the
plantation permitted the expansion of production on smaller farms.
These farms attracted white labor, whether by a shift from alternative
agriculture, as in the southern United States, or by immigration from
Europe, as in Brazil.

In cotton and coffee, the transition was easier because small-scale production, with some decline in efficiency, was possible—and indeed had
been attempted with limited success while slavery was still legal. In sugar
areas, however, until the late nineteenth century there seemed to be no
small-scale alternative, and as in the British Caribbean, the choices were
to grow sugar on plantations or not at all. Toward the end of the nine-

teenth century, the development of central milling permitted a system of small farms to develop, as an alternative (or complement) to plantation production. Thus the late date of Cuban emancipation (the 1880s) and its highly successful sugar-producing economy allowed a rapid adjustment in that country. The introduction of white-owned and -operated cane farms and of a labor force drawn partly from whites already in Cuban agriculture and partly from emigrants from Spain helped to increase postemancipation sugar output despite the declining plantation sector and the withdrawal of ex-slave labor. Thus, where the production of crops had been expanding and where the existing or developing new technology permitted it, production was either maintained or recovered rapidly, but almost always through the entrance of a new group of agriculturalists to supplement or replace ex-slaves, many of whom left the plantation sector.

For many reasons, the most commented-upon example of adjustment to emancipation, both in nineteenth-century debates concerning slavery and emancipation and more recent debates, is the case of Haiti. St. Domingue was the richest colonial island and the world's largest sugar and coffee producer prior to the successful slave uprising of 1791–1804. Following slaves' freedom and independence, Haitian sugar production fell to near zero, coffee production declined sharply, and the plantations disappeared. Ex-slaves resisted all attempts to reintroduce the plantation system. They worked on small farms, producing mainly foodstuffs for sale in local markets. The economic and political difficulties of Haiti in the mid–twentieth century may or may not be traceable to the choices made in response to world and local conditions in the earlier part of the nineteenth century; but the sharp contrast between Haiti and areas of the Americas where slavery persisted longer remains of interest in all discussions on the meaning of freedom.

The wide range of economic responses to the ending of slavery has significant implications for social and political outcomes, as well. Even in places with a dominant preemancipation plantation sector, outcomes varied with the particulars of crop production technology, the land-labor ratio as determined by natural resources, prior settlement, political controls, and the availability of emigrants from elsewhere. There are few constants in the process, except for some initial decrease in plantation output and a decline in plantation residence. Given the variation in areas undergoing initial decline, broad explanations of similarity in direction are less interesting than explanations of the differing magnitudes of direction. Moreover, even allowing for long periods of adjustment, few ex-slave areas adopted modern manufacturing. However, this lack of manufacturing was not only characteristic of ex-slave areas in the Americas; it was, and remains, a feature of countries in the tropical zones today. Indeed, the nexus of climate, staple production, limited economic growth, and a limited nonagricultural sector is one of the major concerns in an examination of the outcome of emancipation.

Land and Labor in the Postemancipation World

There are two key constraints on economic opportunities, available labor and available land. These are affected by natural conditions, by laws, and by the behavior of ruling political coalitions. Land-labor ratios are not set merely by nature but also by human intervention. Nevertheless, as is clear from the varying outcomes of emancipation, these ratios help explain changes in plantation output, the nonplantation opportunities open to ex-slaves, the standards of living of the ex-slaves, and even the success of political controls in influencing the distribution of incomes among members of society.

Ex-slaves often wanted to own land, which provided an alternative place to live and work, a change from living on land owned by others and laboring for others on their land. Restrictions on who could purchase land and on minimum (or maximum) acreages and prices helped determine the ability of individuals and groups to achieve meaningful landownership rather than be forced into laboring for others. The financial return from laboring for others may have exceeded that from landownership, but the desire to own land may have outweighed the impact of such considerations. (Peasant demand for land, however, may reflect either a desire for security and nonmarket production, or an attempt to benefit from increased land values and market production.) And the control of land, of economic value in itself, could also be used by landowners as a device to control labor, either by precluding any landownership by labor or allowing small allotments to ex-slaves in exchange for their availability as a plantation labor force.

The controls over labor took two distinct forms in the postemancipation period, both influencing the size and nature of the labor force and labor inputs, the choice of time spent at work and the location of work, and the ability to migrate to seek economic alternatives. The control of labor via vagrancy laws, debt provisions, and coercion against migration was frequently attempted—legally or nonlegally—to restrict the possibilities open to ex-slaves. Restricting ex-slaves to specific employers was one form of limiting mobility, and the measures that limited ex-slaves' exodus out of the regional economy prevented large-scale outward mobility. If these were not sufficient, subsidized immigration of free workers was undertaken to replace the ex-slaves who left the plantation sector. In the British (and, less dramatically, the French and Dutch) Caribbean, indentured workers from overseas were brought in under multiyear contracts for the specific purpose of plantation labor. At times, return passage was provided after the expiration of the contract period; at times none was provided. The role of indentured labor was dual. First, during the contract period, these laborers were the basis of the plantation labor force, replacing, or perhaps competitively driving out, the ex-slaves from the plantation. In either case, this reduced the opportunities for, and the wage rates of, the freed laborers. Second, even after the indenture period, if these laborers remained (as most did), the local labor supply was increased, usually generating increased competition for employment or land, thereby lowering the returns to the ex-slaves. Thus immigration, whether of free workers or contract workers, was one way the ruling elite raised their own incomes and lowered those of the ex-slaves. Where possible, immigration was used to control the outcome of economic conflict. Where immigration was limited, as in the U.S. South, the outcome had more aspects of a market-bounded compromise between the two groups than it did in those areas where immigration was able to tip the planter-laborer balance.

There are several points to note in this brief summary of land and labor conditions after emancipation. First is the general importance of the initial land-labor ratio as well as the general conditions of economic productivity at the time of emancipation. Generally, emancipation did not reverse the economic fortunes of declining areas, while plantation recovery usually followed preemancipation experience and the land-labor ratio. This applies both to changes in overall plantation output and in the relative wage rates of plantation workers after emancipation. This does suggest that the differences in income redistribution with emancipation were significant, the greater benefits going to ex-slaves in areas of relatively higher economic productivity. However, since plantation production is not necessarily a direct measure of the ex-slaves' per capita income, we should not confuse these two variables. Often, declines in plantation output and regional incomes may have left the ex-slaves better off in consumption terms than under slavery, as a result of the redistribution from owners (in addition to the direct welfare gains from ending slavery). This need not, however, have been the case in all areas, and there are too few estimates to make appropriate comparisons. What is clear is that, no matter what the changes in absolute levels of living, ex-slave incomes have long been significantly below those of whites in the same regions and in the European metropoles, and in probably no area have the conditions of the descendants of the formerly enslaved risen to equal those of the resident descendants of those never enslaved.

As discussed above, there were important changes in some areas in the nature of the plantation labor force; at times this was a change in the size of the agricultural unit. In Trinidad and British Guiana, the sugar plantation economy was restored but with a labor force primarily from contract labor from India, China, and elsewhere. In Brazil, the coffee sector expanded with primarily white immigrant labor. In the United States, resident white farmers became a much larger component in cotton production. And in Cuba, resident and immigrant white labor became more important in the production of cane sugar. Ex-slaves stayed in export crop production in the United States and Cuba, although their relative importance as labor in that sector declined as that of white labor increased.[4] Where the ruling elites found export production profitable but ex-slaves either unavailable or too expensive given world market conditions, the elites were willing to invest in attracting labor from elsewhere.

This desire to attract contract labor from elsewhere in the last half of the nineteenth century was not only found in those places where slavery had ended but was characteristic of all areas producing sugar. Without significant slavery in their histories (at least for the production of sugar), Fiji, Natal, Hawaii, Peru, and Australia drew upon immigrant indentured labor for sugar plantation work. And the late expansion of sugar production in the Dominican Republic was based upon attracting annual and seasonal labor from Haiti. The hard work of plantation production existed even in areas that never had slaves, but these areas were able to enter world sugar markets with the ending of slavery elsewhere. Thus, whether slavery had been important in a given area or not, the late nineteenth-century sugar plantation was often dependent on contract labor from overseas for its labor force.

Labor Choices After Emancipation

The expansion of rights that came with the end of slavery, particularly with regard to choice of work and its location, seems to have persisted despite the frequent attempts of ex-planters and ruling elites to induce governments to favor the continuation of plantation labor. Despite frequent conflicts over social and economic matters, the ex-slaves could abandon the plantations producing for export markets and settle on smaller farms and produce for self-sufficiency or local markets. Conflicts limited the material gains achievable by ex-slaves, but the most undesirable and abhorrent work patterns under slavery were changed. Ex-slaves were frequently highly mobile, exercising their independence by moving from their plantations. Further, within the constraints, ex-slaves exercised enough choice in working conditions in most areas to produce a decline of the plantation system. Thus the ending of slavery significantly changed the nature and organizations of plantation production.

It is not clear, however, what, why, and how much ex-slaves actually produced in the postemancipation world. Some worked for others as laborers on small farms or, in the United States, as sharecroppers on small farms. Others worked their own farms, producing either for their own consumption or for sale in local markets. Although these alternatives may suggest quite different things about the economic motivations of ex-slaves, it is clear that the change in working conditions alone, even if ex-slaves consumed less, was an overall welfare gain.[5] There is a related debate about when and why ex-slaves left the plantations. Was it immediately after the legal end of slavery, or was it after a number of years—and only in reaction to changing wage and employment conditions? These clearly imply quite different patterns of desires and behavior adopted during the period of slavery.

Similarly worthy of systematic examination is the choice made by ex-slaves between hours of work (needed to produce income and output) and hours of leisure, or nonwork. Hours of work per year may change, and patterns on a daily, weekly, and monthly basis vary. Less output and income are produced than the maximum possible, but if these are voluntary reductions in labor time, there is a clear welfare gain. Frequently, ex-slave women and children participated less in the labor force than previously, with, again, a possible trade off of income and consumption for free time. These decisions on labor force participation influenced the overall supply of labor and, thus, wage rates and helped to determine the limits of the ex-slaves' food consumption and other material conditions of life.

Withdrawal from the labor force may have provided short- or medium-term welfare gains, but it also constrained the growth of income and wealth over time. This constraint, in turn, affected diet and nutrition as well as the mortality of ex-slaves.[6] Intergenerational opportunities for education, literacy, and freedom from debt are further implications of the work and leisure and working condition choices of the first generation for subsequent generations of ex-slaves. These choices were made under difficult constraints, with many limits imposed by white or metropolitan society. The limited alternatives, even in freedom, meant that, whatever was chosen, opportunities were constricted. Yet in trying to understand the choices made under freedom and to balance the two historical views of the ex-slave — as victim and as actor — an awareness of the implications of such choices is important.

A focus on the economic issues and on the limited choices permitted to and negotiated by ex-slaves perhaps presents too dismal a view of what the freedom of choice accompanying emancipation meant in terms of other aspects of life, such as social life, religion, family life, and education. Ex-slaves were permanently freer to gather together, to locate in their own communities, and to live free from the most intrusive extremes of white control that had persisted under slavery. Forced sales, family separations, and corporal punishment by owners were no longer possible, and migration was now a choice to be made by the freed, not by their former owners. (There were, of course, some difficulties in realizing these gains after emancipation, but the situation differed in obvious ways from that prior to emancipation.) There were, perhaps, more gains to the ex-slaves in their social and cultural life than in their narrowly defined economic life. There, both landowners' concern with profits and their ability to introduce new political constraints, despite their own losses, had a pronounced impact.

The Benefits of (and Limits to) Freedom

Any attempt to evaluate the outcome of emancipation will seem either very simple or very complex. Very simple because, in one obvious sense, emancipation was a great success. There was no call by those freed to return to their previous condition as slaves. More curiously, perhaps, there were few calls to return to legal slavery even on the part of planters and other whites. They accepted the basic legal changes even while attempting to introduce myriad measures to control labor, to limit ex-slaves' access to land, to restrict their political liberties, and to otherwise seek to recover the gains that slavery had granted them.[7] It is this failure to call for the revival of slavery, even with the economic and social problems generated by emancipation, that suggests the full tri-

umph of the ideology of the antislavery movement in the nineteenth century. So dominant was that ideology among abolitionists and their rivals
that even an awareness of its economic consequences in particular areas
did not permit any major deviation from the triumphant free-labor ideology. But for the ex-slaves, emancipation and freedom were clearly a
big gain, even if their legal rights were still less than those granted whites
(except, of course, in Haiti) and even where policy retrenchment and
limited enforcement further weakened them. Obvious and trivial as it
is to say, for the ex-slaves there was absolutely no question that freedom was desired and welcome, a necessary step, which served to open
up opportunities then and in the future that would otherwise not have
been possible.

Yet, clearly, in all cases there has been only a rather limited sense
of success, and not as much was achieved by emancipation as could
have been or "should have been." The initial achievements are generally seen as having been quite limited, and still more was left to be
achieved over the longer term. After the sharp, initial legal gain, there
was a sense that much afterward was downhill and disappointing, limited in what was accomplished. But limited compared to what? And,
even if the desired ends are agreed upon, could any feasible political
or legal measures have been taken at that time that, in conjunction with
the social, cultural, and economic realities of the period, would have
provided for a more positive set of outcomes?[8] Were legal and political
measures sufficient to bring success in a world in which a more virulent
form of ideological racism often accompanied postemancipation development and in which the most extreme form of racial apartheid was
not reached until a full century after the ending of slavery? Could the
difficulties of adjusting to changing world market demands or the development of alternative sources of supplies have been avoided even if
slavery had not existed in the past? In other words, what else could and
should have been done at emancipation? What would one have liked
to have seen accomplished? In any event, many free whites were not
spared the economic and political difficulties that confronted ex-slaves.
The economic crisis of the 1890s and the rise of southern Populism in
response to the cotton collapse in that decade indicate that even "forty
acres and a mule" would not have solved the problems of ex-slaves,
since even with "more acres and more mules" many whites were still
vulnerable to the changing world market.

Moreover, until the late nineteenth century, the lower and working
classes in much of western Europe also lacked the right to vote, and

labor movements in Europe and in North America also suffered from political and legal restrictions on their right to organize protests and expand their membership. Restrictions on religious minorities and educational freedom persisted in many parts of the world; slavery persisted in parts of Africa and Asia into the twentieth century; and serfdom in Europe disappeared only slowly over the course of the nineteenth century. Peter Kolchin compares the changes upon emancipation of the slaves in the U.S. South with that of the serfs in Russia at the same time, where racism was not as pronounced as in the United States (chapter 11). For several reasons, the initial impact of emancipation, at least in its economic implications, was more favorable for the ex-slaves in the United States, who had more rights to mobility and at least did not have to, in effect, overpay for land to accompany their deferred freedom (Gerschenkron 1968:140–248; Domar 1989). Thus, even with the limited changes accompanying slave emancipation, the gains to the ex-slaves of the New World often went beyond the range of liberties in other parts of the world, even while the ex-slaves were not granted other benefits, some of which were still denied the previously free elsewhere. These points do not discount the remaining injustices within most societies after emancipation (and otherwise) but point to the complexity of inequality.

Overall rates of economic growth in most ex-slave societies were low, below those of western Europe and its overseas settler offshoots. Even in the exceptional case of the U.S. South, income relative to that in the rest of the nation remained low until the middle of the twentieth century. In most other cases, per capita income in postemancipation societies fell behind that in the developed parts of the world. Per capita income in most of the ex-slave societies of the Caribbean came to resemble that in parts of Africa and Asia, even those parts where slavery was never important. Thus, whether a society was nonslave or ex-slave, the economic impact of European imperialism, direct or indirect, on economic structure and performance remains central. Few ex-slave societies have experienced modern economic growth; but then again, neither have any tropical countries, even those outside direct European imperial control.

In short, with emancipation the gains of freedom have not been as rapid as desired, and some have never been realized. Some gains came very late, only with mobility to new regions; some gains came early, and then were taken away over time. Witness the segregation wave after the 1890s in the American South against the previous political and social gains of the black ex-slaves there, to be reversed only three-quarters of a century later. Thus the meaning of freedom changes over time. And with all the political, economic, and ideological changes of the nineteenth and twentieth centuries, how realistic were the desired benefits that "just freedom" was expected to provide?

Summary, Conclusions, and Further Questions

There are several major problems in the study of the economic and cultural effects of emancipation that I wish to note briefly in concluding. Some relate to the permanent impact of emancipation, others to its short-term incidence. Some relate to only a few areas, others are more general. Since all of the ex-slaves freed in the Americas were black or colored, the role of white racial attitudes and racial controls in limiting the gains of emancipation is crucial. Racism's emergence, its causes, and class origins are central to understanding emancipation, as are its changes over time. For some understanding of the adjustment to emancipation, we could examine changes with abolition in Africa and Asia, where some similarities to plantation areas can be seen, and where racism of the severity found in the New World was not present. Nevertheless, there are few other areas where plantation slavery was of sufficient magnitude to provide meaningful comparisons.

There is also debate about the relative roles of race and class and the interaction of the two in emancipation's impact. In some areas of emancipation, the ex-slave population was over 90 percent of the total; in the United States it was about 14 percent (over one-third in the southern slave states of 1860). In some cases, political power remained with white European nations; in others, ex-slaves did not participate fully in the national political process. Yet the relative numbers and political role of ex-slaves as members of the working class could have helped determine the importance of the working class and influenced working class incomes. As it was, the economic interests of working-class whites, in the short run, frequently conflicted with those of working-class ex-slaves, although it has been argued that if a coalition of these workers had been permitted, workers of both races would have gained in the long run against the ruling elites. Was the general failure of such coalitions to occur and endure due to a self-generated lower-class racism, or was it, rather, a hegemonic imposition by the upper class? Examination of conditions in areas that did not have slavery and had not been dominated by European-introduced slavery will be more important in

understanding the impact of emancipation in the New World slave societies. These concerns pertain directly in situations where we divide
societies into black and white. Yet such divisions are inappropriate for
nations such as Haiti, where the fissure has long been between black
and mulatto, a reminder that even where black versus white is the key
distinction, perceived shadings within the ex-slave population can have
a long and persisting impact.[9]

There has been frequent discussion of the legacy of slavery, how long
it may have lasted, and even if some positive cultural patterns under
slavery could have caused undesired outcomes in the postemancipation
world. Many similar issues persist about the legacy of emancipation
and its meaning over the next century. In some aspects, the two come
together; in others, they diverge. Thus, for example, E. Franklin Frazier's (1939) initial discussions of the weakness of the black family in
the middle of the twentieth century points both to legacies of slavery
and to the immediate impact of emancipation, with its increased geographic mobility, as well as to the northward movement in the twentieth century. More puzzling, perhaps, for the issue of legacies, is whether
either of these, or any one single set of past factors, could explain the
changes in the black family, which dramatically accelerated after the
late 1950s.[10]

In tracing the legacy of slavery into the future, other questions arise.
What was the relation between the booming slave sugar economy of
the mid–nineteenth century and the continued dependence of twentieth-
century Cuba on sugar production, even with the dramatic political
changes accompanying the rise of Fidel Castro? And, in surveying nearly
two centuries of Haitian history, it is difficult to categorize a legacy of
slavery, a legacy of emancipation, and the general changes over the subsequent period. Were economic circumstances as dire there in the 1880s
as in the 1980s? Was cultural life more vibrant during either of these
decades?

These comments focus mainly on the economic aspects of emancipation, the economic choices made by ex-slaves, and the probable long-
term consequences of these choices. There is, however, another point.
The cultural and psychological impacts upon the ex-slaves and their descendants may depend on whether their life as freed people is in a society over 90 percent nonwhite—as in the British and French West
Indies—or in a nation that is 14 percent black, as in the United States.
One puzzle arises from the relatively rapid income growth of the U.S.
black population after emancipation in comparison with the relative

stagnation or slow income growth in the rest of the Americas, particularly the Caribbean. Yet, when both areas sent migrants to the northern United States after World War I, there seems to have been relatively little overall difference in economic performance. This result persisted even when migration from both the South and the Caribbean greatly expanded (Sowell, 1981).[11] What, if anything, such comparisons say about the economic and cultural implications of emancipation in specific areas remains unclear. But these comparisons serve to point both to the gains achieved and to the gains yet to be achieved, even in those areas in where such progress seemed most accessible.

NOTES

This essay draws upon evidence and interpretations presented elsewhere, and rather than repeat the citations to my work and that of others, I refer the reader to the following published articles: Engerman (1982), Engerman (1983), Klein and Engerman (1985), and Engerman (1986). I am indebted to Seymour Drescher, David Eltis, and James Irwin for comments and discussions on drafts of this chapter.

1. At least fifty distinct geographic areas were involved, even without considering the variations within the countries and islands in which slavery had persisted. The total number of slaves freed in the nineteenth century was about seven million.

2. For the United States, see, most recently, Fogel (1989) and its three companion volumes; on Latin America and the Caribbean, see Klein (1986). Both contain excellent bibliographies to the recent literature.

3. In terms of the current historiographic phrasing, slaves are now seen as actors in creating their world, not just as victims of the power of white society.

4. In the U.S. South, for example, about 90 percent of all cotton output was produced by slave labor in 1860; their share fell to about 60 percent in 1876.

5. Welfare is defined to include both pecuniary and nonpecuniary components yielding utility to individuals. It consists of, among other items, material consumption, the value of leisure, and the benefits of avoiding unfavorable working conditions. It also includes changes in mortality and morbidity.

6. In the U.S. South, for example, life expectancy apparently declined relative to that of whites with the initial impact of emancipation. See Farley and Allen (1989).

7. This, of course, excludes the relegalization of slavery in the French Caribbean in 1804. Otherwise, once slavery was terminated, former slaveowners worked to get maximum advantage from the new system, not to reinstate slavery.

8. For the most recent discussion of emancipation in the United States, see Foner (1988), which also contains an excellent bibliography.

9. For an important discussion of fissures within the black community in South Carolina during Reconstruction, see Holt (1977), and for a similar set of issues for Jamaica, see Heuman (1981).

10. For a recent discussion of the additional problems caused by the depression of the 1930s, see Lieberson (1981).

11. For an alternative view, see Farley and Allen (1989).

REFERENCES

Domar, Evsey D. 1989. Were Russian Serfs Overcharged for Their Land by the 1861 Emancipation? The History of One Historical Table. In *Agrarian Organization in the Century of Industrialization: Europe, Russia, and North America,* edited by George Grantham and Carol S. Leonard, 429–39. Greenwich: JAI Press.

Engerman, Stanley L. 1982. Economic Adjustments to Emancipation in the United States and British West Indies. *Journal of Interdisciplinary History* 12:191–220.

———. 1983. Contract Labor, Sugar, and Technology in the Nineteenth Century. *Journal of Economic History* 43:635–60.

———. 1986. Slavery and Emancipation in Comparative Perspective: A Look at Some Recent Debates. *Journal of Economic History* 46:317–39.

Farley, Reynolds, and Walter R. Allen. 1989. *The Color Line and the Quality of Life in America.* New York: Oxford University Press.

Fogel, Robert William. 1989. *Without Consent or Contract: The Rise and Fall of American Slavery.* New York: W. W. Norton.

Foner, Eric. 1988. *Reconstruction: America's Unfinished Revolution, 1863–1877.* New York: Harper and Row.

Frazier, E. Franklin. 1939. *The Negro Family in the United States.* Chicago: University of Chicago Press.

Gerschenkron, Alexander. 1968. *Continuity in History and Other Essays.* Cambridge: Belknap Press.

Heuman, Gad J. 1981. *Between Black and White: Race, Politics, and the Free Coloreds in Jamaica, 1792–1865.* Westport, Conn.: Greenwood Press.

Holt, Thomas. 1977. *Black Over White: Negro Political Leadership in South Carolina During Reconstruction.* Urbana: University of Illinois Press.

Klein, Herbert S. 1986. *African Slavery in Latin America and the Caribbean.* New York: Oxford University Press.

Klein, Herbert S., and Stanley L. Engerman. 1985. The Transition from Slave to Free Labor: Notes on a Comparative Economic Model. In *Between Slavery and Free Labor: The Spanish-Speaking Caribbean in the Nineteenth Century,* edited by Manuel Moreno Fraginals, Frank Moya Pons, and Stanley L. Engerman, 255–69. Baltimore: Johns Hopkins University Press.

Lieberson, Stanley. 1981. *A Piece of the Pie: Blacks and White Immigrants Since 1880.* Berkeley and Los Angeles: University of California Press.

Miers, Suzanne, and Richard Roberts, eds. 1988. *The End of Slavery in Africa.* Madison: University of Wisconsin Press.

Sowell, Thomas. 1981. *Ethnic America: A History.* New York: Basic Books.

JAY R. MANDLE

Black Economic
Entrapment After Emancipation
in the United States

Throughout the New World, slave emancipation threatened economic catastrophe for former slave owners. Sugar planters in the Caribbean and cotton planters in the United States, deprived of their most valuable asset, were faced with the need to reorganize their production processes. What is remarkable is how successfully the planters accomplished this transition. Everywhere in plantation America, with the exception of Haiti, the momentous transformation that the ending of slavery seemed to promise turned out to be far less than revolutionary. The slave-owning classes, by and large, were able to accomplish the transition from being what Gavin Wright calls labor lords to becoming landlords and, in the process, continue in their former role as the dominant class in society (Mandle 1982:1–8; Wright 1986:17–50; Mandle 1989:229–36).

In the U.S. South, the fact that with the ending of slavery the composition of the planter class changed only slightly raises the question of how thoroughly emancipation transformed that region's social structure (Wiener 1978:3–34). If the rulers of the society changed little, then perhaps the society also had changed only minimally. Critical to this issue is the extent of mobility achieved by the former slaves. The antebellum plantation economy flourished because slavery provided labor in larger numbers and at lower costs than would have been the case if black workers had been free to choose their own occupations (Fogel and Engerman 1974:236–38). A functional substitute for slavery—a continued limiting of black occupational choice to plantation labor—would have permitted continuity in the region's social structure. Alternatively, if after the Civil War black labor no longer was predominantly confined to plantation work but exercised industrial and geographic choice, the South's plantation way of life would have been profoundly undermined.

69

As Gerald David Jaynes formulates it for the United States, "the crucial question which must be answered about the southern agricultural labor force [after the Civil War] is, how free was the laborer?" (Jaynes 1986:302).

The question of the extent to which emancipation implied freedom was not confined to the United States, of course, but was raised with the ending of property rights in persons throughout plantation America. Everywhere, the salient issue was the extent to which former slaves were able to exercise in fact what was theirs juridically — freedom in occupational choice. As Eric Foner has written, "every plantation society undergoing emancipation experienced a bitter conflict over labor control . . . that is, the definition of the rights, privileges and social role of a new class, the freedmen" (Foner 1983:10). In open-resource territories such as Guyana and Trinidad, a considerable degree of such freedom was experienced, at least in the period immediately after emancipation. Since these British colonies possessed abundant unused land, with freedom in 1838 former slaves were able to vacate the plantations in large numbers and establish themselves as peasant proprietors. So successful were they in depleting the plantations' labor supply that the planters were forced, in concert with the colonial power, to import a whole new population, largely from India, to provide themselves with workers.

It was not until the 1870s that the planters in these colonies were fully able to replenish their stock of labor from overseas sources and establish conditions of relative labor abundance. Their success in this regard, however, undermined the bargaining power that the former slaves had been able to exercise in the determination of wages. Further, with the reviving of profitable production on the estates, the availability of plantation land for sale to peasant cultivators declined. Thus, by the 1870s or 1880s the growth of an independent West Indian peasantry, and the options that growth represented, slowed considerably. With that, the region's sugar plantations were able to restore their once-jeopardized hegemony (Engerman 1986:225–44; Mandle 1973:17–31; Marshall 1985: 1–14; McLewin 1987:124–51).

In the closed-resource islands of the Caribbean, the threat to plantation dominance symbolized by emancipation was more easily contained. The fact that on an island like Barbados very little land was not already controlled by large plantations meant that the opportunity to escape estate life was largely foreclosed. There, juridical freedom did not provide former slaves with wider employment options. Because squatting was not feasible and the plantations were not in distress, the terms of the bargaining relationship between worker and planter remained one-sided, in favor of the latter. As a result, after only a short period of adjustment, plantation agriculture became reinvigorated and continued its hegemonic position in society (Engerman 1986:335; Beckford 1972:90).

The U.S. South faced many of the same issues confronted by the Caribbean. There, as in the West Indies, the ending of slavery raised the question of the terms under which former slaves would work on the plantations. The greater the employment options, the more demanding those terms would be. Conversely, without these options, the planters would have the upper hand in determining the conditions of post–Civil War agricultural employment in the South.

Some recent scholarly literature argues that, with emancipation, a considerable degree of autonomy and freedom was achieved by former slaves. Gavin Wright's views in this regard are representative. Wright denies that blacks remained in the South because of "heavy-handed legal barriers or debt peonage or the convict labor system." The South, he writes, "was not a prison and there was no smoking gun to keep blacks and poor whites in the region." Efforts to recreate slavery, according to Wright, "did not succeed." Sharecropping, the new organizational form widely adopted after the Civil War in southern agriculture, was not a system of coercion. Instead it represented "a balance between the freedmen's desire for autonomy and the employer's interest in extracting work effort and having labor when it was needed." Wright concludes that "all things considered, blacks made remarkable progress in accumulating wealth in the post bellum South" (Wright 1986:91, 85–86, 101).

In contrast, Gerald David Jaynes is not as sanguine. He details the impediments to labor mobility that were present in the region and concludes that "the competition of convict labor, the legal crushing of a free market for mobile wage labor, the landlord-merchant lien, and control of the productive and distributional process to the exclusion of laborers all confined the southern laborer within a system that bred exploitation." In that system, Jaynes concludes, "the state had legally seized about as much control of its agricultural labor force as was possible in the absence of total ownership" (Jaynes 1986:63, 314). Jaynes' interpretation of the postemancipation adjustment in the U.S. South is strikingly similar to the way the transition from slavery in other parts of plantation America has been characterized. Philip J. McLewin writes with regard to planters in Guyana and Jamaica that "having lost the coercion of the whip, the key issue was how to build a labor force using some other mechanism of coercion. The sale of land in small plots and the use of indentured immigrants in Guiana, and the withholding of land, the use of white immigrants, and, most overtly, the passage of harsh labor laws in Jamaica support the conclusion that planters desired to effect a solution using coercion" (McLewin 1987:211–12).

In attempting to adjudicate between Wright's and Jaynes's views, it is necessary to operationalize what is meant by freedom or its lack in a way that is susceptible to empirical measure. As argued above, the extent to which occupational and geographic mobility was exercised by the former slaves is a reasonable indicator of the degree to which the lack of economic freedom associated with slavery had been overcome. In this way, the ability of African Americans to achieve what slavery had prohibited—the exercise of their own preferences in employment choice—can be measured. In this perspective, I examine the extent to which the African-American labor force after the Civil War actually widened its spatial distribution, the diversity of industries it was employed in, and the range of its occupations.

Cast in these terms, it is hard to avoid the conclusion that the black population experienced very little change in the years between the ending of slavery and the beginning of the twentieth century. For example, between 1870 and 1910 the proportion of the black population residing in the South remained virtually stationary, standing at 91 percent in 1870 and 89 percent in 1910 (U.S. Census Bureau, n.d., table 5). In this period, almost half of the country's black population lived in five states of the Deep South: Alabama, Georgia, Louisiana, Mississippi, and South Carolina. This percentage actually increased slightly between 1870 and 1910. Such concentration suggests continuity, since these were precisely the states in which the cultivation of cotton was most heavily concentrated (see table 1).

The extent of change in the industrial structure of the black labor force in the years immediately after slavery is impossible to estimate, since the earliest year for which data are available in this regard is 1890. As late as 1910, however, 87.8 percent of the black labor force in the five plantation states discussed above worked in the plantation-dominated sectors of agriculture and domestic and personal services, and only 12.1 percent worked in nonplantation manufacturing and other categories. By contrast, 34.3 percent of the white labor force in these states was employed in the latter two sectors. Thus, black labor by 1910 had only to a very limited extent been able to move outside of the industries that characterized black work under slavery (see table 2).

Table 1
The Black Population of Selected Southern States,
1870, 1910 (1,000s)

State	1870	1910
Alabama	476	908
Georgia	545	1,177
Louisiana	365	714
Mississippi	444	1,009
South Carolina	416	836
TOTAL	2,246	4,644
TOTAL as percentage of U.S. black population	46.0	47.3

SOURCE: U.S. Census Bureau, n.d., table 11.

Occupationally, as well, these years saw little change in the black labor force. In their sample of counties in the Cotton South, Ransom and Sutch estimate that only 3.5 percent of the black labor force was in skilled crafts, a figure they contrast with the 5.6 percent of slaves that they estimate filled such occupations in 1860. Data for 1890 on occupations by race—the earliest available—reveal a continuing clear pattern of exclusion of blacks from high-income, high-status trades. Constructing an index of racial balance, Ransom and Sutch find that "all the skilled occupations other than masonry were predominantly white" and that "all or nearly all of the professional mercantile and commercial occupations effectively excluded blacks" (Ransom and Sutch 1977:16, 33–36, 38). Thus, in the decades before World War I the black labor force's industrial and occupational structure, as well as its geographic location, closely resembled those that had existed under slavery.

Of course, these indicators of economic mobility do not measure the entire content of emancipation. In his recent history of reconstruction, Eric Foner justifiably emphasizes that with the ending of slavery important changes occurred in the family, in schooling, and in black religious and community life (Foner 1988:82–102). Further, the substitution of sharecropping tenantry for coerced gang slave labor represented a substantial reorganization of production, one that did at least partially speak to the preferences of the labor force (Woodman 1979:319–37). And of course the ending of property rights in persons was the precondition that had to be satisfied before any substantive civil or human rights

Table 2
The Industrial Structure of the Labor Force by Race,
Selected Southern States, 1910[a]

Sector	White	Black
Agriculture, forestry, fishing, and mining	63.4	74.7
Manufacturing and mechanical industries	14.7	6.6
Domestic and personal services	2.2	13.1
Other	19.6	5.5

SOURCE: U.S. Census Bureau 1914, table 7.
a. Alabama, Georgia, Louisiana, Mississippi, South Carolina.

could be won. Nonetheless, it is also true that, despite all of these changes, by 1910 not much had changed with regard to the roles filled by black labor in the U.S. economy.

It was this stability that allowed the South's plantation economy to survive juridical emancipation. A limited growth in black landowner-ship had occurred, and comparable increases in the per capita value of black wealth in the South had been experienced (Marable 1979:142–52; Higgs 1982:725–37). But continuity was salient. Black labor had been brought to the United States to work in large-scale southern agricul-ture, and more than in any other activity, it continued to do so in the years before World War I. This continuity gave new life to the South's plantation system after the Civil War.

In accounting for the continuity in the black economic experience and the southern social structure, it is useful to consider plausible his-torical scenarios likely to have resulted in a significantly different out-come. By examining why such scenarios were not realized, it is possible to identify the variables that militated against an alternative emerging to the plantation economy in the South. In this connection, the fact that, unlike the islands of the Caribbean, the South was not a colony but an integral part of the United States meant that the possibility of a thorough break with plantation agriculture was greater in the United States than elsewhere. The potential range of employment options avail-able to former slaves in the United States was much greater than in the West Indies.

New employment opportunities could have become available to the ex-slaves either in the South or in regions of the country where economic growth was proceeding rapidly. In the North, these employment oppor-tunities could have taken the form of manufacturing jobs. In the South, the possibilities for alternatives lay primarily in agriculture. The federal government could have endowed former slaves with land and resources, perhaps as compensation for their years of work under coercion. If either northern jobs or southern land had become available, the result would have been, as it was in the open-resource territories of the West Indies, a strengthened bargaining position for the now-freed blacks of the South relative to the plantation sector. In such a context, blacks would have been provided with an alternative to being primarily the providers of cheap labor for the South's cotton plantations. With that, the labor supply basis of the South's plantation economy would have been undermined and a new point of departure would have opened for the African-American population in the United States.

The relationship of black labor to the South's plantation sector, in short, depended crucially on how successfully black labor was able to compete for alternative employment both in the South and throughout the rest of the nation. The fact that land was not provided to the former slaves and that southern black workers did not secure northern manufacturing employment in the years before World War I thus was central to the continuity of the black experience in the United States in the aftermath of slavery.

If a program of land redistribution had resulted in the creation of a black small-farm sector, income and occupational differentiation would have been the likely outcome. Those farmers possessing an appropriate combination of good land, skills, and luck would have prospered. At the same time, less fortunately endowed farmers would have suffered in the competitive agricultural market. In the meantime, the white planter class would almost certainly have been damaged, since it was their land that would have been reallocated to the new black farmers. Not only would this have had economic consequences, its political implications would have almost certainly been even greater, for the continuity in landownership provided the basis for the dominance of the southern planters (O'Brien 1986:55–75). If the planters had not continued to own most of the land, their influence on the course of southern history would likely have been substantially less than it was. Thus the fact that land reform was not carried out had profound implications for both black freed persons and white former slave owners. Virtually nothing in the South would have been the same if the ex-slaves had been endowed with land at the expense of their former owners.

A number of actions suggested to the former slaves that land would be turned over to them. In June 1863 federal troops in Clark County,

Alabama, allowed the ex-slaves to measure off their former masters' land. In 1864, as Sherman's troops advanced they told the former slaves that land would be made available to them. This talk seemed to come to fruition with Sherman's Special Field Order Number 15, issued in January 1865, which created a reserve of land for the exclusive use of the former slaves. Forty acres were to be allocated to each slave family, with horses and mules to be loaned to them as well. In addition, according to Claude Oubre, the initial circulars and orders issued by the Freedmen's Bureau also "convinced freedmen that they would receive land." Oubre, in this regard, quotes an assistant commissioner of the bureau as telling a negro convention that "they must not only have freedom, but homes of their own thirty or forty acres, with mules, cottages and school houses" (Oubre 1978:182–84).

But of course neither the slaves, the army, nor even the Freedmen's Bureau would decide the question of land reform. The decision of whether to confiscate the planters' land and provide it to former slaves was to be made in the Congress. There, led by Thaddeus Stevens, a small group of Republicans struggled in favor of such a program, and as Eric Foner reports, as the war progressed their support grew. Confiscation was defended as the only means to break the power of the southern plantocracy and as the way to create a new class of black and white property owners, who would provide a new foundation for southern society. As Foner writes, this view could be defended as "the corollary of a traditional widely shared value — the conviction that democratic institutions must rest on an industrious middle class." Thus Stevens and his associates were able to appeal to generally accepted values within the Republican party: restricting the power of the planters, protecting the rights of the former slaves, and transforming the southern social structure (Foner 1980:132, 134). In this regard, the radical Republicans in the United States seem to have sought more from emancipation than did English abolitionists. W. A. Green writes that the latter judged the success of abolition not in terms of changing the social system in the colonies but rather "in terms of the ability of emancipated labour to preserve and enhance existing plantation economies" (Green 1985:186).

While the idea of providing land to former slaves was consistent with at least some of the values that animated the congressional Republican party, the problem was that taking land from the planters for this purpose was in conflict with other, and more deeply felt, principles. Fundamental to the world view of many who were opposed to the southern way of life was the belief that free labor should rise or fall only according to the diligence of its effort. In this perspective, the risk in giving land to the former slaves was that the government would indicate, in the words of the *Nation,* "there are other ways of securing comfort or riches than honest work." Similarly, the *New York Times* argued against confiscation because it would violate "the fundamental relation of industry and capital. . . . An attempt to justify the confiscation of Southern land under the pretense of doing justice to the freedmen, strikes at the root of all property rights." Thus congressional Republicans were caught between their commitment to property rights and their hostility to southern planters. Having deprived the planters of what the Republicans viewed as illegitimate property in persons, northern politicians could not bring themselves to deprive them of what were acknowledged to be legitimate property rights in land. Although, Foner writes, as late as the spring and summer of 1867 confiscation was still a contentious issue, this was its high-water mark, and a radical land reform never came close to serious implementation (Foner 1980:132, 143, 144).

While land confiscation was being debated and defeated, however, a Southern Homestead Act was passed. Introduced in January 1866 and passed in June of that year, this law specified that in the distribution of southern public lands in homesteads none be allocated to southerners who had taken up arms against the North. At the same time, the fact that the homesteads were relatively small in size meant that the Southern Homestead Act was not attractive to northern whites or European immigrants. In effect, therefore, the Southern Homestead Act was designed principally to benefit former slaves. As the chair of the Senate Committee on Public Lands put it at the time, "the object of the bill is to let them [the Negroes] have land in preference to people from Europe or anywhere else" (Pope 1970:203).

The problem was that the land in the public domain was generally of poor quality. The best land in the South had long since been put into cultivation by white southern landowners. As a result, as Pope writes, heavy capital expenditures and labor were necessary for cultivation to be successful on the land that remained. But it was precisely capital that the former slaves lacked. As a result, according to the Freedmen's Bureau reports, only about 4,000 freedmen had made homestead applications by October 1869. As Pope summarizes the act's results, "despite the fact that the bill was passed expressly for the benefit of freedmen, only an insignificant percentage of the four million Negroes in the South were able to take advantage of the law." In combination, the failure of land reform and the ineffectiveness of the Southern Homestead Act

meant that an overwhelmingly large proportion of the black population remained landless (Pope 1970:204, 208).

In addition to southern land, northern employment possessed the potential to allow the former slaves to escape plantation work. But like
land reallocation, this option was not realized either. The African-
American population remained in the South, distanced from the jobs
created through northern industrialization. Black net migration from
the South to the rest of the country remained at relatively low levels
from 1870 until the 1910–1920 decade. It was not until World War I
that emigration to the North became large enough that the percentage
of the black population in the South started to decline at a substantial
pace (see table 3).

Black geographic immobility prevailed before World War I despite
intense northern demand for labor. These were the years in which net
international migration to the United States stood at peak levels. Between 1870 and 1920 immigration averaged in excess of 500,000 per
year, or almost seven immigrants per 1,000 of the population. Almost
all of this inflow were people who secured employment in the industrial
North (Davis et al. 1972:138–39). Furthermore, the North's per capita
income was roughly twice that in the South, making it a potentially attractive alternative to southern employment (U.S. Census Bureau 1975:
Series F 287–96).

The question that arises, then, is why southern blacks did not become part of the growing northern industrial labor force in those years.
Insight into this issue is provided by the information in table 3, indicating that there was an inverse relationship between black migration from
the South and European migration to the United States. As Richard A.
Easterlin notes, "immigrants and nonwhites were to some extent substitute sources of labor" (Davis et al. 1972:137). The same point is made
by Brinley Thomas: "within the unskilled sector there was a high degree
of competition between the Negro and immigrants from South Eastern
Europe" (Thomas 1973:134). Thus the explanation of why blacks remained in the South lies in the answer to the question of why European
immigrants secured northern jobs but southern blacks did not.

An explanation of the different migration rates of Europeans and
southern blacks might lie in their ability to learn of available jobs. Alternatively, the difference might be accounted for on the demand side.
That is, although Europeans and southern blacks were comparable in
their ability and desire to fill available jobs, employers might have pre-

Table 3
Southern Black Migration and Net Immigration to the United States, 1870/80–1920/30

Period	Black Migration from South (1,000s)	Migration Rates to United States (per 1,000)
1870–1880	−60	5.1
1880–1890	−70	8.0
1890–1900	−168	3.7
1900–1910	−170	6.5
1910–1920	−454	3.2
1920–1930	−749	2.8

SOURCES: U.S. Census Bureau, n.d., table 52; Davis et al. 1972.
NOTE: The correlation coefficient between black migration and international migration rates is 0.73, statistically significant at the .05 level.

ferred one group to another. It is plausible that in the immediate after-math of emancipation former slaves may not have known about employment opportunities outside of the South. Slavery had meant that job search was not possible. As a result, channels of information with regard to finding work undoubtedly were poorly developed. It might be anticipated that, with freedom, the new-found mobility of the black population would be exercised narrowly, in a geographically circumscribed area.

But with the passage of time, the handicap that inadequate information represented must have declined. There was some South-to-North black population movement — albeit in limited numbers — a flow that undoubtedly increased knowledge concerning labor market conditions in the North. A further indication that knowledge of employment opportunities was present among southern blacks was the effort of state legislatures in the region to staunch the flow of such information. Anti-enticement and anti-recruitment legislation indicates a concern that would not have been present unless significant numbers of black workers were showing an interest in securing employment elsewhere.

The response of the southern black population to the curtailing of international migration at the time of World War I, however, is the most convincing indicator that the black population possessed considerable insight into the dynamic of the northern labor market. Once the flow of labor from Europe was disrupted because of the war, the flow of labor from the South surged. The population-weighted black emigration rate from Alabama, Georgia, Louisiana, Mississippi, and South Carolina in 1910–1920 was almost three times the level it had been in 1900–1910 (U.S. Census Bureau 1975: Series C 25–75). In contrast, the emigration rate for southern whites increased by about 60 percent. As Taeuber and Taeuber report, black age-specific migration rates during this period, in particular for the category of those aged fifteen to thirty-four, "are almost beyond belief" (Taeuber and Taeuber 1966:112). The clear inference is that the black labor force did not lack either information or the desire to move north. With Europeans no longer available, the black population responded with alacrity to the demand that had been satisfied by international migrants in the past. The pattern of European employment domination in the North, in short, does not seem to be supply-side determined.

Evidence concerning differential demand-side preferences has been provided most thoroughly in the work of Stanley Lieberson. Lieberson provides important support for the hypothesis that northern employers preferred European immigrants to southern blacks. He writes, "there is no rigorous study that I know of which examines employers' attitudes toward blacks and SCE [Southern, Central, and Eastern European] groups, but the evidence I have patched together seems to indicate a more favorable disposition toward the latter." In this regard, he cites survey data from the 1920s that ranks racial groups on a continuum from good to bad and shows blacks at the bottom of the list. In addition, a survey carried out in Minneapolis at about the same time shows that "the vast majority of employers surveyed indicated that they would not employ blacks if any were to apply." A president of a steel company is cited as saying, again at the same period, that "it would be better . . . if the mills could continue to recruit their force from [Europe]. The Negro should remain in the South." Lieberson comments that what seems to have happened is that an etiquette or set of norms developed among whites concerning the proper behavior of blacks. It defined "black efforts to reach equality as inappropriate." He goes on, "this emphasis called for blacks to remain in their status," whereas European immigrants were expected to achieve upward mobility. Lieberson concludes that there is "no way of avoiding the fact that blacks were much more severely discriminated against in the labor market and elsewhere" (Lieberson 1980:348, 31, 348–49, 35, 369). Precisely the same conclusion is reached by Robert Higgs in his statistical analyses of European and black wage rates. The evidence seems clearly supportive of the hypothesis that the reason blacks remained in the South before World War I was not out of preference, but rather because they were largely barred from effective participation in the northern labor market (Higgs 1971:114–22).

Thus neither of the two alternatives that would dramatically have altered the role played by the black population in the United States came to fruition. The former slave population became neither a landowning class of farmers nor an urban working class. Instead, the largest fraction of this group was left to seek its livelihood as non-landholding agriculturalists, overwhelmingly still resident in the South. The foreclosing of alternatives meant that after emancipation, as before, the role of the black population remained different and separate from that of the rest of the population. Unlike other groups, the range of employment opportunities available to the black labor force was narrowly constrained.

It was in this way, through the foreclosing of occupational alternatives, that the black postemancipation experience resembled that of slavery. Plantation owners continued in the postbellum, as in the antebellum, period to benefit from a substantial and low cost black labor force. Such would not have been the case if these workers had open to them a wide range of employment opportunities, which they would have had with an allotment of southern land or an opportunity to get a northern job. Because this was not the case, planters were provided with labor on the terms and in the numbers that permitted large-scale, labor-intensive agriculture to be profitably restored. Plantation agriculture in the U.S. South thus survived slave emancipation.

But the restoration of plantation agriculture was not simply an economic phenomenon. It also meant that the authoritarian character of plantation life was allowed to persist. Although sharecropping substituted for direct coercion, an extensive anthropological and sociological literature on the postbellum plantation is in agreement concerning the continued, racially based authoritarianism of plantation life. A variety of sources can be cited in this regard. For sociologist Edgar T. Thompson, the "southern plantation has always had the character of a coercive institution," while anthropologist Morton Rubin observes that the power of the planter allowed for control "to a degree far exceeding comparable institutions in a democratic society." Police powers were typically delegated to plantation officials. A 1931 study of lynchings, for example, reports that "to the planter and his overseer [was left] the settlement of any trouble which arises on the plantation." Both Thompson and

Gilbert Fite point to the planters' control of the tenant's food supply as an important lever of coercion. Because food self-sufficiency on the postbellum plantation was markedly lower than it had been on the slave plantation, the potential for choking off a cropper's food by limiting the availability of credit provided the planter an important means of social control. M. B. Hammond concludes that "authority little short of compulsion is often exercised by the planters" on large plantations in the period. Thus, though the tenant plantation was not the same as the slave plantation, it nonetheless provided the context in which black subordination was perpetuated in the South (Thompson 1975:98, 94, 235, 256; Rubin 1951:27; Fite 1984:25; Hammond 1966:186).

Planter authority was typically cast in racial terms. After emancipation, as before, as Thompson writes, "capital and labor relations on the plantations are commonly at the same time race relations." As late as 1936 Monroe Work was still able to write that "the legal attitudes of tenancy are on the basis of race" (Work 1936:214). All of this meant that, in the plantation South generally, as Ronald Davis reports for Natchez, Mississippi, blacks became "a subordinate caste of people hopelessly subjugated to all whites as inferior people." Thompson concludes: "everywhere the plantation appears as a race-making situation," constituting the "physical basis of traditional race relations" (Thompson 1975: 217, 203, 83; Mandle 1978:xii; Davis 1982:179).

Despite its persistence, however, the plantation economy that survived emancipation was weaker than the system that had been constructed before the Civil War. With slavery, the South's social system had been based on a labor supply mechanism that it authored and implemented. After the war, southern planters' control of labor was contingent upon conditions and policies initiated and carried out by the North. If the North had chosen either to provide land to the freed persons or to offer employment in large numbers to blacks, the South and its plantation agriculture would have been thrown into crisis and forced to change its methods of production and pattern of labor relations.

But, of course, neither land nor northern jobs in large numbers were made available to the black population. The consequence was that the plantation system was permitted a rebirth after the Civil War. With the persistence in the plantation way of life, the behavioral, as differentiated from the juridical, content of freedom largely was denied to the African-American population in the United States. Blacks continued to suffer the multidimensional deprivations associated with the hierarchic and racist class relations characteristic of plantation agriculture. Slavery had been abolished, but northern policies and prejudice meant that blacks remained entrapped in the South's plantation economy.

REFERENCES

Beckford, George L. 1972. *Persistent Poverty: Underdevelopment in Plantation Economies of the Third World.* New York: Oxford University Press.

Davis, Lance E., et al. 1972. *American Economic Growth: An Economists' History of the United States.* New York: Oxford University Press.

Davis, Ronald L. F. 1982. *Good and Faithful Labor: From Slavery to Sharecropping in the Natchez District, 1860–1890* Westport: Greenwood Press.

Engerman, S. L. 1986. Slavery and Emancipation in Comparative Perspective: A Look at Some Recent Debates. *Journal of Economic History* 46:317–39.

Fite, Gilbert C. 1984. *Cotton Fields No More: Southern Agriculture, 1865–1980.* Lexington: University Press of Kentucky.

Fogel, Robert William, and Stanley L. Engerman. 1974. *Time on the Cross: The Economics of American Negro Slavery.* Boston: Little, Brown.

Foner, Eric. 1980. *Politics and Ideology in the Age of the Civil War.* New York: Oxford University Press.

———. 1983. *Nothing But Freedom: Emancipation and Its Legacy.* Baton Rouge: Louisiana State University Press.

———. 1988. *Reconstruction: America's Unfinished Revolution, 1863–1877.* New York: Harper and Row.

Green, W. A. 1985. Was British Emancipation a Success: The Abolitionist Perspective. In *Abolition and Its Aftermath: The Historical Context, 1790–1916,* edited by David Richardson, 183–202. London: Frank Cass.

Hammond, M. B. 1966. *The Cotton Industry: An Essay in American Economic Growth.* New York: Johnson Reprint.

Higgs, Robert. 1971. *The Transformation of the American Economy, 1865–1914: An Essay in Interpretation.* New York: John Wiley and Sons.

———. 1977. *Competition and Coercion: Blacks in the American Economy, 1865–1914.* New York: Cambridge University Press.

———. 1982. Accumulation of Property by Southern Blacks before World War I. *American Economic Review* 72:725–37.

Jaynes, Gerald David. 1986. *Branches Without Roots: Genesis of the Black Working Class in the American South.* New York: Oxford University Press.

Lieberson, Stanley. 1980. *A Piece of the Pie: Black and White Immigrants since 1880.* Berkeley: University of California Press.

McLewin, Philip J. 1987. *Power and Economic Change: The Response to Emancipation in Jamaica and British Guiana, 1840–1865.* New York: Garland.

Mandle, Jay R. 1973. *The Plantation Economy: Population and Economic Change in Guyana, 1838–1960.* Philadelphia: Temple University Press.

———. 1978. *The Roots of Black Poverty: The Southern Plantation Economy after the Civil War.* Durham: Duke University Press.

———. 1982. *Patterns of Caribbean Development: An Interpretive Essay on Economic Change.* New York: Gordon and Breach.

————. 1989. Caribbean Economic History: An Interpretation. In *The Modern Caribbean,* edited by Franklin W. Knight and Colin A. Palmer, 229–58. Chapel Hill: University of North Carolina Press.

Marable, Manning. 1979. The Politics of Black Land Tenure. *Agricultural History* 53:142–52.

Marshall, Woodville K. 1985. Peasant Development in the West Indies since 1838. In *Rural Development in the Caribbean,* edited by P. I. Gomes, 1–14. Kingston, Jamaica: Heinemann Educational Books.

O'Brien, Gail Williams. 1986. *The Legal Fraternity and the Making of a New South Community.* Athens: University of Georgia Press.

Oubre, Claude F. 1978. *Forty Acres and a Mule: The Freedmen's Bureau and Black Land Ownership.* Baton Rouge: Louisiana State University Press.

Pope, Christie Farnham. 1970. Southern Homesteads for Negroes. *Agricultural History* 44:201–12.

Ransom, Roger L., and Richard Sutch. 1977. *One Kind of Freedom: The Economic Consequences of Emancipation.* New York: Cambridge University Press.

Rubin, Morton. 1951. *Plantation County.* Chapel Hill: University of North Carolina Press.

Taeuber, Karl E., and Alma F. Taeuber. 1966. The Negro Population in the United States. In *The American Negro Reference Book,* edited by John P. David, 96–160. Englewood Cliffs: Prentice Hall.

Thomas, Brinley. 1973. *Migration and Economic Growth: A Study of Great Britain and the Atlantic Economy.* Cambridge: Cambridge University Press.

Thompson, Edgar T. 1975. *Plantation Societies, Race Relations and the South: The Regimentation of Populations.* Durham: Duke University Press.

U.S. Census Bureau. 1914. *Occupational Statistics,* vol. 4 of *Thirteenth Census of the United States.* Washington, D.C.: Government Printing Office.

————. 1975. *Historical Statistics of the United States, Colonial Times to 1970.* Bicentennial Edition. Washington, D.C.: Government Printing Office.

————. n.d. *The Social and Economic Status of the Black Population in the United States: An Historical View, 1790–1978,* in Current Population Reports, Series P-23, no. 80. Washington, D.C.: Government Printing Office.

Wiener, Jonathan M. 1978. *Social Origins of the New South: Alabama, 1860–1885.* Baton Rouge: Louisiana State University Press.

Woodman, Harold. 1979. Post Civil War Southern Agriculture and the Law. *Agricultural History* 53:319–37.

Work, Monroe. 1936. Racial Factors and Economic Forces in Land Tenure in the South. *Social Forces* 15.

Wright, Gavin S. 1986. *Old South, New South: Revolutions in the Southern Economy Since the Civil War.* New York: Basic Books.

GAVIN WRIGHT

The Economics and Politics of Slavery and Freedom in the U.S. South

Slavery and freedom have meant many different things to different people at different times and places. The rise of antislavery thinking in England and the northern United States after 1790 was so rapid and thoroughgoing, and slavery as it was then known came to seem so far outside the boundaries of human decency, that *freedom* needed no precise or rigorous definition. Former slaves, southern planters, and northern officials had widely varying conceptions of acceptable meanings for *freedom* after 1865. Because of a similar absence of accepted criteria, historians have debated ever since whether the freedom of the postbellum South was a real freedom or merely the illusion of freedom, a legalistic veneer over a new form of slavery. The words *slavery* and *freedom* slip so readily into rhetorical formulations for countless purposes that it is easy to lose track of distinctions between political metaphor and social reality. One way to avoid being controlled by our own abstractions might be to examine a number of transitions from slavery to freedom within a reasonably standard framework, avoiding prepackaged concepts of what real freedom was or might have been. This is the strategy proposed by the organizer of the conference on "The Meaning of Freedom."

The comparative approach has its dangers, however. There is a built-in temptation to find parallels and similarities in situations that may in reality be different in their fundamentals. In an effort to contribute to the discussion, therefore, this essay begins by trying to identify those features of the nineteenth-century U.S. South that set it apart from other examples of slavery and emancipation in the Americas. Some of these are well known, while others are commonly overlooked. I then consider the character of labor and land tenure institutions in the postbellum South and interpret the political and economic forces that shaped

the meaning of freedom for southern blacks in the half century following emancipation.

The Economic and Social Context of U.S. Slavery

In many important respects, the character of North American mainland slavery was distinctive from its beginnings in the seventeenth and
eighteenth centuries. It is well known that mortality conditions on the
mainland were favorable. Long before the African slave trade was terminated in 1807, natural population increase was the primary source
of growth of the slave population, which grew at rates roughly similar
to those of the free population. By the time of emancipation, the slaves
were overwhelmingly American rather than African; more so, in fact,
than any other large ethnic group in the country. As the literature on
comparative slave systems has established, material conditions of slavery in the United States were uniquely favorable; at the same time, legal
rights and potential access to free status were uniquely limited. This
contrast has been seen as paradoxical, yet both sets of conditions flowed
from the same underlying context: scarce and valuable slave labor in
a setting of strong demand, land abundance, relatively favorable health
conditions, and (after 1807) restrictions on new imports from Africa
or other slave countries. Whereas in the Caribbean, Brazil, Cuba, and
elsewhere, closing the African slave trade was a decisive blow against
slavery itself, in the United States the identical step helped to create the
largest and strongest slave system in the New World. By conventional
measures, the South was far more advanced economically than Brazil
in the mid–nineteenth century (Graham 1981).

In these respects, slavery in the U.S. South was extremely profitable
and firmly established at the time of secession, providing a solid economic basis for that bold political step. In another sense, however,
North American mainland slavery was less essential to the economy than
was true for most other major slave systems. North American slavery
grew up around the demands for two major staple crops, tobacco and
cotton, neither of which was intrinsically linked to slavery on either a
technological or geographic basis. Tobacco is the great exception, re-
futing attempts at a purely staples-based interpretation of the original
economic basis for slavery: it was a high-value, care-intensive crop without major capital requirements or scale economies in production and
has continued to be the very epitome of a family farm cash crop until
modern times. Yet North American slavery in the eighteenth century

was primarily tobacco slavery, production on plantations coexisting with production on small farms with few slaves or none. When cotton emerged as an alternative cash crop in the 1790s, it filled a nearly identical economic and social niche. It is a standard interpretation among American historians that Eli Whitney's cotton gin, which allowed the successful commercial cultivation of upland cotton, broke down the economic barrier between the coastal plantations and the small-farm interior, giving both groups a common interest in cotton markets and giving the institution of slavery a new lease on life.

Slavery thus fits very differently into North American economic history than it does elsewhere. In the sugar colonies of the Caribbean and Brazil, slavery made possible the development of commercial production in locations and under conditions that could not have attracted free labor (Eltis 1987:14, 24, 165). But in the U.S. South, the expansion of slavery displaced what would otherwise have been an expansion of small cotton-growing family farmers on the pattern of the North, and one can analyze the effects of slavery as an institution in terms that are at least meaningful in historical context (which is not to imply that this alternative history almost happened).

There is more here than hypothetical histories-without-slavery. The nonessentiality of slavery to commercial agriculture is also reflected in the fact that U.S. slavery was embedded in a society with a large free white farming population, displaying a full range of stratification, from wealthy planters to landless tenant farmers, and a developed political culture. Unlike the British and French sugar islands, the antebellum South was not a society in which a small planter elite exercised authority over a vast slave-majority population. Wealth holding in the South was more concentrated than in the agricultural North, to be sure. But in 1860 there were 380,000 slave owners in the southern states, averaging ten slaves each. The great majority (88 percent) were small-to-moderate farmers owning between one and twenty slaves. In the cotton areas, more than half of the farm operators owned slaves, a level of dispersion substantially broader than (for example) stock ownership in the United States today (Olsen 1972; Wright 1978). Interpretations of the postwar fate of the "planter class" often lose sight of this much larger, politically important group. Though the slave societies of Cuba and Brazil also had large coexisting free populations, in both cases there was a close link between plantation slavery and export crops (Klein 1986: 94–96; Engerman 1986b:328).

At the same time, there were on the periphery of the 1860 cotton belt large numbers of nonslaveholding farmers, most of them landowners but participating only marginally in the market economy. In the east these areas had been left behind as backwaters when slave owners leap-frogged onto the best cotton-growing soils further south and west. In the Southwest, the vast potential of Texas and Arkansas as cotton states had barely been tapped at the time of secession. Though the region thus had great potential for agricultural expansion, commercial cultivation was limited in many areas by poor transportation and an absence of local credit and marketing facilities. The black population, however, was heavily concentrated in the plantation region of the Deep South, a reasonably well-defined belt running from South Carolina to Louisi-ana, with smaller concentrations in Virginia and Tennessee.

For all of these reasons, concepts like land availability or the land-labor ratio are not very well defined or meaningful when applied to the U.S. South. Local conditions varied greatly, but populations were not confined to local areas except by reasons of culture and familiarity. The southern population as a whole was more or less closed to outside inflows and outflows (though this fact, too, is something to be explained rather than a technical specification); but realistic accessibility of new lands and new farming opportunities depended on the development of transport and credit, which was beyond the scope of individual farmers. Further-more, with the demise of the Confederacy there was no government en-tity in position to make decisions based on the land-labor ratio for this aggregated southern region as a whole. All of this is merely to say that, when we ponder the adjustments that emancipation required of all of the parties involved, we should not picture it as a well-defined zero-sum game of strategy between former slaves and former slaveowners.

This last point is reinforced by one further respect in which the U.S. South differed from other cases of slavery and emancipation. By the 1820s this region had become the dominant cotton supplier for the world. With the admission of Texas to the Union in 1845, virtually the whole of the world's production of good-quality medium-staple cotton was contained within the borders of one country. The geopolitical poten-tial of this fact was not lost on the secessionists of 1861, though they badly miscalculated its strategic impact. Though Brazil later attained comparable dominance of the world coffee supply, at the time of eman-cipation, Brazilian slave owners had no such illusions about the uses of market power (Drescher 1988:447). In contrast to Brazil, the collapse of the Confederacy meant that there was no political entity in position to negotiate or calculate collectively on the basis of this regional cotton interest. But the uniqueness of the U.S. South as cotton country none-theless had two major implications for the postbellum experience of the freedmen and other southerners. On the one hand, the value of up-land cotton to the world cotton market meant that manufacturers, ship-pers, and financial agents had a strong interest in the restoration of the southern supply. There is no law of history that a country or region cannot simply remove itself from the international economy, no matter what the cost. But such an outcome is much less likely when that region is a large and uniquely valuable supplier of a major raw material. Cot-ton production did increase in India, Egypt, and Brazil during the pe-riod of the Civil War and Reconstruction (1861–1876), but only at prices high enough to be an irresistible temptation to farmers in the U.S. South (Wright 1974). So there were strong market pressures to bring labor into cotton growing, and the South was unique among postemancipa-tion cases in increasing the share of the export staple in production (Engerman 1986a:333). The largest share of this increase, however, was attributable to small, white, family farms.

Though cotton clearly was the best immediate opportunity for farmers in the region, there was a second implication. Cotton growing was so much more profitable than alternative uses for southern resources that the economic prosperity of the region was highly dependent on cotton demand. Dependence on external demand conditions was of course a common feature of slave and postslave economies, but in the South de-mand fluctuations were often obscured by confusing market signals and political events, especially in the immediate postwar years. This situa-tion lends a certain air of unreality to much of the economics of south-ern politics. Issues were debated in an atmosphere of class and race con-flict over the distribution of resources or rights, and historians have typically interpreted events in these terms. But the background condi-tions that generated these conflicts were often global in origin, well be-yond the poor powers of southerners to add or detract. This does not mean that southern politics had no economic causes or effects. It means that the causes and effects are often not to be found in the overt ob-jects of political debate.

The Economic and Political Context of Reconstruction and Redemption

The basic political facts of postslavery southern history are familiar. Slaves in the rebellious states were legally freed by the Emancipation

Proclamation on New Year's Day 1863. Emancipation was reaffirmed by the Thirteenth Amendment to the U.S. Constitution in 1865 and by the first postwar constitutions of the states under Presidential Reconstruction. As a practical matter, slavery had crumbled in wide areas of the South during the war, as slaves by the thousands abandoned their masters as word came that the Union army had arrived (Robinson 1985). Though the shape of the future was far from clear, abolition itself was swift and thorough; in contrast to all other emancipations but Haiti, there was no protracted legislative debate and no room for delay, compensation, or such pretexts as apprenticeships to cushion the blow.

Though the southern states acquiesced in the demise of slavery, they returned to the Union initially under constitutions that denied blacks the vote and severely restricted their rights. The infamous Black Codes were unmistakably intended to control black labor and restore much of the condition of slavery through enticement and vagrancy laws and convict labor systems for nonpayment of taxes or other offenses (Novak 1978: chapter 1). However effective these measures might have become, they were quickly overturned by the Reconstruction Acts of 1867. Ratification of the Fourteenth Amendment, which granted citizenship to the freedmen and guaranteed them equal protection of the laws, was made a condition for reentry of the states into the Union. The Fifteenth Amendment, guaranteeing blacks the right to vote, was ratified in March 1870. Between 1868 and 1877, vigorous two-party competition prevailed in most of the southern states, with blacks represented mainly in the Republican party, which shaped significant legislation concerning taxes, labor contracts, transportation, schools, and other matters. One by one the Republicans were toppled in each of the states by various combinations of political mobilization and violent intimidation, giving way to conservative Democratic "Redeemers." The formal demise of Congressional Reconstruction in 1876–1877 largely ratified what was already defacto home rule in the South, with black political effectiveness reduced to near insignificance. The downward trend in black political participation continued until formal disfranchisement after 1890 (Kousser 1974).

Postslavery agricultural arrangements therefore took shape during a period when southern landowners could not exercise effective political power. All accounts agree that planters were unable to restrain the mobility of laborers, who refused to accept a return to the work regime of slavery and vigorously pressed for better terms (Davis 1982; Foner 1983; Ransom and Sutch 1977; Wayne 1983). Attempts at collusion by groups of planters to restrain wages or specify contract terms were virtually all failures (Shlomowitz 1984). But the limits on political power in southern economic affairs went well beyond the inability to effect the reenslavement of black laborers. As emphasized in a recent article by Hahn (1990), emancipation coincided in the United States with a marked centralization of federal political authority at the expense of the states. This trend contrasts with Brazil, where states gained the power to tax exports and planters were able to dictate national policy in support of the coffee market. Both before and after Redemption, state governments had no power over international trade policies, and southern representatives could not reverse the dramatic move toward protectionism that the country had taken during the war. State government power over banking and credit was severely circumscribed by the regulations of the National Bank Acts of 1863, 1864, and 1865. Perhaps most importantly in comparative perspective, the southern state governments did not have the power to establish and administer large-scale immigration programs, such as the contract labor systems that replaced slavery in many other postemancipation cases (Engerman 1984:1986a,b). A flurry of postwar interest in immigration recruitment in Europe met with little success, and later attempts at organizing contract labor from Asia foundered on competition with employers in California and conflict with federal laws (Erickson 1984:47, 53–57). Most of these limitations on political power followed directly from the absence of a regional government with sovereign powers.

Even within the bounds of their formal powers, the range of true state authority in economic affairs was distinctly limited by some harsh facts of economic life. Several recent studies have found that policy differences between Republican and Democratic-Redeemer administrations in such matters as taxation, debt adjustment, and government support for railroads were far less pronounced than the rhetoric of the times would indicate. Virtually every Republican policy had been tried by the Democrats during 1865–1867, if on a smaller scale (Summers 1984:11). State administrations of any party were confronted with a fiscal crisis, owing to the loss of revenue from taxes on slaves, which had accounted for anywhere from 30 to 60 percent of receipts before the war (Thornton 1982; Wallenstein 1987:188–89). At the same time, land values had collapsed from prewar levels, so that substantially higher rates were required in order to raise the same state revenue. Since states were now required to provide schools and other services to blacks as well as whites, inevitably white landowners felt that they were bearing a heavier tax burden and receiving a smaller share of the benefits than ever before.

In terms of public finance, 1865 was a more fundamental break with the past than Redemption in the 1870s (Wallenstein 1987).

The strategy of the southern Republicans rested on the belief that freedom and railroads would unleash a new burst of prosperity into the region, a self-justifying, virtuous circle of towns, markets, manufacturing centers, and thriving commercial farms on the northern pattern. They avoided radical distribution measures, to be sure, but they made a real effort to use economics to bury the race issue (Summers 1984: chapters 6–9). And railroads were politically popular, virtually demanded as a matter of right by newly invigorated towns and localities. Railroads were not thrust on an unwilling South by powerful outside invaders: a survey of ten major lines and their presidents during 1865–1880 shows that virtually every one had strong local ties and investments in local enterprises (Klein 1970:7–12). With all of the wastefulness and corruption, the fact is that tracks were laid, towns did spring up, and small farmers responded to the new opportunities. Yet prosperity did not come either to the old plantation belt or the new small-farm cotton districts. Republicans, out-of-state bondholders, and black voters were convenient scapegoats when the state subsidy programs soured and collapsed in the 1870s. As important as political competition was for the future of black political influence, broad economic policies and trends were largely driven by forces and pressures external to the South. In this respect, the South was similar to many other slave and postslave economies — its distinction was perhaps more in the depth of its illusion that freedom and prosperity would go hand in hand.

The most basic of these economic trends was stagnation or decline in demand for U.S. cotton throughout the Reconstruction period. Problems in production were real enough, both from organizational turmoil and from the withdrawal of black female labor from field work (Ransom and Sutch 1977:44–47, 232–36). But so critical was southern supply to world cotton markets that when production was down, prices were up. When production recovered in the 1870s, prices slipped steadily downward, channeling all the new energies into an aggregate wheel-spinning exercise rather than into a productive stimulus for the region, and undermining the political and economic promise of the Republican program. A railroad-led boom could not succeed if the major customers were sliding into poverty and debt.

The central point for present purposes is that the political power that was restored at the time of Redemption did not represent a thoroughgoing control of the regional economy and its future. There were severe limits on the capacities of any political alliance to influence economic change, given the realities of world and national markets, and given the political status of the South as a regional cluster of separate states located within the much larger political entity (and free trade area) of the United States. Nor does this mean that effective control over the southern economy was exercised by identifiable outside political or economic interests. These interpretations may apply with reasonable appropriateness to some postemancipation regimes, but in the U.S. South they have to be understood metaphorically, as short-hand characterizations of what was in reality a much less premeditated politicoeconomic equilibrium that emerged after 1880. Institutions and expectations developed and solidified over time, and political defenses grew up around the interests at stake. In this process, the race issue surely had a logic of its own, but in the formative phases of the postbellum world, it was an open question how race would cut across such basic institutions as land tenure and labor markets.

Landownership and Postbellum Development

American historians have long argued that the best opportunity for a favorable economic future in the South was lost with the failure to redistribute land to the freedmen after the war. There is more to this story than is commonly appreciated. The idea that access to plots of land would make all the difference between success and failure was no mere historians' pipedream; it was an active part of contemporary thinking. The policy of assigning confiscated lands to former slaves gained majority congressional support during the war. In contemplating postwar adjustments, many Republicans argued that homesteads would be more effective protection of black rights than would the right to vote, and a redistribution policy was actively planned by the Freedmen's Bureau in 1865. The land issue could hardly have been of greater importance to the freedmen themselves. Expectations of land allotments caused many to be reluctant to enter into labor contracts for that season. Though the bureau and many southern whites later attributed these beliefs to naive quasi-religious euphoria among the blacks, in fact the rumors had been fostered by federal authorities in the sincere belief that this was the natural outcome of the war effort (McFeely 1970: chapter 5). In the end, however, most confiscated lands were returned to the previous owners.

Some have questioned the importance of the land issue alone, on the grounds that an illiterate and vulnerable black population would not have been able to maintain landownership in the midst of a hostile white majority without continued quasi-military outside enforcement, a policy that was politically unsustainable (Belz 1973). While no one can safely predict an alternative political history in a revolutionary atmosphere, such a dismissal seems to underestimate both the intensity of black desire for land and the strategic value of legal and physical possession. In those few areas where the former slaves did gain plantation lands, such as the sea islands of South Carolina, their possession was remarkably tenacious and the course of local history altogether different (Strickland 1985). Contrary to much vivid political rhetoric of the postwar period, most white small farmers (many of whom were also illiterate) did not lose their land over the next half century; the absolute number of landowners continued to grow, even while increasing numbers of new young men became tenants. Long after Redemption and the triumph of white supremacy, blacks aspired to landownership, and the number and acreage of black owners increased (e.g., Banks 1905:69, table B). They were always a small percentage, and their holdings were often small and of poor quality, but their legal status as owners was generally respected.

Indeed, the reluctance to abrogate established property rights in land was one important reason that so few blacks received any. Congressional Republicans were perfectly willing to offer homesteading opportunities to blacks on land still in the public domain and voted with near unanimity for the Southern Homestead Act of 1866. This act opened up more than forty-five million acres to settlers in five states (Alabama, Arkansas, Florida, Louisiana, and Mississippi), with preference to loyal whites and blacks until 1867. The acreage amounted to one-third of the total area of the five states. Since the sponsor of this legislation, George Julian of Indiana, was a militant advocate of land redistribution and enforcement of black rights, there is little reason to view the act as fraudulent in its intentions. In actuality, however, it was a dismal failure. By the end of 1869, only 4,000 freedmen had filed entries (19 percent of the total). Though others may have lived on public lands without attempting to obtain formal title, taking up land on the public domain was apparently either unattractive or unfeasible for most blacks in 1866–1869. The accounts of the time suggest some of the reasons: only one land office per state was opened; the land itself was remote from the plantation belt and of poor quality; no means of finance was available for seed, implements, work stock, and subsistence rations prior to the first crop; there were few opportunities to combine wage-earning employment with part-time homesteading (Pope 1970).

These events offer important insights on the U.S. South in comparative perspective. On the one hand, *land availability* is not a phrase to be taken literally. The viability of small farming, even on a subsistence basis, requires a minimum of working knowledge and a network of social support for all but the hardiest, either through community assistance or channels of credit. In this sense, mere land availability was hardly enough. But on the other hand, redistribution of good cotton-growing acreage in family-sized plots, with a modicum of transitional assistance, was well within the realm of technical (if not political) feasibility. Far from being unhistorical, this is exactly the alternative that the freedmen and a small number of Radical Republicans favored. What difference would it have made?

Land distribution would clearly not have generated the prosperous midwestern-style family-farm agriculture that the Republicans hoped for. It could not have affected cotton demand nor the underdeveloped character of the economic infrastructure and human resources of the southern population, white as well as black. Historians differ on the character of black work norms and leisure preference at the time of emancipation, some arguing that premodern or preindustrial habits were in fact prevalent (Fields 1985:163–165), while others reject such complaints out of hand as planter prejudice and propaganda. There is no easy way to resolve this issue. But up-country white farmers are also renowned for their premodern antebellum cultural heritage (McDonald and McWhiney 1975), and this class of small owners was the major locus of the postbellum reallocation of resources from subsistence to commercial farming (McDonald and McWhiney 1980). It is a fair guess that a postbellum class of black small farm owners in the cotton belt would also have been lured and pressured into heavy reliance on cotton as a cash crop and that their descendants, like their white counterparts, would have experienced rising rates of tenancy, declining farm size, and contentious struggles with landlords and merchants.

The near-term economic future for the region would have been little different, but land distribution might have changed the racial and class basis of southern politics, quite possibly a more important factor over the long haul. As it was, the incipient interracial cooperation in the farm insurgency of the 1890s, celebrated so eloquently fifty years ago by C. Vann Woodward (1938), never had a serious chance, because the economic circumstances of the two races were so different. This is not to deny the potency of racism as a factor with its own force, but only to suggest that the character of U.S. racism as it came to be known in the twentieth century could hardly have been unaffected by the economic structures and incentives of the nineteenth century (e.g., Fields 1982). Not least among these structures was the disproportionate political power of the large black-belt planters, a class with a strong interest in black farm labor, which in turn gave them an interest in the racial basis of politics and social organization.

In the debate over the continuity of the planter class from antebellum to postbellum times, this key point has been underappreciated: emancipation served to increase the relative power of black-belt planters, by changing the basis for political representation and by redirecting taxes from slaves onto land. Though they could no longer control the movement of black labor, large-scale planters took a far more intense interest in local and state political issues then they had as slave owners (Wright 1986: chapter 2). This shift offers a material base for the proposition recently put forward by James Oakes, that the crystallization of the planters as a politically conscious class was more advanced in the twentieth century than it had been in the nineteenth (Oakes 1986). It is a consideration missed by Hahn (1990), who argues that the postbellum status of U.S. planters compares unfavorably to that of other landed elites. The central weakness of his argument is that terms like *planter class* and *landed elite* do not distinguish the small elite group of black-belt planters from the much larger segment of the white population who were slave owners and who shared the economics and politics of that status. Instead of ranking former slave-owning classes on a kind of power scoreboard, a better approach to comparative emancipation history is to put the reconfiguration of classes at the center of the stories.

Tenancy, Cropping, and Labor Markets

As it happened, landownership was a distant dream for most freedmen, who had to come to terms with the need to find employment on someone else's land. Several recent studies trace the path of employment relations in minute detail for the period roughly from 1865 to 1880, so that we now have a reasonably clear picture of how things happened (Curie 1980; Davis 1982; Harris 1982; Jaynes 1986; Ransom and Sutch 1977; Shlomowitz 1982; Wayne 1983). Continued debate represents not so much disagreement over the historical evidence as an excess dose of essentialism, the belief that contract forms like sharecropping must have a deep philosophical character such as "bourgeois social relation" or "dependency." In the absence of specific historical comparisons, it is not clear that such discussions are really about history. What we can now say with some confidence about the postwar South is that sharecropping and coexisting contract forms emerged out of an interaction between desires and constraints, on the part of workers as well as landowners. It was a competitive market process, but within a political and financial context that was anything but normal. The main open question is not so much why things happened as they did, but to what extent the abnormal conditions of the immediate postwar environment shaped the institutional development of southern agriculture and, in so doing, had lasting impact on southern economic history.

As recounted most recently by Jaynes (1986), the process was something like this. Plantations were initially reorganized on the same centrally managed basis as under slavery, under labor contracts initially supervised by the Freedmen's Bureau. These were not, however, cash-wage but share-wage contracts, or less frequently, "standing wage." In the first, the entire labor force contracted for a share of the crop; in the second, a significant portion of the wage was withheld until after the harvest. Both systems were mainly postharvest payments, reflecting the landowner's effort to secure the continuity of labor through the harvest and his desire to reduce his own credit requirements in the disrupted postwar credit environment. Both systems broke down over time. The centralized operation was incompatible with share payments and gave way to intermediate "squad system" arrangements and, ultimately, to family-based sharecropping. The standing wage might have been an alternative, but in the atmosphere of 1865–1867, crop failures and falling prices caused widespread planter default on wage payments. This experience led the freedmen to put first priority on the security of their earnings, which was also a central concern of the Freedmen's Bureau. The popularity of shares after 1867 is largely to be explained by the legal status of the shareholder's lien on such contracts, which gave the worker property rights in his share of the crop. These rights, in turn, allowed workers to borrow from third parties using the crop lien as collateral. Jaynes concludes: "The entire evolution provides a superb lesson in the force of the law" (1986:157).

But does it? The immediate pressures toward shares seem clear. What is less clear is why this temporary context of crop failure, falling prices, disrupted credit, and mutual suspicion should have "made payment by a share of the crop a permanent institution" (1986:156). Jaynes refutes the common argument that the freedmen refused to work under centralized wage-paying systems that reminded them of slavery. He points out that workers were never offered the option of "cash wages promptly paid," because the severe scarcity of credit made such payments an unacceptable financial risk for the planters. This is an important corrective to those accounts that casually invoke rigid preferences for autonomy on the part of the freedmen, as though these preferences would have been independent of the other terms of the employment package. Freedmen pressed for share contracts in an attempt to safeguard their claim to the proceeds of the crop. But why did they continue to sign such contracts long after credit conditions had stabilized and property rights in the crop had been firmly reassigned to landlords by Redeemer legislatures? (Woodman 1979).

My view is that there was a logic to sharecropping, and that logic represented not just the credit and production conditions of the postwar years, but a more lasting balance of forces. Sharecropping was only one among several alternative contract forms that coexisted in most parts of the South long after the demise of the Freedmen's Bureau. Agricultural wage labor, for example, did not disappear after 1870 but continued to be an option for substantial numbers of young black males (Flynn 1983:68–69). The form of wage labor that emerged, however, was not attractive to married men with families, because it offered neither security nor work autonomy. Flynn quotes one planter to this effect: "Disobedience, idleness, dishonesty, neglect, or insolence, I punish on the spot with dismissal" (ibid., 69). True tenancy, on the other hand, with tenure secured by contract, legal title to the crop, and managerial autonomy on the farm, was the preferred option for anyone with the assets or creditworthiness to obtain it. Sharecropping was in the middle — a contract form suited for married men with families but possessing no property. It is true that the legislatures and courts might have endowed sharecroppers with more extensive rights, just as they might have endowed the freedmen with landownership. But that hypothetical possibility does not change the fact that sharecropping, as it came to be defined in the South, was little more than the logical corollary to the status of *propertylessness* as defined in the mainstream of Anglo-American legal history (Karsten 1990).

In fact, sharecropping was not a new institution after the war. The term itself is an Americanism, which has been traced to the turpentine fields of North Carolina in the 1830s. In that state, court decisions clearly recognized the distinction between cropper and tenant: the tenant has a lease and possession of the land, holds title to the crop, and pays rent. The cropper has none of these rights but is only a laborer subject to the landlord's favored position with respect to crop liens (Applewhite 1954). The term *cropper* implies that the laborer works only on the crop, and does not do the general maintenance work that a tenant would do (Shlomowitz 1984:593). This designation was employed by some census enumerators in Georgia in 1860 and appears to have had the same meaning in that state (Bode and Ginter 1986). The fact that sharecropping existed prior to emancipation does not, of course, imply that most southerners knew of this contract form and its legal character. But it supports the view that sharecropping represented a form suited to the particular circumstances of southern agriculture in the presence of imperfect credit markets and workers without property.

Among the distinctive features of cotton agriculture was the dual peak seasonality in labor requirements. Figures 1 through 3 contrast the seasonal patterns of cotton, wheat, and fruit farming as of the early twentieth century. In the premechanized era, the heavy demands for chopping and cultivating cotton early in the season posed special problems for credit markets and labor relations. Any landowner who offered "cash wages promptly paid" and hired labor by the day, week, or month, was taking on much more financial risk than his counterpart in wheat or fruit farming, who could wait until the harvest and hire only the labor required for that task. Situations like these give rise to a demand for tied labor contracts, in which the worker binds himself for the harvest as a condition of work in the earlier part of the season (Bardhan 1983). Labor tying was one of the main features of sharecropping. Though the share aspect has received extensive attention from economic theorists, in the South it may have been more significant that sharecropping was an annual contract. As such, the legal treatment of sharecropping fell under the long Anglo-American legal tradition regarding annual labor contracts, which held that workers who left employment before the end of the year could not recover payment for the time they had put in. Between 1824 and 1875, English agricultural laborers were subject to upwards of three months imprisonment for breaches of agreement with employers, and this threat was not entirely removed thereafter (Morgan 1982:124–26). Thus the claim that such criminal punishments for breach of contract and labor enticement were "exclusively Southern" (Novak 1978) is misleading. It is true that by 1900 the law of labor contracts in the South looked very different from that in the northern states and in England; but it was they who had changed, not the South.

Figure 1. Patterns of Seasonality: Corn Belt (Illinois) versus Winter Wheat Region (Washington)

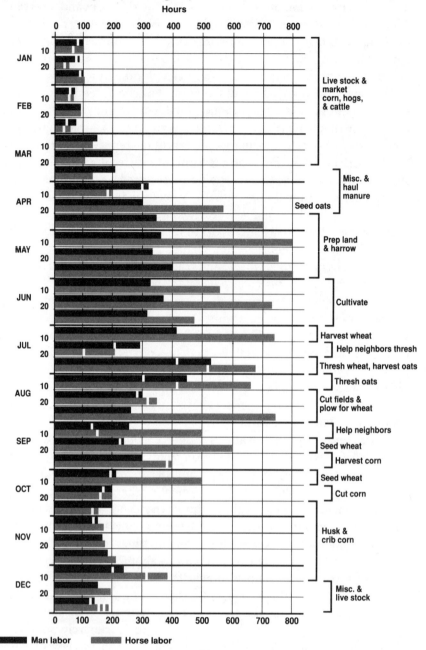

S O U R C E : Yearbook of the Department of Agriculture, 1917, pp. 544-45.

N O T E : 270-acre corn and small-grain, southwestern Illinois.

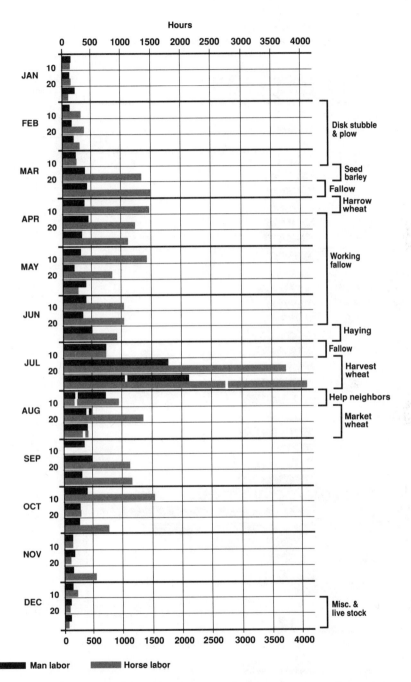

Hours

Man labor   Horse labor

N O T E : 800-acre wheat and summer fallow, Walla Walla, Washington

Figure 2. Seasonality in Fruit Farming, Western New York

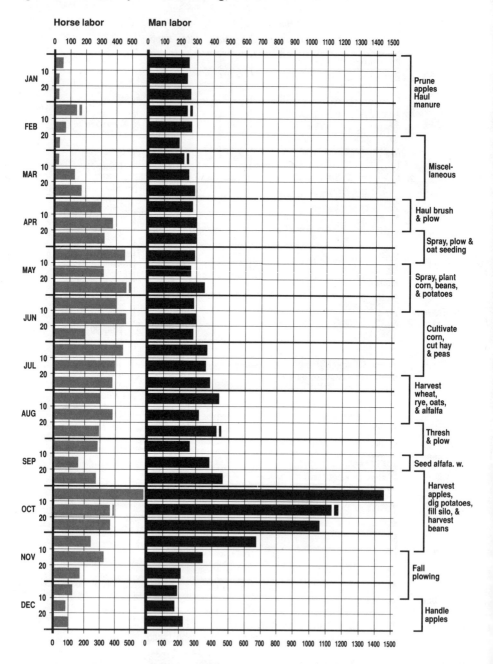

SOURCE: Yearbook of the Department of Agriculture, 1917, pp. 543.

NOTE: 256-acre diversified farm, apples, hay, beans, wheat, potatoes, peas, oats corn & pasture, western New York.

Figure 3. Cotton Belt: Seasonal Distribution of Field Labor on a 522- acre Cotton, Corn, and Oats Farm, Southern Georgia

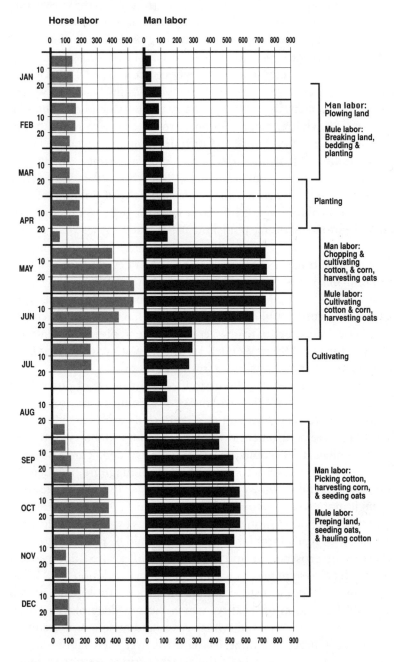

SOURCE: Yearbook of the Department of Agriculture, 1917.

Of all the conceptions of freedom that contributed to the rise of anti-slavery forces, the idea of an absolute right to quit one's work at any time was insignificant. What could be wrong with mere enforcement of a voluntary contract, provided that workers have the right to move freely from one workplace to another between contracts? The evidence is clear that workers did so in the postbellum South, blacks as well as whites. Is enforcement by criminal penalty too harsh and class-biased? Perhaps so, but what else are employers to do in the case of laborers without property? A 1905 Supreme Court decision held that "free labor" meant the right to break the labor contract at any time, subject only to "action for damages" (Novak 1978:50). But what is the use of action for damages against a worker with no assets? To avoid violation of state constitutional prohibitions of imprisonment for debt, southern states passed legislation providing punishment for fraud rather than breach of contract in such cases, failure to provide services being presumptive evidence of such fraud. Novak writes that "the effect of such a statute on the labor market is obvious." (1978:39). But he does not say what that effect is, and indeed it is not obvious. Why should enforcement of the terms of a contract be onerous, if workers have the right to choose a new employer and negotiate new terms at the end of the growing season? That is the way Oliver Wendell Holmes saw it, in his dissent from the antipeonage *Bailey* decision of 1912 (ibid., 59).

The reader who takes this discussion to be a defense of postbellum southern labor practices will have missed my point by approximately 180 degrees. There is no question that conditions were harsh and that the threat of severe punishment was intended to impel laborers into contract arrangements they would otherwise have avoided. Those who ran afoul of the law could fall into the nightmarish quagmire of indefinite penal servitude. And if you were black, there was always a danger that such a nightmare could become reality in response to the merest acts or gestures of insubordination to whites. This was by no means the typical experience of black farm laborers, but it would be pointless to deny that the risk of prosecution and the absence of assured due process through the legal system had a chilling effect on negotiations and labor arrangements. My point instead is that the process took place within an established tradition of legality, which did not deny blacks access to labor or credit markets and which gave landowners and creditors only the most indirect and imperfect control over their labor supply. In pointing to coercive aspects of the system, critics are not so much indicting the hypocrisy and lawlessness of the South as pointing up one of the deep internal contradictions in the very conception of freely operating competitive labor markets.

The essence of the problem is that a labor contract is also a credit arrangement; the seasonality of agriculture elevates the credit aspects to the forefront, and the peculiar seasonality of cotton made credit all-important. If the employer must absorb the entire amount of the financial risk, as he would if workers received "cash wages promptly paid" all year, or if propertyless tenants were given a secure first lien on the earnings of the crop, it is not clear that the entire transaction would be financially viable, even if capital markets in the South had been as well-developed as those in the rest of the country. In declaring that share-croppers without property had no first claim on the crop, one can argue that "the law only crystallizes the actual economic facts as they have worked out," as the southern writer R. P. Brooks asserted (Brooks 1914:67). Without such protection, lenders would have been far more eager to do business with the one class of producers who clearly had no laborer's lien: small family farmers. The credit and crop lien issues, in other words, are the landownership issue in disguise. If you accept one, the others follow logically.

The legal and financial dimensions of postemancipation labor systems have been understudied in comparative terms. In the absence of a good international literature, it is instructive to compare the southern system with those that came to prevail elsewhere in the United States. The heartland of the Midwest is known as the epitome of family farm agriculture, but in fact there was a significant trend toward the use of wage labor in the harvest during the late nineteenth century, so much so that the saying "wheat farms and hobos go together" became something of a byword (Taylor 1981:62). In California, the strong single-peak seasonality of labor requirements in fruits and vegetables gave rise to flows of migrant labor, initially from China, then from Japan, Hawaii, and the Philippines, but eventually evolving into a regular annual migratory cycle by Mexican families. In both of these cases, acute political and social tensions developed wherever farm laborers went. They were always considered outsiders and rarely enjoyed basic protection from the legal system, to say nothing of social and educational services. In the Midwest, the problem was ameliorated over time by mechanization. In the far West, that route was closed for technological reasons, and the migrant system persisted only within a network of institutions and barriers that kept migrants firmly isolated from the cities, schools, and labor markets of the rest of the country (Wright 1988).

The main contrast between California and the South is that the southern farm labor force was a resident labor force. This may have been partly for historical reasons, but it almost had to be so, given the year-round character of the labor requirements and the lack of access to international contract-labor supplies. Within this basic distinction, systems that appear to have been very different had an underlying similarity. Landowners could not directly control the mobility of labor, but networks emerged to serve the labor demands of these owners, and a political interest grew up to preserve these networks and isolate them from outside influences. In the West, the barriers were linguistic and cultural, but also educational and legal. In the South, the barriers were all of these, except language; in addition, the line became increasingly racial with the course of time.

Reintegrating the White South into the United States

In Cuba and Brazil the ex-slaves quickly lost identity as a distinctive class or political faction (Scott 1988). The opposite was true in the U.S. South, where racial distinctions were uncompromising and became even more rigid over time. By the end of the century, the more appropriate parallel for economic and social relations in the South was no longer the former slave societies of Latin America and the Caribbean, but South Africa. What these two cases had in common was the coexistence of blacks with a large white small-farming and laboring class. Though their formal political structures were very different from each other, in both cases there were strong links between the white society and Anglo-American legal and political culture, and increasing political pressures to modernize; that is, to reduce the economic and educational gap between the region and the metropolitan centers of Europe and the northern United States. In South Africa, the labor movement targeted a "European standard of living" as an explicit goal. As Cell (1982) argues, formalized racial segregation was the instrument for accommodating coexistence between a progressive industrial and educational development program and the demands of planters (and other large employer interests) for cheap unskilled labor. The segregationists were in many ways progressive, supporters of active government programs and by no means committed to brutal antiblack policies. But they could not let the economic problems and political vulnerability of blacks stand in the way of their program. There was considerable communication and imitation between South Africa and the U.S. South on these matters during the early twentieth century.

Like all such parallels, this one can be overdone. Unlike South Africa, the U.S. South was a white-majority region with a large class of whites whose basic living standard was not much different from the norm for blacks. Prior to World War I, whites who found themselves in the unskilled labor market received a wage very close to the black wage, and the status of black sharecroppers overlapped that of large numbers of poor white farmers (Wright 1986:104–05). Industrial job segregation systems were primarily implicit and informal, rather than explicit and legally enforced (though they could be no less tenacious and effective for that, as in the textiles industry). As has been often pointed out, large numbers of whites lost the vote in the process of black disfranchisement between 1890 and 1910, a development that was probably not favorable for positive government programs of any kind.

Despite these facts, there was an underlying trend toward closing the gap between the white South and the rest of the United States, leading eventually to an explicit racial wage gap by the 1920s, even for unskilled labor. Trends in education were an essential part of this story. Expenditures per pupil by race were nearly equal in many southern states in 1890. By 1910, the figures for whites were higher by factors of two, three, four, or more (Margo 1985: table I–1). In many cases, the absolute level of spending on schools for black children went down over this twenty-year period. the connection between this development and black disfranchisement is obvious. But almost immediately in the wake of disfranchisement, a major campaign to upgrade southern schools took off, led by the Southern Education Board, an alliance of southern moderates and northern philanthropists (Harlan 1958: chapter 3). These forces were not opposed to upgrading black schools, but the price of their success in state-level campaigns was acquiescence in the black-belt planters' demands for segregation and local control of expenditures. Expenditures on white schools in the black-belt counties were invariably among the highest in the South. The evidence is clear that obtaining education greatly increased the probability of leaving the area and leaving agricultural employment altogether, and planters were well aware of these considerations.

In these ways, the racial basis for the politics of southern agricultural labor issues should be thought of as something that emerged and crystallized only over the course of the half century after emancipation. For the most part, neither planters nor their creditors ever had control of their labor supplies; competition and labor mobility prevailed most of the time. But a regional system emerged that settled into a kind of institutional and political equilibrium, in which racism and racial segregation played increasingly important roles. The disproportionate political representation of black-belt planters in state politics (and hence, in the U.S. Senate) gave them veto power over basic policies (especially education), which might have threatened this status quo. The racial attitudes of white urban dwellers and industrial workers facilitated this accommodation, and race came to be the accepted reason for deviations between the South and the rest of the country, allowing white southerners to feel that in other respects they were making steady progress toward national cultural and economic norms. In this view they were joined by most of the rest of the nation. In much the same way, acceptance of racism in the late nineteenth century served as the solution to the problem of reconciling bourgeois ideology with the apparent failure of abolitions throughout the hemisphere (Holt 1982).

REFERENCES

Applewhite, Marjorie Mendenhall. 1954. Sharecropper and Tenant in the Courts of North Carolina. *North Carolina Historical Review* 31:134–45.

Banks, Enoch. 1905. *The Economics of Land Tenure in Georgia.* New York: Columbia University Press.

Bardhan, Pranab K. 1983. Labor-Tying in a Poor Agrarian Economy: A Theoretical and Empirical Analysis. *Quarterly Journal of Economics* 98:501–14.

Belz, Herman. 1973. The New Orthodoxy in Reconstruction Historiography. *Reviews in American History* 1:106–13.

Bode, Frederick, and Donald Ginter. 1986. *Farm Tenancy and the Census in Antebellum Georgia.* Athens: University of Georgia Press.

Brooks, R. P. 1914. The Agrarian Revolution in Georgia, 1865–1912. *Bulletin of the University of Wisconsin, 639.*

Cell, John W. 1982. *The Highest Stage of White Supremacy.* New York: Cambridge University Press.

Currie, James T. 1980. *Enclave: Vicksburg and Her Plantations.* Jackson: University Press of Mississippi.

Davis, Ronald L. F. 1982. *Good and Faithful Labor: From Slavery to Sharecropping in the Natchez District, 1860–1890.* Westport, Conn.: Greenwood Press.

Drescher, Seymour. 1988. Brazilian Abolition in Comparative Perspective. *Hispanic American Historical Review* 68:429–60.

Eltis, David. 1987. *Economic Growth and the Ending of the Transatlantic Slave Trade.* New York: Oxford University Press.

Engerman, Stanley. 1984. Economic Change and Contract Labor in the British Caribbean: The End of Slavery and the Adjustment to Emancipation. *Explorations in Economic History* 21:133–50.

———. 1986a. Slavery and Emancipation in Comparative Perspective: A Look at Some Recent Debates. *Journal of Economic History* 46:317–39.

———. 1986b. Servants to Slaves to Servants: Contract Labour and European Expansion. In *Colonialism and Migration: Indentured Labour Before and After Slavery*, edited by P. C. Emmer, 263–94. Dordrecht: Martinus Nijhoff.

Erickson, Charlotte. 1984. Why Did Contract Labour Not Work in the Nineteenth Century United States? In *International Labor Migration*, edited by Shula Marks and Peter Richardson, 34–56. London: Maurice Temple Smith for the Institute of Commonwealth Studies.

Fields, Barbara Jeanne. 1982. Ideology and Race in American History. In *Region, Race and Reconstruction*, edited by James M. McPherson and J. Morgan Kousser. New York: Oxford University Press.

———. 1985. *Slavery and Freedom on the Middle Ground*. New Haven: Yale University Press.

Flynn, Charles L. 1983. *White Land, Black Labor*. Baton Rouge: Louisiana State University Press.

Foner, Eric. 1983. *Nothing But Freedom: Emancipation and Its Legacy*. Baton Rouge: Louisiana State University Press.

Graham, Richard. 1981. Slavery and Economic Development: Brazil and the United States South in the Nineteenth Century. *Comparative Studies in Society and History* 23:620–55.

Hahn, Steven. 1990. Class and State in Postemancipation Societies: Southern Planters in Comparative Perspective. *American Historical Review* 95:75–98.

Harlan, Louis R. 1958. *Separate and Unequal: Public School Campaigns and Racism in the Southern Seaboard States, 1901–1915*. Chapel Hill: University of North Carolina Press.

Harris, J. William. 1982. Plantations and Power: Emancipation on the David Barrow Plantations. In *Towards a New South,* edited by O. V. Burton and R. C. McMath. Westport, Conn.: Greenwood Press.

Holt, Thomas C. 1982. "An Empire Over the Mind": Emancipation, Race and Ideology in the British West Indies and the American South. In *Region, Race and Reconstruction*, edited by James M. McPherson and J. Morgan Kousser. New York: Oxford University Press.

Jaynes, Gerald David. 1986. *Branches Without Roots: Genesis of the Black Working Class in the American South, 1862–1882*. New York: Oxford University Press.

Karsten, Peter. 1990. "Bottomed on Justice": Breaches of Labor Contracts by Quitting or Firing in Britain and the United States, 1630–1880. *American Journal of Legal History* 34:213–61.

Klein, Herbert S. 1986. *African Slavery in Latin America and the Caribbean*. New York: Oxford University Press.

Klein, Maury. 1970. *The Great Richmond Terminal: A Study in Businessmen and Business Strategy.* Charlottesville: University Press of Virginia.

Kousser, J. Morgan. 1974. *The Shaping of Southern Politics: Suffrage Restriction and the Establishment of the One-Party South, 1880–1910.* New Haven: Yale University Press.

Margo, Robert A. 1985. *School Finance and the Economics of Segregated Schools in the U.S. South, 1890–1910.* New York: Garland Press.

McDonald, Forrest, and Grady McWhiney. 1975. The Antebellum Southern Herdsman: A Reinterpretation. *Journal of Southern History* 41:147–66.

———. 1980. The South from Self-Sufficiency to Peonage: An Interpretation. *American Historical Review* 85:1095–118.

McFeely, William S. 1970. *Yankee Stepfather: General O. O. Howard and the Freedmen.* New York: W. W. Norton.

Morgan, David Hoseason. 1982. *Harvesters and Harvesting, 1840–1900: A Study of the Rural Proletariat.* London: Croom Helm.

Novak, Daniel A. 1978. *The Wheel of Servitude: Black Forced Labor After Slavery.* Lexington: University Press of Kentucky.

Oakes, James. 1986. The Present Becomes the Past: The Planter Class in the Postbellum South. In *New Perspectives on Race and Slavery in America: Essays in Honor of Kenneth M. Stampp,* edited by Robert H. Abzug and Stephen E. Maizlish. Lexington: University Press of Kentucky.

Olsen, Otto. 1972. Historians and the Extent of Slave Ownership in the Southern United States. *Civil War History* 18:101–16.

Pope, Christie Farnham. 1970. Southern Homesteads for Negroes. *Agricultural History* 44:201–12.

Ransom, Roger, and Richard Sutch. 1977. *One Kind of Freedom: The Economic Consequences of Emancipation.* New York: Cambridge University Press.

Robinson, Armstead L. 1985. "Worser dan Jeff Davis": The Coming of Free Labor during the Civil War, 1861–1865. In *Essays on the Postbellum Southern Economy,* edited by Thavolia Glymph and John J. Kushma. College Station: Texas A&M University Press.

Scott, Rebecca. 1988. Exploring the Meaning of Freedom: Postemancipation Societies in Comparative Perspective. *Hispanic American Historical Review* 68: 407–28.

Shlomowitz, Ralph. 1982. The Squad System on Postbellum Cotton Plantations. In *Toward A New South,* edited by O. V. Burton and R. C. McMath. Westport, Conn.: Greenwood Press.

———. 1984. 'Bound' or Free? Freedman Labor in Cotton and Sugar Cane Farming, 1865–1880. *Journal of Southern History* 50:569–96.

Strickland, John Scott. 1865. Traditional Culture and Moral Economy: Social and Economic Change in the South Carolina Low Country, 1865–1910. In *The Countryside in the Age of Capitalist Transformation,* edited by Steven Hahn and Jonathan Prude. Chapel Hill: University of North Carolina Press.

Summers, Mark W. 1984. *Railroads, Reconstruction and the Gospel of Prosperity: Aid Under the Radical Republicans, 1865–1877.* Princeton: Princeton University Press.

Taylor, Paul. 1981. *Labor on the Land.* New York: Arno Press.

Thornton, J. Mills. 1982. Fiscal Policy and the Failure of Radical Reconstruction in the Lower South. In *Region, Race and Reconstruction,* edited by James M. McPherson and J. Morgan Kousser. New York: Oxford University Press.

Wallenstein, Peter. 1987. *From Slave South to New South: Public Policy in Nineteenth-Century Georgia.* Chapel Hill: University of North Carolina Press.

Wayne, Michael. 1983. *The Reshaping of Plantation Society: The Natchez District, 1860–1880.* Baton Rouge: Louisiana University Press.

Woodman, Harold D. 1979. Southern Agriculture and the Law. *Agricultural History* 43:319–37.

———. 1982. Postbellum Social Change and Its Effect on Marketing the South's Cotton Crop. *Agricultural History* 56:215–30.

Woodward, C. Vann. 1938. *Tom Watson: Agrarian Rebel.* Reprint 1963. New York: Oxford University Press (1963).

Wright, Gavin. 1974. Cotton Competition and the Postbellum Recovery of the American South. *Journal of Economic History* 34:610–35.

———. 1978. *The Political Economy of the Cotton South: Households, Markets and Wealth in the Nineteenth Century.* New York: W. W. Norton.

———. 1986. *Old South New South: Revolutions in the Southern Economy Since the Civil War.* New York: Basic Books.

———. 1988. American Agriculture and the Labor Market: What Happened to Proletarianization? *Agricultural History* 62:182–209.

O . NIGEL BOLLAND

The Politics of Freedom
in the British Caribbean

One of the principal questions in the comparative study of emancipation is, "How did former slaves give meaning to their freedom?" (Scott 1988:416). Philip Curtin, in a study of the emancipation period in Jamaica, states that the former slave "was not principally interested in economic success" in the terms of the planters, nor even in the terms of those whites who supported the small settlers. "What did make a difference was his escape from the estates—freedom became a reality, and not simply a change in legal status" (Curtin 1970:121). In order to evaluate the extent to which their freedom became a reality, we need to study "the myriad manifestations of worker autonomy, as former slaves and free men and women claimed some 'space' for themselves in the years of emancipation" (Martinez Vergne 1988:50).

In some circumstances, but not all, this search for space or freedom involved an escape from the estates. Spatial mobility for the former slaves was important for a number of reasons, including the search for better terms of employment on other estates as well as escape from the domination of a former master. The search for freedom often involved a struggle over the labor process, in many respects continuing the struggle that had taken place during the period of slavery. The issue of labor was central in the emancipation process, but the meaning of freedom for former slaves was not limited to their gaining control over their own labor. Emancipation, for them, promised something even more, namely the possibility of taking control of their own lives. Many former slaves migrated in order to reunite families that had been broken up during slavery and to create new communities in which they developed institutions such as churches and mutual-aid societies (Scott 1988:417). In such ways, former slaves used their new legal freedom of movement to shape new social relations, relations that not only were unlike those that had been forced on them during slavery, but that also implied a vision of a free society quite different from that held by their former masters.

In one of the most perceptive studies of emancipation, Rebecca J. Scott has warned, "To evaluate the full meaning of emancipation for former slaves requires a careful attention to perspective" (1985:282). She states that, from the vantage point of studies of slavery, the change in legal status, however compromised, is "by definition a liberation," whereas, from the vantage point of the comparative study of systems of labor control, such changes "are almost epiphenomenal, for the essential facts of coercion and hardship remain" (ibid., 282). The former perspective emphasizes the importance of the changes, while the latter emphasizes the continuities associated with the process of emancipation, but the difference between these perspectives is not simply that of choosing to stress changes as opposed to continuities. What is at stake is the weight to be placed on the question of power. A legalistic approach tends to view slavery as a special case in which human beings are defined as objects of property, whereas a sociological approach views slavery as a variant, in extreme form, of relations of domination and subordination.

In order to assess the transition from slavery to freedom, then, we must go beyond the simple recognition of the change in legal status whereby people are no longer defined as legal things. While acknowledging that the apparent promise of freedom made emancipation a great event for the freed people themselves, we must analyze emancipation as a prolonged process rather than an overnight event. We need to evaluate the subsequent struggle over "personal mobility, autonomy, and dignity," and over the obligation to "labor in tasks not freely chosen" (Scott 1985:282). Nevertheless, it is confusing when Scott prefaces this statement with the comment that "slavery was at once a labor system and a social system," as if a labor system is something other than a social system. The social relations involved in the labor process are part of the social system as a whole and are, in fact, the most important social relations in both slave and wage labor societies, insofar as they influence most other aspects of the social system. For example, in a recent study of Reconstruction, Eric Foner states, "the fulfillment of blacks' 'noneconomic' aspirations, from family autonomy to the creation of schools and churches, all depended in considerable measure on success in winning control of their working lives and gaining access to the economic resources of the South" (1988:110). This was also true in the British Caribbean after 1838, where those who had been slaves found themselves struggling against existing power structures and emerging market forces while they tried to forge a new society.

The ability of the former slaves to exercise their initiatives and fulfill their aspirations was decisively affected by the economic forces as well as the political constraints placed on them in the colonial societies. For example, the extent to which former slaves were able to sustain a secure family life was dependent to a large degree, as it was for slaves, upon the predominant relations in the labor process. Edith Clarke argues, in a study completed in Jamaica over thirty years ago, that "the fact of Emancipation did not itself create a set of conditions, social or economic, in which the freed Negro could at once assume the role of father and husband in the new society" (1957:19). Clarke shows that the extent to which a man could own land and sell produce, or the terms on which he could offer his labor, "created conditions in which he could assume the role of father and husband without the threat of external interference in these relationships. Family patterns were, however, already prescribed by status and class structure" (ibid., 20). This class structure, she argues, was responsible for the varieties of family forms, household structures, marital unions, and parental roles observable more than a century after emancipation, because the "conditions which make it impossible for men to perform the roles of father and husband as these roles are defined in the society to which they belong, *persist in present-day Jamaica*" (ibid., 21; emphasis in original).

I do not wish to imply that economic relations or the class structure determine all other social relations or that those people who control the economy thereby have total power over all other people. This is not true even in slave societies. However, it is surely true that, in societies emerging from the era of slavery, the struggle over access to the means of existence, which had been monopolized for so long by so few, was a central struggle in the entire process of adjustment to the abolition of slavery. It is for this reason that I believe we should view the nineteenth century as "a period of transition from one system of domination to another, each involving distinct forms of labour control and patterns of labour resistance" (Bolland 1986:175). To understand the meaning of freedom, therefore, we need to place this struggle — and the question of power — at the center of our analysis of the process of emancipation.

The fact that surplus labor is extracted under capitalism primarily by economic rather than by political means should not be allowed to obscure the fact that there remains a central conflict of interest, and hence location of struggle, between those who hire and those who offer labor power in a free society. The key distinction between the polar types of slavery and free wage labor is not in the existence or absence of compulsion, but rather in the distinction between the *laborer* as a commodity and the laborer's *labor power* as a commodity. The existence of free wage labor "implies the conceptual abstraction of a man's labor power from the man himself" (Finley 1980:68), and this form of hired labor becomes the defining characteristic of capitalist relations of production. The institutionalized system of organizing labor under capitalism depends upon varieties of economic compulsion and exploitation, in which the state continues to play a crucial role, as I will show was the case in the British Caribbean after 1838.

Of the two polar extremes, slavery may be seen as involving the loss of control by the laborer not only over his labor but also over his own person, and even his (and her) children. To conceive of a person as having the status of a marketable commodity is to conceive of "one of the most extreme forms of the relation of domination, approaching the limits of total power from the viewpoint of the master, and of total powerlessness from the viewpoint of the slave" (Patterson 1982:1). Patterson stresses the importance of the deracination of the slave, of his natal alienation, "the loss of ties of birth in both ascending and descending generations. . . . It was this alienation of the slave from all formal, legally enforceable ties of 'blood,' and from any attachment to groups or localities other than those chosen for him by the master, that gave the relation of slavery its peculiar value to the master. The slave was the ultimate human tool" (ibid., 7). Of course, slaves resisted this definition by various means and so were not always "as imprintable and as disposable as the master wished" (ibid., 7).

The other polar extreme, wage labor, cannot be adequately understood simply as the absence of some of the features of compulsion associated with slavery. It needs to be understood in terms of the existence of a variety of mechanisms of economic compulsion, such as rents, taxes, and debts, by means of which laborers are required to sell their labor power to others. We must also examine the many legal, political, and cultural influences upon the interaction of those who offer and those who hire labor power in the market. The transition from slave to free status, seen in this light, occurred "only in ideal terms. In practice it involved a series of ongoing adjustments intended to sustain the economic and political power of those who needed labor over those who provided it" (Mintz 1985:275). The dialectic of power in the master-slave relationship was thus transformed into a new dialectic of power in the relationship between capitalist and wage laborer. What changed in this transition, then, was not the fact of domination and subordination, which persists, but the dimension of the ties between them (Finley 1980:36).

The central and unavoidable issue invoked by the meaning of freedom, therefore, becomes the struggle between those who attempt to depress legally free people into various conditions of dependency and compulsion and those who resist such coercive measures. This is why I urge that "the political dimension of social history, that is, the multiplicity of ways—cultural, economic, military, legal, psychological—by which class authority is formulated, implemented, and resisted, be placed at the center of our analysis of postabolition societies in the Caribbean" (Bolland 1984:125). The former slaves recognized, as surely as did their former masters, that the struggle for political power was a collective struggle and that a person's or family's security and freedom depended very largely on the outcome of this struggle (Scott 1988:423).

In this essay I focus on the political dimension in order to understand those transformations of social relations that constituted the process of emancipation in the British Caribbean in the nineteenth century. After examining the patterns of coercion and resistance in the labor process, and the role of the state in maintaining the planters' hegemony in these colonial societies, I return to the question of the meaning of freedom for former slaves.

Coercion and Resistance in the Labor Process

The architects of emancipation in the British Caribbean, for a variety of motives, sought to abolish slavery without provoking the far-reaching social changes that had occurred in Haiti. The British government and the West Indian planters disagreed about the necessity for slavery, but they agreed that the plantation economies, based chiefly upon the production and export of sugar, should continue. From the viewpoint of the planters, the problem created by the abolition of slavery was one of ensuring the continued existence of an adequate labor force to maintain the plantations. "Planters, assuming blacks were either inherently indolent or simply determined to escape plantation labor, insisted that only coercion of some kind could maintain sugar production after abolition" (Foner 1983:15). The British government soon adopted the planters' view of the postemancipation crisis.

The Abolition Act, passed in the British Parliament in June 1833, contained two important elements calculated to appease the proprietors of slaves. One element was the provision introducing the system called *ap-*

prenticeship, under which all slaves over the age of six years were compelled to become apprenticed laborers for the same masters and were paid wages only for work done in excess of forty-five hours per week. Full freedom was to be received by nonfield-workers in 1838 and by field-workers in 1840. (Antigua and Bermuda rejected the system and conferred immediate freedom on the slaves in 1834.) The other element concerned compensation, not for the unrequited toil of the slaves, but for the loss of property of their owners. The act empowered the treasury to raise 20 million pounds to be paid to the slave owners, a prodigious sum that was not only intended to shore up the planters' enterprises but also to reassure the property-owning classes that the principle of private property was not itself under attack. (An earlier abolition bill had proposed a twelve-year apprenticeship period and 15 million pounds of compensation. The final version was a concession on the first element to the Anti-Slavery Society, which wanted immediate abolition, and on the second element to the planters who, if they could not be assured of continuing control over their laborers, demanded more compensation.) These elements of the Abolition Act were intended, generous and sympathetic as they were to the slave owners, to produce a minimum of social change, "to avoid any significant alterations in the plantation system of agriculture or the hierarchical character of society" (Green 1976:126).

As the apprenticeship system was to last for only a limited period, the planters sought a variety of means of coercion to ensure an adequate, steady, and manageable supply of laborers. The concept of apprenticeship implied that the former slaves were to learn their obligations as wage-earning estate laborers during this period, that they "would continue to work on the plantations, but would gain legal equality while at the same time developing the economic wants, the familiarity with the marketplace, which would ensure their continued, voluntary labor once emancipation was complete" (Foner 1983:16). Meanwhile, the planter-dominated legislatures of the various colonies enacted a series of oppressive laws concerning such offenses as vagrancy, insubordination, and neglecting work, in an attempt to regulate and control labor. Initially, the imperial government struck down many of these measures, which were scrutinized by the Anti-Slavery Society in Britain. Over a hundred stipendiary magistrates were appointed to supervise the equitable functioning of apprenticeship, but many were patronized by the planters, and there were never enough to provide adequate legal protection for the apprentices.

Not surprisingly, the apprenticeship system failed. From its inception, apprenticeship had provoked opposition among the ex-slaves, many of whom considered it a conspiracy on the part of the local elites to keep freedom from them. There were disorders and disturbances in St. Kitts, Montserrat, British Guiana, and Trinidad. As 1 August 1838 approached it became clear that there would be widespread trouble if the praedial apprentices were required to work under the same conditions for a further two years after others had been freed, so the entire system was ended on that date.

The planters were able to maintain their power after emancipation because they continued to control the local legislatures, where these existed, and they had the support of the imperial government. A parliamentary select committee of 1842 accepted the planters' view of the postemancipation crisis, attributing the planters' inability to secure sufficient labor at low wages to "the easy terms upon which the use of land has been obtained by Negroes," and recommended that "planters should exercise greater control over the alienation of estate lands" (Lobdell 1988:196). The committee also urged the immigration of "a fresh labouring population, to such an extent as to create competition for employment, thereby containing or possibly even reducing wage rates," recommended the revision of labor laws, and particularly urged that "steps should be taken to control vagrancy and eliminate squatting by freedmen on abandoned estates or crown lands" (ibid., 196).

The Bentinck Committee of 1848 expressed similar views. Richard Lobdell concludes that, "by the middle of the nineteenth century, most British officials appear to have shared the view of Lord Grey, Secretary of State in 1847: 'the highest interests of the Negroes require that the cultivation of sugar should not be abandoned, and that the proprietors of European race should be enabled to maintain their present place in the society . . . which can only be done by giving them a greater command of labour'" (ibid., 198). Until the late nineteenth century, when some officials favored the West Indian peasantry over the sugar plantations, the Colonial Office argued that "West Indian prosperity might be rejuvenated if planters were afforded more effective control over wage labour" (ibid., 199).

The masters, as they still thought of themselves, tried a variety of techniques of labor control after 1838 throughout the British Caribbean (Bolland 1981). These included the enactment of laws to restrict emigration and vagrancy, various forms of taxation to pressure people into wage labor, the use of wage-rent and advance-truck systems to make laborers dependent, and the development of systems of police, magistrates, and prisons to punish those who broke the new labor laws. Several of these techniques had already been tried in Antigua, and planters in other British colonies commonly sought to benefit from the Antiguan experience.

One such technique was the use of contracts to ensure regular and obedient supplies of labor. According to an act passed in the Antiguan legislature on 29 December 1834, labor contracts were not required to be written but needed only to be made orally in the presence of two witnesses. If a laborer under contract absented himself from work, even with a reasonable excuse, he forfeited his wages for the lost time, and if absent without such an excuse for half a day or *less* (a term sufficiently elastic to be used to enforce promptness), he forfeited the whole day's wages. If absent for two successive days, or for two whole days within any two-week period, the laborer would be liable to a week's imprisonment with hard labor. Other offenses, such as drunkenness or the careless use of fire or the abuse of cattle, could be punished with up to three months' imprisonment with hard labor. In contrast, the maximum punishment for an employer, for any violation of a contract, was a fine of five pounds.

The imperial government, still sensitive to the criticisms of the antislavery party, disallowed this Antiguan act, but it was replaced the following year by another only slightly less severe. The new act provided that verbal or implied contracts should be for a year, terminable only at a month's notice, and that the occupation of a tenement should be prima facie evidence of the existence of such a contract between the tenant and his landlord. Under this act, Antiguan laborers worked nine hours a day, with one day free in a week or sometimes only one in every two weeks, for wages of ninepence a day. Not surprisingly, it has been concluded that "the purely material condition of the Antiguan labourers showed little real advance over that of the days of slavery" (Hall 1971:28). Such contract systems were widespread and persistent in the British Caribbean. In Belize, a worker who failed to perform according to the labor contract could be apprehended by the employer, without warrant, and forcibly removed to his place of work. A century after emancipation, workers who infringed their contracts were treated as criminals and were subject to imprisonment with hard labor for three months (Bolland 1986:180).

Antigua introduced another mechanism of labor control, the wage-rent system, which was adopted, with variations, by many planters elsewhere. This system combined the roles of employer and landlord, on the one hand, and those of employee and tenant, on the other. The ex-slaves found that they had to pay rent for access to the provision grounds and family homes, often built by themselves, that they had occupied as slaves. The employer-landlords were able to threaten their laborer-tenants with eviction if they did not work to the master's satisfaction on the estates. The ex-slaves frequently desired to continue to occupy the grounds and houses to which they had customary rights of usage, supplementing a peasant livelihood with occasional cash earnings from casual estate labor. The masters, however, wanted regular and continuous labor, especially during crop time, and used their property rights over the houses and grounds to coerce such labor from their former slaves. The conflicting interests of these groups thus clashed in the wage-rent system: the planters continued to require plentiful and regular supplies of cheap labor, which they were accustomed to controlling in a coercive manner, and their former slaves sought to avoid the limitations estate work persistently imposed on their autonomy.

The application of the wage-rent system varied considerably from one colony to another. In Barbados, a house was often occupied rent free on the condition that the tenant work on his landlord's estate five days a week. Those who worked less were fined, and the fine effectively constituted a rent. In order to prevent their tenants from paying rent with money earned by marketing provisions or laboring elsewhere, the planters deducted the rents from estate wages, thereby obliging the tenants to work for wages on the home estates, on pain of eviction. Until the mid-1840s, rents and wages were generally associated, in Barbados, with resident laborers being paid 10d. daily and nonresidents 1s. or 1s. ½d., making the rent effectively 2d. or 2½d. daily. If such tenants did not work satisfactorily they could be evicted, and if they refused to leave when evicted they were subject to arrest (Levy 1980:79).

There were wide variations in the rents charged. In Jamaica, the average was 2s. a week, but it was sometimes as high as 6s. 8d. per household. In some cases in Jamaica, rent was charged "*per capita* against husband, wife, and each of the children, as a *penal exaction,* to compel labor" (Gurney 1840:79, emphasis in original). In Trinidad and British Guiana, however, ex-slaves who worked on the estates continued to enjoy their houses and grounds rent free and also had the customary allowances and relatively high wages. When considering rents as a percentage of wages, there was wide variation among colonies. In Tobago and Barbados, rents were about 20 percent of wages, in St. Vincent they were 33 percent, in Grenada 35 percent, and in Jamaica as high as 48 percent (Riviere 1972:7–8). There was also great variation in the planter's ability to collect rents. On Worthy Park estate in Jamaica, £342, more than 10 percent of the total wages, was deducted directly from the laborers' pay in 1839, but in the following year, when the total rent on houses and provision grounds was assessed at £2,827, attempts to collect it proved futile. "Those from whom rents were collected proved even less willing to work, and those who did not work had no money to pay" (Craton and Walvin 1970:217). In 1842, less than £50 was collected for all rents on Worthy Park, "and within a few more years it was nothing at all. In effect Worthy Park was then offering rent-free cottages and land to its regular workers. But even this did not effectively tie cottagers to the estate . . . until it was backed up by a fairly ruthless policy of evictions" (Craton 1978:288).

The wage-rent system varied considerably in its ability to promote continuous supplies of reliable labor. In some colonies, the planters maintained control over labor supplies, but in others the system became self-defeating. While the threat of eviction might coerce some tenants to work on the estate, implementation of the threat would throw laborers on the general market and alienate them still further from the landlord and would-be employer who had evicted them. Often, as in Jamaica, the coercive nature of the tenure arrangements was sufficient to cause the newly freed slaves to reject the system and flee the estates. Whether they fled or were evicted, the planters lost their labor force. By the mid-1840s, Jamaican planters had recognized the failure of the system and grudgingly abandoned it.

The reasons why the wage-rent system worked in some instances and not in others are complex. Variations in the success of the system in securing labor supplies for the estates depended to a large extent on the availability of alternatives for the ex-slaves. Though some former slaves became artisans and small traders, the chief option was peasant farming on a small scale to produce a variety of crops for family consumption and for sale. Sidney Mintz has called these people a "reconstituted peasantry," in order to draw attention to their origins in the "proto-peasantry," who originated a peasant style of life while they were still enslaved (1974:151). An important factor in determining whether peasant agriculture could become an alternative to estate labor was the availability of land. The explanatory importance of population density in this analysis has been debated at some length (Bolland 1981; Green 1984; Bolland 1984).

In my view, the availability of land, though important, is not the only factor affecting the planters' ability to secure a labor supply, nor is it determined by population density. The availability of land for a peasantry is chiefly determined by the degree of monopolization of land by the planters. Indeed, the plantation monopoly of land is generally one of the chief means of the coercion of labor. This helps to explain why much of the land held on large estates is not utilized for agriculture. In Trinidad in 1838, for example, it was estimated that only 43,265 acres of the 208,379 acres in private ownership were in cultivation (Wood 1968:49). Andre Gunder Frank has argued that "one primary purpose of the ownership of large amounts of land, both on the individual and on the social level, is not to use it but to prevent its use by others. These others, denied access to the primary resource, necessarily fall under the domination of the few who do control it. And then they are exploited in all conceivable ways" (1971:288).

This has been shown to be the case even in a colony with such a low population density as Belize, where the emergence of a peasantry after emancipation was severely inhibited by the extreme monopolization of landownership (Bolland and Shoman 1977). The point is, simply, that the availability of land is primarily determined by the power structure—by the ability of the planters, through their control of local legislatures and with the support of the imperial government, to control access to land in the interests of the plantation economy (Beckford 1972:96).

Credit and truck shops were important means of labor control in St. Lucia, Belize, the Bahamas, and some other colonies in the nineteenth and early twentieth centuries. H. Breen, writing in 1844, said that in St. Lucia, "on the abolition of slavery almost every planter was induced to establish a shop upon his estate, with the two-fold object of attaching the labourers to the property, and of drawing back in exorbitant profits a portion of the exorbitant wages he was compelled to give them" (Fraser 1981:329).

Belizeans who worked in the forest industry were given advances on their wages when they signed contracts at the beginning of the season, around Christmas time. Ostensibly, the advances were intended to enable the laborer to purchase supplies prior to going to the forests for the season, but the money was generally spent in "keeping Christmas" with his family and friends in Belize Town. The result was that laborers had to purchase their supplies on credit and at exorbitant prices from the employers' truck shops at the camps in the forest. Often, the balance of the wages a worker received was insufficient to meet his expenses, and he ended his season in debt to his employer. To work off his debt, the laborer would sign another contract with that employer the next season, with the result that the advance and truck system effectively bound the laborers to their employers in a form of debt servitude. Fifty years after emancipation, the colony's handbook admitted that, by this system, the laborers "become virtually enslaved for life" (Bristowe and Wright 1888:199). Though the custom of giving advances declined as the supply of laborers came to exceed the demand, the truck system, and even the partial payment of workers in rations and commissary tickets, was still widespread in the mahogany camps of Belize in the 1930s (Bolland 1986:180).

A comparable system of credit and truck in the Bahamas left the lower classes in debt and, according to the governor in 1884, in a position of "practical slavery." Howard Johnson has described "the control mechanisms which enabled a white mercantile minority to consolidate its position as a ruling elite in the postemancipation period. Rather than a monopoly of land, the important elements in this elite's economic and social control were a monopoly of the credit available to the majority of the population and the operation of a system of payment in truck" (1986:729). Johnson points out that such systems were also known in the sugar colonies of Trinidad, Tobago, British Guiana, and Jamaica. He concludes, "The need for advances to cover subsistence made the labourer vulnerable to control and manipulation by the employer class and facilitated the emergence of credit and truck systems. It may be argued that these systems of labour control appeared in those British West Indian colonies where the roles of employer, landlord, or entrepreneur and of supplier of subsistence and production loans were combined in a single individual and where there were few alternative opportunities for employment" (ibid., 752).

The chief purpose of the credit and truck systems appears not to have been to make a profit directly, though the exploitation of captive consumers undoubtedly contributed to that result, but rather to limit the opportunities of the ex-slaves and thus to make them dependent upon the employers. Wherever such dependency could not be maintained and alternatives to estate labor were available, there seems to have been a substantial flight from the estates. Michael Craton has observed that there was no great change in the population of Worthy Park estate until tumbling sugar prices made a resident population impractical from the viewpoint of the planters, and wages became too low from the viewpoint of the former slaves.

The old cohesion of the plantation's population was not lost until 1846, when the transition began to the modern system of employing the minimum number of workers, and only when needed, for minimal wages. This naturally increased the ex-slaves' preference for peasant cultivation, making them more than ever determined to work for wages only when they had to. . . .

Carefully avoiding the suggestion that a defense of chattel slavery is being proposed, it is still clear that the wage labor system substituted was in many ways even more degrading and exploitative. (Craton 1978:293)

Since the surviving records tell us little directly about the ex-slaves' responses to the conditions of their emancipation, the indirect evidence of their avoidance of plantation labor and the rise of a peasantry is extremely important (Hall 1978; Marshall 1985).

Sidney Mintz has shown that the cultivation of provision grounds came to be perceived by slaves as a customary right and that the experience of this protopeasantry in producing and marketing crops and livestock was an important aspect of their transition to emancipation. Both during slavery and after, the rise of such peasantries constituted "some kind of resistant response" to the plantation system (Mintz 1974:132). Ex-slaves valued peasant farming as a basis for their independence. Even during slavery, cultivation of the provision grounds was largely free of supervision, and during the apprenticeship period, "apprentices guarded closely the labour time in their control" (Marshall 1985:211). The problem for the slaves, apprentices, and ex-slaves was how to secure their access to land and how to increase the amount of work they did, without supervision, on their own account. The plantation and peasant spheres of activity, though in some sense coexistent, competed for resources—in particular, for land and labor.

When employer-landlords asserted their property rights over the houses and grounds of their former slaves, demanding rent and the labor of their tenants, some ex-slaves contested the claim. In Grenada, for example, estate residents told the magistrates and constables who tried to evict them at the end of apprenticeship that "they would not surrender their houses and grounds because these had been 'given them by the Queen'" (Marshall 1985:219). When the workers were told they had no right to the provision grounds if they left the plantation residence, the conflict sharpened. The labor crisis that Marshall describes in the Windward Islands resulted from a conflict between what the ex-slaves expected and what the employers offered. Marshall suggests that slaves' participation in own-account activities fostered the growth of attitudes to plantation labor that affected labor relations during and after the apprenticeship period:

From the slaves' perspective, their own-account activities were as important as coerced labour in defining their status, their humanity and their notions of freedom. Perhaps it is not too fanciful to suggest that humanity and freedom may have been equated by them with own-account activities. Further, they may have concluded that their forced involvement in plantation labour was the factor which constrained their exploitation of the potential in proto-peasant activities, and was therefore the critical limiting factor on their acquisition of freedom and full expression of humanity. . . . Both apprentices and ex-slaves utilized the greater control of the labour time, which slavery abolition conferred, to de-emphasize regular plantation labour and to emphasize own-account activities (1988:38–39).

The extent to which ex-slaves achieved greater control of their labor time within the confines of the plantation, or alternatively, left the estates and formed an independent peasant class, varied a great deal from one colony to another throughout the British Caribbean. In Antigua, St. Kitts, and Barbados, for example, there was little change in the patterns of land tenure after 1838 — the plantations continued more or less intact, and sugar production actually increased after emancipation. In Jamaica, Trinidad, and British Guiana, however, peasant communities arose rapidly, and the plantation system entered a prolonged crisis. In Jamaica, the number of estates fell from 646 in 1834 to 330 in 1854, and in British Guiana they declined from 308 in 1838 to 196 in 1849. In British Guiana, plantation production fell dramatically between 1838 and 1844: sugar production was down by 25 percent, rum by 36.5 percent, and molasses by 25 percent (Moore 1987:33). Meanwhile, many ex-slaves in these three colonies purchased land (and presumably many more were squatting on land without acquiring legal title). In Jamaica, the number of freeholds of less than ten acres increased from 883 in 1840 to 20,724 in 1845 (Hall 1959:162) and to about 50,000 in 1861, when it was reported that "there are possibly forty thousand laborers in all who give transient work to the estates, but at one and the same time the number actually at work, or the number that can be commanded, does not average more than twenty thousand. These twenty thousand laborers, taking them *en masse,* do not work for estates more than one hundred and seventy days in the year, sometimes three and sometimes four days in the week" (Sewell 1861:265). Certainly, some people were engaged in both own-account farming and estate work from time to time, but by 1861, there were more peasant proprietors in Jamaica than there were people employed in casual estate labor.

In Trinidad, the number of proprietors, mostly smallholders, increased from about 2,000 in 1832 to over 7,000 in 1849, while only 3,116 laborers were said to work regularly on the plantations in 1851. Moreover, squatting, which "rankled with those who wanted to see disciplined labourers working regularly on the estates," was widespread (Wood 1968:50). An attempt by the authorities to evict squatters, and to imprison them for up to six months if they did not remove themselves, was largely ineffective because there were not enough police, and, ironically, "planters themselves were unwilling to lay information before the Magistrates about those squatters who were a source of labour for their own estates" (ibid., 51).

British Guiana, meanwhile, "witnessed one of the greatest expressions of land hunger among the ex-slaves of the region" (Moore 1987: 35). By 1848, some 32,717 people resided on freehold lands in British Guiana, and the total value of property (including buildings and other improvements as well as land) in the hands of ex-slaves was estimated to amount to almost $2.5 million. Remarkably, these ex-slaves bought not only small plots of land but also whole plantations, which they worked cooperatively. By 1851, there were 11,152 small holdings in British Guiana, and 46,368 people lived in villages formed since emancipation. Nevertheless, about 38,000 ex-slaves, or about 43 percent of the labor force at emancipation, still worked on the estates in the mid-1840s (ibid., 37).

Why did so many ex-slaves leave the estates in Jamaica, Trinidad, and British Guiana in the years following 1838? For years it was simply assumed that they fled because of the association of the estates with slavery, or because the ex-slaves, like most people, preferred to work on their own account than for others. Though it is reasonable to assume that these factors played a part, the motives and interests of the ex-slaves must also be seen as more complex than these simple explanations suggest. Douglas Hall concludes in *The Flight from the Estates Reconsidered,* "The movement of the ex-slaves from the estates in the immediate post-emancipation years was not a flight from the horrors of slavery. It was a protest against the inequities of early 'freedom'" (1978:23). Walter Rodney goes one step further when he argues that the former slaves left the estates in order to undermine the planters' ability to dictate to them. The flight from the estates, he argues, "did not occur in order to run away from plantation labor, but to strengthen the bargaining position of labor in dealing with planter capital by putting the laborer in a position where one would be unafraid of the threat that one might be kicked out of the house" (Scarano 1989:69).

In the months after emancipation, the chief issue in labor relations appears to have been a struggle over the terms of work, occupancy, and other rights on the plantations. The employers, who were used to a captive and coerced labor force, "wanted a regular and docile force with a low turnover but instead they had mobile labourers who would not be bound by any contract and who would leave to seek better conditions if they pleased" (Wood 1968:54). The planters' desire for a regular and disciplined supply of labor led them, quite predictably in the circumstances, to find new means of coercion, while the ex-slaves, equally predictably, continued to take advantage of opportunities to increase their autonomy. What this perspective emphasizes is that the crisis in labor relations that occurred after 1838 reflects continuities with slavery and apprenticeship. As Marshall points out,

The factors which created the crisis indicate the existence of continuities which affect the comprehension of post-slavery labour problems. Planters held fast to coercion as the means of extracting a sufficient quantity of labour from what appeared to be a reluctant labour force, and they were not deflected either by evidence of apprentices' alienation or by the creation of a wage labour force. For their part, ex-slaves, deeply influenced by participation in the provision ground/marketing complex, apparently drew the conclusion from their experience during the Apprenticeship that they could secure some insulation from coercion as well as greater rewards for their labour power by emphasizing proto-peasant activity (1985:221).

The clash between ex-slaves and planters resulted not only in a flight from the estates and the rise of a peasantry but also in endemic labor struggles on the plantations. Indeed, the latter was a major cause of the former. The laborers were generally in a weak bargaining position on the plantations, particularly in those colonies where the concentration of land ownership limited their options away from the estates. The availability of land was a crucial factor in the labor struggle, and such availability was determined primarily by economic and political factors, not merely by population density (Bolland 1981). If the ex-slaves could purchase land, especially good land that was close to markets and not poor and remote Crown lands, their independence increased, and, hence, their bargaining power as laborers on the estates grew. The planters knew this, of course. Conversely, the deteriorating economic conditions that many planters experienced in the 1840s weakened their control over land, forcing some of them to sell out and to make land available to the ex-slaves, thereby weakening their control over labor. The ex-slaves valued their ability to choose, bargain, and organize their labor as independently as possible, not only because it reduced the onerous aspects of plantation work and white supervision, but also because it provided the basis for more autonomous family and community life. Access to land did not lead to wealth for the ex-slaves, but it could improve the circumstances in which they entered the labor market and positively affect their conception of themselves.

In British Guiana, emancipation and the subsequent rapid growth of an independent peasantry soon resulted in a scarcity of labor on the sugar plantations and a rise in wages, especially for the heavier tasks like digging canals. On the already overburdened estates, the wages bills rose to form at least half of total currency outlay (Adamson 1972:162). When planters tried to reduce wages and discipline the workers in 1842, the ex-slaves struck and "won a quick and easy victory" (ibid., 166). In 1847–1848, when workers again struck against a concerted effort to reduce their wages by 25 percent, they were defeated, in part because new immigrant workers did not maintain solidarity. Some 15,000 immigrants entered the colony between 1848 and 1851, and wages declined. An initial surge of people into the villages after the 1847–1848 strike was followed by a drop in village population, as many former slaves settled up the rivers and creeks of the interior, moving away from both the villages and the plantations (ibid., 36–37). With a continued flow of indentured immigrants in the 1850s, the planters in British Guiana recovered control of the labor market. The withdrawal of ex-slaves from estate labor in the 1840s reversed as the number of nonresident laborers at hire rose from 17,252 in 1852, to 18,469 in 1861, and to about 22,000 in 1868. The black villagers, who could not maintain their families on small subsistence plots, were compelled to return to estate work at reduced wages in the 1860s. The 1870 Commission of Enquiry concluded simply that Creole estate workers had not shared in the "growing material prosperity of the Colony" (ibid., 72).

Eric Foner's evaluation of the promise and limits of landownership for the former slaves in the postwar South of the United States is applicable to the West Indies after 1838: "Where political power rests in hostile hands, small landowners often find themselves subjected to oppressive taxation and other state policies that severely limit their economic prospects. In such circumstances, the autonomy offered by land ownership tends to be defensive, rather than the springboard for sustained economic advancement" (1988:109). The ability of the plantocracy to recover control of the labor market and, frequently, to intimidate their workers depended to a large extent on their control of the state.

The Role of the State:
Planter Hegemony in Colonial Societies

In the context of the bitter struggle over the control of land and labor, the continuing political influence of the planters in the colonial power structure was central. On the issues of wage rates and rights of occupancy to houses and grounds, the ex-slaves faced not only their employer-landlords but also the power of the colonial state. In the first months after emancipation, prolonged strikes occurred in Grenada, Tobago, and St. Vincent. "Troops were sent to the aid of the civil authorities and to overawe labourers in districts of Grenada and St. Lucia" (Marshall 1985:220). The civil authorities (governors, police magistrates, and stipendiary magistrates) actively toured the districts to explain to the ex-slaves that they would be breaking the law if they tried to retain possession of their houses and grounds, properties that the ex-slaves knew to be the fruits of their own labors.

In the Windward Islands, however, the "Labourers' protest effected no real change on the crucial questions of wage rates and secure rights of occupancy because their tactics of withholding labour while maintaining themselves on the provision grounds were robbed of their effectiveness when they were forced to accept the legality of planters' ownership of house and ground" (ibid., 220). West Indian planters "made full use of the machinery of state to compel the freed workers to labour on the plantations" (Moore 1987:40), and where this failed or provided an inadequate labor supply they resorted to the sponsored immigration of thousands of Asians, who worked as indentured or contract laborers.

The Colonial Office, represented by Lord Glenelg and James Stephen, initially defended the freedmen's liberty against the attempts of the colonial legislatures to keep them working on the estates through vagrancy and contract laws. But whenever the plantation economy was threatened by crisis, the British government rallied to support the planters, and after Lord Stanley returned to the Colonial Office in 1841, numerous concessions were made to the planter-dominated colonial governments. Even William Green, who claims that "the Colonial Office constituted a third force in Caribbean affairs, standing between the colonial oligarchy and the emancipated population" (1986:160), acknowledges that in this crucial period of struggle the imperial government sided with the planters. "On every issue the British Government retreated from positions it had taken during the initial year of freedom, conceding points of principle and positions of power to the planter elites. . . . In every category of legislation the imperial Government modified its initial formula for the free society in order to accommodate the needs of an increasingly distressed planter class" (1976:176, 187). For example, legislation passed in the colonies to raise the property qualifications for the franchise to exclude black voters and to strengthen the organization of police, militias, and colonial judiciaries was approved by the British government.

A series of masters and servants acts was passed in the Caribbean colonies, the chief purpose of which was to control and discipline the estate workers. Laborers who broke their contracts, or who were convicted of "wilful misconduct," "ill-behavior," or "disobedience" while at work were fined or imprisoned. Magistrates in British Guiana were empowered to stop all or part of a convicted laborer's wages and to hand it to the employer (Moore 1987:41), and in Belize much of the time and effort of district magistrates seems to have been taken up with enforcing the labor laws in a way that favored the employers and served as a means of disciplining and intimidating the laborers. The Corozal magistrate, for example, reported that in 1869 all of the 286 cases he decided under the colony's labor laws were against employees: 245 were punished for "absenting themselves from work without leave," 30 for "insolence and disobedience," 6 for "assaults on bookkeepers," and 5 for "entering into second contracts before the expiry of the period of former ones." Such infringements of the labor laws were commonly punished with three months' imprisonment with hard labor (Bolland 1977:149).

Expenditure on prisons and courts rose sharply after emancipation. In Barbados, between 1835 and 1840, prison costs doubled and the expenses of the judiciary trebled, while in British Guiana the amount spent on police and jails rose from £812 in 1833 to £27,796 in 1840. Total public expenditure in British Guiana increased in those years from £53,996 to £125,209 (Green 1976:184), and the chief burden of taxation fell on the ex-slaves. In British Guiana, in 1833, direct taxes in the form of property and income taxes produced 76.5 percent of the colonial government's revenue, but by 1845 customs duties and excise taxes, which fell disproportionately on the poorer consumers, brought in 74.3 percent of the vastly enlarged revenue (Moohr 1972:605). In Jamaica, similarly, two-thirds of the revenue raised for the colony in the mid-1840s was derived from import duties (Green 1976:185). By increasing import duties, especially on the basic necessities, the authorities not only raised more revenue and shifted the cost of various responsibilities formerly borne by the owners of slaves, but in so doing they also sought "to stimulate the freedmen to perform wage work on the estates" (ibid., 184). Earl Grey, who administered the Colonial Office from 1846 to 1852, "advocated heavy capitation taxes which would force freedmen to perform steady wage work in order to satisfy the tax collector. Those who could not pay, he argued [in 1848], should be forced to labour on the roads or be hired out in gangs to the planters" (ibid., 186).

The ex-slaves sometimes resisted tax increases and the colonial administration generally lacked the means to collect unpopular taxes. In Jamaica, attempts to collect a tax on hereditaments "led to serious altercations in which a collector and police constable were beaten" (ibid., 188). In British Guiana, the increase of taxes on consumer goods and imported commodities that were in general demand, such as wheat flour, tobacco, tea, cornmeal, dried codfish, pickled beef and pork, soap, and salt, caused considerable distress among ex-slaves. In addition to import duties, licenses were required for porters, hucksters, and shopkeepers, and a poll tax of $2 per annum for males (equivalent to two months' wages) and $1 per annum for females was imposed in 1856. Brian Moore concludes, "High indirect taxation thus remained a major instrument in suppressing the Creole population and in perpetuating their dependence on the plantation system" (1987:117).

The most dramatic attempt to replace slave labor on the plantations, and at the same time to make the ex-slaves more tractable by reducing their bargaining power, was a massive immigration scheme. Even before 1838, the West Indian planters sought to encourage white immigration, both to augment the white population for security reasons and to create a middle class that would help keep the ex-slaves dependent. Between 1834 and 1838, British Guiana received over a thousand, and Jamaica over two thousand, European immigrants, but their mortality rate was high, and they were unwilling to stay on the estates. In 1841, British Guiana supported the cost of passage for immigrants from Madeira, and up until 1850 some 17,000 Portuguese migrated there, with a further 13,535 following between 1851 and 1882 (ibid., 43). A few thousand Portuguese immigrants went to Antigua, St. Vincent, and St. Kitts-Nevis, but European immigration did not meet the labor requirements of the plantation system after emancipation in the British Caribbean.

Some Africans who had been liberated from slave ships and the slave centers at Rio and Havana, along with others recruited in West Africa, were brought to the British Caribbean. In all, 36,120 "liberated" Africans immigrated to the British Caribbean between 1841 and 1867 (Green 1976:273), some 12,800 of these going to British Guiana, 11,000 to Jamaica, and 8,000 to Trinidad. These Africans made an important contribution to the continuing operation of the plantations in the post-emancipation years (Laurence 1971:14–15). Between 1839 and 1847, over 1,300 black Americans migrated to Trinidad, and there was a substantial migration from the smaller Caribbean islands—some 10,278 West Indians going to Trinidad and 7,582 to British Guiana between 1839 and 1849 (Wood 1968:66). However, attempts by the most labor-hungry colonies to entice former slaves from other British West Indian colonies were discouraged. Barbados, the Windward and Leeward islands, and the Bahamas made it illegal for immigration agents to act on those territories, and on several islands, "laborers who did register for emigration were presented with accounts for false debts to prevent their going" (Adamson 1972:44).

It was the massive immigration of Asian laborers that revived the West Indian plantation system, particularly in Trinidad and British Guiana, where the cultural and social effects of this influx have been profound and permanent. In 1838 a group of 396 Indians was brought under five-year contracts into British Guinana, but due to reports of their ill treatment and high mortality rates publicized by the Anti-Slavery Society, further emigration was suspended by the Council of India (Moore 1987:45). By the mid-1840s, West Indian planters had persuaded the British government to support Indian immigration (a loan of half a million pounds helped finance the scheme) and by 1851 it was well under way. British Guiana received 238,909 Indians, Trinidad received 143,939, Jamaica 36,412, St. Lucia 4,354, Grenada 3,200, St. Vincent 2,472 (Laurence 1971:21–26), and small numbers went to other sugar colonies and to Belize, which began to produce sugar after emancipation. Immigrant workers were also brought from China, about 13,000 of them going to British Guiana between 1852 and 1879 (Moore 1987:45–46). The black and colored Creoles constituted 93 percent of the population of British Guiana in 1841, but with the influx of Asian immigrants the Creole proportion diminished to 52 percent by 1891 (ibid., 110).

The introduction of these indentured laborers was intended to solve two problems for the planters: the short-term problem of providing enough dependable laborers to maintain plantation production after emancipation, and the long-term problem of increasing the potential plantation labor force. The first problem was solved by the terms of the contracts that bound the Asian laborers for a period of years, nor-

mally five. The second problem "was expected to be solved by having
the time-expired workers remain as settlers" (Engerman 1985:234), thereby
expanding the pool of available laborers and, not coincidentally, reducing their bargaining power and hence their wage rates. As one British
Guiana planter explained, "So long as an estate has a large Coolie gang,
Creoles must give way in prices asked" (Foner 1983:22). The ex-slaves
in the British Caribbean contributed through their taxes to the local immigration funds that were supported from the general revenue. Ironically, "Indian immigration was thus financed to a considerable extent
by those with whom it was intended that the Indian immigrants should
compete" (Williams 1970:358). While the planters persistently complained
that the available labor force was inadequate, these indentured and, subsequently, time-expired Asian immigrants enabled them to revive the plantations by recapturing control of the labor market and reducing the price
of labor (Moore 1987:46).

According to Foner, "The use of government-sponsored immigration
to transform the labor market and labor relations is a striking example
of how the power of the state helped to determine the ultimate fate of
planters and freedmen in the postemancipation Caribbean. . . . Emancipation in the British Caribbean did not challenge the local political
hegemony of the planter class" (1983:23). Such political hegemony was
maintained in a variety of ways, not least by the severely restricted franchise that excluded most of the ex-slaves. Planters dominated the legislative assemblies in such colonies as Antigua, and Jamaica. In Barbados
the number of registered voters in 1857 was 1,350 in a population exceeding 135,000. In 1854, Grenada, with a population of 32,600, had
191 electors; St. Vincent, with a population of 30,125, had 273; and
Tobago, with 14,500 persons, had 135 electors. In the 1863 election for
the Jamaican Assembly, only 1,457 votes were cast out of a population
exceeding 440,000 (Green 1976:176–77). In British Guiana, the number
of voters increased from 561 in 1847 to 962 in 1851, but restrictive qualifications ensured that the electorate remained less than 1 percent of the
total population. When there appeared to be a chance that some of the
freedmen, urban as well as rural, could meet the property qualifications,
the planters excluded many of them by adding a literacy qualification.
The maintenance of an electoral college further preserved planter dominance (Moore 1987:55–56).

Not only were legislation, taxation, and expenditures controlled by
the planters and manipulated in their interests, but "local judicial authority remained completely in the hands of planters. With emancipa-

tion . . . the judiciary became a major means of disciplining the black labor force. Heavy fines for vagrancy, theft, and trespass were routinely imposed on the freedmen" (Foner 1983:24). That members of the judiciary could not act independently is attested by Joseph Beaumont, the former chief justice of British Guiana, who wrote in 1871 that, "when acts of the Executive Government or the interests or privileges of the planters come into question, no judge or magistrate can decide adversely to them, without being exposed to the risk of punishment" (Moore 1987:61). Further, through their control of the vestries, statutory boards, and village administrations, the planters' control over local government was pervasive. When such means were insufficient to intimidate and discipline the ex-slaves, the planters controlled the local armed forces in the form of the police, militia, and volunteer forces. In British Guiana, in the wake of disturbances in 1856, when the predominantly white militia had proved inadequate, the Estates' Armed Force was created, Composed mainly of white employees of the planters, this force strengthened "the security and coercive power of the planters on individual estates" (Moore 1987:204). Though the militia and Estates' Armed Force virtually disappeared in the 1870s, a Volunteer Force established in 1878 was sufficiently strong to aid in suppressing the Georgetown riots in 1889. Moore concludes, "Above all, white authorities placed great emphasis on coercion—the show and actual use of armed force—to promote social stability by instilling fear and awe of white power in the minds of the subordinate population. They never equivocated about the absolute need for military force to keep these subordinates in submission to the lawful authority of the ruling white minority" (ibid., 203).

Coercion was emphasized by the white minorities in the British Caribbean and was a key element in the maintenance of social stability, both during and after slavery. It is harder to assess the part played by cultural hegemony in social control. The planters and colonial administrators certainly recognized that organized religion, and the schools that were run by missionaries, could contribute to a value consensus, though they had often been concerned about the effects of conversion and religious education on their slaves. In 1835, the Reverend John Sterling, in a report on the moral and religious education of the ex-slaves, argued that the churches and schools could play an important role in the West Indies:

For although the Negroes are now under a system of limited control [apprenticeship] which secures to a certain extent their orderly and industrious conduct, in the short space of five years from the 1st of next August, their performance of the functions of a labouring class in a civilized community will depend entirely on the *power over their minds* of the same prudential and moral motives which govern more or less the mass of the people here. If they are not so disposed as to fulfil these functions, property will perish in the colonies for lack of human impulsion. . . . There has been since the 1st of August a great increase of the desire for knowledge . . . its certain result where the minds of the people are at all in movement will be a consciousness of their own independent value as rational beings without reference to the purposes for which they may be profitable to others (Gordon 1968:59–60, emphasis added).

The British government agreed with Sterling, and from 1835 to 1845 the Negro Education Grant subsidized the religious bodies and missionary societies to pay teachers and build schools in the West Indies. When the foundations of the elementary school system had been established, the British government decided that West Indians could henceforth pay for their own education.

The Anglican and Methodist clergy intended to foster among the ex-slaves a deference to authority, an acceptance of their own subordinate social position, and industrious, disciplined work habits. Even the more independent missionaries, who insisted on the rights of the ex-slaves and were often involved in campaigns for political reforms and the establishment of free villages, nevertheless stressed white cultural superiority in their teaching. Their paternalism, however benevolent in its intentions, was oriented toward fostering dependency among the ex-slaves, and the system of teaching, in which rote learning and authoritarian relationships were backed by corporal punishment, promoted passivity and habits of obedience rather than a critical intellect and a sense of self-worth and autonomy. Thomas Holt points out that both British and American authorities promoted education, especially religious and moral education, as a way to transform ex-slave cultures and characters. "Education seemed to offer the paradoxical possibility of encouraging greater material aspirations as well as inculcating social restraint and acceptance of the status quo in social relations" (Holt 1982:296).

It is reasonable to conclude that, even if the religious and education system did not systematically indoctrinate the ex-slaves, it contributed to their continued subjugation to the plantation system by buttressing the colonial authority structure and helping to maintain the so-called good behavior of the working people. Nevertheless, it is true that "the results of schooling and religious proselytization in instilling the superiority of white culture, religion and values among the Creole population were at best ambiguous" (Moore 1987:198). The widespread persistence of Afro-Caribbean beliefs and customs, as well as the continuing resentment of and resistance to the authority systems of the colonial plantation society, are eloquent testimony to the ultimate failure of the indoctrination process among the ex-slaves in the British Caribbean.

This brings us to the pervasive but elusive factors of race and racism. At the same time that the British were attempting to assimilate the ex-slaves into the postemancipation society by emphasizing the supposed superiority of English culture, they excluded them from equal participation in that society on racial grounds. The obvious, but crucial, point is that an important element of the English culture was (and is) its racism. Raymond Smith emphasizes the conflicts and contradictions that existed in the process of creolization after emancipation:

The basic facts about creole society are that it was rooted in the political and economic dominance of the metropolitan power, it was colour stratified and was integrated around the conception of the moral and cultural superiority of things English. . . . It was an integral part of the process of 'creolization' to stress the differences between groups identified as 'racial' groups, despite tendencies toward cultural assimilation. This resulted from the fact that the value standards pertaining to the whole society were 'English' or 'white' people's and thus total conformity to them was impossible for non-whites no matter how well they commanded the culture of the mother country (1967:234–35).

The racial factor affected not only the status of the ex-slaves within the British Caribbean colonies after emancipation, but also the status of the colonies vis-à-vis the imperial government. Without attempting here to explore the complex relations of slavery to racism, it is clear that the legacy of slavery left a mark in the social consciousness of race and thus also in the social status of the ex-slave. "While his powerlessness and rightlessness as a slave may be seen as related to the juridical idea of the slave as property, his continued powerlessness and rightlessness as a free person was related to his racial identity" (Sio 1979:271). At the same time, the exclusion of the vast majority of the people of the British Caribbean colonies from the political process, while ostensibly on the basis of property and literacy qualifications, was intended to maintain some form of white rule. British ideas of representative government in the nineteenth century were always tainted by racism. The earl of Newcastle, in a speech in the House of Lords in 1858, said that self-government was "only applicable to colonists of the English race" (Williams 1970:399). So, in Jamaica, just two years before Canada achieved dominion status on its road to democracy, the assembly was abolished and Jamaica became governed as a Crown colony.

The British government accepted the dominant political influence of the planters within a colonial power structure in which the imperial Crown remained the supreme authority. The periodic local struggles between the planters and colonial administrators were resolved (except in Barbados) in the form of Crown colony rule, most dramatically in Jamaica in 1865. Rather than extending political participation to the ex-slaves, who were deemed unfit for representative government, the old legislative assemblies were replaced by autocratic Crown colony regimes, in which planters continued to have political influence. Moore concludes that the factors of race and imperialism determined the predominant form of colonial polity in the British West Indies after emancipation. "The issue of race was used to deny the black and coloured majority the right of political participation, while their consequent non-representation was in turn used to justify the need to maintain the supremacy of the authority and power of the imperial Crown in the colonial polity. Thus race and imperialism went hand-in-hand with the preservation of white political domination in the colonial society" (1987:78–79).

Though the elective principle was reintroduced subsequently in some West Indian colonies, the franchise remained extremely narrow until the great outbreak of labor disturbances in the 1930s ushered in the modern era of politics, democratic reforms, and, eventually, independence. Crown colony status kept political power out of the hands of the freedmen and their descendants, "the better to guarantee the survival of the plantation system" (Foner 1983:29), for over a century after the abolition of slavery.

The Ordeal of Free Labor: Struggle and Accommodation

Each day in the life of a member of the working population was a day on which there was both struggle and accommodation. Struggle was implicit in the application of labor power to earn wages or to grow crops, while accommodation was a necessary aspect of survival within a system in which power was so comprehensively monopolized by the planter class. Some persons resisted more tenaciously and consistently than others; but there was no simple distinction between those who resisted and those who accommodated (Rodney 1981:151).

In studying this dialectic of domination, resistance, and accommodation in the period after legal emancipation, it is appropriate to focus attention on the labor process as the central location of the struggle, and on the issues of the control of land and the state in connection with that struggle. In the transition from slavery to capitalist relations of production, the degree to which the former slaves were able to acquire and retain access to land was important, not only in affecting whether they would sell their labor power on the plantations, but also in affecting the prevailing wage rates. Moreover, for many of the plantation laborers, who experienced only seasonal employment, their access to the means of subsistence was often crucial to survival. In their search for employment and the means of subsistence, former slaves moved in ever increasing circles, first temporarily and then permanently, to neighboring estates and provision grounds, to more remote villages and lands in the hills or the interior, to other colonies or countries in the Caribbean and Central America, until, in this century, their descendants have extended the perimeters of migration to the metropolitan centers of Europe and North America.

The ability of former slaves to undertake this search for the means of subsistence was, of course, one of the chief consequences of their legal emancipation, but their desire to undertake the search was fostered by the continuing attempts of their former masters to coerce them into plantation labor. Moreover, as Woodville Marshall suggests, "their own-account activities were as important as coerced labour in defining their status, their humanity and their notions of freedom" (1988:38). So, while we should evaluate the economic options of the former slaves, including their ability to choose employment, to move in search of work, to rise in the occupational scale, to bargain for better wages and working conditions, and to have more autonomy at the workplace, we must not neglect the noneconomic aspects of their freedom. In other words, when we ask the question, how free was the ex-slave? we must not, like former masters, think of him or her only as a laborer. While for many of the former slaves the labor process was to be, unavoidably, the focal point of their struggle for freedom, there is abundant evidence that freedom meant more for them than the freedom to sell or to withhold their own labor power in the marketplace.

Walter Rodney suggests that, "Over the course of the nineteenth century Creole laborers had developed a conception of themselves that was incompatible with an increasing number of estate jobs and, ultimately, with field labor as a whole . . . *given the terms on which estate labor was organized*" (1981:162, emphasis in original). If we take as given the place of the plantation within the world economy and the racist and authoritarian ideologies and institutions of the colonial polities, then the "terms on which estate labor was organized" in the nineteenth-century

Caribbean were pretty much inevitable. The features of a plantation system (which include monocrop production for export, strong monopolistic tendencies, a rigid system of social stratification, which includes a high correlation between racial and class hierarchies, and a weak community structure) conspire to ensure that estate labor will be casual and seasonal, poorly paid, closely supervised, socially degraded, and hard to organize.

As several features of the plantation system are common to both the period of slavery and after, we should not be surprised that the people caught in this system have continued to resist it. Though it took a considerable amount of time, the experience of resistance to estate labor has given rise, throughout the Caribbean, to increasing class consciousness and the creation of a range of working class institutions, including trade unions. But, again, these features of the proletarianization of West Indian workers, though key to understanding their social and political history, do not exhaust what Rodney calls their "concept of themselves."

Former slaves, like former masters, brought a whole complex of attitudes, values, self-images, and notions of rights and entitlements out of the period of slavery. The meaning of freedom, for both masters and slaves, was historically and dialectically interconnected with the system and experience of slavery, but in different ways, so we should not assume that the former slaves shared the dominant conception of freedom. The concept of personal freedom or autonomy, and the antithetical concept of dependence, is culturally and historically variable. The liberal concept of freedom, which has predominated in Western societies at least since the nineteenth century, stresses not only the absence of human restraint on the individual but also the supposedly inherent need or desire of the individual for autonomy. This nonprescriptive meaning of freedom contrasts with prescriptive freedom, which accepts limits on personal behavior as a consequence of acknowledging that freedom is bestowed as a gift on the individual by a superior power. In the context of this distinction, Orlando Patterson draws attention to the sociohistorical connection between slavery and freedom in modern Western consciousness: "Personal freedom in the liberal sense, even more than its illiberal prescriptive counterpart, requires the menace of an endangering power to be meaningful. Slavery and the dread of social death was once again that menace, both symbolically and realistically. In political terms we find a growing tendency to identify the state with slavery during the late eighteenth and nineteenth centuries" (1985:26).

This latter identification may be associated with the fact that, with the transition from slave to free status, the locus of authority and social control passes from an individual master to the impersonal state, as personal relations of domination are transformed into a bureaucratic structure of domination. Within this transformation of systems of domination, the former masters conceived of market relations as compatible with, or even as the guarantors of, their own personal freedoms, including their freedom to hold and dispose of private property and to hire and fire labor power without interference. But it would be naive to assume that former slaves shared this liberal-bourgeois concept of freedom.

We know that many former slaves had goals and priorities that were compatible with a concept of personal autonomy, and as we have seen, many of these were dialectically connected to their past and present experience of oppression and exploitation at the workplace. We know also that former slaves had important goals connected with family life, with conceptions of the home and of domestic authority, with religious and cultural life, and with education, and these goals were affected by, but certainly not determined by or limited to, the ex-slaves' work situation. As Rebecca Scott reminds us, even while it is appropriate to "place particular emphasis on the search for land and for control over one's own pace of work," we should bear in mind that "it is not simply the autonomy of the individual that is at stake, but the degree of achievement of several goals by an entire family" (1987:576). She also points out that "former slaves often placed goals of family and community above the assertion of simple individual autonomy. . . . Moreover, family welfare and individual well-being were frequently intertwined, making the concept of individual autonomy misleading" (1988:423).

The need to look beyond the liberal notion of freedom and its association with the political economy of the bourgeois marketplace is apparent when we focus on the former slaves' attitude toward land. We must consider not only the economic and material importance of land to the former slaves, both as a means of subsistence and as a base from which to bargain with the former masters, but also the symbolic significance of land. Jean Besson's historical anthropology of family land in Jamaica is highly suggestive:

Freehold land was not only of obvious economic importance to those ex-slaves who managed to obtain it, giving some independence from the plantations and a bargaining position for higher wages when working on them, but it also had considerable symbolic significance to a people who had not only once been landless, but property themselves. For such land symbolized their freedom, and provided property rights, prestige, and personhood. Family land was also the basis for the creation of family lines and the maximization of kinship ties, in contrast to the kinlessness of the enslaved. (1987:18)

Here lies the key. Insofar as slavery involved the natal alienation of the slave and his social death through the loss of kinship ties, the transcendence of slavery must recover or reestablish such ties. Family land, then, is not limited to a bit of material security but becomes, more significantly, a means of creating and maintaining just such a network of ties and mutual obligations as slavery had denied.

An ideal slave society as conceived by the masters is really the very negation of sociality, insofar as it consists merely of dehumanized tools who have become isolated from each other and denied their human, social existence. The negation of this society, then, is not a liberal society of autonomous citizens, an aggregate of self-interested individuals, but rather a genuine community of people linked by kinship and other social ties. Family land emerged as a "resistant response" (Mintz 1974:132–33) to the slavery-plantation system, and as a symbol and potential core of a different kind of society, in which the relation between personal autonomy and dependence seems to be conceived in ways that differ from those predominating in the liberal-bourgeois society. Constance Sutton and Susan Makiesky-Barrow suggest that "for women as well as men a wide network of social relations and supports provides an important basis for independence and autonomy. In contrast to the western concept of individual autonomy and equality, which implies a shedding of social attachments, the Afro-Caribbean and black American concept of autonomy is linked to a strong sense of interpersonal connectedness—an involvement in the lives of others" (1977:322). Personal autonomy, rather than being defined over and against the rights of others, becomes achievable only in connection with others. In this vision of society, the principles of mutuality, cooperation and interdependence, in contrast to social hierarchy, competition, and the dependency of subordinates, are deemed to be the very fabric of society itself. For the former slaves, then, the process of emancipation involved a struggle to recover or reestablish a lost birthright, usually established through kinship, that included notions of association, property, and personhood that differed from those held by their former masters, because they were linked to an alternative set of values and visions of society.

The continuing struggle over the control of land and labor, and later of the state, was always crucial precisely to the degree that it offered to the former slaves opportunities to gain some control over their own lives and their own communities. It is in this much broader sense, and not in the narrow calculations of political economy, that we should seek the myriad ways that the former slaves gave meaning to their freedom. For the abolitionists, the meaning of freedom appeared in the context of the rise of the liberal state and the capitalist economy. "Slavery meant subordination to the physical coercion and personal dominion of an arbitrary master; freedom meant submission only to the impersonal forces of the marketplace and to the rational and uniform constraints of law" (Holt 1982:286). But these market forces and colonial laws of the British Caribbean in the mid–nineteenth century helped to perpetuate the poverty and powerlessness of the ex-slaves and their descendants, who were denied the civil rights of liberal society for over a century. This kind of freedom — where the ex-slaves were conceived primarily as free labor in free markets — was really a new form of domination, albeit one more limited and disguised than the naked domination of slavery. Those who had formerly been slaves, it seems, aspired to a kind of freedom that their legal emancipation appeared to promise, but that could not be achieved in the societies where they lived. Hence, a central aspect of the struggle between the former slaves and masters was concerned with their respective visions of a free society.

REFERENCES

Adamson, Alan H. 1972. *Sugar Without Slaves: The Political Economy of British Guiana, 1838–1904.* New Haven: Yale University Press.

Beckford, George L. 1972. *Persistent Poverty: Underdevelopment in Plantation Economies of the Third World.* New York: Oxford University Press.

Besson, Jean. 1987. A Paradox in Caribbean Attitudes to Land. In *Land and Development in the Caribbean,* edited by Jean Besson and Janet Momsen, 13–45. London: Macmillan Caribbean.

Bolland, O. Nigel. 1977. *The Formation of a Colonial Society: Belize, from Conquest to Crown Colony.* Baltimore: Johns Hopkins University Press.

———. 1981. Systems of Domination after Slavery: The Control of Land and Labor in the British West Indies after 1838. *Comparative Studies in Society and History* 23:591–619.

———. 1984. Reply to William A. Green's "The Perils of Comparative History." *Comparative Studies in Society and History* 26:120–25.

———. 1986. Labour Control and Resistance in Belize in the Century after 1838. *Slavery and Abolition* 7:175–87.

———. 1988. *Colonialism and Resistance in Belize: Essays in Historical Sociology.* Belize City: Society for the Promotion of Education and Research.

Bolland, O. Nigel, and Assad Shoman. 1977. *Land in Belize, 1765–1871: The Ori-*

gins of Land Tenure, Use, and Distribution in a Dependent Economy. Kingston: Institute of Social and Economic Research.

Bristowe, Lindsay W., and Philip B. Wright. 1888. *The Handbook of British Honduras for 1888–89.* London: Blackwood.

Clarke, Edith. 1957. *My Mother Who Fathered Me: A Study of the Family in Three Selected Communities in Jamaica.* London: Allen & Unwin.

Craton, Michael. 1978. *Searching for the Invisible Man: Slaves and Plantation Life in Jamaica.* Cambridge, Mass.: Harvard University Press.

Craton, Michael, and James Walvin. 1970. *A Jamaican Plantation: The History of Worthy Park, 1670–1970.* London: W. H. Allen.

Curtin, Philip D. 1970. *Two Jamaicas: The Role of Ideas in a Tropical Colony, 1830–1865.* New York: Atheneum.

Engerman, S.L. 1985. Economic Change and Contract Labour in the British Caribbean: The End of Slavery and the Adjustment to Emancipation. In *Abolition and its Aftermath: The Historical Context, 1790–1916,* edited by David Richardson, 225–44. London: Frank Cass.

Finley, M. I. 1980. *Ancient Slavery and Modern Ideology.* New York: Viking.

Foner, Eric. 1983. *Nothing But Freedom: Emancipation and Its Legacy.* Baton Rouge: Louisiana State University Press.

———. 1988. *Reconstruction: America's Unfinished Revolution, 1863–1877.* New York: Harper & Row.

Frank, Andre Gunder. 1971. *Capitalism and Underdevelopment in Latin America: Historical Studies of Chile and Brazil.* Harmondsworth: Penguin Books.

Fraser, Peter. 1981. The Fictive Peasantry: Caribbean Rural Groups in the Nineteenth Century. In *Contemporary Caribbean: A Sociological Reader.* Vol. 1, edited by Susan Craig, 319–47. Maracas: Susan Craig.

Gordon, Shirley C. 1968. *Reports and Repercussions in West Indian Education, 1835–1933.* London: Ginn and Company.

Green, William A. 1976. *British Slave Emancipation: The Sugar Colonies and the Great Experiment, 1830–1865.* Oxford: Clarendon Press.

———. 1984. The Perils of Comparative History: Belize and the British Sugar Colonies After Slavery. *Comparative Studies in Society and History* 26:112–19.

———. 1986. The Creolization of Caribbean History: The Emancipation Era and a Critique of Dialectical Analysis. *Journal of Imperial and Commonwealth History* 14:149–69.

Gurney, Joseph John. 1840. *Familiar Letters to Henry Clay of Kentucky Describing a Winter in the West Indies.* Reprint 1969. New York: Negro Universities Press.

Hall, Douglas. 1959. *Free Jamaica, 1838–1865: An Economic History.* New Haven: Yale University Press.

———. 1971. *Five of the Leewards, 1834–1870.* Barbados: Caribbean Universities Press.

———. 1978. The Flight from the Estates Reconsidered: The British West Indies, 1838–42. *Journal of Caribbean History* 10/11:7–24.

Holt, Thomas C. 1982. "An Empire Over the Mind": Emancipation, Race, and Ideology in the British West Indies and the American South. In *Region, Race, and Reconstruction,* edited by J. Morgan Kousser and James M. McPherson, 283–313. New York: Oxford University Press.

Johnson, Howard. 1986. "A Modified Form of Slavery": The Credit and Truck Systems in the Bahamas in the Nineteenth and Early Twentieth Centuries. *Comparative Studies in Society and History* 28:729–53.

Laurence, K. O. 1971. *Immigration into the West Indies in the Nineteenth Century.* Barbados: Caribbean University Press.

Levy, Claude. 1980. *Emancipation, Sugar, and Federalism: Barbados and the West Indies, 1833–1876.* Gainesville: University Presses of Florida.

Lobdell, Richard S. 1988. British Officials and the West Indian Peasantry: 1842–1938. In *Labour in the Caribbean From Emancipation to Independence,* edited by Malcolm Cross and Gad Heuman, 195–207. London: Macmillan Caribbean.

Marshall, W. K. 1985. Apprenticeship and Labour Relations in Four Windward Islands. In *Abolition and Its Aftermath: The Historical Context, 1790–1916,* edited by David Richardson, 203–24. London: Frank Cass.

———. 1988. Provision Ground and Plantation Labour: Competition for Resources. Paper presented at the twentieth annual conference of the Association of Caribbean Historians, St. Thomas, V.I.

Martinez Vergne, Teresita. 1988. New Patterns for Puerto Rico's Sugar Workers: Abolition and Centralization at San Vicente, 1873–92. *Hispanic American Historical Review* 68:45–74.

Mintz, Sidney W. 1974. *Caribbean Transformations.* Chicago: Aldine.

———. 1985. Epilogue: The Divided Aftermaths of Freedom. In *Between Slavery and Free Labor: The Spanish-Speaking Caribbean in the Nineteenth Century,* edited by Manuel Moreno Fraginals, Frank Moya Pons, and Stanley L. Engerman, 270–78. Baltimore: Johns Hopkins University Press.

Moohr, Michael. 1972. The Economic Impact of Slave Emancipation in British Guiana, 1832–1852. *Economic History Review* 2d Ser., 25:588–607.

Moore, Brian L. 1987. *Race, Power and Social Segmentation in Colonial Society: Guyana after Slavery, 1838–1891.* New York: Gordon and Breach Science Publishers.

Patterson, Orlando. 1982. *Slavery and Social Death: A Comparative Study.* Cambridge, Mass.: Harvard University Press.

———. 1985. Slavery: The Underside of Freedom. In *Out of Slavery: Abolition and After,* edited by Jack Hayward, 7–29. London: Frank Cass.

Riviere, W. Emmanuel. 1972. Labour Shortage in the British West Indies after Emancipation. *Journal of Caribbean History* 4:1–30.

Rodney, Walter. 1981. *A History of the Guyanese Working People, 1881–1905.* Baltimore: Johns Hopkins University Press.

Scarano, Francisco A. 1989. Labor and Society in the Nineteenth Century. In *The Modern Caribbean,* edited by Franklin W. Knight and Colin A. Palmer, 51–84. Chapel Hill: University of North Carolina Press.

Scott, Rebecca J. 1985. *Slave Emancipation in Cuba: The Transition to Free Labor, 1860–1899.* Princeton: Princeton University Press.

———. 1987. Comparing Emancipations: A Review Essay. *Journal of Social History* 20:565–83.

———. 1988. Exploring the Meaning of Freedom: Postemancipation Societies in Comparative Perspective. *Hispanic American Historical Review* 68:407–28.

Sewell, W. G. 1861. *The Ordeal of Free Labor in the British West Indies.* London: Harper & Brothers.

Sio, Arnold. 1979. Commentary on "Slavery and Race." In *Roots and Branches: Current Directions in Slave Studies,* edited by Michael Craton, *Historical Reflections,* special issue, 6:269–74.

Smith, Raymond T. 1967. Social Stratification, Cultural Pluralism and Integration in West Indian Societies. In *Caribbean Integration: Papers on Social, Political and Economic Integration,* edited by S. Lewis and T. Mathews, 226–58. Rio Piedras: Institute of Caribbean Studies.

Sutton, Constance, and Susan Makiesky-Barrow. 1977. Social Inequality and Sexual Status in Barbados. In *Sexual Stratification: A Cross-Cultural View,* edited by Alice Schlegel, 292–325. New York: Columbia University Press.

Williams, Eric. 1970. *From Columbus to Castro.* London: Andre Deutsch.

Wood, Donald. 1968. *Trinidad in Transition: The Years after Slavery.* London: Oxford University Press.

MICHEL-ROLPH TROUILLOT

The Inconvenience of Freedom

Free People of Color and the
Political Aftermath of Slavery in Dominica
and Saint-Domingue/Haiti

It is obvious that abolition, however it eventuated, disturbed the power balance within the various plantation societies of nineteenth-century America. It may be less obvious that it also transformed profoundly both the vision and the options of those who were already free before it came. With abolition, the meaning of freedom ceased to be an abstract issue—if indeed it ever was one. More importantly, it ceased to be an issue that had direct relevance only for the slaves. To be sure, freedom meant different things to different groups and, perhaps, different things to individuals within the same group. But whatever freedom meant, its practical definition (its actual content) was not derived in isolation by any single person or group. Rather, the significance of freedom for each and every subgroup of any slave society was the complex product of an exchange within and across group boundaries.

This essay deals with the reaction of freedmen to the breakdown of the slave order in two Caribbean territories, the British-dominated island of Dominica and the French colony of Saint-Domingue which became, in 1804, the independent state of Haiti.[1] Chronologically, it divides each case into three moments: (1) a prefreedom sketch of the evolution of the free colored people in each society; (2) their immediate reaction to the fact of emancipation; (3) a postfreedom moment, which, in both cases, overlaps the recognition of the downfall of the plantation system. Thematically, it explores the conjunction of race, color, and class in plantation America and the significance of the state in the post-plantation era.

Free people of color belonged to highly stratified societies, the polarities of which their very existence defied. Whether they owned slaves or not, their interests, their objectives, their goals, and their self-definitions had been shaped by the fact of slavery. What happened to this complex stratification once slavery was abolished? Obviously, color-cum-social categories did not disappear with the end of slavery. But how were they transformed? Or more precisely, can we generate rules for their transformation?

Just as the rigid stratification of slavery was constantly backed by the daily threat and actualization of violence, so was state power—colonial or not—verified constantly by the physical subjugation of the labor force. That subjugation survived the end of slavery in many plantation societies (the U.S. South comes to mind); it dwindled elsewhere, notably in areas such as Dominica and Haiti, where the land-labor ratio and the determination of the cultivators signaled the end of the plantation system. How significant, then, is it that in both Dominica and Haiti individuals who would have dreamed to be plantation owners in the heyday of slavery invested the bulk of their energy into the control of the state machinery? What happens to the state when the plantations fall apart?

For the people who were neither slave nor white in Saint-Domingue and Dominica, the abolition of slavery was an inconvenience. Affront was felt deeper in the case of Saint-Domingue: here, colonial decrees notwithstanding, freedom was imposed by the slaves themselves in the midst of a revolutionary war (1791–1803). Moreover, at the start of the revolution, the mulatto-dominated group of *affranchis* or *gens de couleur* controlled a valuable share of the colony's property, including a significant proportion of its slaves and some of its prosperous coffee plantations (Raimond, Perrier and Lamothe-Aigron 1791; Raimond 1792).[2] Finally, the early years of the French Revolution had renewed their hope of achieving political equality with the whites. Dominican freedmen, for their part, were not simply hoping for political equality when freedom finally came. They thought that they had already achieved it—and reasonably so. Many "coloreds" occupied prominent positions in the island state apparatus even before the beginning of apprenticeship. A majority of nonwhite members sat in the Dominica House of Assembly by the time freedom finally came to the slaves in 1838.

In short, free people of color may not have been satisfied with the slave system as it stood, but they had learned to take that system for granted, and they had reason to believe that they had mastered its rules. While they did not expect to reach the summit of their respective social pyramid—proof indeed that they understood its mechanics—they had devised ways to climb some of its most coveted tiers. Freedom changed the rules of the game; and that, for them, was an inconvenience.

The new rules were not the same in the two territories if only because of the basic differences in the way freedom was imposed on the two societies. Hence it is the more interesting that, in retrospect, the reaction of the former freedmen presents similarities that transcend periods and locales. In both cases, former freedmen were first reluctant to admit the fact that the end of slavery signaled the slow replacement of the plantation system by a peasant-based society. In both cases, they tried to overcome the obstacle that the growing peasantry represented to their pursuit of wealth and prestige by resorting to politics and, to a lesser degree, to commerce. In both cases, they met with qualified success.

That the postemancipation rivalry for control of the state opposed colored to whites in the case of Dominica, and *mulâtres* to *noirs* in the case of Haiti; that the former was still a British colony at the end of its slave career, and the latter an independent country newly liberated from the French yoke; that the imposition of freedom came by force of arms in the case of Saint-Domingue, while Dominican abolition was essentially engineered overseas, only make the dual story a worthier case to tell. For the determinant factor, in both places, was not so much the meaning of freedom for those who had already been free but the reluctance of the ex-slaves to return to the plantations. That was the inconvenience that prompted many among the colored elites, both in Dominica and in Haiti, to turn to state politics as a major source of livelihood.

Groping for a Niche (1685–1763)

In both Dominica and Saint-Domingue, the first era of the history of the free coloreds as a distinguishable social category overlaps with the beginnings of official French control. In both cases, the long-term political and social consequences of that long initial period, which ended around 1763, were not immediately visible. Yet it was a period of demographic growth for the free coloreds. Between the last decade of the seventeenth century and 1763, their numbers increased more than tenfold in Dominica and more than twentyfold in Saint-Domingue. Such rates of increase were phenomenal, even though the existence and growth of a free colored population were by no means unique to Dominica or Saint-Domingue.

Indeed, though the plantation slave societies of the Americas were predicated upon rigid socioracial categories, there emerged in all of them individuals who, by virtue of their birth, did not easily fit the white-black dichotomy. In the French Antilles, the initial reaction of the dominant group to that emergence was not so much surprise as annoyance. Mulattoes, like courtesans and prostitutes—with whom, indeed, the females of the genre soon became associated—were an inevitable sore, the living proof of the licentiousness of life in tropical climates if not universal testimonies to the sinful nature of man (e.g., Du Tertre 1667, 2:477ff.; Girod de Chantrans 1980:152–56).

But French lawmakers and planters also realized quite early that the introduction of a third voice in a score originally written for two created a danger. The white-black dichotomy overlapped the more fundamental divide between free people and slaves, and the emergence of the mulattoes threatened that division. However inevitable the sore, its damage had to be limited. Still, up to the latter part of the seventeenth century, local whites never reached full agreement on the procedures of damage control. At times, they tried to curtail most of the mulattoes' rights; more often, they allowed them conditional freedom. Later, the 1685 Code Noir, imposed by the metropolis, advocated the full assimilation of free nonwhites and equated acquired freedom and freedom at birth in its major clauses. But from the point of view of most colonists, the overarching legal framework that the code supposedly provided only muddled issues that were best treated at the local level. Hence, the code's most liberal provisions, especially in regard to the rights of *affranchis* (in the original and strictest sense of freedmen) or *ingénus* (freeborn), were not always applied. When they were, their enforcement occurred in a segregationist context molded by local traditions as well as present-day political and economic issues.

Hence, by the end of the seventeenth century, the trichotomous hierarchy developing in the French territories had a middle stratum ambiguously defined in terms of both color and legal status. Neither the emergence of a recognizable third tier nor its ambiguous status was unique to the French Caribbean (Cohen and Green 1972); but the early indecision of the locals and the pretense of an overarching legal framework imposed by the Code Noir emphasized two consequences. On the one hand, the issue of the freedom of all nonwhites became inextricably mixed, in practice, with that of the status of the mulattoes who came to dominate the free nonwhite group. Thus, mulatto leaders in Saint-Domingue sometimes distinguished explicitly *hommes de couleur* from *nègres libres* (free blacks), but they gave the former group the right to set up the pace and conditions of any political coalition (Raimond 1793; Bonnet 1798a; Tarbé 1792). On the other hand, all free nonwhites, and mulattoes in particular, tried as much as possible to rely on the legal system, especially as interpreted from the metropolis, to back up economic and political claims. Again, those tendencies may have not been exclusive to the French Caribbean; but their existence in Dominica and Saint-Domingue may not be unrelated to the fact that France solidified its grip on both territories soon after the publication of the code. The Code Noir was published in 1685. France obtained from Spain formal control of the western third of Hispaniola, which became officially Saint-Domingue, twelve years later, at the Peace of Ryswick. Likewise, the 1690s saw the end of the uneasy balance that the French and British shared in Dominica, which became, for all practical purposes, an uncontested French territory from 1700 to 1763 (Boromé 1972a, 1972b).

We do not know for sure why the demographic growth of the free colored population, a general phenomenon in the French Caribbean at the time, was so exceptionally high in both Saint-Domingue and Dominica. Various analysts, including some who witnessed that growth, have offered multiple explanations, often recycling arguments first voiced in the seventeenth century. The near-total absence of white women, migratory movements, and the military potential that a free colored population, enrolled in the militia, constituted for France are all good explanations for the rise of the free coloreds (Du Tertre 1667:428–32; Moreau de Saint-Méry 1958:84–85; Atwood 1971:207–19; Girod de Chantrans 1980:152–56 and passim; Malouet 1802, 4:139–43). But one still needs to show why those factors, which are after all valid for many other colonies, would have produced such remarkable effects in Saint-Domingue and Dominica, two territories otherwise quite dissimilar. What is sure for now is that, by the middle of the century, in Saint-Domingue, where the stakes were higher and the demographic growth of the free coloreds was most impressive, some white planters and officials were already worried. In 1755, the sieur de Vaudreuil, then governor of Saint-Domingue and a planter at Torbeck, was writing to the metropolitan administration: "The *gens de couleur* are beginning to multiply; they are sometimes taking over the whites" (Brutus n.d.: 153). By then, there were 4,861 *gens de couleur* and 14,317 whites in Saint-Domingue (table 1).

We do not yet have comparable figures for the Dominica of the 1750s,

Table 1
Population of French Saint-Domingue,
1681–1789

Year	Slaves	Gens de Couleur	Whites
1681	2,102	210	4,336
1687	3,358	224	4,411
1700	9,082	500	4,074
1713	24,146	1,117	5,709
1715	30,651	1,404	6,668
1717	37,474	1,335	7,264
1720	47,528	1,573	7,926
1730	79,545	2,456	10,449
1739	109,780	2,527	11,699
1751	148,530	3,478	13,741
1754	172,548	4,861	14,317
1764	206,000	(a)	16,000
1771	239,698	6,180	18,448
1775	261,365	6,897	20,361
1780	252,357	10,427	20,203
1786	340,000	15,000	25,000
1788	405,564	21,808	27,717
1789	465,429	27,548	30,826

a. Not available

which would help us flesh out the demographic evolution of the free colored under French control. However, a few estimates can help us fix the end points of the Dominican curve. The registered number of free coloreds grew from about 30 in the early 1730s to about 300 in 1763 (table 2). Those are small absolute numbers, but they take significance in relative terms. With 1,718 whites and 5,872 slaves on the island in 1763, Dominican freedmen accounted for 4 percent of the total population, a high proportion in the Caribbean context of the times.[3] In that same year, Dominica became a British possession.

The 1763 Peace of Paris, which ended the Seven Years' War, also signaled a reorganization of the Atlantic world. Colonies changed hands: while France retained Saint-Domingue, Guadeloupe, and Martinique, it officially relinquished control of most of the territories contested by Britain, including Dominica. Peace also brought the restoration of French maritime travel, much disturbed by Britain's fleet. The reshuffling ushered in new opportunities to various New World populations. Both in Saint-

Domingue and in Dominica, the most ambitious free coloreds seized theirs.

Seizing the Chance:
Saint-Domingue's Coffee Revolution

For Saint-Domingue's *affranchis,* the chance was in the growing European demand for coffee. Commercial cultivation of the crop in the northern parishes of the colony dated as far back as the 1730s. But European demand had been slow, and the difficulties of transport during periods of international warfare had prevented expansion. After the Peace of Paris, many *gens de couleur,* taking advantage of rising European demand and the frequency of transport, established coffee estates in the mountains hitherto neglected by the sugar plantocracy. The crop required much less capital than sugarcane and a labor force often ten times smaller than that of many sugar plantations; it thus suited very well the means and objectives of marginal groups such as *gens de couleur* and recent immigrants of modest means. Analysis of population and production figures for the 1770s and 1780s shows a strong correlation between the proportion of *gens de couleur* and the importance of coffee in many parishes of Saint-Domingue. The coffee revolution, as some

Table 2
Slaves, Free Coloreds, and Whites in Dominica, 1632–1832

Year	Slaves	Free Coloreds	Whites	Sources
1632	338	23	349	Dominica Almanac 1862:47
1763	5,872	300	1,718	CO/101 in Boromé 1972b:94
1773	18,753	750	3,350	Dominica Almanac 1862:49
1778	14,309	574	1,574	Ms. in Boromé 1972c:105
1780–81	12,713	543	1,066	Dominica Almanac 1862:50; Boromé 1972c:110
1787	14,967	545	1,236	Dominica Almanac 1862:50
1805	22,083	2,882	1,594	Dominica Almanac 1862:52; Hamilton 1894:48
1811	21,728	2,988	1,525	Myers 1987, 1:9
1815	18,862	2,666	1,123	CO 71/55 in Trouillot 1988:99
1826	15,392	3,606	840	Myers 1987, 1:11
1832	14,387	4,077	791	Myers 1987, 1:11[a]

a. Higman (1984:433) records 720 whites and 3,814 free coloreds for 1833.

observers called the boost in production, secured the economic position of the freedmen (M.-R. Trouillot 1982).

Whites in Saint-Domingue offered mixed reactions to the rise of the freedmen. In the mid-1760s, Governor d'Estaing treated them with unusual tolerance (Raimond 1791). The reactions of white planters tended to vary according to locality and economic rivalry. In some parishes, including many remote ones where new immigrants had engaged in coffee production alongside many *affranchis,* whites and mulattoes developed forms of cooperation and sometimes intermarried. In parishes where mulattoes had prospered before the coffee revolution, the general improvement at times encouraged resentment, at times strengthened alliances with whites. Meanwhile, both whites and mulattoes kept the blacks at a distance. Indeed, most of the light-skinned free coloreds shared the prejudices of the French colonials: they just thought that the dominant bigotry should not be directed against them.[4]

Most whites, however, saw the mulattoes as lesser beings; and as the economic power of the *gens de couleur* grew, so did segregationist practices, fueled in part by administrators in Saint-Domingue and in France. The duke de Rohan, who came to the colony to replace d'Estaing (thought to be too favorable to the freedmen), had received from Choiseul, his cabinet minister and direct superior, clear instructions to stop the interracial alliances: "If [wrote Choiseul] through these alliances, the whites achieve cohesion with the freedmen, the colony could easily escape from the King's authority and France would lose one of the most powerful cells of its trade" (Frostin 1975:303).

From the mid-1760s to the late 1780s, a systematic reinforcement of Saint-Domingue's age-old racism, engineered by the colonial officials and supported by a coalition of rich planters and urban *petits blancs,* prevented the freedmen from cashing in the social and political returns of their demographic and economic growth.[5] But that growth did not stop. By 1775, there were nearly three times as many *gens de couleur* as there were in 1730 (see table 1), and by the late 1780s, whites openly voiced their anger about the wealth of some mulattoes and the ostentatious way they displayed it. The mulattoes' consumption patterns may have exaggerated the perception of their affluence; but the decades immediately preceding the French Revolution were, nevertheless, an economic success story for many of Saint-Domingue's freedmen. Their numbers kept growing accordingly, nearly tripling between 1780 and 1789, when nonwhites came to account for an amazing 47 percent of the nonslave population.[6]

Seizing the Chance: Dominica's Colored Militia

The configuration of race, color, and legal status in Dominica was no less amazing. Here as well, the ratio of free nonwhites within the total population was high, and nonwhites represented an unusually high proportion of the nonslave population. Here as well, the end of the Seven Years' War marked the beginning of a new era.

In 1763, nonwhites totaled 15 percent of the free population of Dominica. That in itself was significant, as it was a higher percentage even than in Saint-Domingue at that time.[7] More important, in the context of Anglo-French rivalry over Dominica (a rivalry that the Peace of Paris failed to end), the demographic growth of the free coloreds entailed social prestige and political power because it gave them easy access to a militia courted by both powers. If coffee was the opportunity for Saint-Domingue's *gens de couleur,* the ambiguities of the international reshuffling that followed the Seven Years' War gave Dominica's freedmen their chance. They seized it.

Throughout the eighteenth century, in almost all the slave colonies of the Americas, the militia used freedmen, and freedmen used the militia (Cohen and Greene 1972; Raimond 1793). But in Dominica, the near total absence of permanent standing troops made the militia even more important than elsewhere. Neither France nor England deemed the island important enough to require a large standing army, but both assiduously coveted the place, if only to stop the other from fully securing it.[8] The militia played a key role in those rival strategies, though the French held a distinct advantage. Free people of color were "chiefly of French extraction" (Atwood 1971:219).[9] Their allegiance went generally to the French Crown both before and after the Peace of Paris. Most supported a successful French invasion, launched from Martinique by Marquis Duchilleau, in 1778, in violation of the 1763 treaty. During the ensuing occupation, which lasted until 1784, French officials and free coloreds established a close and mutually beneficial relationship aimed at curtailing both the political and economic power of the few remaining British residents. Duchilleau posted colored Frenchmen in many key positions, created a new "militia of French inhabitants that consisted mainly of free Negroes" (Boromé 1972c:106), and encouraged the coloreds' growing arrogance vis-à-vis British planters and officials.[10]

By the time the British took control again, in 1784, Dominican-born free coloreds and the free nonwhite immigrants who joined them from both British and French neighboring islands constituted a recognized power. British officials did not dare exclude them from the militia, which, by the 1790s included, by law, white and free people of color eighteen to fifty years of age (Atwood 1971:202). By the end of the century, free people of color composed the bulk of the military and paramilitary forces on the island.

That chore was not without heavy burdens and contradictions of its own, and British commanders always lived with the implicit threat of a colored rebellion. In June 1795, amidst an otherwise insignificant attack by French forces from Guadeloupe, many coloreds—including a majority of the Colihaut militia—revolted. In April 1802, pressed by the arduous tasks they performed for the state and worried by rumors that they were to be sold as slaves, soldiers of the 500-man Eighth West India regiment rebelled. Some were hung by Brigadier General Johnstone; others may have joined maroon slaves in the mountains (*Cobbett's Annual Register* 1802:24–25, 760–61). Three years later, the participation of the militia and of the West India regiments in repelling another French invasion exemplified clearly the dilemma of European colonists: one could not secure Dominica without nonwhite support (*Cobbett's Political Register* 1805:763–67). Demographics alone guaranteed some degree of equality for the coloreds. Despite the numerous population movements that punctuated those troubled times (with planters coming and going—sometimes with their slaves—according to the swings of the geopolitical pendulum), the recorded number of free nonwhites grew considerably faster than that of any other category between 1784 and 1834.

By 1805, the year of the last and unsuccessful French invasion, the number of free nonwhites was 2,882, surpassing for the first time that of the white inhabitants (table 2). By 1815, there were twice as many nonwhites as there were whites within the free population (table 2); by 1821, the ratio was more than one to five in favor of the 3,814 freedmen, a rarity in the British Caribbean (Higman 1984:433).[11]

Demographics, thus, were on the side of the Dominican free coloreds; or rather, on the side of a tiny minority among them who saw the political potential of those numbers in the volatile context of a half-neglected island. By the 1830s, it was clear that an informal political elite of free coloreds had emerged. It steadfastly filled positions left vacant by the departure of European-born residents. In 1833, three colored men used the new political and civil rights granted throughout the region by the Brown Privilege Bill to successfully contend for seats in the local House.[12] Others were magistrates with enough clout to be among those assigned to monitor the condition of the laboring population immediately before and after emancipation.[13] Others performed various administrative functions. By 1835, the self-proclaimed leaders of the free coloreds had gained enough political recognition in Dominica and in England itself to successfully petition the Crown against a census bill originally favored by the Colonial Office, on the grounds that by making racial categories official, census taking would only succeed in "perpetuating the distinctions between the whites and the coloureds" (Great Britain 1845:31–32). Two years later, a group of free coloreds started their own independent newspaper.

But the prize that the free colored elite had their eyes on was the Dominican legislature itself. They had blocked the 1835 census, in part to prevent an accurate listing of eligible candidates and voters. Requirements for voters at that time were the freehold of ten acres, a leasehold worth £20 a year in land, or £20 in building. The colored leaders successfully filled the lists of registered voters to control the House after the 1837 election, a move never forgiven by the whites who witnessed it (M.-R. Trouillot 1988:100). To be sure, in spite of that visibility, the corporate economic success of Dominica's coloreds never equaled that of Saint-Domingue's *affranchis*. But that was, in part, because the plantations of prerevolutionary Saint-Domingue mattered much more on the map of international commerce than the few cultivated square miles of Dominica. Within the boundaries of their own society, however, some Dominican nonwhites achieved a political success unmatched even by the Saint-Domingue mulattoes.

Thus in both cases, though in different terms, the end of slavery was — to say the least — untimely for the growing number of individuals, neither white nor slave, who had struggled to create for themselves a niche in the interstices of an otherwise rigid system. With the haphazard help of demography, they managed to become important forces in societies that, at first, refused to recognize their very existence. Freedom meant, at best, a detour in their course. Even in Dominica, where the apprenticeship period prepared them for abolition, they did not really know how it would affect their plans. In Saint-Domingue, their surprise was total.

Coping with Freedom: The Haitian Revolution

In 1788, Louis XVI's decree summoning the States General in France severed the tenuous links that maintained a semblance of cohesion within the free population of Saint-Domingue. While most whites saw in events in France the opportunity to present their claims for greater autonomy, *gens de couleur* saw in them the chance to gain the political rights they had been denied (Raimond 1790; 1791; 1792). In March 1790, an ambiguous decree of the French National Assembly called for "everyone" over the age of twenty-five in the colony to participate in the formation of a representative body. Local mulattoes interpreted the decree as including all free individuals; whites claimed that it referred only to the white population. Mulatto Vincent Ogé, a member of the free colored lobby in France, returned to the colony secretly and tried to organize the *affranchis* of the northern province, with his friend Jean-Baptiste Chavannes.

In the last months of 1790, under Chavannes's increasing influence, the group threatened to back their interpretation of the decree with the force of arms. Whether they meant it or not is not clear: most were butchered by white colonial troops, and the two leaders were publicly executed on the wheel on 25 February 1791. Three months later, the metropolitan assembly clarified its earlier decree, granting political rights to everyone born of two free parents; but the shedding of mulatto blood had forever sullied the myth of a natural and spontaneous alliance between whites and free coloreds, which many among the latter had come to cherish (Tarbé 1792; James 1962; Dorsinville 1986; Debbash 1967).[14]

By 1791, *gens de couleur* in Saint-Domingue had created for themselves a political cul-de-sac. They were too close to revolutionary France to be able to bargain with the metropolitan leaders over a support many took for granted (e.g., Brissot 1791). Yet they were also too far from the revolutionary momentum to be considered its unconditional supporters (Stein 1985). They led the groups of free coloreds, which included a substantial number of dark-skinned individuals, but they continued to behave as if they were superior to all *nègres* by virtue of their immediate proximity, both physical and cultural, to whiteness. Indeed, their view of political equality was one step behind that of many white metropolitan politicians. In 1789, Julien Raimond, their most important lobbyist in France, wanted the French National Assembly to grant or recognize the freedom of "all the mulattoes and people of color *except the negroes*" (Debbash 1967:153). Both Raimond and Ogé saw free blacks as a threat to mulatto power, and they considered slavery as an utmost necessity (Raimond 1790; 1792). In 1790, Ogé balked at Chavannes's suggestion of using the slaves of the northern province to fight against the whites. Raimond wrote many pamphlets on the origins and causes of the whites' antimulatto prejudices and on the political turmoil on Saint-Domingue in which he managed not to mention slavery either as a cause or even as among the important ingredients of the situation (Raimond 1790; 1791; 1792; 1793). Raimond and Rigaud later backed the southern mulattoes' claims that civil equality for the former slaves should not mean the end of a regimen of harsh labor on the plantations (Lejeune et al. 1796; Bonnet 1798a; Raimond 1797). Likewise, in 1791, *affranchis* of the western and southern provinces increasingly used black slaves in their many fights against the whites but never took positions against slavery (Fick 1985; Raimond 1792). By August 1791, time had run out on them anyway: the slaves of the northern province had entered the battle for themselves.

From the slave insurrection of 1791 to the end of 1802, the free coloreds of Saint-Domingue had little breathing time during which to decide upon a coherent course of action. They consistently lagged behind events forced upon them by others. Their participation in the politics of the day was often parochial, almost always reactive. White planters, colonial officials, and especially the slaves in revolt were the principal actors shaping the country's future, and *gens de couleur* were constantly thrown off balance. Between 1791 and 1793, growing groups of slaves liberated themselves by force of arms. *Gens de couleur* wanted to use the slaves, but they wanted to maintain slavery: they wavered (Baillio 1791; Tarbé 1792; Madiou 1989). On the day following the slave outbreak in the north, prominent free coloreds, including the brother of martyred Jean-Baptiste Chavannes, volunteered to crush the revolt for the whites. Other free nonwhites, including some mulattoes, in turn joined the rebels (Tarbé 1792). In the west and south, some *gens de couleur* took more seriously the elder Chavannes's old suggestion of raising a slave army, still without taking a position against slavery. In the end, neither group made a clear and winning choice: the slaves were liberating themselves with or without freedmen's help. On 4 April 1792, the French Assembly granted full political rights to all *gens de couleur* and free blacks. Free coloreds turned in mass against the slaves; but by then, many whites thought these free coloreds as big a threat as the rebel slaves. Sixteen months later, in part as a political response to the de facto freedom of those slaves, colonial officials sympathetic to the ideals of the French Revolution legally confirmed the abolition of slavery. *Gens de couleur* resigned themselves to the inevitable. By 1794, the leading force in Saint-Domingue was the party of ex-slaves dominated by Toussaint Louverture, whose stated goal was the dismantling of the slave system. By 1795, *gens de couleur* were outmaneuvered by Louverture's party. By 1797, Louverture had become general in chief of Saint-Domingue's army, with the reluctant approval of France.[15] *Gens de couleur* saw that as an affront.

Color prejudice among the nonwhites probably dates from the emergence of the *gens de couleur* themselves. But until the rise of the Louverture party, that prejudice was often nuanced by contempt. As whites felt toward mulattoes, so mulattoes felt toward blacks. They feared the blacks' alleged brutality, lack of reason, dignity, and objectivity, all the alleged impediments that made them lesser beings on the great ladder of God's creatures. In short, if and when they showed apprehension, it was, or it was meant to be, in a manner akin to one's fear of an animal. Ideally, the very fact that blacks were considered lesser beings made them also less threatening in other regards. From the mulatto viewpoint, for instance, blacks were not expected to be masters at the game of politics. The Louverture party shattered all those assumptions. Blacks were still threatening physically, not because they were barbarians but because some of them (Toussaint Louverture, Jean-Jacques Dessalines, Moïse Louverture, Henry Christophe) had amazing talents for military strategy. More important, blacks' political skills enabled them to beat whites and mulattoes at their own game.

Not surprisingly, mulatto resentment against the blacks grew considerably after 1795. The growing gap between the mulatto-dominated former freedmen (*anciens libres*) and the newly liberated slaves (*nouveaux libres*) amplified the political competition between various *mulâtre* factions and the Louverture party. Under the leadership of André Rigaud, the *anciens libres* of the south revolted in the summer of 1799, contesting Louverture's authority and launching a civil war that was to last a year.[16]

Haitian historian Antoine Michel (1929) devoted an entire book to the suggestion that the special agent of the French government, General Joseph Hédouville, created purposely the enmity between the two men (Rigaud and Louverture), who were at least on speaking terms before Hédouville's mission. Indeed, many French leaders did their best to divide blacks and *gens de couleur* (Raimond 1797; Bonnet 1798a; 1798b). But Hédouville's success only brings out the fertility of the grounds in which he planted the seeds of suspicion. At stake were, in fact, two views of Saint-Domingue: that of Louverture, aiming at greater autonomy, and that of Rigaud, more tied to the dictates of revolutionary France (M.-R. Trouillot 1977:123–51; James 1962:224–25). To that, the color question added renewed passions. Rigaud had black followers, black siblings, and black friends, just as Ogé had black relatives still in slavery. Further, contrary to Ogé, by the mid-1790s, Rigaud publicly opposed slavery. But he was a caste-minded *ancien libre* convinced of the superiority of his category. In 1797, after four years under his military leadership, the entire southern province had only one dark-skinned officer (Bonnet 1798a: 28). As late as 12 September 1795, Rigaud wrote in a public letter to mulattoes of the south: "It is by sermonizing on equality that some perverse individuals want to annihilate your caste; the successes they gained in the north give them hope of easily achieving their goal in the west and in the south. But believe me, they are mistaken" (Dorsinville 1986:121).

But when the mulatto Lapointe, an infamous con man and avowed reactionary, wrote to him in derogatory terms about Louverture, Rigaud replied: "I must reprimand your insolence and criticize the arrogant tone you speak about the French General Toussaint Louverture. It is not proper for you to call him a coward, since you were afraid to measure swords against him; neither can you call him a slave since a French Republican cannot be a slave" (Bonnet 1798a: 22–23; E. Trouillot 1961:31).

Rigaud was thus caught in the contradictions between his origins, his love for France, and the republican ideals he espoused. His complex world view included a hierarchy of skin colors, a hierarchy tamed by his personal ties with many blacks, but one that nevertheless returned to the surface when he felt personally threatened.[17] After all, he was part of a crowd that felt itself different than the free blacks, used the word *nègre* to mean *slave* and worried quite loud about the future of their properties in the south after the liberation of the slaves denied them the privilege to extract labor at will (Bonnet 1798a; 1798b; Lejeune et al. 1796).

To be sure, in 1799, Louverture was the one who introduced the color question in his public polemic with Rigaud, probably to decrease Rigaud's popularity among southern blacks (M.-R. Trouillot 1977). Further, the conflict between the two men cannot be reduced to color, as the most placid observers rightly argue (E. Trouillot 1961; James 1962; Nicholls 1979).[18] But color was part of the conflict, even before Louverture made it obvious; and after Louverture used the prejudice argument against Rigaud, color became the favorite idiom of the conflict.[19] Thus, by the time the civil war was over, the general perception was that the mulattoes had lost. Rigaud and many *gens de couleur* left for France.

Some were to return to Saint-Domingue in 1802 with the French army that Napoleon sent to reestablish slavery in the colony.[20] After Toussaint's capture, however, a majority of *anciens libres,* influenced by Alexandre Pétion, recognized the authority of Jean-Jacques Dessalines, a former slave and a Louverture follower of the early days, and joined the fight against the French around December 1802.[21]

The period between December 1802 and December 1803 was most crucial for Haiti's future. First, the French army was defeated. Second, in spite of the fact that both the commander of the revolutionary army, Dessalines, and his second in command, Henry Christophe, were black veterans of the Louverture party, the mulatto-dominated *anciens libres* used those twelve months to control strategic positions within the native forces.[22] We do not know for sure the mechanisms of this takeover; but it is a fact that a disproportionate number of light-skinned *anciens libres* signed the Haitian declaration of independence in 1804.

A bitter struggle for power between *anciens* and *nouveaux libres* followed independence when Dessalines became the first Haitian chief of state. Though the main issue was the control of the plantations left by the French, color again became the favorite idiom of that contest. To be sure, there were blacks and mulattoes for and against Dessalines's rule, and the first Haitian chief of state himself did his best to deflect the color issue (M.-R. Trouillot 1990). But the conspiracy against him was perceived as (and was indeed) directed by a *mulâtre* party, consisting mainly of light-skinned individuals and their cronies. They murdered Dessalines on 17 October 1806. Soon after, Haiti was divided into two states, with Christophe ruling the north and Pétion establishing in the south and the west a republic controlled by the mulatto-dominated *anciens libres.*[23] After Christophe's suicide, in 1820, Pétion's long-time secretary and friend, General Jean-Pierre Boyer, reunited the two states. The mulattoes had finally come to power.

But power itself had come to mean something else in post-slavery Haiti, because of what freedom meant to the ex-slaves. Since the days of the Louverture regime, the laborers had demonstrated consistently their reluctance to engage in plantation work. To them, freedom implied the disappearance of the plantation system altogether. In contrast, the mulatto-dominated elite who controlled the state aimed at restoring that system. Politics to them was not an end unto itself; they wanted control of the state—and had killed Dessalines to obtain such control—because the state had the power to decide who was to run the plantations. Their most cherished dream, which they shared with the competing elite that emerged among the black *nouveaux libres,* was to be plantation owners. But freedom was seriously interfering with that dream.

Haiti: The Making of an Oligarchy

That the ex-slaves associated the plantations with slavery was clear since the Louverture regime. What was less obvious before independence was the extent of their determination to avoid estate labor. Louverture had revitalized the export-oriented production of both sugar and coffee mainly by militarizing agriculture. His system was forced labor, even though cultivators were remunerated; the ex-slaves saw it as slavery with another name. Jean-Jacques Dessalines and Henry Christophe, in turn, had preserved estate labor also by using force.

But Louverture, Dessalines, and Christophe were national heroes, and they were black. The *mulâtres* who dominated the west and the south after Christophe's death could not afford to alienate the masses of cultivators on the issues of land and labor without seeing the color question revived by the most ambitious *nouveaux libres.* Likewise, the fact that France did not recognize Haitian independence until 1825 forced the *mulâtres* to court a majority, which they would need militarily in case of a French invasion. Further, France's 1825 recognition entailed an indemnity of 500 million francs. Thus, for political as well as economic reasons, both Pétion and Boyer ended up selling or granting to many blacks more land than they would have wished. Between 1807 and 1825, many mulatto leaders came to accept the rise of an independent peasantry as a condition of their control of the state. Indeed, some of them had anticipated that situation.

Alternate roads to riches outside of plantation ownership were not plentiful, however. The conditions under which independence had been achieved, the lack of capital, and most important, the ostracism imposed on the black republic by white western powers (M.-R. Trouillot 1990) made it impossible for most Haitians to engage in international commerce. Some did become wholesale traders but as early as 1807, the more ambitious *anciens libres* started to turn the state into a machine that would suck off the peasant surplus, which was becoming more difficult to obtain through mere ownership of the plantations.

The mechanisms that the mulatto-led Senate and presidents Pétion and Boyer set up between 1807 and 1825 revolved around a fiscal policy that unfairly taxed the peasantry through a multilayered package of import and export duties (ibid.). From then on, successive Haitian governments would draw most of their revenues from indirect taxes, most of which were collected at the customhouses. In part because of the domination of the import-export trade by foreign merchants, in part because of the new leaders' own insensitivity toward the needs of the country, the funds accumulated by the state did not stay long in the treasury, nor were they transformed locally into capital. The rulers tended to spurn investment in commerce and, especially, in agriculture (H. Trouillot 1963). Rather, they passed on to foreign merchants, through state expenditures on consumer goods or through private consumption of luxuries, the funds collected from the peasantry at the customhouses.

But the color question was not gone. Boyer's regime had been openly prejudicial to dark-skinned individuals (Nicholls 1979:71–73), and by 1843, the elite of black *nouveaux libres* that had emerged during the regimes of Louverture, Dessalines, and Christophe felt shortchanged. Like their mulatto counterparts, they had dreamed of being plantation owners. But unlike most *anciens libres,* they had been unwilling to accept the peasants' reluctance to work on the estates. The mulattoes' admission of defeat on the issue of the work regimen, inherent in the fiscal system, in some of the land concessions of Pétion and Boyer, and in the move toward wholesale commerce, left many black generals dissatisfied, especially since the higher echelons of the state apparatus were occupied by mulattoes both during the long reign of Boyer (1818–1843) and the short one of Charles Rivière Hérard (December 1843–May 1844). Color became, once more, the favorite idiom of political struggle within the elite, which became divided between *mulâtre* and *noir* factions, largely—though by no means exclusively—identifiable by the complexion of their members.[24] The *noirs* wanted their share of the spoils; and after 1843, some mulattoes were willing to compromise.

After the fall of Boyer, the most cunning of the *mulâtres* realized that their survival required a minimum of power sharing with some of the black leaders, if only to nullify the color argument. Between 1844 and 1849, the *mulâtre* clique, which had dominated the Senate since the days of Pétion, connived to install a series of dark presidents, whom they easily manipulated or dismissed. Haitian historians have labeled this strategy *la politique de doublure* (government by understudies) and have noted that it turned against its architects when Faustin Soulouque (1847–1859), handpicked because he looked blockheaded, destroyed the very individuals who had placed him in power. More important is the fact that, long after the death of the individuals who set up the system, the vast majority of Haitian presidents have been dark-skinned individuals, often associated with the *noirs*.[25] At the same time, the legislature has been dominated largely by *mulâtres* until the first two years of the regime of François Duvalier (1957–1971), at which point it lost even a semblance of autonomy. Nineteenth-century constitutional debates and changes often reproduced the opposition between the two factions, with emphasis on the power of the legislature overlapping periods of *mulâtre* supremacy.[26] The peasantry itself, pushed to the background, remained politically marginal, while *noiriste* leaders loudly claimed power in its name by virtue of sharing the same complexion.

Recent history has changed some of the particulars of Haitian politics, of course. But in retrospect, the mulatto-dominated group of *anciens libres,* who first formulated the codes governing the relationship between state and nation in Haiti during the Pétion regime, had created a viable alternative for themselves and their descendants. Since freedom meant the end of the plantation system, they turned to state politics as their most important means of livelihood. In this particular case, they had to share the spoils with the members of the black elite. Further, the ultimate beneficiaries of the system were the foreign-born merchants—who pumped out that surplus to Europe and the United States—and their metropolitan patrons. The ultimate loser was the Haitian peasantry, which was forced to subsidize a state over which it had no control. The consequences, as we know, were disastrous. But the welfare of the Haitian masses was never the major concern of the *anciens libres.* By setting the mechanisms of state control, by shaping the function of the state, and by investing early in the higher tiers of its apparatus, they made sure that they and their descendants would be, for a long time, part of a two-pronged oligarchy.

It is interesting that the Dominican story is fundamentally similar, even if the particulars differ. For in postabolition Dominica as in postindependent Haiti, the most difficult issue faced by the free coloreds was the reluctance of the former slaves to engage in estate labor. At about the time that the *mulâtre* clique that revolved around Boyer and his lightskinned Senate were resigned to accept the rise of the peasantry, the Dominican free colored elite was discovering that freedom might imply the end of their plantocratic dreams.

Coping with Freedom:
The Flight from the Estates in Dominica

The political elite that developed among the Dominican coloreds in the early 1830s did not at first see itself as exclusively engaged in politics. Rather, it aimed at aping white attorneys, planters, and merchants who occupied powerful positions within the state apparatus while running their businesses or plantations. Many white government officials, including the lieutenant governor and the attorney general, were planters. Likewise, some of the prominent coloreds who first entered the higher echelons of the state apparatus had private sources of income quite significant by local standards. James Garraway, for instance, one of the first three coloreds elected in 1832, was a successful merchant and insurance agent who managed various enterprises while occupying diverse elective or appointive offices.[27]

Most colored leaders did not have Garraway's fortune, but a few had acquired control of substantial estates during and after apprenticeship, and many others expected to as more whites left the colony (Gurney 1840). Accordingly, they generally backed authoritarian measures, which were passed by both house and council between 1836 and 1838, in an effort to maintain the ex-slaves on the estates during the last two years of apprenticeship and after (M.-R. Trouillot 1988:103–06). Likewise, we find some coloreds among the planters and estate attorneys who tried to organize a unified front against laborers' demands in 1838–1839.

But the plantation system was never as firmly planted in Dominica as in Saint-Domingue. Dominican free coloreds were not as rich as the *gens de couleur* of the much more valuable French colony. Further, the end of slavery was announced years ahead and was imposed by the metropolis. With lower stakes, a more peaceful transition, and — to a certain extent — less turbulent past relations with both blacks and whites, Dominican free coloreds did not react as violently to the coming of freedom as did Saint-Domingue's mulattoes. Some free coloreds were members or supporters of the local antislavery society, but participation in the society — well known for its disorganization and its ineffectiveness — was rather a matter of ideological standing. To be sure, some of the most liberal among the educated freedmen saw abolition as an improvement for the masses. But at first, few in that tiny minority saw the end of slavery as something that concerned them directly.

Most were to learn, some faster than others, that freedom in fact meant an end to their dream of joining in the plantocracy or the merchant class. Some, of course, rejected that realization until the very end; but the evidence was there to see. To start with, coffee, their favorite crop, was on the decline. In the late 1830s, a blight (*Cemiotosa coffelum*) devastated many of the coffee plantations. The blight affected all kinds of coffee planters, but it bore more heavily on the coloreds as a group. Most colored estate owners were engaged in coffee production, and most coloreds who hoped to become planters had their eyes on that crop because its production required much less capital than sugar. Meanwhile, the dominant European-born segment of the plantocracy was turning away from coffee production, trying by all means to encourage exports of sugar and sugar derivatives. Finally, freedom had put an end to the practices of gang labor favored by coffee planters (Prestoe 1875). Accordingly, coffee exports, which amounted to more than 1,600,000 pounds by 1838, declined 88 percent in three years (M.-R. Trouillot 1988:54–56). Yet the decline of coffee as an export crop, severe as it was, did not constitute the fundamental obstacle to the free coloreds' dreams. Beyond the coffee decline (and indeed a partial explanation of that decline itself) was the fundamental fact that a substantial number of ex-slaves abandoned plantations on the very first day of emancipation, many of them never to return.

Debates of the last two decades on the so-called flight from the estates in the British Caribbean have been flawed, in part by ideological assumptions, in part by lack of specific evidence.[28] In the case of Dominica, some of that evidence was preserved by a member of the rising free colored elite, one William Lynch, stipendiary magistrate for the parishes of St. George, St. Luke, St. Mark, and St. Patrick South. Lynch's observations were entered into a volume of the Accounts and Papers of the House of Commons (Great Britain 1839). In a report dated 13 September 1838, Lynch described the labor population of more than fifty estates within his jurisdiction. For forty-seven estates listed by name, he provided the number of laborers on the estate on 31 July 1838 and the average number of laborers during the month of August, the first month following the end of apprenticeship. Lynch's numbers are telling. On 31 July 1838, those forty-seven estates counted 2,951 laborers. Within one month, they had lost more than half of their labor force, with 1,560 laborers choosing to leave.

Lynch gives similar numbers elsewhere in his reports for the months of September, October, and November. These data suggest that some ex-slaves returned to the plantations between August and the end of the year.[29] However, a majority of those who fled did not return. Lynch's consistent data for forty-one of the estates over those four months show that they registered a decrease of 39 percent of their labor force between 31 July and 1 December 1838. Figures from the 1891 census show that only twenty-eight of the estates on Lynch's original lists survived by name; by then, despite the much larger population, and despite the fact that laborers were resident sharecroppers rather than wage laborers, the surviving estates managed to reduce their loss to 25 percent of the 1838 labor force (M.-R. Trouillot 1984; 1988:77–81; 95–96).

Lynch's figures — as well as qualitative reports from other magistrates — suggest clearly that in Dominica, the much debated flight from the estates was a painful reality to most actual and aspiring planters. A majority of ex-slaves abandoned the estates in the days immediately following apprenticeship. Many gradually returned, but by the end of the 1830s, the labor loss was still substantial and would remain significant for a long time to come. Moreover, even when laborers agreed to work on estates as such, the work regimen they imposed on the owners was not the plantation labor process but some form of sharecropping (Hamilton 1894; M.-R. Trouillot 1988:84–87). For them, as for their Haitian counterparts, freedom meant control of the land and of the work regimen.

Not only did freedom bring down many former freedmen's dream of establishing successful estates, it also reduced the opportunities to start a career in large-scale commerce. The ex-slaves' reluctance to engage in estate labor — even at higher wages — and the subsequent spread of the peasant labor process meant a decline in import-export activities. In short, the usual roads to economic success were blocked by the former slaves' use of their freedom. That was the unexpected inconvenience that forced the most ambitious among the new colored elite to view state politics as their principal and often sole means of livelihood.

Dominica: The Mulatto Ascendancy

It took the Dominican colored elite sixty long years to fully complete the shift from plantation to politics. The process was much more gradual than in Haiti: it reflected migratory movements, individual histories, and most important, the pace at which the peasantry itself was expanding its control of the land and the labor process.[30] Further, whereas in Haiti independence had rescued the political elite from direct colonial interference, Dominica was still a British colony, where the opinions of the Colonial Office, of the resident white planters, and of the local executive branch of government often mattered more than those of the legislature. And until the beginning of the twentieth century, many officials at the Colonial Office (who had no direct knowledge of Dominica) still believed in the possible restoration of the plantation system (M.-R. Trouillot 1989).

Still, because of their preabolition history, some former freedmen were in good positions to make the move to full-time politics as early as the 1840s. They occupied high ranks in the militia, which by then was "chiefly composed of colored men who were free before emancipation" (Great Britain 1845:81). Some dined at the lieutenant governor's table (Gurney 1840:58). Others, patronized by the lieutenant governor or other high colonial officials, occupied middle-level positions within the state apparatus. Not all of those positions entailed a salary, but most were stepping-stones from which the coloreds could launch successful political or administrative careers.[31]

Up to the mid-1840s, however, the colored elite lacked leadership and direction. James Garraway, the most prominent among them, was a merchant too close, perhaps, to the white planters and bureaucrats to unify the coloreds into a coherent front. But by 1845, the colored elite had started to rally under the leadership of Charles Gordon Falconer, an immigrant from Barbados who, in less than six years, had established a reputation as the most intransigent colored politician in Dominica.[32] Under Falconer's leadership, they curtailed the influence of the Crown's Council and gnawed at the power of the executive branch, which was forced to share control of government with them up to the mid-1860s. By then, the Falconer coalition was broken, in part because many of the colored politicians of the early days, worn out by legislative fights, were quite content to rubber-stamp colonial decisions if their own positions remained secure. Falconer himself had become quite subdued, hoping not so secretly to gain a high-level appointment in the civil service. And indeed, in 1868, he was named colonial registrar. (He was under contract as printer for the assembly since 1865.)

The colored individuals born after the end of apprenticeship, who entered the political scene in the 1860s and 1870s, refurbished the political maneuvers of the 1840s and 1850s, with largely the same results.[33] They loudly opposed measures from the Colonial Office or the local executive branch that they thought limited Dominica's autonomy. They voted for liberal public expenditures. They vociferously criticized the elders, from whom they had learned their rhetoric and their tactics, for being now too soft in regard to Britain.[34] Not surprisingly, they tired even faster than those who had preceded them. By 1898, convinced that their place within the local apparatus was secure, the Mulatto Ascendancy, or rather what remained of it, dropped all rhetorical pretense.[35] The local assembly abrogated itself, and Dominica became a Crown colony, governed by England without an elected native representation (Boromé 1972d).

Dominica gained little from those sixty years of colored ascendancy. Even the tradition of electoral politics owes more to the labor movement of the 1930s than to the electoral gymnastics of the nineteenth-century mulattoes. From the end of apprenticeship to the late 1880s, white planters and officials set voting requirements that precluded the vast majority of the population from participating in the electoral process. The minuscule colored elite often preferred to bypass those requirements with illegal maneuvers rather than change them officially. After all, what they came to enjoy were the spoils of power. As late as 1884, the entire roll of the voting register comprised only 612 names for a total population exceeding 27,000 (Hamilton 1884:xix). In 1886, the executive branch lowered voting requirements, extending the franchise to allow poorer members of the population to participate in the elections. The not-so-secret goal was to modify the composition of the electorate in the hope that new and different voters, not tied to the mulatto elite, would get rid of the most vocal members of the Mulatto Ascendancy and bring Dominica under closer British control. The strategy failed: the ascendancy returned to power after the elections. Many of the newly eligible voters had not bothered to cast their vote. As in Haiti, the elitist practices of the native leaders had resulted in the political marginalization of the peasantry, a marginalization which, in this case, was to last until the middle of the twentieth century.

The mechanisms were different, of course. One could argue that the Dominican marginalization occurred under a cover of constitutionality. Further, while a small, dark-skinned elite emerged early in Haiti and staunchly refused to be marginalized by the free coloreds to the point of becoming an accepted segment of the oligarchy, Dominican politics were for a long time a game played primarily between white and light-skinned individuals. But from the viewpoint of the majority, the result was the same: they were being kept away from the centers of decision while two equally estranged parties pretended to argue about how best to rule them.[36] The early rise of the native elite opened a gap between light- and dark-skinned individuals and, for a long time, the majority of the latter (that is, the peasantry) saw politics as a reserved terrain of the more urban, more educated coloreds.

The lieutenant governor in the 1840s, though by no means an impartial witness, accurately reported on that gap as early as 1844. According to him, black laborers "have since [abolition] witnessed many of the colored people appointed to places, and brought into public notice, without any elevation of the kind toward any of them since the abrogation of apprenticeship. . . . It is a well-known fact that the lately emancipated negroes have looked upon their colored brethren for some time back with much jealousy, and have not been backward in giving vent on several occasions to expressions, that showed there was not a very good feeling existing betwixt them" (Great Britain 1845).

The lengthy evidence gathered on La Guerre Nègre (a series of riots that occurred in June 1844, as enumerators started to take a new census of the population) seems to back Laidlaw's views. Rioters—most of whom were former slaves—did not distinguish between colored and white owners, or colored and white officials.[37] Disturbances occurred in and around estates owned by whites and mulattoes alike. Witnesses reported threats against both coloreds and whites, and some of those threats targeted groups rather than individuals. William Ellisonde, of Stowe Estate, for instance, testified that he had heard African-born Remy, an alleged insurgent, telling another laborer that "all the people of colour will weed our canes and that this country must be similar to St. Domingo," a reference to the Haitian revolution.[38]

The coloreds' responses to the 1844 census riots also show their own ambivalence: they saw the obvious gap between them and the majority of the peasantry. Indeed, they welcomed it. At the same time, they needed to claim some special link with that majority that was out of reach of British-born officials and that would give legitimacy to their thirst for power. They alluded to that link and presented themselves as the defenders of black civil rights, for instance, during the trial of Charles Leathem, a white attorney accused of the brutal murder of a laborer during the riots. Time and again, from the 1860s to the 1890s, the rhetoric of the ascendancy would claim greater control for the natives in the name of greater familiarity and closer fraternity with the masses.

The needs of the masses, in fact, were rarely met. In practical accordance with the strategies mapped out by the Colonial Office, the coloreds contributed to the passage of tax laws that stymied the commercialization of typical peasant crops as soon as slavery ended. In 1839, for instance, taxes on arrowroot at the rate of six shillings per one hundred pounds took the lead among export duties. Taxes on coffee, cacao, plantains, and manioc flour, accepted or sometimes pushed by the coloreds, also crushed peasant producers. And a list of licenses, the longest one in the British Caribbean, tried to bar peasants from alternative sources of income (M.-R. Trouillot 1988:106–12). Here, as in Haiti, the former freedmen and their descendants sucked off peasant surplus through an unfair tax policy. Only British control—with the political "stability," the grants, and the commercial preferences it entailed—and an extremely low population density preserved Dominica from some of the worst dramas of nineteenth-century Haiti.

Conclusion

I have tried to recapture three moments of the life history of two Caribbean societies and to emphasize the role that people of color played in each. Those moments are, of course, heuristic devices; another observer could have found good reasons to separate the material differently. But it seems to me that what freedom meant cannot be severed from what existed before and what came after. Thus, I have distinguished a prefreedom moment, during which, in both cases, free people of color, strengthened by an extraordinary demographic growth, seized upon the new opportunities brought forward by the 1763 Peace of Paris. In Saint-Domingue, those opportunities were mainly economic. In Dominica they were more of a political and military nature. Freedom itself exposed the ambiguities of both groups, despite the very different ways in which it was achieved in the two cases. But because of the earlier ascent, in both cases also, it became increasingly an inconvenience, a detour in the course of the free coloreds, and especially an end to their dream of securing a firm niche within the plantocracy. In the postfreedom moment, the Haitian *mulâtre* elite as well as the Dominican ascendancy tried to carve for themselves a new niche in the state, from which they hoped to inherit the spoils. In both cases, they were successful, but they also had to share with other contenders; and they had to do so against the background of increasing peasant control over the labor process.

As it should, this dual story raises more questions than it answers, both about free coloreds in the Afro-Americas and about the role of the state in postslavery societies. Does the fetishism of state power characteristic of nineteenth-century Dominica and Haiti bear any similarity with later developments in, say, Louisiana or Alabama? Are there enough similarities between these and other societies for us to speak of a postplantation state? We need to know more about intermediate groups in other Antillean societies and on the mainland to learn the full lesson of the comparison sketched here. Behind this dual story is the history of Caribbean peasantries reconstituting themselves, the history of ex-slaves who rejected the plantation labor process and forced the free coloreds of Dominica and Haiti to take the course they did. It was ex-slaves who gave meaning to some alternatives opened to the free coloreds and closed the door on others. At the heart of this story is their Freedom, or rather, what they took it to mean.

NOTES

I thank Drs. Drexel G. Woodson, John D. Garrigus, and Professor Robert Forster for comments on an early version of this chapter. My research in England was funded by the Inter-American Foundation, and that in France by the John Simon Guggenheim Foundation. I remain responsible for the final result.

1. This essay bears some of the limitations inherent in comparative studies. Published works on Dominican history are extremely rare even though British record keeping, the most important source for that history, is proverbially good. On the other side of the comparison, accounts and interpretations of the Saint-Domingue revolution and the emergence of the Haitian state are numerous but uneven. More important perhaps, Dominica is a small and neglected country, even by Caribbean standards, with a population that will still be below 200,000 by the end of the twentieth century. In contrast, by 1791, the slave population alone was near the half-million mark in Saint-Domingue. By then also, Saint-Domingue had contributed the largest share of France's colonial profits for half a century. In contrast, since the mid-1700s Dominica derived its importance mainly from the fact that it was sandwiched between the two French sugar colonies of Guadeloupe and Martinique. This chapter reflects those fundamental differences in the two situations, the methods of record keeping, and the published record.

2. I follow the local usage of the times in using, interchangeably, many of the terms referring to color or legal-status-cum-social categories. In Saint-Domingue, *affranchi* never had a precise phenotypical referent and lost early its original meaning of *manumitted*. I use it with *gens de couleur* much as I use the term *free colored* interchangeably with *freedman* to refer to a free person in Dominican slave society, manumitted or freeborn, of which the assumed racial ancestry was mixed or Negroid. Although in both cases, free people of assumed African ancestry were politically and often demographically dominated by individuals considered to be of lighter skin, in the local context, the categories used here do not refer to skin color but to a mixture of perceived phenotype and social status.

3. At that time, freedmen represented only 2.3 percent of the total population of Martinique, Dominica's southern neighbor. Four years later (1767) in Guadeloupe, Dominica's northern neighbor, free colored "numbered only 762, or less than 1 percent of the total population" (Elizabeth 1972:149–50; see also Frostin 1975). In 1768, the 448 freedmen of Barbados represented only 0.5 percent of the total island population (Handler 1974:18); the 3,500 of Jamaica, only 1.3 percent.

4. On the castelike stratification of Saint-Domingue and the position of the *affranchis* within it, see Nicholls (1979: chap. 1). Nicholls makes a useful distinction between racism and color prejudice, but his differentiation works better for post-independent Haiti than for Saint-Domingue.

5. The term *petit blanc* refers indifferently to white residents who did not belong to the plantocracy, the elite of higher government officials, or to the merchant class. The three latter categories comprised the *grands blancs*. Raimond (1791) suggests that this systematization was due, in part, to recent female immigrants from France — a suggestion on which I cannot comment except to say that the connection between gender and racism in the making of the Afro-Americas remains unexplored. In a finely researched thesis, John Garrigus (1988) shows how *gens de couleur* in a southern parish used local conditions — and especially the power vested in public notaries — to maintain both rights and social recognition in spite of the colonywide context of oppression.

6. The factors mentioned in explaining that second period of growth do not much differ from the ones discussed above in relation to the pre-1763 period. Moreau de Saint-Méry (1958:84–85), among others, emphasizes the local government's growing need for the manumission fees, the role of the militia, and an extraordinary increase in legal unions between free — white and nonwhite — people and slaves in Saint-Domingue after 1770. For the social and economic changes connected with those trends, see M.-R Trouillot (1982).

7. In spite of the fact that the number of free nonwhites grew throughout the Caribbean in the last quarter of the eighteenth century, many Caribbean territories reached proportions similar to 1763 Dominica only in the 1830s (Higman 1984:77).

8. From 1699 to 1763, most armed encounters between British and French troops involved less than 200 — and often less than 100 — individuals, many of whom were civilians (Boromé 1972b). Eyewitness Thomas Atwood (1971:109) sets at 94 the number of British regular troops, inclusive of officers, on the eve of the French 1778 attack from Martinique.

9. Free blacks from Martinique were among the first "French" settlers in Dominica (Boromé 1972b:95–96), and as we have seen, the demographic growth of the colored population was particularly impressive during the French occupation.

10. Free coloreds felt so secure during French occupation that they stopped showing any respect whatsoever for British planters and officials. Atwood (1971:152) notes the case of "a Frenchman of colour" who "had the audacity to strike the English Chief Justice."

11. I suspect that the rise was due to a combination of factors, among which manumission may have been predominant (M.-R. Trouillot 1988:99). But one should not dismiss the fact that, in the early 1800s — even more than before, perhaps — many free nonwhites from *both* the British and French neighboring islands saw Dominica as a land of political and economic opportunity. The economic opportunities never materialized for most. In the early 1800s, nonwhites owned only 22 percent of the slaves and controlled an even lower proportion of the export crops. Many specialized in coffee, as did many *gens de couleur* in Saint-Domingue. Yet, at best, the free colored controlled 19.1 percent of the coffee, 3 percent of the sugar, and 2.7 percent of the rum produced in the island in 1820 (Green 1976:15). Those proportions probably grew in the 1830s, to an extent yet unknown. But even then,

as in the rest of the Caribbean, the vast majority of freedmen were traders, crafts-men, or small landowners, still poorly fitted within the plantation economy.

12. They were Michael Bolland, James Garraway, and J. Lawrence Lionne.

13. One of the most respected stipendiary magistrates of the times, whose care-ful records I have used here and elsewhere (M.-R. Trouillot 1984) was a colored man by the name of William Lynch, an early advocate of civil rights for the labor-ers, who later became a member of the House of Assembly and of Her Majesty's Council (*Dominica Almanac* 1864:15; Gurney 1840).

14. The death of Ogé and Chavannes convinced many free coloreds that armed force was the sole means to enforce the decree of March 1790. But the many local-ized combats in which they engaged never gave them a decisive victory in spite of significant temporary successes.

15. Interestingly, Louverture's most daring political gamble was made possible by one of the few occasions during which the *affranchis* tried to take an indepen-dent initiative and came close to uniting under a colonywide leadership. On 20 March 1795, they orchestrated the kidnapping of General Lavaux, the white commander in chief of the French troops. Toussaint promptly liberated Lavaux, who named him second in command. A few months later, Toussaint engineered Lavaux's depar-ture, clearing his way to supreme power.

16. Benoit Joseph André Rigaud was born on 17 January 1761, in Les Cayes. His mother, Rose Bossy Depa, was probably an African-born Arada woman. His French father, André Rigaud, legitimized him and sent him to Bordeaux, where he trained as a goldsmith. He returned to Saint-Domingue in 1773, and fought under Lafayette and d'Estaing in New York and Savannah in the U.S. War of Independence. He first became a general in the Saint-Domingue colonial forces, together with Louverture, but was then left behind as Louverture made his extraordinary ascen-sion. He left the colony after losing the civil war to Louverture. He returned to independent Haiti in 1810 and started a secessionist republic in the south in 1810, which collapsed when he died of natural causes in September 1811 (see E. Trouillot 1961:25–36; Woodson, 1990).

17. Rigaud seems to have been very close to his black brother, General Augustin Rigaud, who was a witness at his wedding (E. Trouillot 1961:29). But among the witnesses, besides another Rigaud brother, probably a mulatto, was also Guy-Joseph Bonnet, André Rigaud's trusted secretary, who later became a prominent ideologist of the *mulâtre* party in independent Haiti.

18. Picking up from Haitian historian Pauleus Sannon, James (1962:230), as in the case of many Marxists working on Haiti, cuts the color conflict down to an epiphenomenon, which I think is dead wrong. What we are dealing with here is a metaevent, encapsulating many contradictory trends, a complex expression of class, color, and personal oppositions. Hence a black leader like Pierre Michel backed Rigaud, as Nicholls (1979:29), among others, points out; but he was also a personal enemy of Louverture, whom he envied.

19. I have pointed elsewhere to the speech made by Toussaint Louverture in the cathedral of Port-au-Prince, on 21 February 1799, as the first use of the color argument in a *noiriste* (hence demagogic) manner. By reducing the conflict to an opposition between bigots (which, in his claims, included all mulattoes) and free-dom and equality seekers (read, all blacks), Louverture created one of the worst

precedents of Haitian history. He of course knew, as did most *noiristes* after him, that the fundamental issue was not color. Some mulattoes occupied high positions within his own troops before, during, and after the war. Rigaud, of course, whose army was highly segregated at the top, was weak enough to reply in the same terms, and from then on, color became the language of political polemics (M.-R. Trouillot 1977:140–43; on color and politics in postindependent Haiti, see Nicholls 1979; M.-R. Trouillot 1990).

20.   To Rigaud's credit, he did not return with the invading French army, though some of his followers, including future presidents Pétion and Boyer, did.

21.   Pétion was the son of a resident Frenchman and a free mulatto woman, which technically made him a *quarteron* rather than a mere mulatto in Saint-Domingue's white-dominated scale of race and color categories. He was nevertheless rejected, and perhaps mistreated, by his father. A goldsmith by training, he was active on the side of the *gens de couleur* in the military campaigns of 1791 against the whites, during which his talents as a gunner were very useful to the mulattoes. Later, he joined the regular French troops and received many promotions under Toussaint Louverture. In the midst of the civil war against Rigaud, he sneaked out of the Louverture camp to become the commander of the mulatto army in Jacmel. After a heroic resistance, he was forced out of Jacmel by no one less than Jean-Jacques Dessalines, then commander of Louverture's second most powerful battalion. In August 1799, he fled to France with Rigaud to return in 1802 with the antirevolutionary expedition. On 13 October 1802, he abandoned the French army and started to work for the establishment of the military unity of *anciens* and *nouveaux libres* under Dessalines' command (E. Trouillot, personal communications; Woodson, 1990; Ardouin 1958).

22.   Henry Christophe himself was a former freedman, born on the island of Grenada, but he never associated with the mulatto-dominated clique of *anciens libres*. Further, *mulâtre* leaders tended to demarcate themselves from the *nègres libres* whom they saw as a different category (Bonnet 1798a).

23.   For a brief period, there were in fact four statelike entities, if one counts the short-lived, secessionist Meridional Republic Rigaud tried to install in the south, in 1810–1811, and the separatist enclave maintained by the peasants of the Grand'Anse area from 1807 to 1820. Not much has been written about those, but see Woodson (1990).

24.   This is not the place to discuss the relation between phenotypes and Haitian social categories. I will simply note that the Haitian terms used here do not simply refer to skin color, nor even to phenotype alone, but to socioideological and political groupings, within which color plays an important role as a marker but operates *only* in relation to other symbols, never by itself. Thus, both factions often had individuals who were phenotypically similar, even though the *mulâtres* were visibly lighter and tended to be dominated by individuals who were thought to be of the "mulatto" type—a type that, itself, has darkened considerably since independence (see M.-R. Trouillot 1990, chap. 5).

25.   Leyburn's listing of the color of Haitian presidents (1941:316–17) provides a sense of this evolution, even though his categories ("light," "black," "dark") may be more U.S.-based than Haitian-based, and even though he is wrong on some individuals, regardless of the margin allowed for cultural translation.

26. One can read in such light the evidence on constitutional and presidential politics in the recent book by Haitian historian Claude Moïse (1988), though Moïse himself does not voice that argument.

27. Garraway's career was extraordinary. By the 1850s, besides his import-export firm and interests in insurance agencies (the Colonial, which he personally controlled, and the Royal, of Garraway and sons), he was engaged in shipping, probably transporting provisions to neighboring Caribbean islands. In 1865, he held the only recorded wholesale license in Dominica and owned at least two boats (M.-R. Trouillot 1988:108). He also broke successive political records as a nonwhite. He was one of the first three coloreds elected to the Assembly in 1832. In 1840, he was one of the first nonwhites appointed to the Queen's Council (with Police Magistrate Thomas Rainey). He occupied diverse and increasingly high positions in the magistrature, to which his position as council member had given him automatic entry. As senior council member, he thrice became temporary chief executive of Dominica, the first person of known African ancestry to exercise that function in any British Caribbean colony, and perhaps in any colony within the British empire. He died in 1873 at the age of seventy-four. International trade and services attracted equally the former freedmen in both Dominica and Haiti, but only a few were as successful as Garraway in Dominica and, in Haiti, access to the merchant class did not stop them from venturing in politics (M.-R. Trouillot 1990).

28. I have commented on that debate elsewhere, underlining some of those assumptions and suggesting some methodological prerequisites (M.-R. Trouillot 1984).

29. We do not know, of course, whether or not the same individuals were involved. There are reasons to believe that many ex-slaves did not return to the same estates.

30. The individual histories and the many migrations in and out of Dominica underline Suzan Lowes's point (Lowes 1987) that we cannot simply assume continuity from the coloreds of slavery days to the postabolition middle classes of the Caribbean. In Haiti, of course, such continuity is exceptional. But in Dominica — in spite of the migrations (and in spite of the fact that individuals more closely related to the British than to the French, and usually associated with the Methodists, came to dominate the colored elite) — personal histories suggest that they were integrated in a continuing flow.

31. Some of the coloreds started a career in the civil service in the 1840s. By 1844, Theodore Francis Lockhart, who started as a notary public in 1843, was sergeant at arms in Chancery. He became visiting justice of the prisons in April 1852, commissioner of education, justice of the peace, and Registrar General in the 1850s and 1860s, and sat in the legislature as a Crown nominee in 1865 (*Dominica Almanac* 1859:18, 1864:28). Wm. Thomas Rainey, nominated police magistrate after he reached the Crown's Council in the 1840s, was one of the first colored men to reach that distinction, along with James Garraway (Great Britain 1844:XXI). William Lynch, Esq., stipendiary magistrate in 1838, elected member of the assembly, also sat on Her Majesty's Council in the 1860s (*Dominica Almanac* 1854, 1864:15).

32. Born in 1819, in Barbados, where he trained as a printer, Falconer came to Dominica in 1839, one year after the colored majority first sat in the assembly. He started a newspaper, the *Dominican,* in October of the same year (Boromé 1959:11). By 1842, he was appointed printer of the legislature. By 1845, he was elected

to the assembly. In 1848, he became an ensign of the Royal St. George's militia and a marshall bailiff. By 1850, he was justice of the peace and judge of the Supreme Courts of the Criminal Judicature. By 1853, he became the uncontested leader of the Mulatto Ascendancy at the House of Assembly. This group of representatives included, besides Falconer himself, his brother-in-law, John Bellot Fraser, three of his uncles-in-law from the Bellot family, his half brother, C. Herbert, Thomas P. Trail, assistant editor to the *Dominican* and nephew of one of his sisters, and John Hopkins Fillan, a colored merchant. The white colonists dubbed it the Family Party. In 1868, he became colonial registrar. He died on 29 March 1872. See Boromé (1959).

33. A striking figure among this new generation of colored leaders was William Davies, the mulatto son of a Welsh planter, educated in Winchester. In the mid-1860s, he already controlled several estates. Elected member of the legislature in 1881, he soon became the leading voice of the colored group, which was fragmented after the deaths of Garraway and Falconer. Contrary to most colored politicians, he refused to accept the demise of the plantation system, which he tried unsuccessfully to revive with technological improvements (Boromé 1972d:126; M.-R. Trouillot 1988:108, 193–95, 309–10).

34. Even then, continuity was not broken. Alexander Ramsey Capoulart Lockhart, for instance, one of Davies' allies, was the son-in-law of Galvan Bellot, which ties him directly to many of the predecessors he criticized—including Falconer, who had also married into the Bellot family.

35. In his 24 February 1874 message to the assembly, Governor Henry Turner Irving specifically envisioned the systematization of the public service to create employment opportunities "outside of the domain of agriculture and trade" (M.-R. Trouillot 1988:117). In 1893, the Dominica Grammar School opened with the explicit aim of preparing Dominican boys for a public career. With the indulgence of the executive, colored people used their positions to perform various paid services for the government. Because of Dominica's tortuous topography, the Department of Public Works was, and remains, a source of graft and political patronage. Nineteenth-century politicians such as Falconer and William Davies sat at various times on the Road Board, from which they gained substantial economic power. Falconer's appointment as colonial registrar also proved that colonial officials could easily forget the most virulent anticolonial rhetoric.

36. Quite interestingly, the legislative debates between Liberal and National parties during the brief period that Haiti came close to modern electoral politics (1870–1883) shared strong similarities with arguments voiced in Dominica at the peak of the ascendancy. Whites in Dominica and the mulatto-dominated Liberals in Haiti emphasized their competence and their integrity. Haitian Nationals and mulattoes in Dominica emphasized a representativeness implicitly or explicitly based on phenotype and the fact that they had in mind, or so they said, the good of the majority. The motto of the journal *Dominican,* Falconer's organ, was exactly the same as that of the Haitian National party: "The Greatest Possible Good for the Greatest Number." (On Liberals and Nationals in Haiti, see Nicholls 1979; Moïse 1988; M.-R. Trouillot 1990.) Likewise, just as Haitian mulattoes claimed that the Haitian color question did not exist before black leaders used an alleged color prejudice for demagogic purposes (which is of course half false, since the prejudice existed long before the demagoguery), so did H. A. Alford Nicholls, white British resident

of Dominica. He rightly criticized the coloreds' hypocrisy but wrongly claimed that racial harmony prevailed on the island before the Mulatto Ascendancy. See Ardouin (1958) for Haiti; Hamilton (1894) on Dominica. Nicholls' memorandum is in Hamilton (1894:69).

37. Note that, at that time, the militia, which went after the protesters, was composed mainly of light-skinned former freedmen, even though whites dominated the higher ranks. The police magistrate, Thomas William Rainey, a member of the legislature, was a colored man.

38. Remy was, of course, mistaken about the evolution of the Haitian situation. In 1844, "people of colour" were not weeding anyone's canes in Haiti. Quite the contrary.

REFERENCES

Ardouin, A. Beaubrun. 1958 [1853–1860]. *Etudes sur l'histoire d'Haïti.* Port-au-Prince: François Dalencour, éditeur.
Atwood, Thomas. 1971 (1791). *The History of the Island of Dominica.* London: Frank Cass. Reprint of the first J. Johnson edition, 1791.
Baillio, M. 1791. *Un Mot de vérité sur les malheurs de Saint-Domingue.* Paris: J. B. Chemin.
Bonnet, Guy-Joseph, 1798a. *Exposé de la conduite du général Rigaud, dans le commandement du Département du Sud de Saint-Domingue.* Paris: Imprimerie J. F. Sobry.
———. 1798b. *Au Directoire Exécutif et au Corps Législatif.* Paris: Imprimerie J. F. Sobry.
Boromé, Joseph Alfred. 1959. George Charles Falconer. *Caribbean Quarterly* 6:11–17.
———. 1972a. Spain and Dominica. In *Aspects of Dominican History,* edited by D. Taylor et al., 67–79. Roseau: Government Printing Division.
———. 1972b. The French and Dominica, 1699–1763. In *Aspects of Dominican History,* edited by D. Taylor et al., 80–102. Roseau: Government Printing Division.
———. 1972c. Dominica During French Occupation, 1778–1784. In *Aspects of Dominican History,* edited by D. Taylor et al., 103–19. Roseau: Government Printing Division.
———. 1972d. How Crown Colony Government Came to Dominica by 1898. In *Aspects of Dominican History,* edited by D. Taylor et al., 120–50. Roseau: Government Printing Division.
Brissot, J. 1791. Letter to M. Raymond. In J. Raimond, *Observations sur l'origine . . .* Paris: Belin, Desenne, et Bailly, libraires.
Brutus, Edner. N.d. *Révolution dans Saint-Domingue.* Brussels: Editions du Panthéon.
Cobbett's Annual Register. 1802. London.
Cobbett's Political Register. 1805. London.
Cohen, David, and J. Greene, eds. 1972. *Neither Slave nor Free: The Freedmen of African Descent in the Slave Societies of the New World.* Baltimore: Johns Hopkins University Press.

Debbash, Yvan. 1967. *Couleur et liberté. Le jeu du critère ethnique dans un ordre juridique esclavagiste.* Annales de la Faculté de Droit et des Sciences Economiques de Strasbourg. Paris: Dalloz.

Dominica Almanac (spelling varies). 1814–1879.

Dorsinville, Roger. 1986 (1965). *Toussaint Louverture ou la vocation de la Liberté.* Montreal: Les Editions du CIDHICA.

Du Tertre, Jean-Baptiste. 1667. *Histoire générale des Antilles habitées par les français.* 2 vols. Paris: Th. Jolly.

Elizabeth, Leo. 1972. The French Antilles. In *Neither Slave nor Free: The Freedmen of African Descent in the Slave Societies of the New World,* edited by D. Cohen and J. Greene, 134–71. Baltimore: Johns Hopkins University Press.

Fick, Carolyn. 1985. Black Peasants and Soldiers in the Saint-Domingue Revolution: Initial Reactions to Freedom in the South Province (1793–4). In *History from Below: Studies in Popular Protest and Ideology in Honour of Georges Rudé,* edited by F. Krantz. Montreal: Concordia University Press.

Frostin, Charles. 1975. *Les révoltes blanches de Saint-Domingue.* Paris: L'Ecole.

Garrigus, John D. 1988. A Struggle for Respect: The Free Coloreds of Pre-Revolutionary Saint Domingue, 1760–69. Ph.D. diss. Johns Hopkins University.

Girod de Chantrans, Justin. 1980 (1785). *Voyage d'un suisse dans différentes colonies d'Amérique.* Paris: Tallandier.

Great Britain. 1845. Copies or Extracts of Despatches Relating to the Disturbances in the Island of Dominica. Colonial Office, Downing Street, 17 March 1845. G. W. Hope. In PP 31 (146).

———. 1839. Papers Relative to the West Indies, pt. 3. Papers on the Condition of the Labouring Population, West Indies. In Accounts and Papers 8. Colonies, West Indies, &c. Leeward Islands. . . . Parliament Session 5 February–27 August 1839. Vol. 37, 1839 (PRO ZHC1/1266).

Green, William E. 1976. *British Slave Emancipation: The Sugar Colonies and the Great Experiment.* Oxford: Clarendon Press.

Gurney, John Joseph. 1840. *Familiar Letters to Henry Clay of Kentucky, Describing a Winter in the West Indies.* New York: Press of Mahlon Day.

Hamilton, Robert. 1894. Report of the Royal Commission (appointed in September 1893) to Inquire into the Conditions and Affairs of the Island of Dominica and Correspondence Relating Thereto. Presented to both Houses of Parliament by the Command of Her Majesty. August 1894 (PP, 57 or PRO, ZHC1/5667).

Handler, Jerome S. 1974. *The Unappropriated People: Freedmen in the Slave Society of Barbados.* Baltimore: Johns Hopkins University Press.

Higman, Barry. 1984. *Slave Populations of the British Caribbean, 1807–1834.* Baltimore: Johns Hopkins University Press.

James, C. L. R. 1962 (1938). *The Black Jacobins: Toussaint Louverture and the San Domingo Revolution.* New York: Vintage.

Legislative Assembly Minutes. From January 1860 to January 1880. U. K. Public Record Office. CO 74/33.

Lejeune, Fradin, Blanchard, et al. 1796. *Mémoire adressé par les citoyens de la commune des Cayes, Département du Sud de Saint-Domingue, au Corps Législatif, et au Directoire Exécutif.* Aux Cayes: De l'Imprimerie de Lemery.

Leyburn, James G. 1941. *The Haitian People.* New Haven: Yale University Press.

Lowes, Susan. 1987. Time and Motion in the Formation of the Middle Class in Antigua, 1834–1940. Paper presented at the annual meeting of the American Anthropological Association, Chicago, November.

Madiou, Thomas. 1989 (1847). Histoire d'Haiti. Vol. 1. Port-au-Prince: Editions Henri Deschamps.

Malouet, V. P. 1802. Collection de mémoires et correspondances officielles sur l'administration des colonies. 5 vols. Paris: Baudouin.

Michel, Antoine. 1929. La mission du général Hédouville. Port-au-Prince: Imprimerie La Presse.

Moïse, Claude. 1988. Constitutions et luttes de pouvoir en Haïti. Vol. 1, La faillite des classes dirigeantes (1804–1915). Montreal: Les Editions du CIDIHCA.

Moreau de Saint-Méry, Médéric Louis Elie. 1958 (1797–98). Description topographique, physique, civile, politique et historique de la partie française de l'isle Saint-Domingue. Paris: Société d'histoire des colonies françaises.

Nicholls, David. 1979. From Dessalines to Duvalier: Race, Colour and National Independence in Haiti. Cambridge: Cambridge University Press.

Official Gazette, 1865–1968. Public Record Office CO 75/1.

Prestoe, Henry. 1875. Report on Coffee Cultivation in Dominica. Trinidad: Government Printing Office.

Raimond, Julien (spelling varies), 1790. Réflexions sur les véritables causes des troubles et des désastres de nos colonies. Paris: Imprimerie des Patriotes.

———. 1791. Observations sur l'origine et les progrès du préjugé des colons blancs contre les hommes de couleur; sur les inconvéniens de le perpétuer; la nécessité de le détruire. Paris: Belin.

———. 1792. Véritable origine des troubles de S.-Domingue, et des différentes causes qui les ont produit. Paris: De l'Imprimerie du Patriote Français, and Desenne.

———. 1793. Lettres de J. Raimond, à ses frères les hommes de couleur. Paris: Imprimerie du cercle social.

———. 1797. Rapport de Julien Raimond, commissaire délégué par le gouvernement français aux Isles-sous-le-vent, au Ministre de la Marine. Au Cap Français: P. Roux.

Raimond, Perrier, and Lamothe-Aigron. 1791. Première lettre écrite de la partie de l'ouest. Paris, Rue Meslée.

Stein, Roger Louis. 1985. Léger Félicité Sonthonax: The Lost Sentinel of the Republic. Toronto: Associated University Press.

Tarbé, Charles, ed. 1792. Pièces justificatives du Rapport sur les troubles de Saint-Domingue. Paris: De l'Imprimerie Nationale. 3 vols.

Trouillot, Ernst. 1961. André Rigaud. In Prospections d'histoire: choses de Saint-Domingue et d'Haïti, 25–36. Port-au-Prince: Imprimerie de l'Etat.

Trouillot, Hénock. 1963. Les anciennes sucreries coloniales et le marché haïtien sous Boyer. Port-au-Prince: Imprimerie de l'Etat.

Trouillot, Michel-Rolph. 1977. Ti dife boule sou Istoua Ayiti. New York: Koleksion Lakansiel.

———. 1982. Motion in the System: Coffee, Color, and Slavery in 18th-Century Saint-Domingue. Review 5:331–88.

———. 1984. Labour and Emancipation in Dominica: Contribution to a Debate. Caribbean Quarterly 30:73–84.

————. 1988. *Peasants and Capital: Dominica in the World Economy*. Baltimore: Johns Hopkins University Press.

————. 1989. Discourses of Rule and the Acknowledgment of the Peasantry in Dominica, W.I., 1838–1928. *American Ethnologist* 16:94–108.

————. 1990. *Haiti: State against Nation. The Origins and Legacies of Duvalierism*. New York: Monthly Review Press.

Woodson, Drexel. 1990. Tout mounn se mounn men tout mounn pa menm: Microlevel Sociocultural Aspects of Land Tenure in a Northern Haitian Locality. Ph.D. diss. University of Chicago.

JEAN BESSON

Freedom and Community
The British West Indies

One of the most far-reaching aspects of the aftermath of full emancipation in the British West Indies was the establishment and growth of free Afro-Caribbean communities. This occurred through both dispersed settlement and nucleated villages and laid the foundations of rural life in the Commonwealth Caribbean today. This chapter, written to commemorate the 150th anniversary of full freedom in the Commonwealth Caribbean, addresses this important theme. It does not, however, attempt an exhaustive treatment of this subject; constraints of knowledge, time, and space prohibit such a task. Instead, it seeks to highlight and explore certain controversial issues regarding the origin and development of these free communities.

First considered is the origin of the British West Indian free communities, set within the wider contexts of continuity and change in the interrelationship of people, land, and labor in 1838. Were these communities forged in opposition to the plantations, or did the ex-slaves wish to remain in symbiotic relationship with the estates? This question entails a further reconsideration of the flight from the estates debate (cf. Hall 1978). It is argued that, while postemancipation planter policies were indeed significant in triggering the exodus of former slaves from the British West Indian plantations (ibid., Marshall 1979; cf. Besson 1981, 1984a, 1984b, 1987a:13–18), an overemphasis on this factor, and on the postslavery era, underplays the significance of the long history of slave resistance based on the interrelated themes of kinship, community, and land. The emergence of British West Indian free communities is then examined against these background themes.

The essay next explores the central role of customary land rights in perpetuating British West Indian free communities. Most significant are the kin-based tenures, rooted in the protopeasant past of the plantation slaves who created a peasant life-style while still enslaved (cf. Mintz 1974a:151–52), that emerged in the free communities and persist within

183

them to the present day. The controversial issues of their origin and function are considered, as is their interrelationship with other customary tenures and with legal freehold. It is then argued that the evolution of Afro-Caribbean customary tenures provides a powerful model for understanding other controversial aspects of rural life in British West Indian free communities. Finally, the disputed characterization of the inhabitants of these communities is considered against the background themes of freedom, community, and land.

An underlying contention throughout the chapter is that the emergence of British West Indian free communities must be set within wider parameters of time and space. The postemancipation era should be seen as a point on a continuum of change and continuity in the interrelationship of people, land, and labor from slavery to the present time and the British West Indian case seen as a variant on Caribbean regional themes.

The Origin of British West Indian Free Communities

British West Indian free communities emerged with the exodus of former slaves from the plantations in the aftermath of full emancipation in 1838. The question of their origin must therefore be set within the wider contexts of the flight from the estates debate. A useful starting point is the "reconsideration" by Hall (1978) who summarizes the extant views: "The prevailing impressions conveyed in the general body of literature on the history of the [British West Indian] post-emancipation period are: that the majority of ex-slaves wished to remove themselves from the estates on which they had suffered so much in the days of bondage; that the ex-slaves were, apparently with some reluctance, forced to leave the estates because of the harsh attitudes and demands of their masters, the ex-slave owners; and, in either case, that their movements clearly depended on the availability of somewhere else to go" (ibid., 8). These impressions, as Hall shows, derive respectively from the opposing views of Farley (1964) on British Guiana and Paget (1964) on the Jamaican case.

Hall's reconsideration, based on the examination of evidence given before the Select Committee of the House of Commons on the West India Colonies in 1842, develops his earlier view, following Paget, of the Jamaican case (Hall 1959). Hall argues that the ex-slaves who left the British West Indian plantations were not rejecting the horrors of the slavery system but the inequities of early freedom, reflected in planter

policies restricting the ex-slaves' use of estate houses, gardens, and provision grounds in order to keep the ex-slaves as a dependent labor force
tied to the estates. This involved either imposing high rents on houses
and provision grounds, thus diminishing earnings from the sale of ground
provisions, or rendering continued occupation dependent on providing
daily work for the plantations (Hall 1978:17). Hall further concludes
that while there was hatred of the plantation, there was love of home
on the estate (ibid., 23–24). For Hall, the crucial factor in the flight from
the plantations was therefore planter policy regarding land and labor
among the former slaves.

The debate reconsidered by Hall surfaces again in two complemen-
tary publications by Mintz and Marshall in 1979. In "Slavery and the
Rise of Peasantries," Mintz (1979) elaborates his earlier thesis that Caribbean peasantries represent a mode of resistant response to the plantation system (1974a:132–33), exploring the rise of the postslavery peasantries against the backdrop of postemancipation planter power and in
terms of the link with the protopeasant past. Marshall's (1979) commentary concedes Mintz's thesis that the reconstituted Caribbean peasantries
represent a resistant response to the plantation system. However, citing
Hall (1978) and focusing on the anglophone Caribbean, Marshall (1979:
247) argues that Mintz underplays the significance of labor recruitment
policy, the ex-slaves' response to planter policy, and the role of the provision grounds, in this context, in understanding the flight from the
estates. If these were stressed, Marshall contends, rather than the ex-
slaves' wish for independence from the plantations, "the patterns of development [of the postslavery peasantries] would emerge more clearly"
and the resistant response could be seen in more complex terms (ibid.,
245).

Marshall's argument is that the ex-slaves expected to have continued
access to the plantation yards and provision grounds and perhaps intended to increase provision ground cultivation to the detriment of
labor on the estates. This conflicted with planter interests, which focused on retaining a cheap full-time labor supply, and the planters therefore introduced a labor recruitment policy based on "long contracts,
low wages and conditional occupancy of houses and provision grounds"
(ibid., 246) to keep the ex-slaves tied to the estates. The conditional
occupancy of provision grounds, dependent on supplying cheap regular
plantation labor and sanctioned by eviction, was the key element in this
policy. However, while planter policy succeeded in the short-term, it
backfired as a long-term strategy; the ex-slaves responded by challeng-

ing wage rates, by striking, sometimes violently resisting and, eventually, by leaving the estates (ibid., 247). Marshall also argues that "where planters sold surplus estate land or rented land to ex-slaves there was no significant desertion" of labor from the plantations (ibid., 248). Like Hall (1978), Marshall therefore focuses on the conflict of interests between planter policy and the expectations of the former slaves, and the peaceful coexistence of plantation and peasantry where this conflict did not occur (1979:245–48). In a detailed study of the emergence and development of an estate-based peasantry in Dominica, Chace (1984) also argues Hall and Marshall's case.

Marshall, Hall, and Chace contribute valuable perspectives in stressing the role of planter policy regarding land and labor in triggering and shaping the exodus from the plantations and in highlighting the significance in this context of the role of the provision grounds (cf. Besson 1981, 1984a, 1984b, 1987a:13–18). However, to focus too closely on these factors, and on the postemancipation era (e.g., Marshall 1979:243; cf. Marshall 1968:252–53), underplays the significance of the long and complex history of slave resistance in the ex-slaves' flight from the estates (cf. Besson 1984a, 1984b, 1987b; Mintz 1974a:131–250). Moreover, Marshall's evidence shows that the ex-slaves' attachment to estate provision grounds was rooted in their belief that these lands were, in fact, their own—or in their actual purchase of these lands (Marshall 1979:246, 248; cf. Berleant-Schiller 1987; Craton 1987). Nor is it a sharper focus on postemancipation planter policy, the ex-slaves' response to such policy, and the role of the provision grounds, in this context, which would have sharpened Mintz's overview of postslavery peasant development (Marshall 1979:245). Mintz's focus on these issues is sharp enough, and he has pioneered our understanding of the link between protopeasants and postslavery peasantries (1974a:146–224, 1979:218, 241). Instead, the contours of postslavery peasantries would have emerged more clearly if Mintz had drawn more fully on his earlier comparison regarding the plantation-peasant interplay in the Hispanic and non-Hispanic variants of the region. For while the declining plantation system in the nineteenth century non-Hispanic Caribbean enabled the transformation of protopeasants into postemancipation peasants, the simultaneous burgeoning of the Hispanic Caribbean plantations destroyed the squatter peasantries and constrained the subsequent emergence of postemancipation peasantries (1959, 1971a:29, 1974a:146–56; cf. Besson 1987a:36).[1]

Drawing on these background themes of slave resistance and the differential plantation-peasant interplay in the Hispanic and non-Hispanic

Caribbean, this essay reasserts and develops Farley's view on British Guianese free communities and its wider relevance to the British West Indies and other non-Hispanic areas of the region. For as Farley argues:

The rise of the village settlements is usually recorded as a post-emancipation phenomenon. Considered as such, the exciting story of the settlements becomes a mere record entirely drained of its real historical colour. The roots of the village settlements are to be found in the days of slavery. The forces which were fundamental to the establishment of these settlements were, *for the most part,* the same economic and social forces which led to the end of slavery as such on August 1st, 1838.

The most decisive and continuous of these forces was the desire, on the part of the slaves, for personal liberty and for land of their own. (Farley 1964:52, emphasis added; cf. Besson 1974:12).

The essay, therefore, argues that British West Indian and other non-Hispanic postemancipation free communities are indeed a resistant response to the plantation system (Mintz 1974a:132–33), rooted in slave resistance and their desire for freedom and land. In developing this thesis, the essay also elaborates Farley's perspective on "land of their own" by revealing the significance of customary as well as legal rights to land in the complex history of slave and postslavery resistance. Evidence for this thesis comes from both sides of the flight from the estates debate.

Land, Community, and Slave Resistance

From the very inception of plantation slavery in the British West Indies, as elsewhere in the Caribbean region, the slaves sought to establish autonomy and community, often based on customary as well as legal rights to land (cf. Craton 1985:111; Heuman 1985:7; Mintz and Price 1976). This was manifested in various forms of slave resistance: rebellion, protopeasant adaptations, and marronage (cf. Mintz 1974a:75–76, 131–250). Long and continuous histories of slave rebellion typified the Caribbean region and Brazil and, to a lesser extent, the southern United States (Genovese 1981). Slave rebellion particularly typified the non-Hispanic Caribbean, where the early development of large-scale plantation slavery was most pronounced (Mintz 1959). This was especially so in the British West Indian colonies, which were the vanguard of European overseas agricultural capitalist development, and "the greatest slave revolts in the Western Hemisphere, except for the world-shaking revolution in Saint-Domingue, took place in Guiana and Jamaica" (Genovese 1981:33; cf. Craton 1985; Patterson 1973:273).

Marronage — escaping slavery and founding autonomous communities—also typified the entire span of New World slavery and was widespread throughout Afro-America, especially where inaccessible topography enabled the establishment of customary rights to land (Price 1973; cf. Genovese 1981:52). In other cases, maroons hid in towns or escaped by sea (Heuman 1985:5). The most pronounced and longest lasting maroon communities were in the non-Hispanic Caribbean territories of Jamaica and Surinam (Genovese 1981:51; Price 1973:227). Here (and elsewhere) customary land rights were transformed to freehold by treaties establishing the maroons' legal rights to land (cf. Price 1976:2).

The widespread protopeasant adaptation was a more subtle mode of slave resistance, based on customary rights to land. Here a peasant life-style was established within the constraints of the plantation system by plantation slaves (Mintz 1974a:151–52). Protopeasantries especially typified the non-Hispanic Caribbean, particularly the British West Indies—the vanguard of plantation slavery—where planter policy and topography allowed. With the early burgeoning of the plantation system in the non-Hispanic Caribbean, the planters faced the problem of feeding their slaves (Mintz 1959, 1974a:180). There was no clear policy on this issue (ibid., 182) but, as Mintz has noted for the British Caribbean:

The alternative extremes were either to have the slaves produce as much as possible of the food they ate or to import all of their food. Of these two courses the first, though not always practicable, was the more desirable. If the slaves could feed themselves, the estates would save the cost of imported foods and avoid the risks contingent upon importation. When warfare disturbed merchant shipping, a frequent occurrence in the eighteenth century, and shortages of imported food resulted, food prices rose. . . . Moreover, when import shortages existed, the slaves could not be adequately fed even if the planter could afford high food prices. Prolonged interference with the importation of food introduced a vicious circle of high prices, malnutrition, and reduced production and profits. (Ibid., 180–81)

The choice of food production by the slaves or the importation of food was largely determined by the suitability of land for growing sugarcane: "Generally speaking, where land was flat and fertile, the cane was planted; where it was not, food was grown for the slaves and dependence on food imports was considerably reduced" (ibid., 181).

Protopeasantries, therefore, emerged in the more mountainous British West Indian islands such as Jamaica, St. Vincent, Dominica, and Grenada, while flatter islands such as Barbados, Antigua, and St. Kitts were almost entirely devoted to sugarcane (Chace 1984; Marshall 1979: 245; Mintz 1974a:181; Patterson 1973:216–30; Rubenstein 1987b:35–37). British Guiana also developed a protopeasantry (Farley 1964:54–55), as did French Saint-Domingue (Mintz 1960) and Danish St. John (Olwig 1985). The protopeasant adaptation was based especially on the provision grounds in the mountainous backlands of the plantations. Here, in addition to the yards in the slave village, plantation slaves were required to cultivate their food (e.g., Mintz 1974a:184–94).

Evidence of the significance of the protopeasant adaptation as a mode of slave resistance comes from both sides of the flight from the estates debate. Mintz (ibid., 131–250) explicitly interprets the protopeasantry as a form of slave resistance (cf. Farley 1964), showing how plantation slaves developed the system of yard and ground beyond the planter strategy of feeding the slaves, producing surpluses for sale in internal markets. Thus in Jamaica, the largest of the British West Indian islands, the free population became dependent on the slaves for food and, by 1774, at the zenith of Jamaican slavery, the slaves controlled 20 percent of the island's currency (Mintz 1974a:194–206). Hall (1978: 24) also refers to the "self-asserted independence" of the slave "in the privacy of his house and garden and the circle of his family," and to "reports of the slaves' attachment to their dwelling-places and to the burial plots of their relatives and their sense of belonging to the 'negro-house' community of the estate" (cf. Paget 1964:40). Thus, customary rights to yard and ground, and the interrelationship of kinship and land, became important and creative bases of slave identity and resistance.

British West Indian Jamaica, where the protopeasant adaptation was most pronounced (Mintz 1974a:181–224; Patterson 1973:216–17), provides clear evidence of such customary rights to land as a basis of slave autonomy and community. There John Stewart observed the significance of customary rights to yards, provision grounds, and family burial grounds: "Adjoining to the house is usually a small spot of ground, laid out into a sort of garden, and shaded by various fruit-trees. Here the family deposit their dead, to whose memory they invariably, if they can afford it, erect a rude tomb. Each slave has, beside this spot, a piece of ground (about half an acre) allotted to him as a provision ground. . . . If he has a family, an additional proportion of ground is allowed him, and all his children from five years upward assist him in his labours in some way or other" (Mintz 1974a:187). And as early as 1793, Bryan Edwards noted a system of customary inheritance among the Jamaican slaves: "I do not believe that an instance can be produced of a master's interference with his Negroes in their peculium thus acquired. They are permitted also to dispose at their deaths of what little property they possess; and even to bequeath their grounds or gardens to such of their fellow-slaves as they think proper. These principles are so well established, that whenever it is found convenient for the owner to exchange the negro-grounds for other lands, the Negroes must be satisfied, in money or otherwise, before the exchange takes place. It is universally the practice" (ibid., 207).

These customary land rights provided the basis for kinship and community even among the newly arrived slaves (ibid., 209). Mintz also highlights the widespread link between kinship, community, and customary rights to land among the protopeasantries throughout the non-Hispanic Caribbean: "It seems quite likely that the provision ground-marketing complex, which turns up over and over again, reduced the hunger of the slaves, increased their autonomy *while still slaves,* allowed them to accumulate (and bequeath) wealth, *enabled them to link patrimony to genealogy, possibly encouraged the stability of kin groups"* (1979:241, emphasis added).

Data from the Danish Virgin Island of St. John throw further light on the interrelationship between kinship, community, and customary land rights among the Caribbean protopeasantry. Olwig notes that among the St. Johnian slaves, "the bush lands were not foreign territory but their own land, where they could make their gardens in small clearings and create an existence for themselves outside the direct control of the planters" (1985:46, cf. 43–44). In addition, Olwig's data implicitly suggest that the cognatic descent system that emerged in postemancipation Caribbean family land was rooted in these customary protopeasant rights to land (see Besson 1989a). For while Mintz (1974a:216–17) "found no evidence that 'land use was ever afforded other than to male slaves—though their families . . . commonly helped them on the provision grounds'" (Olwig 1985:49), Olwig shows that in St. John both male and female slaves had rights, and a strong attachment, to land and a "particular preference for living and being buried on their place of birth" (ibid., 41; cf. ibid., 49).

Returning to the British West Indies, unusually isolated protopeasant adaptations, bordering on marronage, emerged in the Bahamas and Barbuda at the margins of plantation slave society in a situation of benign neglect. These cases provide a pronounced illustration of the interrelationship of kinship, community, and customary rights to land and their role in Caribbean slave resistance. For here, well-developed customary tenures, based on actual or fictive kinship and commonage, provided the foundations of autonomous communities among the protopeasantry. These customary tenures were also the basis of the slaves' resistance to

formal work and to their owners' attempts to move them to more profitable plantation areas in the region (Berleant-Schiller 1987; Besson 1987a:
38–40 n5; Besson and Momsen 1987:4–5; Craton 1987:93–97).

Against this background, estate-based peasantries and the flight from
the estates in the postemancipation British West Indies can be seen as
transformations of two modes of slave resistance — protopeasantry and
marronage, both rooted in customary rights to land (cf. Greenwood and
Hamber 1980:86; Mintz 1974a:151–54). Protopeasants evolved into estate-
based peasantries when ex-slaves were able to retain customary rights
to yards and grounds, or when topography or planter policies regarding land and labor constrained movement off the estates. Free communities beyond plantation boundaries were established where planter
policies, availability of land, and peasant capital combined with the traditions of slave resistance to trigger a flight from the estates (cf. Besson
1984a, 1984b, 1987a). In many colonies, both variants coexisted as did
the protopeasant and maroon adaptations in the slavery past. The next
section outlines the emergence of British West Indian free communities
against these background themes.

The Emergence of British
West Indian Free Communities

Jamaica, the largest of the British West Indian islands, provides the
most pronounced example of the emergence of Caribbean postemancipation free communities (Besson 1984a, 1984b; Greenwood and Hamber
1980:86–87; Paget 1964). There the exodus of former slaves from the
plantations was rooted in strong traditions of slave rebellion, protopeasantry, and marronage, and was triggered by planter legislation
obstructing the ex-slaves' customary rights to land on the estates (cf.
Besson 1981, 1984a, 1984b; Paget 1964). A pronounced protopeasant
adaptation ensured that many ex-slaves had marketing and cultivation
skills to establish free communities and sufficient capital to purchase
land (cf. Mintz 1974a:157–213). The potential availability of land was,
however, severely constrained by planter policies designed to keep the
ex-slaves tied to the estates. These included the ejectment and trespass
acts, which imposed high rents on estate houses and provision grounds
sanctioned by ejection and imprisonment, and were designed to create
dependency on the low wages paid by the estates, and a virtual veto
on selling land to former slaves (Besson 1984a:64–65; Knox 1977; Marshall 1972:31; Paget 1964:39; Wright 1973:167). Therefore, while some

estate-based peasantries remained through choice (Hall 1978; Marshall 1979), planter opposition constrained, as well as triggered, the flight from the estates (Besson 1984a:65–66; Robotham 1977:50–51). Land scarcity was further exacerbated by the absence of Crown lands (Wright 1973:167).

In this context, the Baptist Church, under the leadership of James Phillippo and William Knibb, played a major role in Jamaican post-emancipation rural settlement through the purchase and subdivision of properties to establish church communities (Mintz 1974a:157–79; Paget 1964). In addition, "from the impetus provided by church sponsorship, other free villages grew without the deliberate patronage of the missionary churches" (Mintz 1974a:161). By 1840, Knibb estimated there were nearly 8,000 cottages in 200 free villages throughout the island. By 1845, Knibb's estimate was that 19,000 ex-slaves had purchased land and were erecting cottages, with Trelawny, the parish where he was stationed, at the center of these developments (Greenwood and Hamber 1980:87; Paget 1964:51).

The parish of Trelawny had been the heart of Jamaican slave society and slave resistance, and Trelawny's former slaves had strong traditions of slave rebellion, protopeasantry, and marronage. In the aftermath of emancipation, Trelawny's fertile land continued to be engrossed by the plantation system, as it is to the present day (Besson 1984a, 1984b, 1987b, 1988). The free village movement in Trelawny was rooted in the ex-slaves' traditions of slave resistance and was triggered by oppressive planter policies designed to tie a landless labor force to these estates. These policies included notices to quit plantation lands and the sale of plantation backlands, used as provision grounds, in an attempt to destroy the production of the former slaves (Paget 1964:42). With this background, and under the sponsorship of Knibb, who led the British nonconformist antislavery struggle, Trelawny's emancipated slaves became the vanguard of the British West Indian postemancipation village movement (Besson 1984a, 1984b, 1987b, 1988).

Alps (New Birmingham) was Trelawny's first free village (Besson 1984b). It was founded by the Rev. Dexter in 1838 under the sponsorship of Knibb and was located in the foothills of the Cockpit Country—the stronghold of Trelawny marronage. The village was established on a former coffee plantation and was settled by ex-slaves from that estate. Laid out around a Baptist mission house, Alps—along with Sligoville, St. Catherine, Jamaica's first free village—served as a model for the island's free village system. Other Trelawny villages—such as Refuge

(Wilberforce), Kettering, and Granville, which were established in 1838, 1841, and 1845, respectively, and studied by the present writer in 1983 — were founded directly by William Knibb himself (ibid.). Like Alps, and Sturge Town in the neighboring parish of St. Ann (Mintz 1974a:157–79), they were established by subdivision of properties purchased by the Baptist Church and resold to members of their congregations. Refuge, Kettering, and Granville, like other villages elsewhere in Trelawny, absorbed dispossessed plantation slaves from nearby sugar estates. They also provided reservoirs of labor for these plantations and, established around a Baptist chapel or prayer house and school, congregations for the Baptist Church. Above all, however, they gave the ex-slaves some independence and a bargaining position for higher wages when working on the estates. The village of Martha Brae, established by ex-slaves from surrounding plantations on the ruins of a former planter town, was another variant on Trelawny's free village theme (Besson 1984a, 1984b, 1987b, 1988).

Although Jamaica was the most pronounced example of the British West Indian postslavery peasant movement, free communities were established in varying degrees throughout the British Caribbean. In British Guiana, a long history of slave resistance (rebellion, protopeasantry, and marronage), accumulation of peasant capital, and relative availability of land combined to trigger and sustain a major movement from the estates (Farley 1954, 1964; Mintz 1979:234–35). By 1852, there were some 10,000 Negro village freeholds, and between 1842 and 1854 "village populations rose from about 16,000 to about 49,000" (Mintz 1979:234). The villages were established on the narrow empoldered coastal plain, and joint stock companies formed by the ex-slaves for purchasing joint freeholds played a major role in their establishment (Farley 1964). Others were founded in a more pronounced maroon tradition through squatting on Crown land (Greenwood and Hamber 1980:87). Like the Jamaican free villages such as Alps (New Birmingham), Refuge (Wilberforce), Kettering and Granville in Trelawny, and Sturge Town in St. Ann, the naming of Guianese free villages such as Unity and Buxton reflect the emancipation theme (Besson 1984b, 1989b:23, 162 n37; Mintz 1974a:157–79; R. T. Smith 1962:35).[2] By the 1860s, however, planter legislation to control the sale of land and "clearly intended to decapitate the peasant movement" stemmed the establishment of Guianese free villages (Mintz 1979:235).

In Trinidad, although the free village movement was less marked than in Jamaica and British Guiana (Greenwood and Hamber 1980:87) and "there was no mass disappearance into the bush" (Brereton 1981:80), there was a substantial exodus of former slaves from the estates and an establishment of villages. This was due to a desire on the part of the ex-slaves "to make freedom meaningful, to achieve a measure of economic and social independence of the planter . . . accentuated by the tenancy system, the withdrawal of allowances in 1842, the reduction in wages after 1846, and countless other irritants" (ibid.). It was estimated that of the 11,000 field slaves in Trinidad in 1834,

4,000 remained on the estates by 1859, while 7,000 had left. The majority of the ex-slaves who left the estates remained in agriculture. They bought, leased or squatted on parcels of land, becoming small cultivators, giving part-time labour to estates, and living in new villages close to existing plantations which sprang up in the years after 1838. . . . Ex-slave villages developed near Port of Spain (East Dry River, Laventille, Belmont) and San Fernando (Rambert and Victoria Villages), and a ribbon development of settlements along the Eastern Main Road between Port of Spain and Arima. (Ibid., 80; cf. Henshall 1976:39)

This ribbon development included Tacarigua, Arouca, and Arima, all preemancipation Amerindian settlements that became transformed into postemancipation Negro villages (Besson 1989b:154–55; Brereton 1981: 5–7, 21, 89). Other free villages were established "in the Montserrat Ward in the centre of the island" (Greenwood and Hamber 1980:87). In Tobago, "ex-slaves settled round the pre-emancipation church, . . . although their farmland might be some miles away" (Henshall 1976:39). By 1846 it was estimated that 5,400 Trinidadian ex-slaves "were living in these new villages, and by 1847 the resident estate labour force had shrunk by 40 per cent. Sewell estimated that five-sixths of those who had left the estates had become land-owners by 1859 holding 1–10 acres" (Brereton 1981:80).

This relative availability of land through squatting on Crown lands or on abandoned estates and from the sale of some estates was, however, constrained by the general reluctance of planters to sell land to the ex-slaves, by high land prices, and by state policy obstructing the sale of Crown lands to former slaves (Besson 1989b:17–18, 157 n21; Brereton 1981:81, 88–89). This at least partially accounts for the 60 percent of ex-slaves remaining on estates in 1847, though planters did initially adopt the strategies of task work and high wages to induce ex-slaves to remain on the plantations (ibid., 78–80).

While the larger territories of Jamaica, Trinidad, and British Guiana provide the best examples of British West Indian free communities (cf.

Greenwood and Hamber 1980:86), settlements were also established in
the Windward Islands and, to a lesser extent, in Barbados, the Leewards,
and the Bahamas. Along with Jamaica, Trinidad, and Guiana, the mountainous Windward Islands provided most opportunity for postemancipation peasant settlement, and both dispersed and nucleated settlements
occurred (ibid., 88; Henshall 1976:38; Marshall 1968:245–55).

In the Windward Island of St. Lucia, "emancipation in 1838 unleashed
the tendency of the population to be independent of the plantation" and
"despite tremendous odds, there was a gradual movement away from
the estates" (Acosta and Casimir 1985:36). Although there were only two
new villages by 1849, ex-slaves augmented the populations of older villages
and also attempted unsuccessfully to reestablish the old ruined town
of Dauphin — paralleling, to some extent, the Jamaican case of Martha
Brae (Besson 1984a, 1984b, 1987b; Henshall 1976:38). However, most
postemancipation settlement in St. Lucia was dispersed, on both rented
and purchased land (ibid.). The desire for independence from the plantations in St. Lucia was reinforced by planter policy restricting wages
and rights to land on the estates, and the number of freeholders rose
steadily from 1845 to 1861:

The planters, anxious to safeguard their entire labour force, attempted by various means to keep all the ex-slaves on the estates in relationships which closely
approximated to their earlier servile condition. Insecurity or lack of tenure,
as well as relatively low wages for plantation labour, and sometimes high rent
and long contracts, reinforced the determination of the ex-enslaved to seek new
and better opportunities away from the estates. . . . They attempted to buy
land, even at prohibitive prices. By the 1840s the changing trends of land tenure
were already apparent. For example, the estimated numbers of freeholders between 1845 and 1861 indicate the trend: 1845, 1,345; 1846, 1,390; 1849, 1,920;
1853, 2,343; 1857, 2,045; 1861, 2,185. (Acosta and Casimir 1985:36)

Constraints on postemancipation freehold settlement were, however,
severe due to planter opposition to the purchasing of land. This led to
the establishment of peasantries on rented and leased land on the periphery of the plantations, which were tied through tenancy to the estates.
The state also monopolized extensive areas of land and introduced discriminatory land taxes to deter peasant settlement through squatting,
renting, or purchasing of land (ibid., 36–37).

Dominica, the largest and most mountainous of the British Windward Islands, showed both similarities and contrasts with St. Lucia. By
1851, only seven postemancipation villages had been founded, "but many
people had moved into the old-established villages especially on the

leeward coast" (Henshall 1976:38). While the Dominican ex-slaves did not face the obstructive planter legislation of most other British West Indian colonies, the coastal plantations encompassed most of the island's cultivable land. In addition, the planters ensured that the ex-slaves remained tied to the estates through introducing task work and manipulating plantation waste lands for provision grounds through metayage and rental (Chace 1984; cf. Gomes 1985). This suggests, in contrast to Chace's (1984:9) thesis that Dominica's former slaves were not concerned with independence from the plantations, that the ex-slaves, in fact, had little opportunity for a flight from the estates.

In Grenada, where postemancipation planter legislation restricted wages, discouraged squatting, and legalized the eviction of tenants to ensure a continued supply of labor for the plantations, most ex-slaves remained tied to the estates as tenants-at-will in the immediate aftermath of emancipation. These estate-based peasantries provided plantation labor in return for customary rights to yards and provision grounds (Brizan 1984:126–28). The desire for independence was, however, strong: "The dearest wish of the freed-man was to have his own independent plot; this signified to him in a very real way his transition from slavery to freedom. Ownership of land, no matter how little, became the most important criterion of freedom to the Grenadian. Work on the estate, if and when it was done, was a necessary evil in that it provided some needed money" (ibid., 129). Accordingly, "as the years passed, the number of people residing and working on estates decreased" and "concomitantly, the peasantry and village settlers increased" (ibid., 126). Following this exodus from the plantations, ex-slaves purchased land (for example, from abandoned estates in the parish of St. George) or leased and rented land from the estates. By 1852, 22 percent of Grenada's population (7,127 persons) were living in free villages (ibid., 129). Such villages were both dispersed and nucleated, as in St. Vincent, where the number of plantation laborers decreased from 15,000 in 1838 to 4,500 in 1845 (Rubenstein 1987b:40) and "the number of people living in villages increased from 3,664 in February 1846, to 8,209 in 1857" (Henshall 1976:38; cf. Rubenstein 1987b:43–44).

In Barbados and the Leeward Islands, the establishment of free communities was more constrained due to the greater dominance of plantation agriculture and the denser population of these flatter islands (Greenwood and Hamber 1980:87–88; Marshall 1968:254). However, even here ex-slave communities were established on marginal land. In Barbados, postemancipation located-labor planter legislation, land scarcity, and high land values kept most ex-slaves on the plantations (Greenfield 1960:170). The located-labor legislation, designed to restrict the occupational and physical mobility of the former slaves, required a stipulated amount of cheap labor as a condition for renting working allotments or yards on the estates. Landownership provided escape from the located-labor laws with their low wages and insecurity of tenure, and despite the high land prices, a small peasantry was established on freehold land by 1859. As most of these purchased plots were subdivisions of former plantations, some nucleated villages were established despite the continued dominance of the estates (ibid., 170; cf. Henshall 1976: 38; Marshall 1979:244; Mintz 1979:228–30). "In Antigua, sixty-seven villages containing 5,187 houses and 15,644 inhabitants were built between 1833 and 1858"; and even in St. Kitts, some free villages were established, with names reflecting the significant role of the church in the island's postemancipation settlement (Henshall 1976:38, 39).

However, in Nevis and Montserrat, free villages and the development of an independent peasantry in the immediate aftermath of emancipation was entirely constrained by land monopoly, and estate-based peasantries emerged through sharecropping and tenancy-at-will (Besson and Momsen 1987:6; Momsen 1987; Olwig 1987; Philpott 1973:20–23). Both islands also saw high rates of emigration among former slaves. An independent Montserration peasantry did emerge in the 1850s with the subdivision and sale of some marginal estates (Philpott 1973:23–25), but in Nevis, the stranglehold of the plantation system continued until the 1930s (Besson and Momsen 1987:6).

The cases of Nevis and Montserrat were paralleled, in some respects, by the British West Indian mainland colony of Belize. There, despite the potential availability of land, labor legislation and land monopoly by the mahogany lords stifled the development of a postemancipation peasantry (Bolland 1981:600–11). In Belize, land monopoly, established in the eighteenth century, was maintained after e   ˌⁿation through a unique labor control strategy based on the adva   ⁻tems, which kept the mahogany laborers in permaneɪ ing elite. The advance system involved the adˑ to the laborers in the hiring season in Belize tɾ during the Christmas holidays, "ostensibly to purchase his supplies prior to going to the f 608). However, as anticipated by the emɼ spent on Christmas obligations and celebrɐ ers then had to purchase their supplies on from the employers' stores in the forests, a practice known as the 'truck' system. . . . The effect of the combination of the advance and truck systems, therefore, was to bind the laborer to his employer by keeping him eternally in debt" (ibid., 608).

In contrast to this extreme control of the ex-slaves in most of the Leewards and Belize, there was benign neglect of them in the Bahamas and the Leeward Island of Barbuda, at the margins of British West Indian society (Besson and Momsen 1987:4–5). Emancipation made little difference in Codrington, the only settlement in Barbuda, where the ex-slave community continued its autonomous protopeasant way of life undisturbed until the 1860s (Berleant-Schiller 1977, 1978, 1987). In the Bahamas, legislation designed to restrict the ex-slaves access to land was enacted following emancipation. However, it proved impractical to enforce, and the former protopeasants evolved, relatively undisturbed, into free communities retaining customary rights to land (Craton 1987).

These free communities that emerged in the postemancipation British West Indies were later paralleled by similar developments in other non-Hispanic areas of the region, such as French Martinique (Henshall 1976: 38; Horowitz 1967) and Danish St. John (Olwig 1985). They were also predated by Haiti's postrevolutionary free communities (Mintz 1960, 1974a:267–301). Themes of both continuity and change have marked the evolution of such communities through more than 150 years of freedom, to the present day, and different territories have shown variations on these themes (see e.g., Beckford 1972, 1975; Berleant-Schiller 1978, 1987; Craton 1987; Henshall 1976; Marshall 1968; Mintz 1959, 1985). However, within these contexts of continuity, change, and variation, the interrelationship of freedom, community, and rights to land, rooted in the tradition of slave resistance, have remained a central theme. The remainder of this essay explores this thesis with particular reference to British West Indian free communities.

Land, Freedom, and Community

Within the context of postemancipation rural settlement, land rights emerged as the central theme of freedom and community in the post-slavery British West Indies. As seen above, both dispersed settlements and nucleated villages were generally established through land purchase, though some were based on renting, squatting, or common land. Legal therefore, provided the foundations of most free communities, omary tenures played a supplementary role. Customary land rights soon, however, reemerged as the prime basis of community, as in the protopeasant past. This was especially so with the kin-based tenures of family land, also known as generation property and children's property. Rooted in protopeasant systems of customary tenure and transmission, these customary institutions became fully established in the postslavery era following the purchase of land and the subsequent transformation of legal to customary freeholds (Besson 1979, 1984a, 1984b, 1987a, 1987b, 1988).

These kin-based tenures have persisted throughout Commonwealth Caribbean communities to the present day, through 150 years of freedom. In Jamaica, the largest of the former British West Indian islands, family land has been identified in a wide range of contemporary rural communities, including the Trelawny free villages of Alps, Refuge, Kettering, Granville, and Martha Brae. Similar institutions have also been reported for Afro-Caribbean communities in Guyana, Trinidad, Dominica, St. Lucia, St. Vincent, Grenada, Carriacou, Montserrat, Barbados, and the Bahamas. Family land is also found in anglophone Providencia and among the "West Indian" Black Caribs of Central America's Caribbean Coast. Parallel institutions have also evolved in other parts of the non-Hispanic Caribbean such as Haiti, Martinique, St. John, Curaçao, and Surinam.[3] To my knowledge, family land has not been reported for the Hispanic Caribbean, where the emergence of postslavery peasantries was not pronounced (cf. Mintz 1959, 1971a:28–31, 1979).[4]

These customary institutions of family land have transformed the principles of colonial legal freehold in the context of postslavery free communities. Legal freeholds, introduced to the Caribbean region by the planter class, often comprise extensive tracts of land. Legal freeholds are private property, alienable, marketable in the capitalist economy, validated by legal documents, and acquired through purchase, deed of gift, or testate inheritance. In the British West Indies, intestacy is traditionally defined on the basis of legitimacy, male precedence, primogeniture, and legal marriage. Houses on legal freehold land are considered part of the real estate, and land use is governed by the capitalist values of maximizing profits and production (cf. Besson 1984a:58–60, 1987b:103).

The customary institutions of family land that emerged among the postemancipation peasantry and that persist today contrast in all respects. Generally small in size (often only a few square chains), family land should not be sold and is regarded as the inalienable corporate estate of the family line. Rights to family land are essentially validated through oral tradition and, while initially acquired through purchase, are customarily transmitted through intestacy. In the Commonwealth Caribbean, the definition of intestate heirs differs markedly from the traditional legal system. The definition is based on unrestricted cognatic descent, whereby all children and their descendents in perpetuity are considered heirs regardless of sex, birth order, residence, or legitimacy. Furthermore, marriage is not regarded as a basis for inheritance. Houses are distinguished from family land and considered moveable property and may be either individually or jointly owned. The use of family land is not governed by the values of capitalist monoculture but by a complex of economic and symbolic values forged among the peasantry and protopeasantry. Family land is the spatial dimension of the family line, reflecting its continuity and identity, and provides inalienable freehold rights, housesites, a spot for a kitchen garden, a place for absentees to return to in time of need, and a family burial ground (cf. Besson 1984a: 58–60, 1987b:103–04).

The explanation of the evolution and persistence of these widespread kin-based customary tenures has been the focus of much scholarly attention and controversy (cf. Besson 1979:109–10, 1984a, 1987a, 1987b). For example, Edith Clarke (1953, 1966:40) attributes Jamaican family land to African cultural survivals; namely, the principles of joint inheritance, equal rights of all the family, and the inalienability of land. More specifically, she argues that family land is derived from the Ashanti kinship system (ibid., 48, 71 n26, n27). Greenfield (1960) accounts for Barbadian family land with reference to the English cultural heritage; namely, the upper-class settlement and seed-to-seed inheritance. Family land in St. Lucia, Dominica, Haiti, and Martinique is attributed to the French Napoleonic code of equal inheritance (Finkel 1971:229; Horowitz 1967:29–30; Mathurin 1967:4; Mintz 1974a:274; Momsen 1972: 103; O'Loughlin 1968:102). Despres (1970:280) and R. T. Smith (1971: 245, 254–55) argue that in Guyana children's property is derived from the Roman-Dutch property code of joint rights in undivided land, while M. G. Smith (1960:42, 1965a:261) interprets family land in Carriacou as a functional adaptation to the island's social structure.

However, as I have shown elsewhere, these explanations are both inconsistent and inadequate (Besson 1984a:60–63, 1987a:17–18). They focus on family land in specific territories only, whereas the institution exists on a pan-Caribbean (non-Hispanic) scale. The explanations conflict, providing no coherent explanation at a regional level, and, with the exception of M. G. Smith's account of Carriacou, family land is seen as simply an inert cultural survival from Africa or Europe—a static approach that underplays the Caribbean context in which the institution evolved and persists. Nor does Clarke's Africanist thesis, the most plausible of the cultural survival explanations, stand up to closer scrutiny; for the Ashanti transmit land rights matrilineally, while Caribbean family land is based on a cognatic descent system.

These kin-based customary tenures may be better understood by viewing them at a regional level and within the context of Caribbean agrarian relations and the evolution of Afro-Caribbean free communities (cf. Besson 1979, 1984a, 1987a). As seen above, the postslavery peasantries purchased land whenever possible in the flight from the estates, in a context where plantations continued to engross the region's land, and planters obstructed peasant development (cf. Cross 1979:121; Marshall 1972:31). Within this context, the ex-slaves forged customary institutions of family land, rooted in protopeasant customary systems of inheritance, to transmit freehold rights to land. For in the postemancipation Caribbean, "freehold land was not only of obvious economic importance to those ex-slaves who managed to obtain it, giving some independence from the plantations and a bargaining position for higher wages when working on them, but it also had considerable symbolic significance to a people who had not only once been landless, but property themselves. For such land symbolized their freedom, and provided property rights, prestige, and personhood" (Besson 1987a:18; cf. Besson 1984a, 1984b).

Moreover, in the context of postemancipation land scarcity, the principle of unrestricted cognatic descent at the heart of family land maximized the transmission of these freehold land rights, in contrast to the colonial system of primogeniture in the British West Indies (cf. Craton 1987:96). Unrestricted cognatic descent, whereby all descendants in perpetuity were ensured freehold land rights regardless of sex, birth order, and legitimacy, was more effective for this purpose than African unilineal descent systems. In addition, unrestricted descent ensured that nonresidence on family land would not result in forfeiture of land rights, as in a restricted cognatic descent system (cf. Besson 1979, 1987a). The unrestricted system was also the basis for generating ever increasing and overlapping family lines, rooted in family land, which is the central mechanism for perpetuating the identity of the postemancipation peasant communities (Besson 1984a:18; cf. R. T. Smith 1964:316; Wilson 1973:57). Within these free communities, institutions of family land, therefore, continued the maximization of land rights and family lines forged in the protopeasant customary systems of inheritance and descent. These family inheritance and descent systems were the basis of community on the slave plantations in the face of the masters' legal denial of kinship, identity, and land to the slaves (cf. Besson 1989a; Mintz 1974a:155, 1974b:60).

Therefore, rather than a mosaic of inert survivals from colonial or ancestral cultures, family land emerged as a dynamic Caribbean cultural creation forged by the peasantries themselves in resistant response to the plantation system (Besson 1979, 1984a, 1987a). The transformation of the plantation system through corporate capitalism in the twentieth century exacerbated plantation control in many areas of the region (Beckford 1972, 1975), while postwar development of the mining and tourist industries reinforced foreign monopoly of Caribbean land (Girvan 1975; Henshall 1976:38). Within these contemporary contexts, family land continues its traditional role as a mode of resistant response by the peasantries in the face of inequitable agrarian relations (Besson 1979, 1984a, 1984b, 1987a, 1987b, 1988; cf. McKay 1987).

Since this reinterpretation of family land as a Caribbean institution at the heart of postemancipation peasant communities was first put forward (Besson 1979, 1984a), a reanalysis of the St. Lucian case along similar lines has been advanced by Acosta and Casimir (1985:38–41).[5] The theory of family land as a Caribbean institution has, however, also been challenged on the basis of its institutional approach, its regional perspective, and its apparent dismissal of the African heritage (Carnegie 1987). Carnegie's critique, based on a restudy of the Jamaican free village of Sturge Town (cf. Mintz 1974a:157–79), focuses especially on the institutional approach. He argues that this leads me, along with other writers such as Clarke (1966) and M. G. Smith (1965a), to resort to a rigid demarcation between Caribbean legal and nonlegal tenurial systems. Carnegie argues that the evidence from the regional literature and from Sturge Town points rather to an intersystem or continuum model of Caribbean folk tenure. He cites evidence of a testamentary element, named heirs, specific portions of land, a distinction between legitimate and illegitimate children, subdivision, and a land market, both in Sturge Town and on a regional scale, to support his case. He also, however, identifies instances of family land in Sturge Town and elsewhere in the region. Carnegie further argues that such variation in land tenure invalidates the view of family land as a regional institution. On this basis, he also challenges my dismissal of the African heritage explanation of family land, which he attributes to the institutional regional perspective.

I have answered these arguments in detail elsewhere (Besson 1987b), reasserting the reinterpretation of family land as a Caribbean institution, but showing how this leaves room for both the possibility of African influences on the institution and an intersystem analysis of Caribbean folk tenure. Indeed, these points were made previously (Besson 1974:2:1–113, 1979:110, 1984a:76 n7, n9, cf. 1988). For example, while family land, with its cognatic descent system, cannot be seen as a survival of the Ashanti kinship system, African influences on the institution may include modes of burial and cultural ideas linking kin groups to land (Besson 1974:2:98–99, 1979:110, 1984a:75, 1987b:108; cf. Carnegie 1987; Mintz and Price 1976:39). However, Euro-Caribbean planter burials may also have influenced Afro-Caribbean family burial grounds (Besson 1984b:18, 1987b:108). Moreover, Carnegie's speculation that the inalienability of family land "may have more to do with looking backwards in time towards ancestors (and an African tradition) than forwards to future heirs who would thus be assured of access to freehold land" (Carnegie 1987:96) is questionable, since this would not account for the creation of family land (Besson 1987b:108). The institution of family land may have merged the African theme of landholding kin groups with European legal freehold through the purchase of land. But it has transformed both the African emphasis on unilineal kin groups and European freehold to create new Caribbean customary freeholds with cognatic descent systems for maximizing family lines and freehold rights to land (cf. Besson 1984a:59).[6]

The interpretation of family land as a Caribbean institution also leaves room for an intersystem interpretation of Caribbean folk tenure, as the analysis of land tenure in the Jamaican free village of Martha Brae has shown (Besson 1974, 1984a, 1984b, 1987a, 1987b, 1988). Here, family land emerged as the central theme of village life, at the vanguard of British West Indian free communities, in resistant response to the plantation system. However, the institution of family land also interacts with the legal system, and at least four variants on this theme can be identified. In the first variant, *imposed legal elements,* elements of the national legal code are imposed on family land. *Crab antics* (cf. Besson 1987a; Wilson 1973), the second variant, occur when self-interested individuals draw on the legal system to challenge the customary principles of family land. Third, *selective legal reinforcement* takes place when individuals draw on the legal system to reinforce and adjust the institution of family land. Fourth, *indirect legal reinforcement* occurs, wherein aspects of the legal system indirectly reinforce the customary institution of family land. These variants are explored in detail elsewhere in the analysis of land tenure in Martha Brae (Besson 1974:2:1–113, 1984a: 76 n7, n9, 1987a:38, n3, 1987b; 1988). Rubenstein (1987a) also recently advanced a similar analysis for Leeward Village in St. Vincent, identifying three tenurial systems: an islandwide legal system, a customary folk system including family land, and the modification of both systems through the pragmatic strategies of personalism. The continuum model of Caribbean folk tenure that Carnegie advocates must therefore clearly recognize the Creole institution of family land at one end of the continuum and colonially derived legal systems at the other, with the dynamic intersystem interplay occurring between these two extremes (Besson 1987b).

This interplay between legal and customary tenures in British West Indian free communities, such as Leeward Village, Sturge Town, and Martha Brae, continues the cultural traditions of the protopeasants, the maroons, and the postemancipation peasantries. For, as seen above, these all established autonomous communities in the face of the plantation system through a combination of legal and customary rights to land. This dynamic tenurial tradition is most clearly seen in the institution of family land itself, which draws on customary principles spawned among the protopeasantry on the back of the plantation system to totally transform the principles of legal freehold.

Family land is not, however, the only form of customary tenure to provide the basis of British West Indian free communities. The next section elaborates this theme by considering the interrelationship between family land and other customary tenures in the evolution of these communities.

Family Land and Other Customary Tenures

The interrelationship between family land and other customary tenures in British West Indian free communities is also, in part, a disputed one, as the case of Barbuda shows. In Barbuda, common tenure of inalienable bush lands coexists with the parceling of lands in Codrington, the island's single village. While house and yard are individually owned and can be alienated through bequest or sale, even in the absence of legal title deeds, they are customarily transmitted on the basis of either cognatic descent or household participation (Berleant-Schiller 1977, 1987). The former principle parallels the central feature of family land (Besson 1979, 1987a), while the latter is a variant on the theme of personalism that also typifies Caribbean inheritance (Besson 1974, 1987b, 1988; Carnegie 1987; Rubenstein 1987a). By contrast, with the exception of land immediately surrounding fruit trees, which may be individually owned and bequeathed (Berleant-Schiller 1987:117–18), "bush lands may not be individually owned and may not be bequeathed. All people of socially recognized Barbudan birth, parentage, or ancestry may exercise their use rights, even if they have been absent from Barbuda for a long time" (ibid., 117; cf. Berleant-Schiller 1977).

I have suggested in an earlier essay that Barbudan common tenure may be an extreme variant on the theme of Caribbean family land (Besson 1984a:60, 78 n16), a parallel first drawn to my attention by C. G. Clarke (personal communication, 1982) on the basis of his work on Barbuda (Lowenthal and Clarke 1977, 1979, 1980). Comitas (Berleant-Schiller 1987:119) also suggests that Barbudan commonage may be a variant on the theme of family land. Berleant-Schiller, however, rejects this interpretation and argues that, despite several similarities between Barbudan common tenure and Caribbean family land, the differences outweigh the similarities and are "qualitative and profound" (ibid., 122). This divergence, she concludes, is due to Barbuda's peculiar history, ecology, proprietorship, and slave community. From 1680 to 1870 the island was a private fief of the Codrington family, who owned Antiguan sugar plantations and lived in England, and who were followed by a string of other lessees. With its marginal ecology, Barbuda never had plantations, and its slaves were protopeasants who established customary tenures in the context of benign neglect and isolation. Their postemancipation constraints also differed from those in the Caribbean sugar islands: Barbuda's ex-slaves did not have to find land but only to retain it in the face of successive external attempts to develop commercial agriculture (ibid.; cf. Besson and Momsen 1987:4).

However, a reconsideration of the Barbudan case, along with new evidence from the Bahamas and Nevis (Craton 1987; Momsen 1987), suggests an extension of the hypothesis linking Barbudan common tenure and Caribbean family land and their role in British West Indian free communities (cf. Besson 1987a:38–40 n5). The above three cases all have a mix of customary tenures or attitudes to land involving features of both family land and commonage, and in each case this has been effective in resisting external attempts to impose commercial agriculture (Berleant-Schiller 1978, 1987; Craton 1987:94; Momsen 1987:58–59). This suggests that, in a regional context, family land and commonage are variants on a theme. Both are customary tenures created in resistance to Caribbean agrarian relations and their legal codes. This resistant response has occurred at the margins of plantation society – in Barbuda and the Bahamas – as well as at its core (cf. Besson 1987a:38–39 n5; Besson and Momsen 1987:3–5). From this perspective, Barbuda's unusual proprietorship, slave community, and history may be seen as variations on the regional theme of colonial domination and resistance, with especially strong parallels in the Bahamian case (cf. Lowenthal and Clarke 1977; Craton 1978b).

For, despite the absence of plantations due to its marginal ecology, Barbuda was not totally divorced from the regional plantation scene. The Codringtons, Barbuda's proprietors from 1680–1870, had extensive plantation holdings in Barbados and Antigua and "used Barbuda as an annex to their [Antiguan] sugar estates" (Lowenthal and Clarke 1977:510, 1979:143). Although Christopher Bethel Codrington's hopes that Barbuda might become a nursery for Negroes for his Antiguan plantations did not materialise, there were some labour transfers from Barbuda to Antigua (Lowenthal and Clarke 1977). The Barbudan slaves were property like other slaves, and were aware of the Antiguan threat for "they refused to be sent away" and "died when removed by force to Codrington estates in Antigua" (Berleant-Schiller 1987:123; cf. Craton 1987). Their proto-peasant slave community was thus a variation on a regional theme (cf. Lowenthal and Clarke 1979:145), for proto-peasantries emerged throughout the Caribbean in adaptive resistance to the slave regime (Mintz 1974a:151–52; Olwig 1981a, 1981b). Even in their unusual isolation, the Barbudan proto-peasants were paralleled by those of [the Bahamian island of] Exuma (Lowenthal and Clarke 1977; Craton 1978b, 1987) and by maroon communities (Price 1973; Mintz 1974a:152–54). Indeed, the central theme of Barbudan history emerges as resistance to attempted domination (see Lowenthal and Clarke 1977; Berleant-Schiller 1978). (Besson 1987a:39, n5)

As shown in detail elsewhere in elaboration of this theme, within these contexts the differences of origin, form and function between the Barbudan commons and Caribbean family land appear less qualitative and profound (ibid., 39–40 n5). Moreover, as noted previously, the Barbudan commons coexist with the customary transmission of village yards through cognatic descent, the central feature of Caribbean family land.

Although Berleant-Schiller rejects the interpretation of Barbudan commonage as a variant on the theme of family land, she suggests that "true family land" may emerge in Barbuda "with the advent of deeded property" resulting from the encroachment of Eurocentric tourist development from Antigua and related ideas of legal freehold (1987:130); such encroachment has occurred since independence in 1981, which has tied Barbuda to Antigua. Should this dynamic transformation from commonage to family land occur, Barbudan tenures would be even more clearly seen to be a variant on Caribbean regional themes (cf. Besson 1989a:348).

The parallel between customary tenures in Barbuda and the Bahamas is especially close, for, particularly in the isolated, absentee-owned, ecologically marginal Bahamian Out Islands such as Great Exuma, generational land and common tenure have developed side by side as the basis of postemancipation free communities.[7] This continues the traditions of an isolated protopeasantry that established customary tenures as the basis of autonomous communities in a situation of benign neglect. In the Bahamas, the principles of generational land and commonage are also merged, for rights to the 5,000 acres of Exumian commonage are based on unrestricted cognatic descent (among over 4,000 kin), the central feature of generational land (Craton 1987; cf. Besson 1987a:40 n5; Besson and Momsen 1987:4–5). Furthermore, in both the Bahamas and Barbuda, customary tenures were reinforced by firm beliefs that the land was given to the islanders by their former masters (Berleant-Schiller 1987:117; Craton 1987:93, 96, 104; cf. Marshall 1979:246). In addition, both Craton (1987:108) and Berleant-Schiller (1987:130) point to the potential role of family land as a central feature of nationhood in the Bahamas and Barbuda.

The case of Nevis also provides evidence of a dynamic interplay between the principles of family land and commonage and a further variation on this theme (cf. Besson and Momsen 1987:3; Momsen 1987). In postemancipation Nevis, as seen above, there was little chance for a peasantry or free villages to develop, and the stranglehold of the plantation system continued until the 1930s. However, following emancipation, a sharecropping estate-based peasantry emerged with similarities to the protopeasantry (Momsen 1987:58). In the 1930s, following the decline of plantation agriculture, plantations were subdivided and sold and a peasantry developed independently of the estates. A land settlement scheme was also introduced, and subsequently, sharecropped estates were transformed into land settlements, mostly based on annual rental (ibid., 59).

Despite the absence of freehold tenure and long leases, the Nevisian peasantry has since transformed this externally imposed solution of land settlement into a customary system, rooted in the protopeasant past (ibid., 59, 63–66). For many farmers "could trace their family's presence on a particular estate back through the period of sharecropping to slave days" (ibid., 63); and "even without land ownership settlers have often attempted to ensure that their heirs, resident or absentee, are allowed to

take over occupance of the settlement plot" (ibid., 65). Momsen therefore concludes that the Nevisian peasantry "has recreated its traditional
attitudes to land within the formal structure of the land settlement"
(ibid., 65). The symbolic role of settlement land in providing a basis
for kinship continuity, security, and independence, and its frequent use
as a form of common land for grazing livestock, parallels the roles of
both family land and commonage elsewhere in the region (Besson and
Momsen 1987:3; Momsen 1987:65–66). The transformation of the legally imposed land settlement into a customary tenurial system also parallels the creation of customary tenures within the slave plantations by
Caribbean protopeasants and the creation of family land from legal freehold by the postemancipation peasantries as the basis of autonomous
communities (Besson 1984a, 1987a, 1989a; Mintz 1974a:187, 207, 1979:
241; Olwig 1985:41–49).

Customary Tenures as a
Model for Freedom and Community

This essay has shown that customary tenures have been the central
basis of autonomy, community, and cultural resistance among British
West Indian slaves and their descendants for over 150 years of freedom.
This is especially so with the widespread kin-based tenures, rooted in
the seedbed of protopeasant slave resistance and forged in free communities through the purchase of land. The resilience of these Creole
institutions can be gauged by their long history and by their themes of
continuity and change. Their incipient form among the protopeasantry
provided a basis for autonomy and community within the parameters
of the plantation system (cf. Hall 1978; Karasch 1979), and following
emancipation, the creation of family land challenged the very foundations of this system by transforming the institution of legal freehold.
Family land and other customary tenures rooted in the protopeasant
past have since provided a basis of independence from the plantation
system throughout the years of freedom. In addition to this traditional
role, customary tenures are now playing new roles in Commonwealth
Caribbean free communities, providing a basis for competing in the
foreign-dominated tourist industry and for resisting Eurocentric strategies of development, and serving as a vehicle for Caribbean nationhood
and for maintaining social networks between Caribbean communities
and migrants overseas (Besson and Momsen 1987). The principles of
family land have also transformed the externally imposed institution

of land settlement (Momsen 1987) and are now transforming colonially derived Caribbean legal codes (Besson 1984a:76 n9; Carnegie 1987:86, 97 n3).

The evolution of these Caribbean customary tenures provides a powerful model for understanding other aspects of rural life that have evolved in British West Indian free communities and whose interpretation is a source of much controversy. The relationship of the cultures of these communities to those of Caribbean elites has been explored through a plethora of perspectives: functionalism and pluralism (e.g., Rodman 1971; M. G. Smith 1965a; R. T. Smith 1956); Weberian and neo-Marxist frameworks (Cross 1979; Stone 1973); dependency theory (Beckford 1972); and reputation and respectability (Wilson 1973). The analysis of Caribbean customary tenures as a mode of resistant response to Caribbean agrarian relations suggests, instead, that the cultures of British West Indian free communities are rooted in slave resistance and have evolved through a dynamic process of Caribbean culture building in resistant response to imposed colonial cultures and the plantation system (cf. Mintz 1970, 1971b, 1974a:132–33; Mintz and Price 1976; Schuler 1979).

This theme of Caribbean cultural resistance as the basis of community is illustrated by the Jamican free village of Martha Brae, where, at the heart of British West Indian plantation society, ex-slaves transformed a colonial planter town into a Caribbean peasant village. This village persists today, maintained in the face of the continuing plantation system through the creative process of Caribbean culture building (Besson 1974, 1979, 1984a, 1984b, 1987b, 1988; cf. Mintz 1970, 1974a: 131–250). The themes of family land and family lines form the central threads of Martha Brae's new Afro-Caribbean history (cf. Mintz 1971b: 331). At the core of the village population are the "old families," unrestricted cognatic descent lines of the ex-slave founders of the village. These old families hold family land created by the ex-slave ancestors as a foothold for their descendants in the face of the plantation system, a theme that is explicit in the villagers' oral history. Within the context of persisting land scarcity, some younger members of the old families and immigrants to the village create new family land wherever possible from small plots of purchased land. Other themes, also rooted in the protopeasant and postemancipation past, elaborate the process of culture building. These include language and oral history, house and yard, provision ground and peasant market, a range of tenures for yard and ground, food crops and agricultural techniques, cuisine and architecture, occupational multiplicity and migration, kinship and marriage systems, church and cult, and mortuary ritual and mutual aid (see Besson 1987b; cf. Mintz 1974a:131–250).[8] These themes of cultural resistance are also reflected in other free villages in Trelawny parish, Jamaica (Granville, Refuge, Kettering, and Alps), established and maintained in the face of the plantation system through 150 years of freedom (cf. Besson 1984b).

A Concluding Note: The Definitional Controversy

The case of Martha Brae also throws light on the definitional controversy regarding the inhabitants of British West Indian free communities. For example, while Mintz (1974a:131–250) includes Jamaican villages in his analysis of Caribbean reconstituted peasantries, Comitas (1973:162) concludes that "no viable peasant subculture exists in Jamaica" due to the widespread phenomenon of occupational multiplicity (cf. Fraser 1981; Frucht 1967; Handler 1965, 1966). That the concept of occupational multiplicity is in part derived from fieldwork in Trelawny (Comitas 1962, 1973), at the heart of the Caribbean plantation-peasant interface, underlines the significance in this controversy of the case of Martha Brae.

In Martha Brae—situated only nine miles from Duncans, one of the communities in Comitas's study—while occupational multiplicity exists, it is an aspect of the peasant economy and of the internal differentiation of the peasant community (Besson 1974:1:195–209, 1984a:68, 1987b, 1988; cf. Berleant-Schiller 1977; Mintz 1973; Olwig 1985). This is also the case in other Trelawny villages, including Kettering, which is generally regarded as a part of Duncans town (see Besson 1984b). In the free villages of Trelawny, the concept of occupational multiplicity elucidates both the struggle and creativity of maintaining the peasant economies and the internal differentiation of the peasant communities. However, a historical perspective on these villages reinforces the validity of the concept of reconstituted peasantries for these free communities, for they were established at the vanguard of the British West Indian ex-slaves' flight from the estates in their continuing quest for land of their own (Besson 1984a, 1984b; cf. Farley 1964). That they persist today in a context where, after 150 years of freedom, plantations still engross Trelawny's fertile land demonstrates the validity of the thesis that Caribbean peasantries represent resistance to the plantation system (Mintz 1974a:132–33; cf. Besson 1984b). When the central theme of this cultural resistance is seen to be the evolution of customary tenures reinforcing rights to land (Besson 1987b), the validity of the concept of peasantry is further underlined (cf. Mintz 1974a:132, 155).[9] This is especially so, since the oral history of the Trelawny villagers themselves is based on the interrelated themes of freedom, community, and land (Besson 1984b, 1987b).

NOTES

I thank Rosemary Brana-Shute, Pieter Emmer, and Sidney W. Mintz for their comments, as discussants for the Peasant and Proletarian panel, on an early draft of this chapter presented at the conference, on "The Meaning of Freedom," University of Pittsburgh, August 1988, and Seymour Drescher and Frank McGlynn for their editorial comments. The fieldwork on the Jamaican free village of Martha Brae referred to in this chapter was conducted during the period 1968–1986 and funded in part by the Carnegie Trust and the University of Aberdeen travel fund. The comparative study of the Trelawny free villages was undertaken in 1983 and funded by the Social Science Research Council. My thanks to these bodies for their financial assistance.

1. Mintz (1979:240) suggests that his comparison between the non-Hispanic and Hispanic postslavery peasantries is constrained by lack of data on the Hispanic cases. However, Mintz's data seem adequate to support his earlier contrast on the patterns of peasant development in these two variants of the region (e.g., Mintz 1959). These contrasting patterns of development also clarify the variations in the house and yard complex between Haiti and Jamaica on the one hand, and Puerto Rico on the other (Mintz 1974a:225–50).

2. Birmingham and Kettering in England were the home towns of abolitionists Joseph Sturge and William Knibb, respectively; the villages of Wilberforce, Granville, and Buxton were named after abolitionists William Wilberforce, Granville Sharpe, and T. F. Buxton; while Refuge and Unity highlight the emancipation theme from the perspective of the former slaves.

3. On family land in contemporary Jamaican rural communities see Besson 1984a, 1984b, 1987b, 1988; Carnegie 1987; Clarke 1953, 1966; Comitas 1962; Craton 1978a:355–66; Davenport 1961; D. Edwards 1961:95–97; McKay 1987; M. G. Smith 1965a:162–75. For reports on similar institutions elsewhere in the Commonwealth Caribbean see Despres 1970:280, R. T. Smith 1971 on Guyana; Rodman 1971:135–44 on Trinidad; O'Loughlin 1968:102 on Dominica; Mathurin 1967, Momsen 1972 on St. Lucia; Rubenstein 1975, 1987a on St. Vincent; Brierley 1974:90–91, M. G. Smith 1965b:236–45 on Grenada; M. G. Smith 1965a:221–61 on Carricou; Philpott 1973: 14–18 on Montserrat; Greenfield 1960 on Barbados; and Craton 1987, Otterbein 1964 on the Bahamas. On family land in Providencia and among the Black Caribs see Wilson 1973:53–57 and Solien 1959 respectively. For parallel institutions in other parts of the non-Hispanic Caribbean see Larose 1975 on Haiti; Horowitz 1967:29–30, 45–50 on Martinique; Olwig 1985 on St. John; Henriquez 1969 on Curaçao; and Brana-Shute 1979:64 on Surinam.

4. "Heirs' land" and "family land" does, however, exist in the Sea Islands (Block-son 1987) and north central Florida (Dougherty 1978:12, 43–58), respectively, among descendants of American plantation slaves. This reinforces the hypothesis (Besson 1984a) that family land represents a mode of resistant response by ex-slaves and their descendants to the plantation system.

5. While advancing a reinterpretation along these lines, Acosta and Casimir (1985:39) at one point argue that the St. Lucian case is unique. This is, however, later qualified when they draw a parallel between family land in St. Lucia, Haiti, and Jamaica (ibid., 40 n17).

6. Craton (1987:99) has also argued for the African genesis of Bahamian gen-erational land, especially in the isolated Out Islands, where this form of tenure co-exists with commonage. However, his thesis that the marginal and isolated condi-tions of the Out Islands reinforced an African tenurial tradition is inconsistent with the pan-Caribbean distribution of family land (Besson 1984a, 1987a). This includes Jamaica, which was the center of British West Indian plantation slave society, as Craton's own work has shown (Craton 1978a:355–66; cf. Besson 1984a:69–70).

For a critique of Otterbein's (1964) argument, used by Craton (1987:100) in sup-port of his Africanist thesis, that the unrestricted descent system of the Out Island of Andros is due to the easy availability of land, see Besson (1979). As noted there, it seems more likely that the easy availability of land in Andros has instead "resulted in a situation where the institution of family land itself, and the associated nonunilineal descent group, are insignificant, as Otterbein's later study (1966:129) itself indicates" (Besson 1979:115–16 n27). Indeed, as Craton's study also shows, in the Out Islands, Bahamian generational land coexists with commonage, and Andros was scarcely touched by the plantation system (Craton 1987:100). In addition, in contrast to Craton, Otterbein (1964:34) explicitly indicates that he finds no evidence of an Af-rican influence on family land in Andros. The case of Bahamian family land is there-fore more consistently explained as an attenuated variation on the Caribbean re-gional theme (Besson 1984a).

7. The occurrence of commonage in both Barbuda and the Bahamas, at the margins of plantation society, suggests that this variant may emerge where there is less plantation (or other foreign) engrossment of land in contrast to other areas of the region typified by family land. This hypothesis supports the reinterpretation of Otterbein's thesis on the Bahamian case put forward in note 6 above and is con-sistent with Berleant-Schiller's (1987:130) suggestion that the Barbudan commons may evolve into family land.

8. My fuller account of Martha Brae's historical anthropology, entitled *Martha Brae's Two Histories: Culture-Building in a Caribbean Society,* is in preparation.

9. Rather than challenging the existence of a peasantry, as Comitas (1973:162) argues, the concept of occupational multiplicity is consistent with the definition of peasantry (cf. Besson 1984a:75–76 n3, 1987b:127 n11). Dalton (1967:265–67, 1971) defines *peasant* as a broad middle category between the two extremes of tribal and post-peasant modern farmer, with socioeconomic organization typified by subsis-tence production combined with production for sale; incomplete land and labor markets (the former allowing for the existence of customary tenures, the latter for the sale of labor to augment traditional production—thus generating occupational multiplicity); the virtual absence of machine technology; and a significant retention

Freedom and Community 213

of traditional social organization and culture. Dalton's definition encompasses various subtypes, including the "hybrid / composite peasantries" of contemporary Latin America and the Caribbean. Within this subtype, the "reconstituted peasantries" of the Caribbean (Mintz 1974a:132) may be further distinguished. Mintz highlights the significance of land for both peasantries in general and Caribbean reconstituted peasantries.

REFERENCES

Acosta, Yvonne, and Jean Casimir. 1985. Social Origins of the Counter-Plantation System in St. Lucia. In *Rural Development in the Caribbean,* edited by P. I. Gomes, 34–59. London: Hurst.

Beckford, George L. 1972. *Persistent Poverty: Underdevelopment in Plantation Economies of the Third World.* London: Oxford University Press.

———. 1975. Caribbean Rural Economy. In *Caribbean Economy: Dependence and Backwardness,* edited by George L. Beckford, 77–91. Kingston: Institute of Social and Economic Research, University of the West Indies.

Berleant-Schiller, Riva. 1977. Production and Division of Labor in a West Indian Peasant Community. *American Ethnologist* 4:253–72.

———. 1978. The Failure of Agricultural Development in Post-Emancipation Barbuda: A Study of Social and Economic Continuity in a West Indian Community. *Boletin de Estudios Latinoamericanos y del Caribe* 25:21–36.

———. 1987. Ecology and Politics in Barbudan Land Tenure. In *Land and Development in the Caribbean,* edited by Jean Besson and Janet Momsen, 116–31. London: Macmillan.

Besson, Jean. 1974. Land Tenure and Kinship in a Jamaican Village. 2 vols. Ph.D. diss., University of Edinburgh.

———. 1979. Symbolic Aspects of Land in the Caribbean: The Tenure and Transmission of Land Rights among Caribbean Peasantries. In *Peasants, Plantations and Rural Communities in the Caribbean,* edited by Malcolm Cross and Arnaud Marks, 86–116. Guildford: University of Surrey; Leiden: Royal Institute of Linguistics and Anthropology.

———. 1981. Review of Monica Schuler, *"Alas, Alas, Kongo": A Social History of Indentured Immigration into Jamaica, 1841–1865, Man* n.s. 16:505–06.

———. 1984a. Family Land and Caribbean Society: Toward an Ethnography of Afro-Caribbean Peasantries. In *Perspectives on Caribbean Regional Identity,* edited by Elizabeth M. Thomas-Hope, 57–83. Liverpool: Liverpool University Press.

———. 1984b. Land Tenure in the Free Villages of Trelawny, Jamaica: A Case Study in the Caribbean Peasant Response to Emancipation. *Slavery & Abolition* 5:3–23.

———. 1987a. A Paradox in Caribbean Attitudes to Land. In *Land and Development in the Caribbean,* edited by Jean Besson and Janet Momsen, 13–45. London: Macmillan.

———. 1987b. Family Land as a Model for Martha Brae's New History: Culture-Building in an Afro-Caribbean Village. In *Afro-Caribbean Villages in Historical*

Perspective, edited by Charles V. Carnegie, 100–32. Kingston: African-Caribbean Institute of Jamaica.

———. 1988. Agrarian Relations and Perceptions of Land in a Jamaican Peasant Village. In *Small Farming and Peasant Resources in the Caribbean*, edited by John S. Brierley and Hymie Rubenstein, 39–61. Winnipeg: University of Manitoba.

———. 1989a. Review of Karen Fog Olwig, *Cultural Adaptation and Resistance on St John: Three Centuries of Afro-Caribbean Life, Plantation Society in the Americas* 2:345–48.

———. 1989b. Introduction. In *Caribbean Reflections: The Life and Times of a Trinidad Scholar, 1901–1986*, edited by Jean Besson, 13–30. London: Karia Press.

Besson, Jean, and Janet Momsen (Henshall). 1987. Introduction. In *Land and Development in the Caribbean*, edited by Jean Besson and Janet Momsen, 1–9. London: Macmillan.

Blockson, Charles L. 1987. Sea Change in the Sea Islands: "Nowhere to Lay Down Weary Head." *National Geographic* 172:735–63.

Bolland, O. Nigel. 1981. Systems of Domination after Slavery: The Control of Land and Labor in the British West Indies after 1838. *Comparative Studies in Society & History* 23:591–619.

Brana-Shute, Gary. 1979. *On the Corner: Male Social Life in a Paramaribo Creole Neighbourhood*. Assen: Van Gorcum.

Brereton, Bridget. 1981. *A History of Modern Trinidad 1783–1962*. London: Heinemann.

Brierley, John S. 1974. *Small Farming in Grenada, West Indies*. Winnipeg: University of Manitoba.

Brizan, George I. 1984. *Grenada: Island of Conflict*. London: Zed Books.

Carnegie, Charles V. 1987. Is Family Land an Institution? In *Afro-Caribbean Villages in Historical Perspective*, edited by Charles V. Carnegie, 83–99. Kingston: African-Caribbean Institute of Jamaica.

Chace, Russel E., Jr. 1984. The Emergence and Development of an Estate-Based Peasantry in Dominica. Paper presented at the Eighth Annual Conference of the Society for Caribbean Studies, Hoddesdon, Hertfordshire, May 1984.

Clarke, Edith. 1953. Land Tenure and the Family in Four Communities in Jamaica. *Social and Economic Studies* 1:81–118.

———. 1966. *My Mother Who Fathered Me: A Study of the Family in Three Selected Communities in Jamaica* 2d ed. London: Allen and Unwin.

Comitas, Lambros. 1962. Fishermen and Cooperation in Rural Jamaica. Ph.D. diss. Columbia University.

———. 1973. Occupational Multiplicity in Rural Jamaica. In *Work and Family Life: West Indian Perspectives*, edited by Lambros Comitas and David Lowenthal, 157–73. Garden City: Anchor Books.

Craton, Michael. 1978a. *Searching for the Invisible Man: Slaves and Plantation Life in Jamaica*. Cambridge, Mass.: Harvard University Press.

———. 1978b. Hobbesian or Panglossian? The Two Extremes of Slave Conditions in the British Caribbean, 1783 to 1834. *William & Mary Quarterly*, 3d ser. 35:324–56.

————. 1985. Emancipation from Below? The Role of the British West Indian Slaves in the Emancipation Movement, 1816–34. In *Out of Slavery: Abolition and After,* edited by Jack Hayward, 110–31. London: Frank Cass.

————. 1987. White Law and Black Custom: The Evolution of Bahamian Land Tenures. In *Land and Development in the Caribbean,* edited by Jean Besson and Janet Momsen, 88–114. London: Macmillan.

Cross, Malcolm. 1979. *Urbanization and Urban Growth in the Caribbean: An Essay on Social Change in Dependent Societies.* Cambridge: Cambridge University Press.

Dalton, George. 1967. Primitive Money. In *Tribal and Peasant Economies: Readings in Economic Anthropology,* edited by George Dalton, 254–81. Garden City: Natural History Press.

————. 1971. Peasantries in Anthropology and History. In *Economic Anthropology and Development,* edited by George Dalton, 217–66. New York: Basic Books.

Davenport, William. 1961. The Family System of Jamaica. *Social and Economic Studies* 10:420–54.

Despres, Leo A. 1970. Differential Adaptations and Micro-Cultural Evolution in Guyana. In *Afro-American Anthropology,* edited by Norman E. Whitten and John F. Szwed, 263–87. New York: Free Press.

Dougherty, Molly C. 1978. *Becoming a Woman in Rural Black Culture.* New York: Holt, Rinehart and Winston.

Edwards, Bryan. 1793. *The History, Civil and Commercial, of the British Colonies in the West Indies,* 2 vols. London: John Stockdale.

Edwards, David. 1961. *An Economic Study of Small Farming in Jamaica.* Kingston: Institute of Social and Economic Research, University of the West Indies.

Farley, Rawle. 1954. The Rise of the Peasantry in British Guiana. *Social and Economic Studies* 2:76–103.

————. 1964. The Rise of Village Settlements in British Guiana. *Caribbean Quarterly* 10:52–61.

Finkel, Herman J. 1971. Patterns of Land Tenure in the Leeward and Windward Islands and Their Relevance to Problems of Agricultural Development in the West Indies. In *Peoples and Cultures of the Caribbean,* edited by Michael M. Horowitz, 291–304. Garden City: Natural History Press.

Fraser, Peter. 1981. The Fictive Peasantry: Caribbean Rural Groups in the Nineteenth Century. In *Contemporary Caribbean: A Sociological Reader,* edited by Susan Craig, 1:319–47. Trinidad: S. Craig.

Frucht, Richard. 1967. Caribbean Social Type: Neither "Peasant" nor "Proletarian." *Social and Economic Studies* 16:295–300.

Genovese, Eugene D. 1981. *From Rebellion to Revolution: Afro-American Slave Revolts in the Making of the New World.* New York: Vintage Books.

Girvan, Norman. 1975. Caribbean Mineral Economy. In *Caribbean Economy: Dependence and Backwardness,* edited by George L. Beckford, 92–129. Kingston: Institute of Social and Economic Research, University of the West Indies.

Gomes, P. I. 1985. Plantation Dominance and Rural Dependence in Dominica. In *Rural Development in the Caribbean,* edited by P. I. Gomes, 60–75. London: Hurst.

Greenfield, Sidney M. 1960. Land Tenure and Transmission in Rural Barbados. *Anthropological Quarterly* 33:165–76.

Greenwood, R., and S. Hamber. 1980. *Emancipation to Emigration*. London: Macmillan.

Hall, Douglas. 1959. *Free Jamaica 1838–1865: An Economic History*. New Haven: Yale University Press.

———. 1978. The Flight from the Estates Reconsidered: The British West Indies, 1838–42. *Journal of Caribbean History* 10-11:7–24.

Handler, Jerome. 1965. Some Aspects of Work Organization on Sugar Plantations in Barbados. *Ethnology* 4:16–38.

———. 1966. Small-Scale Sugar Cane Farming in Barbados. *Ethnology* 5:264–83.

Henriquez, E. C. 1969. Familiegronden (tera di famia) en oude fideicommissen (filocommis) op het eiland Curaçao. In *Honderd Jaar Codificatie in de Nederlandse Antillen*, edited by S. Gonda Quint and D. Brouwer En Zoon. Arnhem: Het Huis de Crabbe.

Henshall (Momsen), Janet D. 1976. Post-Emancipation Rural Settlement in the Lesser Antilles. *Proceedings of American Geographers* 78:37–40.

Heuman, Gad. 1985. Introduction. In *Out of the House of Bondage: Runaways, Resistance and Marronage in Africa and the New World*, edited by Gad Heuman, 1–7. *Slavery & Abolition* 6, Special Issue.

Horowitz, Michael M. 1967. *Morne-Paysan: Peasant Village in Martinique*. New York: Holt, Rinehart and Winston.

Karasch, Mary. 1979. Commentary on Monica Schuler, Afro-American Slave Culture. In *Roots and Branches: Current Directions in Slave Studies*, edited by Michael Craton, 138–41. Toronto: Pergamon Press.

Knox, A. J. G. 1977. Opportunities and Opposition: The Rise of Jamaica's Black Peasantry and the Nature of Planter Resistance. *Canadian Review of Sociology and Anthropology* 14:381–95.

Larose, Serge. 1975. The Haitian *Lakou*; Land, Family, and Ritual. In *Family and Kinship in Middle America and the Caribbean*, edited by Arnaud F. Marks and René A. Römer, 482–512. Curaçao: University of the Netherlands Antilles, and Leiden: Royal Institute of Linguistics and Anthropology.

Lowenthal, David, and Colin G. Clarke. 1977. Slave-Breeding in Barbuda: The Past of a Negro Myth. In *Comparative Perspectives on Slavery in New World Plantation Societies*, edited by Vera Rubin and Arthur Tuden, 510–35. New York: New York Academy of Sciences.

———. 1979. Common Lands, Common Aims: The Distinctive Barbudan Community. In *Peasants, Plantations, and Rural Communities in the Caribbean*, edited by Malcolm Cross and Arnaud Marks, 142–59.

———. 1980. Island Orphans: Barbuda and the Rest. *Journal of Commonwealth and Comparative Politics* 18:293–307.

McKay, Lesley. 1987. Tourism and Changing Attitudes to Land in Negril, Jamaica. In *Land and Development in the Caribbean*, edited by Jean Besson and Janet Momsen, 132–52. London: Macmillan.

Marshall, Woodville K. 1968. Peasant Development in the West Indies since 1838. *Social and Economic Studies* 17:252–63.

———. 1972. Aspects of the Development of the Peasantry: Peasant Movements and Agrarian Problems in the West Indies. *Caribbean Quarterly* 18:31–58.

———. 1979. Commentary on Sidney W. Mintz, "Slavery and the Rise of Peasantries." In *Roots and Branches: Current Directions in Slave Studies,* edited by Michael Craton, 243–48. Toronto: Pergamon Press.

Mathurin, D. C. E. 1967. An Unfavourable System of Land Tenure: The Case of St. Lucia. Paper presented at the Second West Indian Agricultural Economics Conference, St. Augustine, Trinidad, April 1967.

Mintz, Sidney W. 1959. Labor and Sugar in Puerto Rico and Jamaica, 1800–1850. *Comparative Studies in Society and History* 1:273–81.

———. 1960. Peasant Markets. *Scientific American* 203:112–22.

———. 1970. Creating Culture in the Americas. *Columbia University Forum* 13:4–11.

———. 1971a. The Caribbean as a Socio-Cultural Area. In *Peoples and Cultures of the Caribbean,* edited by Michael M. Horowitz, 17–46. Garden City: Natural History Press.

———. 1971b. Toward an Afro-American History. *Cahiers D'Histoire Mondiale* 13:317–31.

———. 1973. A Note on the Definition of Peasantries. *Journal of Peasant Studies* 1:91–106.

———. 1974a. *Caribbean Transformations.* Chicago: Aldine.

———. 1974b. The Caribbean Region. In *Slavery, Colonialism, and Racism,* edited by Sidney W. Mintz, 45–71. New York: Norton.

———. 1979. Slavery and the Rise of Peasantries. In *Roots and Branches: Current Directions in Slave Studies,* edited by Michael Craton, 213–42. Toronto: Pergamon Press.

———. 1985. From Plantations to Peasantries in the Caribbean. In *Caribbean Coutours,* edited by Sidney W. Mintz and Sally Price, 127–53. Baltimore: Johns Hopkins University Press.

Mintz, Sidney W., and Richard Price. 1976. *An Anthropological Approach to the Afro-American Past: A Caribbean Perspective.* Philadelphia: Institute for the Study of Human Issues.

Momsen, Janet D. (Henshall). 1972. Land Tenure as a Barrier to Agricultural Innovation: The Case of St. Lucia. *Proceedings of the Seventh West Indian Agricultural Economics Conference,* 103–9. Grand Anse, Grenada.

———. 1987. Land Settlement as an Imposed Solution. In *Land and Development in the Caribbean,* edited by Jean Besson and Janet Momsen, 46–69. London: Macmillan.

O'Loughlin, Carleen. 1968. *Economic and Political Change in the Leeward and Windward Islands.* New Haven: Yale University Press.

Olwig, Karen Fog. 1981a. Women, "Matrifocality," and Systems of Exchange: An Ethnohistorical Study of the Afro-American Family on St. John, Danish West Indies. *Ethnohistory* 28:59–78.

———. 1981b. Finding a Place for the Slave Family: Historical Anthropological Perspectives. *Folk* 23:345–58.

———. 1985. *Cultural Adaptation and Resistance on St. John: Three Centuries of Afro-Caribbean Life.* Gainesville: University of Florida Press.

———. 1987. Children's Attitudes to the Island Community: The Aftermath of Out Migration on Nevis. In *Land and Development in the Caribbean,* edited by Jean Besson and Janet Momsen, 153–70. London: Macmillan.

Otterbein, Keith F. 1964. A Comparison of the Land Tenure Systems of the Bahamas, Jamaica, and Barbados: The Implications It Has for the Study of Social Systems Shifting from Bilateral to Ambilineal Descent. *International Archives of Ethnography* 50:31–42.

——. 1966. *The Andros Islanders: A Study of Family Organization in the Bahamas.* Lawrence: University of Kansas Press.

Paget, Hugh. 1964. The Free Village System in Jamaica. *Caribbean Quarterly* 10: 38–51.

Patterson, Orlando. 1973 (1967). *The Sociology of Slavery: An Analysis of the Origins, Development, and Structure of Negro Slave Society in Jamaica.* London: Granada.

Philpott, Stuart B. 1973. *West Indian Migration: The Montserrat Case.* London: Athlone Press.

Price, Richard. 1973. *Maroon Societies: Rebel Slave Communities in the Americas.* Garden City: Anchor Books.

——. 1976. *The Guiana Maroons: A Historical and Bibliographical Introduction.* Baltimore: Johns Hopkins University Press.

Robotham, Don. 1977. Agrarian Relations in Jamaica. In *Essays on Power and Change in Jamaica,* edited by Carl Stone and Aggrey Brown, 45–57. Kingston: Jamaica Publishing House.

Rodman, Hyman. 1971. *Lower-Class Families: The Culture of Poverty in Negro Trinidad.* London: Oxford University Press.

Rubenstein, Hymie. 1975. The Utilization of Arable Land in an Eastern Caribbean Valley. *Canadian Journal of Sociology* 1:157–67.

——. 1987a. Folk and Mainstream Systems of Land Tenure and Use in St. Vincent. In *Land and Development in the Caribbean,* edited by Jean Besson and Janet Momsen, 70–87. London: Macmillan.

——. 1987b. *Coping with Poverty: Adaptive Strategies in a Caribbean Village.* Boulder: Westview Press.

Schuler, Monica. 1979. Afro-American Slave Culture. In *Roots and Branches: Current Directions in Slave Studies,* edited by Michael Craton, 121–37. Toronto: Pergamon Press.

Smith, M. G. 1960. The African Heritage in the Caribbean. In *Caribbean Studies: A Symposium,* edited by Vera Rubin, 2d ed., 34–46. Seattle: University of Washington Press.

——. 1965a. *The Plural Society in the British West Indies.* Berkeley and Los Angeles: University of California Press.

——. 1965b. *Stratification in Grenada.* Berkeley and Los Angeles: University of California Press.

Smith, Raymond T. 1956. *The Negro Family in British Guiana: Family Structure and Social Status in the Villages.* London: Routledge and Kegan Paul.

——. 1962. *British Guiana.* London: Oxford University Press.

——. 1964. Ethnic Difference and Peasant Economy in British Guiana. In *Capital, Saving and Credit in Peasant Societies,* edited by Raymond Firth and B. S. Yamey, 305–29. London: Allen and Unwin.

——. 1971. Land Tenure in Three Negro Villages in British Guiana. In *Peoples and Cultures of the Caribbean,* edited by Michael M. Horowitz, 243–66. Garden City: Natural History Press.

Solien, Nancie L. 1959. The Nonunilineal Descent Group in the Caribbean and Central America. *American Anthropologist* 61:578–83.

Stewart, John. 1823. *A View of the Past and Present State of the Island of Jamaica.* Edinburgh: Oliver and Boyd.

Stone, Carl. 1973. *Class, Race, and Political Behaviour in Urban Jamaica.* Kingston: Institute of Social and Economic Research, University of the West Indies.

Wilson, Peter J. 1973. *Crab Antics: The Social Anthropology of English-Speaking Negro Societies of the Caribbean.* New Haven: Yale University Press.

Wright, Philip. 1973. *Knibb 'The Notorious': Slaves' Missionary, 1803–1845.* London: Sidgwick and Jackson.

DIANE J. AUSTIN-BROOS

Redefining the Moral Order

Interpretations of Christianity
in Postemancipation Jamaica

The playwright Derek Walcott (1974) suggests in his seminal essay "The Muse of History" that issues of Christianity are central to Caribbean culture. In the Caribbean, the religious sensibility and the moral order it sustains have taken on a markedly Christian form. Citing T. S. Eliot, Walcott observes that any culture requires religion as a central dimension. In literary terms it is the precondition of an epic tradition. What then of the Caribbean, where African and other religious forms have been trampled by Christianity? Does this mean, ponders Walcott, that the New World must remain without an epic sense, with a culture forever depleted through the imposition of alien moral norms? In any summation of emancipation's legacy, this issue of religion remains a central theme. The notions of moral order that prevailed in society following emancipation give insight into the forms of culture that emerged.

In Walcott's view, the slaves did not merely capitulate to Christianity. He notes that the Hebraic tradition offered political parallels to the slaves, though it also brought an ethic of passivity that deflected a challenge of the temporal order. The slaves, however, were better placed than their masters to see in Christianity a potential for new meanings. Walcott (1974:11–13) observes in his inimitable style:

What was captured from the captor was his God, for the subject African had come to the New World in an elemental intimacy with nature, with a profounder terror of blasphemy than the exhausted, hypocritical Christian. He understood too quickly the Christian rituals of a whipped, tortured and murdered redeemer. . . . [No] race is converted against its will. The slave-master now encountered a massive pliability. The slave converted himself, he changed weapons, spiritual weapons, and as he adapted his master's religion, he also adapted his language, and it is here that what we can look at as our poetic tradition begins. Now began the new naming of things.

Walcott's forceful, even romantic, statement of the role of Christianity in Caribbean culture comes out of a careful deliberation on the relations among language, literature, and religion. To disown the history of Christianity within the Caribbean is to disown too much, in Walcott's view. In Jamaica, for instance, music, poetry, and intuitive art, not to mention the work of its celebrated novelist Roger Mais, would present a shattered incompleteness were they divested of the interpretive struggle Jamaicans have sustained with Christianity. Part of emancipation's legacy in Jamaica was to insert Christianity as an integral component into that society's culture. Christianity came not as a permanently alien phenomenon but as a negotiated one, in which Jamaicans themselves have sought to interpret the nature of its message and the values it decrees.

Yet that process has been more complex and arduous than Walcott suggests. The impact of missionaries in Jamaica was probably most profound directly following emancipation. The Christianity that they proposed for the newly emancipated slaves was infused with sectarian ambition for a pietistic culture, fashioned in Europe's image. The interpretive struggle with Christianity began before emancipation but continued after that watershed through the nineteenth century and into the twentieth. Successive generations of Jamaicans have sought to modify the pietism of that early missionary thought and to mold the Christian message to the lives they have led. Still, the victory has never been as complete as Walcott suggests. In social as well as political spheres, Christianity has remained an available tool for modes of domination emanating from both within and beyond the society. The religion has retained the ambiguity of its dual capacities, as constraint and as medium of critique as well. To understand religion in Jamaica and to understand the cultural legacies of the slave plantation period, Christianity cannot be ignored. Rather, it must be treated as a structuring element within the society that has been progressively reinterpreted by Jamaicans themselves.

The literature on religion in Jamaica and in the Caribbean at large has seldom addressed Walcott's theme. Struggle for a Caribbean religious form was interpreted as the struggle simply for African survivals against and separate from European cultural legacies. George Simpson (1956, 1978), following Herskovits, talked of two religious worlds, African and European, which emancipation bequeathed. The study of Jamaican religion became the study of these African survivals (e.g., Moore 1953). Phillip Curtin's (1970) dramatic pronouncement that Jamaica's

1861 revival had "turned African" gave a modern historical imprimatur to this mode of addressing Jamaican religion. It possibly reached its culmination in the works of Leonard Barrett (1968, 1974, 1976). It was followed by a younger generation of writers, Chevannes (1971) and Schuler (1979) among them, who saw in the African survivals a logic of opposition as well. Shifting the emphasis slightly from an Africa remembered through survivals to an Africa asserted through conflict and opposition, they placed Rastafarianism, a quite contemporary construction, in the same line of development as Native Baptists and Revival. And yet the Christian elements in these religious forms, substantial as they have always been, have remained curiously unanalyzed. They have elicited an embarrassment, or perhaps a muted resentment, which Walcott argues must be eschewed if the cultures of the Caribbean are to be charted in their totality.[1]

One further writer on Jamaican religion presents a somewhat different view. In her study of the role of missionaries in the demise of Jamaican slave society, Turner (1982) argues that the missionaries significance stemmed from the fundamental fact that they regarded the slaves as "part of the brotherhood of man, capable of choosing salvation" (1982:196). A similar point is made by Martinez-Alier (1974:4, 68) with regard to the Cuban church and also by Lewis (1983:204) in his general summation of the influence of Christian missions in the Caribbean. Turner observes that the missionaries appealed to the "intellectual and moral qualities" of rational and principled individuals, a status and identity that the regime had denied chattel slaves (1982:199). Coming themselves from the long tradition of Dissenters in England, the missionaries, in Turner's view, passed to slaves like Sam Sharpe crucial political methods of organized opposition. Christian missionization had the latent function of equipping the slaves with ideas and skills, including literacy, which were necessary in their development as political actors. The missionaries did not create a political opposition, but they contributed to its articulation.

Creating a Moral Order

Although Turner's analysis offers considered and very useful insights into the period of the emancipation, it is probably a mistake to overemphasize the role of missionaries as contributors to an emerging form of rational political activity. It may be true that slaves became aware that just as they could choose salvation, they could choose freedom also. That freedom, however, would be for the slaves both a conceptually and institutionally constructed phenomenon about which the missionaries had quite particular ideas. As Turner (1982:72) herself observes, much mission teaching was in direct conflict with the religion and social norms that the slaves had inherited. The Christian notion of sin and the guilt that was meant to accompany sin were alien to the slaves. So, too, was the idea of a constant reinforcement of moral law through right conduct, reflection on the Bible, and the repetitive practice of the sacraments. Moreover, it was as independent cultivators of small landholdings that the missionaries imagined that their neophytes could achieve most readily this spiritual program. From the mission point of view, the free world of the emancipated slaves was, nevertheless, to be a structured one, wherein the strictures of religion would replace the more vicious constraints of the temporal order (see Mintz 1974). William Knibb, the foremost Baptist missionary in the emancipation struggle, observed with regard to the slaves, "To be free you must be independent. Receive your money for your work; come to market with money; purchase from whom you please; and be accountable to no one but the Being above, whom I trust will watch over you and protect you" (Hinton 1847:289).

Here I wish to take a lead from Russell's (1983) observation that the emancipation involved the genesis of a new stereotype, the Christian black, in place of the previous stereotype of Quashie the foolish slave (see Patterson 1967:174ff.). Part of the emancipation struggle involved furnishing an alternative explanation for the situation of African slaves within the New World environment. Their forms of rite, spiritual beliefs, and domestic organization all constituted anathema to the early nineteenth-century missionaries. All of these aspects of their lives had to be changed and had to be seen as amenable to change. Sexual profligacy, belief in ancestor spirits, and blasphemous attention to fetishes to manage the spiritual world were all quite incompatible with a Christian-European mode. Their caretaking, as well as their celebrations at death, remained an affront to Christian mission ideas. If these aspects of slave behavior were to be seen as alterable phenomena, they had to be seen as the product of forces separate from any innate and possibly subhuman African traits. Africans of the Old World and the New World never fully participated in the Rousseauistic romance of the noble savage. Their blackness, which became an integral part of Christian symbolism, and the Islamic allegiance of the Moors and some of the African slaves, constituted double evidence for many a New World European that these people were not merely ignorant savages but depraved and lesser beings (Russell 1983; Lewis 1983; see also Jordan 1969; Davis 1970).

In order that the African slaves might be able to choose salvation and thereby become Christian blacks, these unpalatable aspects of the New World African had to be reconstrued. The ideology of the planters would perforce be replaced, albeit gradually and over almost a century, by the ideology of the mission. That transition would involve a relocation of the sources of the evil that characterized slaves. In order to establish that the African slaves could be saved from practices and beliefs unacceptable to the missionaries, notions of innate evil were denied and redefined as environmental. The source of the evil was seen to be the ignorance of the slave, exacerbated by the slavery system itself. Once liberated from an enslaved state, this ignorance could be dealt with. The emphasis was shifted from an enduring African nature to the historical influence of a New World environment. Indeed, even the ameliorists and defenders of slavery were frequently in agreement with missionaries over the environmental influence of slavery. Stewart (1969:205) observed in his chronicle that "there is in the very nature of slavery, in its mildest form, something unfavourable to the cultivation of moral feeling." Among those missionaries who came to support the antislavery cause, this view was elaborated. One of its most self-confident expressions comes in a postemancipation publication from the Religious Tract Society: "The demoralizing influence of slavery might have been easily foreseen by every right mind, because the system carried on its very front a direct violation of three great moral precepts; that which regards the security of every kind of property, in saying, 'Thou shalt not steal'; that which gives a special recognition to the Divine presence among us, by enjoining a hallowed observance of the sabbath; and that which has a bearing upon all the virtues of social life, by honouring all the rights and relationships of marriage" (1842:117).

Integral to the redefinition of the African as an object of proselytization was the need to pose, in opposition to planter ideology, the vision of a form of economy and social life separate from and alternative to the plantation. If environment impeded the education and salvation of the African, then an appropriate environment for these activities had to be stipulated. Such an environment is stated implicitly in the missionary comments cited above. Knibb emphasizes that the emancipated slave must become a viable, independent economic unit within a cash economy. The Religious Tract Society's statement stipulates further that this must be a system in which property, including the property of the person, is respected; in which temporal life makes room on the sabbath for devotions to the one God; and, in which the missionary model of the family with Christian marriage at its base is the dominant social form.

The Baptist free village system was the concrete embodiment of this alternative social environment that would realize a moral and religious vision (Paget n.d.; Mintz 1974). That system, in turn, has remained in Jamaica a popular model of the social constituents of a viable moral order. Although ideas of property, individual autonomy, correct family forms, and stable ritual gestures to the Christian God have been separated, to a degree, from the rural context of postemancipation society, certainly these social forms and moral values remain prominent. So, too, does the view that disorderly or immoral behavior is connected with the debasement of the "slavery heritage" and with the forms of social disorganization that the system is presumed to have engendered. "The slavery thing is still in them" is a contemporary moral judgment that intertwines the missionary environmental view with a muted notion of biological inheritance that stems from the slavery days (Austin 1979, 1984:149–209; Austin-Broos 1988). The missionaries did not in any simple sense advocate freedom from slavery but, rather, freedom to embrace a definite alternative form of life to the plantation system. The product of this environment would be an individuated and economically rational Christian black ensconced within a European family form. The model superimposed an English petit-bourgeois view of independent Christian producers on the peculiarly complex agrarian legacy of slave plantation society (cf. Russell 1983:57).

The transition the missionaries hoped to achieve was not unlike the transition Horton (1971, 1975) described for Africa. Almost a century after West Indian emancipation, the impact of missions as an integral part of British colonialism in Africa moved religious life among many African peoples from integrated local systems (of ancestor observance, curing cults, and a complex sense of the moral order in a humanly and spiritually inhabited nature) to more abstractly conceived and denatured systems of generalized moral law, anchored in a remote but more prominent high God. The Jamaican case demonstrates, however, that Horton did not go far enough in either the sociological or cognitive dimensions of his analysis. The transition that he describes for Africa would be sustained without variation only to the extent that the social forms introduced by colonialism, or by emancipation in the Jamaican case, were sustained and came to encompass the totality of peoples' lives. Just as the independent African churches now show a marvellous pro-

liferation of variant beliefs and rites following the demise of colonialism in Africa, so in Jamaica the interpretive struggle with Christianity
proceeded as the free village system proved unattainable and remote
from the lives of a majority of Jamaicans. The sociological precondi-
tions of the transition were not sustained. Nor could they ever entirely
dictate the interpretive possibilities of the situation. In the latter half
of the nineteenth century and into the twentieth, Jamaicans struggled
against the stereotype of the Christian black.

The three major religious movements that diverged significantly from
the sectarian norm were Revivalism, Pentecostalism, and finally, Rastafarianism. Each of these religious movements has disputed or rejected,
from diverse perspectives, the postemancipation model of a New World
Christian. That model, in turn, has not been expelled from Jamaican
society but has been confined to a modest but influential section of the
rural and urban petit bourgeoisie. The magical and enthusiastic dimensions of the Revival-Pocomania complex reflect not merely a continuity
with Africa but also the social environmental circumstances of a rural
people intimately engaged with nature and only partly absorbed into
the rationalism of regulated labor and monetarized exchange. The modes
of regulated respectability that the Baptists and others encouraged were
dependent on a form of independent farming or continuous wage labor
that was realized in nineteenth-century England far more easily than
it would be in Jamaica (cf. Hill 1970; Thompson 1963). Pentecostalism
and Rastafarianism, which followed Revivalism, were both reactions
to the increasingly rapid dispersal of Jamaica's small farmer class. The
messianic dimension of these modern movements is typical of religious
forms signaling the fragmentation of a rural order and, also, of the model
of life and morals that accompanies it (cf. Wilson 1975; Anderson 1979).
They mark a further stage, beyond the rise of Revival, in the Jamaican
struggle to interpret a religious life that is Christian but is separated from
the cultural-historical trajectory of nineteenth-century Europe.

Through each of these three religious modes Jamaicans have sought
to adapt dimensions of Christianity to their circumstances in the New
World and to contest a sectarian moral form that was never consistent
with the lives they led. The message of the preemancipation missionaries
should not be seen, therefore, as a simple cumulative step toward a more
rationalized political consciousness but rather as a culturally embodied
move away from the slave plantation in a direction that could accommodate and be meaningful for only some Jamaicans. The following section discusses the missionary James Phillippo's postemancipation im-

228 DIANE J. AUSTIN-BROOS

228 DIANE J. AUSTIN-BROOS

age of the Christian black and compares it to the views of the Anglican and planter ideologue, Reverend George Bridges, writing just fifteen years prior to Phillippo. With this background, the discussion returns to the three religious variants as evidence of the way in which Jamaicans have struggled with Christianity, imbuing it with their own interpretative meanings.

Defining the Moral Order

The whole past history of Jamaica "presents only a succession of wars, usurpations, crimes, misery and vice . . . all is one revolting scene . . . of the abuse of power and the re-action of misery against oppression. Slavery, both Indian and negro . . . has been the curse of the West Indies . . . blasting the efforts of man, however originally well-disposed, by its demon-like influence over the natural virtues with which his Creator had endowed him" (Phillippo quoting Martin, 1843:31). So concludes the Baptist missionary James Phillippo's introductory overview of Jamaican history prior to emancipation. In his account of the slavery system, Phillippo constantly emphasizes the capacity of the system to dehumanize the slave and thereby confer on Africans in the New World a status "not distinguishable from that of passive brutes." He describes the slaves as living in a state of "vassalage" wherein they are "outcasts from the common privileges of humanity, deprived of the essential attributes of man" (Phillippo 1843:256). Among these attibutes, Phillippo lists the ability to command the produce of one's labor, to retain control over a wife and children, and to ultimately control one's own person. Maintaining his male perspective, Phillippo further observes that not only had there been in slavery no sanctions to "guard the chastity of a female slave," there also had been no means for a man to avenge the "violated honour" of a woman. There was, indeed, no protection of the integrity of a slave's domestic life, and at any sign of rebellion against these deplorable conditions, "these poor creatures were shot like wild beasts or hunted down with blood-hounds" (ibid., 157).

The slaves' daily routine, Phillippo observes, was in other countries "performed by horses, oxen and machinery." Consistent with this assimilation of the slaves to beings outside society, their legal rights were hopelessly curtailed and they were denied "all opportunities of Divine worship" (ibid., 158:61). Here Phillippo cites the Consolidated Slave Act of 1816, which required that slaves obtain from a magistrate a license to attend a place of worship. The missionary argues with regard to this situation that the planters and their supporters "had interposed their power between [the slaves] and their Creator, as though determined to retain them in ignorance of the gospel, and the only effectual means of perpetuating the existence of their inhuman system" (ibid., 161).

This statement, along with the summation of Jamaican history cited above, demonstrates Phillippo's view that slavery and its protagonists constituted a humanly embodied force for evil interposed between a divine will and its articulation on earth. The objective of the missionaries was clear—to remove this mechanism that deflected the further elaboration of God's will and to remove this evil mediation of the environment in which the slaves lived. This view is strengthened further in Phillippo's portrait of the Jamaican whites as "the most wretched and corrupt" among the entire population, responsible for the debasement of the slaves, and unable to present a civilized standard for the people of color (ibid., 130). Phillippo also intermittently mentions the continuing affronts against the Dissenters in Jamaica: the inability of sectarians to preach freely, to perform the marriage rite, to derive support from the executive, monetary or otherwise, or to be given due respect as proselytizers of the Christian message. He recounts in detail the retributions against the church following the Baptist War of 1831 and the formation of the Anglican Church Union, hostile both to sectarians and to the idea of emancipation (ibid., 168; cf. Turner 1982). For Phillippo, the planters interposed themselves not only between the slaves and God's will for them but also between the sectarians and their will in response to God.

The tenor of Phillippo's views, however, is revealed more accurately when his withering opinion of slavery is placed alongside his no less critical view of the ignorance and superstition of Africans, which slavery could only exacerbate. Although Phillippo comments adversely on the ideas of Jamaican historian Long, and on those of Montesquieu, that the Africans are an innately inferior people, he nevertheless notes the inability of the African to read, to calculate time, and to arrive at rational decisions (Phillippo 1843:189–92). He comments on Africans under slavery: "Enthralled and bowed down by a system that returned them to the level of the brute . . . they were altogether destitute of taste and genius . . . the dwarfs of the rational world, their intellect rising only to a confused notion and imperfect idea of the general objects of human knowledge" (ibid., 191). Added to this was a debased moral state maintained through ignorance and superstition. Phillippo cites with approval the opinion that the "aggregate character" of the various African peoples "amalgamated into one society under the influence of slavery" was "irrascible, conceited, proud, indolent, lascivious, credulous and very artful"; a "general disposition" that "may safely be asserted to be thieving, lazy and dissimulating" (ibid., 240).

The slaves engaged in "licentious" dancing accompanied by drummed music that was "rude and monotonous." Phillippo assumed the moral depravity of personalities that remained opaque to him. His description of dancing also indicates a total lack of rapport with any element of west African aesthetics: "On some occasions the dance consisted of stamping feet, accompanied by various contortions of the body, with strange and indecent attitudes: on others . . . the lower extremities being held firm, the whole person was moved without raising the feet from the ground. Making the head and limbs fixed points, they writhed and turned the body upon its own axis. . . . Their approaches to each other, and the attitudes and inflexions in which they were made, were highly indecent, the performers being nearly naked" (ibid., 241–42). With regard to elements of slave religion, Phillippo was consistently unsympathetic. He parodied the attempts of slaves to placate the spirit of a dead relative to ensure its welfare in the afterlife while simultaneously protecting the living from the spirit's desires and griefs (ibid., 144–45). If Hogg (1964:61–63) is correct in suggesting that with the demise of larger ancestral complexes African religion in Jamaica became dominated by a cult of the dead, then Phillippo here strikes at the heart of the slaves' beliefs. He also discards as evil superstition the complex of Myal and Obeah beliefs, wherein slaves embraced a world in which human and spiritual forces constantly interact (Phillippo 1843:247–48; cf. Hogg 1964:65ff.).

Clear moral evidence that all these beliefs were simply debasing superstition was found in the fact that the slaves, without the benefit of Christianity, were unable to maintain the cleanliness of their persons or the sanctity of their sexual lives. In fact, he observes, they ridiculed the "sacred institute" of marriage, polygamy was common, and women were especially debased. In Phillippo's view, there was no order in a slave's domestic life: "Licentiousness the most degraded and unrestrained was the order of the day. Every estate on the island—every negro hut was a common brothel: every female a prostitute and every man a libertine" (Phillippo 218–19).

All this could begin to change only following emancipation. After 1838, the newly freed slaves, without doubt felt beholden to the sectarian missionaries and for a while, at least, placed high value on becoming Christians. Phillippo (ibid., 289–92) and later Gardner (1873: 458–63) both confirm the very rapid growth in Christian affiliation in the decade following emancipation. Yet the Congregationalist W. J. Gardner's history of Jamaica, published some thirty years after Phillippo's more polemical work, attests to the enduring lack of compromise with which the sectarian missionaries addressed any evidence of religious or social heritage at odds with their own particular view. Their model of what a Christian black should be was projected enthusiastically onto the free men and women of mid-nineteenth-century Jamaica.

The tools used in the construction of this model New World Christian were conversion, education, and industry, promoted through the private ownership of property. Phillippo (1843:234) notes confidently of the postemancipation experience that "the term indolent can only be applied to the black population in the absence of remunerating employment." Under the new regime, the villages that maintained their own cultivations and also provided the work force for nearby plantations presented, in Phillippo's view, a thriving hive of industry. "On returning from their daily labour the men almost uniformly employ themselves in cultivating their own grounds or in improving their own little freeholds, and the women in culinary and in other domestic purposes until driven to their frugal repast and to repose by darkness and fatigue" (ibid., 235).

Phillippo cautioned against the introduction of more immigrant labor into Jamaica as a threat to the livelihood of those already resident on the island (ibid., 94–98). Nevertheless, his account of peasant life ignores not only the extensive vagrancy and squatting created by landlessness and unemployment but also the fact that women retained and expanded their participation in agriculture (see Cumper 1958; Hall 1959; Eisner 1960; Olivier 1936). Phillippo finds the product of the freemen's industry in neatly organized villages and furnished cottages, which "are in all respects equal, and some of them superior, to the tenancies of labourers in rural districts of England" (220–21). In this setting, which could allow a generalized self-esteem, education was pursued with alacrity. Phillippo estimates that in 1841 there were approximately 186 day schools, 100 Sabbath schools, and 20 to 30 evening schools throughout the island, with an estimated attendance of around 30,000. Children, he reported, studied assiduously, and as a result, the range of occupational skills expanded rapidly to equal that available in England. Phillippo concludes, "the black skin and wooly hair constitute the only difference which now exists between multitudes of the emancipated peasantry of

Jamaica and the tradesmen and agriculturalists of England. Nor are the intellectual faculties of this calumniated and oppressed people in any respect inferior to the rest of the species; *they have simply been suspended from inaction, and the absence of those influences which were necessary to their development"* (1843:201, emphasis added).

Finally, in the religious sphere itself, Phillippo cites the enthusiasm with which school children memorize large tracts of the Bible (ibid., 197). He recounts a village congregation gathering at the call "come to prayers" and families after the Sunday service sitting by their cottage trees engaged in reading scriptures and singing hymns (ibid., 224, 233). In December 1840, the celebration of marriage by missionaries was legalized. As a consequence, Phillippo suggests, marriage came to be associated by Jamaicans "with everything virtuous and honourable in human conduct" (ibid., 232). Phillippo also reports triumphantly that funerals proceed "nearly in accordance with civilized custom" and notes how attendance on the deceased was modified to conform with Christian mores. The sabbath was now observed and the "frantic orgies" of Christmas and other holidays were dispelled. Moreover "attendance at dances, or merry-makings of any description as well as at horse-races, are all sins which are visited with excision in all the Jamaica churches with which the author is acquainted" (ibid., 260–62, 334).

Phillippo's account of Jamaica some five years after emancipation is not so much a description as a blueprint for the Christian black. It envisages a transformation that is startling, not only for its divergence from the previous slave regime but even more for its radical stifling of the folk culture of slaves, with its extensive roots in an Afro-Caribbean rural sedentary life. The missionary was seeking to foist onto emancipated slaves a model of behavior derived from an industrialized and privatized nation. It assumed a radical individuation of the person embodied in a strict moral rationalism. This austere momentary truth of the sectarian Dissenters was understood as the timeless truth of God. The model of the Christian black was therefore presented in a totalistic way that actually sought to duplicate the Dissenters' own social milieu. It would be a futile enterprise. The Dissenters' aims were most likely to succeed among the emancipated who were successful in cultivation or trade. They could, if they wished, simulate the manifest social signs of this Christian culture. Even then, the culture of the Dissenters so profoundly contravened the aesthetics of movement, adornment, and voiced articulation that typified the culture of these African descendants that revolt and modification of the model were inevitable from its beginnings. This

Christianity as introduced by the Dissenters radically denied the Jamaicans' entire "presentation of self."

And yet, to situate James Phillippo within his proper context, it should be underlined that he held few of the views of that prominent Anglican churchman, George W. Bridges. Bridges (1828) argues that although the course of history indicated a movement from slavery to freedom on the part of the various bonded populations of the world—so in Europe slaves became serfs, tenants, and ultimately freeholders—this was not possible for the African with his "generic character of deceit, ingratitude, and cruelty" (2:479). Bridges (2:430) regarded Africa as "the parent of everything that is monstrous in nature" where "the passions rage out of control." As a consequence, Bridges queried whether or not it was possible to convert the slaves, notwithstanding "the enormities of the slave-trade." He comments: "It would be an easy though a tedious task, to prove, from the authority of poets, historians, and philosophers that the human savages of Africa are still the lowest of the species. . . . Is it left for the bishop of the western Indies to work the miracle that is expected of them, and send back their enlightened neophytes as missionaries to their native lands?" (ibid., 2:457). Beginning in 1816, a series of bills from the Jamaica Assembly increased the numbers and the salaries of Anglican curates and rectors who intended to proselytize among the slaves (ibid., 2:455ff.). In time, the model of the Christian black would also be accepted by the Anglican church in Jamaica. Yet, as the church of the ruling class, its judgment of Africans and the role of slavery in curtailing their abilities clearly differed from the sectarians. To this extent, the sectarians were the carriers of a reformist model, which for a time contested the Jamaican status quo.

Contesting the Moral Order

Hall (1959:182ff.) and Eisner (1960:220–21) document the differentiation of Jamaica's small farming class leading up to the period of the Great Revival and the Morant Bay rebellion. Wilmott (1985, 1986; cf. Mintz 1974) details the Baptists' diminishing political influence over poor black Jamaicans during the same period. Gardner (1873) discussed at firsthand the financial difficulties into which the Baptists fell once they declared themselves independent of the Missionary Society in London, and Eisner (1960:326ff.) and Curtin (1970) both relate the rapid curtailing of educational efforts as the economic situation grew worse in the later 1840s and the 1850s. In numerous parts of the island, the environment that would nurture the Christian black was under threat within a decade of its inception. In other parts of the island, it never gained a foothold. Fundamental structural features of Jamaican society would preclude Phillippo's blueprint from becoming a reality. The environment that would proffer an enduring peasant class as the predominant class in Jamaica was never quite realized. But what environments took its place? If one turns to the cultural interpretations of Jamaica's Great Revival, then the answer is that Jamaicans were reverting to a more African mode of being (see especially Curtin 1970:158ff.). Yet this appeal simply to cultural modes does not explain the considerable number of Jamaicans who remained affiliated with orthodox churches or, in the manner that Beckwith (1929:162) reports, sustained a mixed affiliation with orthodoxy and enthusiastic revival religion. A more differentiated approach is required, which considers the developing social circumstances in which Jamaicans found themselves.[2]

The slavery regime had brought together a large agricultural labor force numbering around 220,000 at the time of emancipation (Hall 1959:157; cf. Roberts 1957:40–43). Though many, or even most, of these Jamaicans might have aspired to become small farmers, this course was open only to a limited proportion of the labor force. By 1845 there were 20,724 freehold settlers on properties of less than ten acres (Hall 1959: 162; cf. Paget n.d.:57; Eisner 1960:210). Properties of this size accounted for the vast majority of emancipated slaves able to purchase freehold, and their numbers indicate that Jamaica's rural labor force was only partially converted into Phillippo's "peasantry." Some Jamaicans remained as tenant farmers on larger properties. Others became squatters. Still others became town laborers, or itinerants searching for wage labor or piecework wherever it was available. These Jamaicans constituted a rural labor force rather than a peasantry engaged in dual or multiple occupations (Olivier 1936; Eisner 1960).

The persistence of Myal and Native Baptist traditions that came together in the Great Revival to produce a highly animated, spiritual, magical, and instrumental form of Christianity was but one aspect of this uncertain and varied rural life (cf. Schuler 1979:74; Curtin 1970: 160). The elaborate pantheon that Revival bequeathed signaled the necessity that Jamaicans felt for direct and frequent spiritual intervention in their lives, even when they were situated within a broadly Christian cosmology. This same Revival also incorporated into Christian practice, under the guise of spirit possession, forms of masquerade and dance that were part of an ongoing Jamaican aesthetic to which the Dissenters had been quite insensitive. Jamaicans, in new and innovative ways not especially African and yet not European, challenged the aesthetic constraints contained in European pietism and returned the element of celebration to the mainstream of their religious observance. Revival religion bespoke a rural population beset by the vagaries of nature and living on the margins of a capitalist world, with its homogenizing economy and pervasive state apparatus. The varying degrees of association with Revival and orthodox sectarianism reflect the varying degrees of association with a market economy and an extralocal political system, and a people experimenting with the modes of spiritual expression.

As the century proceeded, the orthodox religion of the emancipist free villages, and Revival itself, became aspects of a more complex historical process. This was the emergence of a large free labor force in Jamaica moving toward major towns and also traveling beyond Jamaica to rural and industrial sites in the wider Caribbean region. The initial impetus for labor migrations beyond Jamaica came when construction of the Panamanian railway, in the late 1840s, gave Jamaicans a new source of wage labor employment (Newton 1984). It became possible to choose an alternative, other than squatting or subsistence farming, to unemployment, underemployment, or depressed wages in Jamaica. The early migrations to work on the Panamanian railway are poorly documented and possibly involved only 5,000 Jamaican workers between 1850 and 1855. The two major periods of labor force migration to Panama occurred between 1881 and 1890 and between 1904 and 1915, when construction of the Panama Canal was in progress. During these two periods, total departures from Jamaica were approximately 78,000 and 91,000, respectively. The loss of Jamaica's population was considerably less, but the important factor was the very high proportion of working men engaged in circulatory migration for the purpose of wage labor (Newton 1984:94). Costa Rica, Cuba, and the United States were other destinations for Jamaicans (Eisner 1960:149–51). Net departures to these three countries in the forty years between 1881 to 1921 were 33,000, 22,000, and 46,000, respectively (Roberts 1957:139).

This migration overseas also occasioned a major population shift within Jamaica itself. Between 1891 and 1911, workers from the west and central sections of the island migrated to the northeast either to work in the expanding banana industry or to emigrate. Census returns indicate that, at this time, the very rapid fragmentation of small and medium freeholds in Jamaica began. Inheritance constantly subdivided land within a finite area, bequeathing to many heirs plots that could not sustain them (Cumper 1958:270). Around 1911, Jamaica's rural labor force thus stabilized at about 75,000 persons (ibid., 271). As this population stabilized, migration began to flow toward Kingston; and when, about 1912, the banana industry began its decline, the movement to Kingston strengthened (Eisner 1960:187; Marshall 1982:8). The repatriation of migrant workers at the onset of the depression increased the flow. So great became the pull of Kingston between 1921 and 1943, that internal migration among all the parishes can be seen as a step-by-step movement toward the Kingston metropolitan area (Roberts 1957:156–57).

In the 100 years since Phillippo produced his blueprint for Christian blacks as independent farmers or localized tradesmen, the entire configuration of Jamaican society changed. This inexorable movement toward an urbanized, waged, and mobile labor force underlined the fact that the Africans had been recruited originally under slavery to constitute a labor force rather than a yeoman class. Phillippo's model of freedom for Jamaicans became progressively less relevant as the character of this labor force reasserted itself. Yet these workers were still not entirely free. The onset of restrictive immigration practices by the United States in 1924, and the mass repatriation of Jamaican labor at the end of the 1920s, demonstrated the continual operation of a racial principle in the labor relations of the Caribbean (see also Austin-Broos 1988).

The more recent developments in Jamaican religion, and especially in their relations to orthodox sectarianism and Jamaican Revival, are best seen against this background of changing forms of society. Pentecostalism and Rastafarianism are both modes of response, in a somewhat different vein, to the crumbling norms and mores of a self-contained rural life. One further element in the situation, however, requires consideration. Prior to the 1880s, women still worked mainly in agriculture. When rural holdings began to fragment near the end of the century, women began to look for other forms of work. The movement of American capital into the region turned some of Jamaica's men into migratory laborers and brought increased wealth to some Jamaican export farmers. With the growth of this indigenous class, domestic and other service work expanded (Eisner 1960:155–62). In 1943 when domestic service was at its peak, 51 percent of black women workers were employed in domestic service; 81.8 percent of all domestic servants were black women (French 1986; Higman 1983). Although the work was less arduous than rural employment, these working women became radically subordinated within middle-class households. Servant's quarters

were often rude huts separate from the employer's house, and the facilities available to them were separated from their employers' (Higman
1983:133). Their choice of religious affiliation at the turn of the century
was between forms of Revival religion and the less satisfying but more
respectable sectarian churches. They very likely engaged in the forms
of compromise Beckwith (1929:126) describes: attendance at an orthodox church for the Sunday morning service and a range of engage-
ments in Revival and curing activities at other points in the weekly and
monthly round. These women would become recruits of the new Pentecostal churches.

During the second half of the nineteenth century and moving into
the twentieth century, Christian proselytization in Jamaica also changed.
The churches of the original sectarian missionaries, including the Mo-
ravians, Methodists, orthodox Baptists, and Presbyterians, did not increase the proportion of the population over which they presided. The
orthodox Baptists had a very rapid rise in membership in the last two
decades of the nineteenth century, which may have reflected the prosperity brought to some by the banana industry. Thenceforth, this increase in membership fell away, so that all of these churches, by 1943,
showed a proportional membership little different from its level 100 years
previously (MacGavran 1962:14–16). Simultaneously, new missionary
initiatives entered the Jamaican field from both England and America.
The first American initiative was the Church of Christ, which was established in 1858. In 1887 the Salvation Army began extensive activities
in Jamaica, and in 1894 the Seventh-Day Adventists arrived (J. Davis
1942:20–22). The Holiness Church of God sent missionaries in 1907,
and 1917 marks the first confirmed presence of a Pentecostal Church
of God in Jamaica (Austin-Broos 1989). The Christian influence among
Jamaica's working class was becoming more fundamentalist. The sectarians, or as they became known, the "denominational" churches, found
their strength within the bourgeois and petit-bourgeois sectors of Jamaican society. Of the new arrivals, the Seventh-Day Adventists and
the Pentecostals were the most successful (Austin-Broos 1987). The Adventists were absorbed mainly into petit-bourgeois society while Pentecostalism became the dominant religion of poor Jamaicans, especially
of working women. Rastafarianism, which first became prominent in
1933–1934, is an indigenous form, nevertheless greatly influenced by
stylistic elements in fundamentalist religion (Barrett 1968; Hill 1983).
Its radical critique of Jamaican society is mediated by a Christian mes-
sianism and reliance on the Bible as text. What were the social milieux

that Rastafarianism and Pentecostalism addressed? How did they challenge the pietism of the older sectarian religion?

The founders of Rastafarianism, who constituted the movement in the 1930s, all had been émigré workers in central America (Smith, Augier, and Nettleford 1960; Hill 1983). Doctrines of the Ethiopian type had been common in Jamaica since the turn of the century (Post 1970). Rastafarianism jelled as a movement not only with the crowning of Haile Selassie but also in the context of a migratory labor experience when Jamaicans confronted what another religious radical called the "white wall" of the region. The solution, from a Rastafarian view, was separation, pan-Africanism, and a return to their own particular place. Steeped in biblical references as Jamaican people had become, Selassie's second coming allowed Rastafarians to conceive themselves on a model with the Israelites led out of captivity. They derived from the Hebraic tradition an individualized hero to put in the place of the respectable villager, the Christian black. Rastafarianism was, and remains, the religion of male itinerant workers. It presents a moral resolution to dilemmas that had their immediate genesis in the postemancipation period.

Pentecostalism, on the other hand, has involved an attempt on the part of a new generation of missionaries, this time mainly American, to subsume Jamaicans within their moral and spiritual world. Notwithstanding the fact that proselytization was soon dominated by black Jamaicans, the initial impact of this Pentecostal thrust never has been overturned. Through proclaiming the possibility of spiritual perfection for all (the state called "holiness" in Pentecostal religion), the movement has promoted a moral order in which issues of race are neutralized (Austin 1981; Wedenoja 1980). Followers are encouraged to reconcile themselves to the hierarchies of the region. The movement has been structurally congruent with the position of Jamaican working women in the 1920s and 1930s. Forced to make their stand in Jamaica, while their men traveled away, many women constituted their households as economic adjuncts to a privileged and lighter-skinned middle class. They embraced a religion that accepted their material and social subordination while promoting a spiritual superordination. Despite its conservative tendencies, this movement celebrates the spirituality of women and proposes ways of being Christian that are alien to the sectarian model. Responsive to the Jamaican sense of a spiritually animated world, Pentecostalism also has given this world a markedly feminine orientation (Austin-Broos 1987). It encourages women in precarious circumstances, both rural and urban, to manage their lives by spiritual means once promoted only by the less institutionalized Revival.

These are the social environments in which the two movements developed: different types of fundamentalism for different types of situations. Yet their differences should not overshadow the fact that Rastafarianism and Pentacostalism both constitute revolts against the pietism of sectarian religion and, therefore, against the respectable image of the Christian black. Each movement has a ritual core that is remote from traditional African practices and yet is still anathema to the pietistic tradition. In the case of Rastafarianism, it is the smoking of ganja, legitimized by them through reference to the Bible. In Pentecostalism, it is vigorous spirit possession with glossolalia, which very often involves male pastors ministering to possessed women. Denominational Christians commonly claim that ganja incites Rastafarians to violence and even to murder. They see in the Pentecostal rite of possession further evidence of the sexualizing and decivilizing force of the slavery tradition.[3] Their concerns are not so different from those Phillippo harbored about the nature of African behavior under slavery.

Where Revival represents a revolt against the sectarian norm by a people still largely rural, Rastafarianism and Pentecostalism present different moments in the same struggle by a people now progressively absorbed into a mobile, urbanizing labor force. Each religion in a different way has borne witness to the limited viability of Phillippo's model for Jamaica. Each religion reveals aspects of an interpretative enterprise in which Jamaicans have been engaged ever since emancipation: the redefinition and ultimate indiginization of Phillippo's Christian black.

Conclusion

Did the slaves and their descendants capture the captor's God? In Jamaica, contrary to Walcott, the struggle really began in earnest when the missionaries sought to create an environment that would civilize and save the African slaves. This environmental view of the missionaries led them to promote a new stereotype: the Christian black, a European Christian who happened to be of African descent and historically situated in Jamaica. This imposition of a European petit-bourgeois form onto the Jamaican social and cultural landscape reinforced the interpretive struggle with Christianity already begun by the Native Baptists. Jamaicans through Revival, Pentecostalism, and Rastafarianism have contested various of the moral and aesthetic forms of sectarian pietism.

They have done this even as they have progressively accepted a Christian rendering of the cosmos and moved away from a specifically African religion.

Each religious form has suggested a moral order for Jamaicans rather different from that proposed by Phillippo. In place of the repressive rules of sectarian piety, Revival proposed the active manipulation by Christians of forces for good and evil. Pentecostalism, to a degree, continues this tradition. It much more explicitly accepts the social hierarchy of the New World environment but more forcefully advocates the spiritual superiority of the descendants of the slaves, and particularly women. Rastafarianism, too, is interventionist, though in a much more direct messianic form. It proposes radical social and cultural separation from the New World order and yet claims for itself a superior Christian spirituality.

Jamaicans have only partly redefined the captor's God. As they have become more nearly integrated into a region dominated by Anglo-America, their religious reflections have been increasingly articulated in terms that are drawn from the Hebraic-Christian tradition. Yet, this very historical circumstance has meant that they would never conform in great numbers to Phillippo's model of the Christian black. They have, through their own experience since emancipation, radically localized the Christian tradition. They have produced a distinctive religious milieu. In religious terms, emancipation did not bring freedom to Jamaicans. It did, however, instigate an enduring interpretive struggle that is today a central component of Jamaican culture.

NOTES

1. Both Hogg (1964) and Wedenoja (1978) display a marked unease in grappling with Jamaica's newer Pentecostal cults. Yet to characterize these cults simply as Anglo-American impositions is no longer appropriate. See Austin-Broos (1987).

2. My own approach to these explanatory issues relies on a sociology of religion, with debts to Max Weber (1958). R. T. Smith (1976) presents a related style. Schuler's (1979:76) description of the latter analysis as "psychological" in the style of George Simpson seems to miss its sociological components.

3. Hogg (1970:14) points to a similar revolt against sectarian proprieties in his discussion of the Convince cult.

REFERENCES

Anderson, R. M. 1979. *Vision of the Disinherited: The Making of American Pentecostalism.* Oxford: Oxford University Press.

Austin, Diane J. 1979. History and Symbols in Ideology: A Jamaican Example. *Man,*
n.s. 14:497–514.

———. 1981. Born again—and again and again: Communitas and Social Change
among Jamaican Pentecostalists, *Journal of Anthropological Research* 37:
226–46.

———. 1984. *Urban Life in Kingston Jamaica.* Caribbean Studies Series, vol. 3.
London: Gordon and Breach Science Publishers.

Austin-Broos, Diane J. 1987. Pentecostals and Rastafarians: Cultural, Political, and
Gender Relations of Two Religious Movements. *Social and Economic Studies*
36, 4:1–39.

———. 1988. Class and Race in Jamaica. Paper prepared for the Conference on
The Meaning of Freedom, University of Pittsburgh, August.

———. 1989. Religion, Economy and Class in Jamaica: Reinterpreting a Tradition. Typescript.

Barrett, Leonard. 1968. *The Rastafarians: A Study in Messianic Cultism in Jamaica.*
Caribbean Monograph Series 6. Rio Piedras: Institute of Caribbean Studies.

———. 1974. *Soul-force: African Heritage in Afro-American Religion.* New York:
Doubleday.

———. 1976. *The Sun and the Drum: African Roots in Jamaican Folk Tradition.*
Kingston and London: Sangster's Bookstore and Heinemann.

Beckwith, Martha. 1929. *Black Roadways: A Study of Jamaican Folk Life.* Chapel
Hill: University of North Carolina Press.

Bridges, George W. 1828. *The Annals of Jamaica.* Vols. 1 and 2. London: Frank
Cass.

Chevannes, Barry. 1971. Revival and Black Struggle. *Savacou* 5:27–37.

Cumper, George E. 1958. Population Movements in Jamaica, 1830–1950. *Social and
Economic Studies* 5:261–80.

Curtin, Philip D. 1970. *Two Jamaicas.* New York: Atheneum.

Davis, David B. 1970. *The Problem of Slavery in Western Culture.* Ithaca: Cornell
University Press.

Davis, J. Merle. 1942. *The Church in the New Jamaica.* New York: Academy Press.

Eisner, Gisela. 1960. *Jamaica 1830–1930: A Study in Economic Growth,* Manchester:
Manchester University Press.

French, Joan. 1986. Colonial Policy Towards Women after the 1938 Uprising: the
Case of Jamaica. Paper prepared for Conference of the Caribbean Studies Association, Caracas.

Gardner, W. J. 1873. *A History of Jamaica.* London: Frank Cass.

Hall, Douglas. 1959. *Free Jamaica.* New Haven: Yale University Press.

Higman, Barry. 1983. Domestic Service in Jamaica, since 1750. In *Trade, Government, and Society in Caribbean History, 1700–1920: Essays Presented to Douglas Hall,* edited by B. Higman, 117–138 London: Heinemann.

Hill, Christopher P. 1970. *British Economic and Social History 1700–1964.* London: Penguin.

Hill, Robert. 1983. Leonard P. Howell and Millenarian Visions in Early Rastafari.
Jamaica Journal 16:24–39.

Hinton, John H. 1874. *Memoir of William Knibb, Missionary in Jamaica.* London:
Houlston and Stoneman.

Hogg, Donald. 1964. Jamaican Religions: A Study in Variations. Ph.D. diss., Yale University.

———. 1970. The Convince Cult in Jamaica. In *Papers in Caribbean Anthropology,* compiled by S. Mintz. New Haven: Human Relations Area Files Press.

Horton, Robin. 1971. African Conversion. *Africa* 41:85–108.

———. 1975. On the Rationality of Conversion. *Africa* 45:219–35, 373–99.

Jordan, Winthrop D. 1969. *White over Black: American Attitudes toward the Negro, 1550–1812.* Baltimore: Penguin Books.

Lewis, Gordon K. 1983. *Main Currents in Caribbean Thought.* Kingston and Port of Spain: Heinemann.

MacGavran, Donald. 1962. *Church Growth in Jamaica.* Lucknow: Lucknow Publishing House.

Marshall, Dawn I. 1982. The History of Caribbean Migrations. *Caribbean Review* 11:6–9, 52–3.

Martinez-Alier, Verena. 1974. *Marriage, Class, and Colour in Nineteenth-Century Cuba.* Cambridge Latin American Series 17. Cambridge: Cambridge University Press.

Mintz, Sidney. 1974. (1958). The Historical Sociology of Jamaican Villages. In *Caribbean Transformations,* 157–79. Chicago: Aldine.

Moore, J. G. 1953. The Religion of Jamaican Negroes: A Study of Afro-American Acculturation. Ph.D. diss., Northwestern University.

Newton, Velma. 1984. *The Silver Men: West Indian Labour Migration to Panama, 1850–1914.* University of the West Indies, Institute of Social and Economic Research.

Olivier, Sidney. 1936. *Jamaica, the Blessed Land.* London: Faber and Faber.

Paget, Hugh. N.d. The Free Village System in Jamaica. In *Apprenticeship and Emancipation,* 45–58. University of the West Indies, Department of Extra-mural Studies.

Patterson, Orlando. 1967. *The Sociology of Slavery,* London: MacGibbon and Kee.

Phillippo, James M. 1843. *Jamaica: Its Past and Present.* London: John Snow.

Post, Ken. 1970. The Bible as Ideology: Ethiopianism in Jamaica, 1930–38. In *African Perspectives,* edited by C. Allen and R. W. Johnson, 185–207. Cambridge: Cambridge University Press.

Religious Tract Society. 1842. *Jamaica: Enslaved and Free.* London: Religious Tract Society.

Roberts, George W. 1957. *The Population of Jamaica.* Cambridge: Cambridge University Press.

Russell, Horace O. 1983. The Emergence of the Christian Black: The Making of a Stereotype. *Jamaica Journal* 16:51–58.

Schuler, Monica. 1979. Myalism and the African Religious Tradition in Jamaica. In *African and the Caribbean, the Legacies of a Link,* edited by M. E. Crahan and F. W. Knight, 65–79. Baltimore: Johns Hopkins University Press.

Simpson, George E. 1956. Jamaican Revivalist Cults. *Social and Economic Studies* 5:321–442.

———. 1978. *Black Religions in the New World.* New York: Columbia University Press.

Smith, M. G., R. Augier, and R. Nettleford. 1960. *The Rastafarian Movement in Kingston, Jamaica.* Kingston: Institute of Social and Economic Research.

Smith, Raymond T. 1976. Religion in the Formation of West Indian Society: Guyana and Jamaica. In *The African Diaspora: Interpretive Essays,* edited by M. L. Kilson and R. I. Rotberg, 312–41. Cambridge: Cambridge University Press.

Stewart, John. 1969 (1823). *A View of the Past and Present State of the Island of Jamaica.* Westport, Conn.: Negro Universities Press.

Thompson, Edward P. 1963. *The Making of the English Working Class.* London: Vintage Books.

Turner, Mary. 1982. *Slaves and Missionaries.* Urbana: University of Illinois Press.

Walcott, Derek. 1974. The Muse of History. In *Is Massa Day Dead?* edited by O. Coombs. Garden City, N.Y.: Doubleday.

Weber, Max. 1958. The Social Psychology of the World Religions. In *From Max Weber,* edited by H. H. Gerth and C. Wright Mills. New York: Oxford University Press.

Wedenoja, M. 1978. Religion and Adaptation in Rural Jamaica, Ph.D. diss., University of California, San Diego.

———. 1980. Modernization and the Pentecostal Movement in Jamaica. In *Perspectives on Pentecostalism,* edited by S. D. Glazier. Washington, D.C.: University Press of America.

Wilmot, Swithin. 1985. From Falmouth to Morant Bay: Religion and Politics in Jamaica, 1838–1865. In *Religion and Society,* Social History Workshop: Sess. 3, Mona. University of the West Indies, Department of History. pp. 1–18.

———. 1986. Baptist Missionaries and Jamaican Politics, 1838–1854. In *Papers Presented at the Twelfth Conference of the Association of Caribbean Historians,* edited by K. O. Laurence. St. Augustine: University of the West Indies.

Wilson, Bryan. 1975. *Magic and the Millennium.* Frogmore, St. Albans: Paladin.

SIDNEY W. MINTZ

Panglosses and Pollyannas; or, Whose Reality Are We Talking About?

Some students of Caribbean slavery find it difficult to imagine a chronicle drearier or more depressing than that of its aftermath—freedom. To be sure, the slaves did become free—overnight, in some cases. From one day to the next, their chains were struck off. There is near unanimity that this yielded some true benefits. The children yet to be born to them would be born free; they themselves were no longer slaves; their legal personalities, as well as their structural relationship to the law, had become fundamentally different. Changed, too, it may be said, was their structural relationship to themselves. They had, in certain complex and perhaps underappreciated ways, become their own persons. That this remains difficult to appreciate may be owing in some measure to the paucity of literary commentary by the newly freed.

Many students of slavery still believe that freedom made an enormous difference. And yet we are told, again and again, that the freedom of the freed did not amount to much—indeed, that it could not possibly amount to much, unaccompanied as it commonly was by the continuing support of the abolitionists, by access to additional economic resources, and by the exercise of political power. The so-called apprenticeships—by which people were to learn how to be free, aided by such gentle devices as ejectment acts and treadmills—were among the techniques employed by planters and their legislatures to punish, to exact labor, and to cheapen the meaning of freedom. Some authorities argue that freedom may even have come at the wrong time—too soon, rather than too late—as the absence of supporting political and economic power at moments of crisis suggests to them.

The insistence on some realistic assessment of freedom, in terms of what it actually made possible for the freed, is fair. We do need to grasp better what free people could realistically aspire to, and what not. Often the freed were subjected to discriminatory and even punitive legislation, which kept them from taking advantage of alternative economic opportunities. In repeated instances, their adjustments to freedom were overtaken by the managed immigration of needy workers from elsewhere, whose presence then drove down the going price of manual labor. What is more, the cost of immigration was sometimes paid for by taxes levied upon the basic necessities of the freed themselves. Almost everywhere, freedpersons were saddled with local governments that could count on at least the tacit approval of their tactics by colonial authorities in the metropolis. Freedom must have been worth something. But in the event, we are told, freedom was not worth much.

On the basis of such claims, it has been argued that freedom not only came too fast, but that it came without real planning or consultation — at least so far as the slaves' opinions are concerned. Does this mean that what the slaves ostensibly wanted was nothing more than a figment of abolitionist imagination? Could being free actually have slowed assimilation to Western cultural and social norms? More to the point, did formal freedom, as bestowed upon the slaves, hinder the acquisition of real freedom? To judge whether these things might be true, we must try to learn what real freedom was, or could have been. Carlyle thought that, for the Caribbean slaves, real freedom was Quashee's freedom — to gorge himself idly on ripening pumpkins. Carlyle, of course, would have none of that:

The Twenty Millions [indemnification to planters], a mere trifle despatched with a single dash of the pen, are paid; and far over the sea, we have a few black persons rendered extremely "free" indeed. Sitting yonder with their beautiful muzzles up to the ears in pumpkins, imbibing sweet pulps and juices; the grinder and incisor teeth ready for ever new work, and the pumpkins cheap as grass in those rich climates: while the sugar-crops rot round them uncut, because labor cannot be hired, so cheap are the pumpkins; — and at home we are but required to rasp from the breakfast loaves of our own English labourers some slight "differential sugar-duties," and lend a poor half-million or a few poor millions now and then, to keep that beautiful state of matters going on. (1853:5)

If working people were entitled to leisure, which Carlyle doubted, they certainly were not entitled to decide when they might have it, nor how much:

And first, with regard to the West Indies, it may be laid down as a principle, which no eloquence in Exeter Hall, or Westminster Hall, or elsewhere, can invalidate or hide, except for a short time only, That no Black man who will not work according to what ability the gods have given him for working, has the smallest right to eat pumpkins, or to any fraction of land that will grow pumpkin, however plentiful such land may be; but has an indisputable and perpetual *right* to be compelled, by the real proprietors of said land, to do competent work for a living. This is the everlasting duty of all men, black or white, who are born into this world. (Ibid., 11)

We can, if we wish, take Carlyle's standard, or at least his conviction that the meaning of freedom to most slaves was the right to eat without working; and that this freedom deprived the slave of his right to be made to work, by "the real proprietors of said land." Even if we do not question Carlyle's opinions on who the real proprietors ought to have been, we may find it difficult to believe that all slaves agreed with Carlyle's definition of freedom. Whether emancipation could bring about their definition of freedom is, of course, a different question. We know far less than we would like to know about what the slaves thought they could achieve for themselves and not that much more about what they expected to be done for them.

So to question, as some have done, the consequences of freedom for the slaves can be a worthy project. However, it involves some imaginative reconstructions, of a sort that we cannot then prove to be right or wrong. This, I think, we need to admit at the outset. We may invent a scenario. But say what we will, we cannot then test it for accuracy. Who can say with certainty, after the fact, that something might better have happened sooner? Or later? Suppose slavery had lasted another hundred years in French St. Domingue. Would the first freed people in 1904 have been better off than were the first freed people in 1804? Are we really able to suppose that the three intervening generations of slaves between 1804 and 1904 would have chosen the alternative of living out their lives in slavery, so that the future of their great-grandchildren might be a happier one — assuming that anyone would have been fanciful enough to promise it? Whence the guarantees? We do not have any answers, and we never will.

It is unfortunate that we cannot ask the slaves' opinions. If they had not been slaves, of course, our chances of learning their opinions at the time would have been better. There is more likelihood that they would have been literate. They would not have been flogged for coming to see us or for talking with us. They would be more candid with their viewpoints. But even if they were slaves, I would add — and despite all the provisos what they would have said might very well have surprised us.

In any case, there is ample documentation from the postemancipation era that should give us some pause, Carlyle's views notwithstanding. We know, for instance, that freedom was coming to a region with a tradition of rewarding, exhausting, and degrading drudgery with mean and trivial rewards. We know, too, that this tradition was grounded in the threat of savage violence. This tradition was one that the planters were fiercely determined to preserve.

At the same time, the newly freed were making desperate efforts to find for themselves any economic alternatives to the plantation regimen that the local situation would permit. Whether we think of postrevolutionary Haiti, where some land soon became available, or postemancipation Barbados, where the freed were neatly tethered to the plantations, there is not much mistaking the intentions of the freed.

These intentions unfolded in a different political climate from that of European countries such as Britain, France, Denmark, and the Netherlands, which, while they were freeing slaves in their Caribbean colonies, were experiencing industrial struggles at home between owners and workers. These struggles were conducted on a playing field a good deal more level than that in the Caribbean. The European divisions between capital and labor were not rooted in a history of slavery, in systems of indenture for imported workers, in divisions of race and ethnicity that corresponded to the division of labor, or in the absence of an indigenous peasantry. Even the belief that there were categories of people absolutely not entitled to their own opinions was less popular in Europe than in the islands. Metropolitan legislatures, though hardly egalitarian, were nonetheless quite unlike their colonial analogues, for they were not composed almost exclusively of the representatives of the only industry extant—which is to say, the sugar industry. In Europe, over time, and Marx notwithstanding, the franchise did come to have at least some moderating influence upon national labor policy.

None of this was true for the colonies. British Guiana is a case in point. Chief Justice Beaumont presided over the Guianese courts during the late 1860s. He oversaw many cases dealing with the obligations of the indentured workers, mainly Indian, in that colony, and he recognized that the sugar industry's task system had been formulated by the planters right after emancipation. When these tasks were set, the planters plainly had "hands" at the peak of their strength in mind—and, as Adamson (1972:112) says, "Negro hands at that. It was generally accepted that East Indians earned on the average about half as much in a given time as a Creole field worker. Under normal conditions, an East Indian could not perform one task a day." The useful contrast for our purposes, however, is not of East Indians and Creoles but of Caribbean labor and European labor. Adamson shows us that Beaumont saw the contrast quite clearly:

Chief Justice Beaumont gave a striking example of the immense effort required to complete certain kinds of work, compared with similar tasks in England. The standard rate in the 1860s for digging a trench was from three shillings and fourpence to four shillings for twenty-seven cubic yards. In England, the minimum price given for ordinary digging in common soils under six feet in depth was sixpence per cubic yard. This would have been equivalent to thirteen shillings and sixpence in terms of the British Guiana task and would have taken the best English laborer between two and three days to complete at five shillings a day. "But," continued Beaumont, "we have no excavating work so heavy as trench digging in Demerara and if the reader were to see a stalwart negro . . . sweltering under the blazing sun throughout the day . . . standing up to his knees and often to his hips in water, not only lifting (or more properly *wrenching*) 4,000 to 5,000 spits of dense clay . . . throwing these twelve or sixteen feet clear on each side—not with a pleasant hammer throwing swing, but delivered straight from the loins at the end of a seven foot shovel . . . I venture to think he would not only wonder at but admire . . . the 'lazy nigger.'" (Ibid., 112)

We must really try to imagine ourselves, each one of us, for a mere moment, to be that freedman, waist-deep in mud under a tropical sun, wielding a seven-foot shovel in order to throw four to five thousand shovelsful of mud twelve to sixteen feet up and to the side, in order to complete a daily "task" at the wage rate of four shillings. And now, would anyone care for a taste of one of Carlyle's pumpkins?

One notes the niggardliness of the planters, the collusion of the legislature, and the cruel confinement of the freed to wage labor on the plantations. Yet none of that explains why freed people were prepared to work so hard, even on the plantations. We know that they worked just as hard, if not harder, in the free villages in Guiana, until these were completely destroyed by planter intent. Some freed people even attempted to acquire plantations that they might then run collectively, but laws were quickly passed to prevent such a frightening development from catching hold (Adamson 1972:57ff.; Mintz 1979:235). What the cunning Carlyle never tells us is of the danger that Quashee might work too hard, rather than not hard enough. That free people preferred not to do it for those Carlyle calls the "real proprietors of said land," but on holdings of their own, is hardly mysterious. Yet they did it for the buckra all the same. All of the work that freed people did, they had to do within systems that only grudgingly took account of the fact of freedom. Meanwhile, the opportunities for change or improvement were limited by planter power, jealous of the land, braying in the legislatures, and lobbying the Colonial Office.

Do we conclude, then, that the more things change, the more they stay the same? I would argue that we do not. The British Guianese case is only one of many, and the outcomes varied substantially. So, for instance, we know that in some places, such as Barbados, where vacant land was scarce and the population dense, freed people continued to accept, *grosso modo*, the traditional work regimen on the plantations. We know that in other places, such as Jamaica, freed people sought and sometimes obtained access to vacant land, produced their own subsistence, and also (but variably) sold their labor to the plantations. In Haiti, when freedom came, most plantations soon withered and disappeared, and the land became occupied in substantial measure by freed people who established a genuinely peasant style of existence (Leyburn 1941; Trouillot 1990; see also Mintz 1979).

The outcomes in Guiana, Barbados, Jamaica, and Haiti varied according to local conditions, available resources, and much else. That none was a bucolic utopia should come as no surprise. To think that the freed people in any Caribbean sugar island were surprised by what happened when freedom came—never mind disappointed and angered—would really tax our imaginations. After all, if anyone knew the planters and the spirit of the metropolitan colonial officials, it was the slaves. Mistaken expectations they no doubt had—but few, one supposes, expected too much. And yet, viewed from a wholly different perspective, perhaps the newly freed did expect too much. The argument proceeds from the possibility that freed people may not have been as knowledgeable about Western society or as accepting of its underlying tenets as some observers may have been led to believe. Is it not possible that they imagined a truly different sort of society?

The cultures of origin of the slaves were not what has, in modern times, come to be called Western. Classics such as Herskovits's *Myth of the Negro Past* and later works by authors such as Fernando Ortiz, Roger Bastide, and Gonzalo Aguirre Beltrán, documenting the African cultural background of the slaves and their descendants, represent one side of this cultural reservoir, this *africanité*. The other side, which is far more familiar, was rooted in racist, rather than cultural, interpretations of slave behavior and is embodied in planters' opinions of the slaves, as well as in the language and documents of colonial legislation and literature. While one body of literature acknowledges the African past as a virtue, the other betrays the planters' pessimism about emancipation. In their view, not only were these Africans and children of Africans dangerous people, quite incapable of absorbing Western civilization, but now they would be permitted to loaf, to "relapse" into their natural state. Both sides take as established fact the persistence and strength of behavioral principles among the freed—that whatever else they may be, they are not Western—though the two sides differed in their optimism about the malleability of the human material. A full development of the implications of these two counterposed (yet oddly united) viewpoints defies summary treatment here and deserves better. But such implications must be mentioned, because a failure to take into account the power and significance of the African past, upon which the New World experience before freedom was built, may lead us seriously to misinterpret what the newly freed may have expected for themselves.

It might be said that enslavement, transportation, and the slave experience, which affected perhaps ten million Africans over nearly four centuries of post-Columbian history, was the single most significant mass acculturational event in world history. Recall that the ten-million figure includes only the enslaved. Were we to add their children and their children's children and all of those who died in the village raids and during transport (or soon after) of disease, starvation, and maltreatment, then the phenomenon begins to assume its real proportions. Certainly, given its scale, the enslavement of Africans was the most brutal and sweeping acculturational phenomenon in the history of our species, alongside which the brutality of the Holocaust dims somewhat. Such an assertion perhaps deserves explanation. Reviewing Stanley Elkins's *Slavery* in 1961, I wrote:

When Elkins turns to compare North American slavery and the concentration camp experience in recent western European history, his treatment is most of all provocative. It seemed effective to this reviewer, especially to the extent that it deals with the shock effects on human personality of certain cruelly repressive episodes, but much less effective as culture-historical analysis. . . . Only for the shortest of time-spans, in cultural terms, was the concentration camp an institution. Its purpose very soon came to be the annihilation of its inmates. The intent of slavery, much to the contrary, was to perpetuate a population in a given status, and to some extent it succeeded. (586)

Thirty years ago, then, I indicated my unease with comparisons of these so-called total institutions—Hitler's concentration camps (much less the death camps) and New World plantations. Yet comparison can teach us more about both. Slavery in the New World lasted nearly four hundred years and directly involved nearly ten million Africans (by conservative estimates) and countless millions of their descendants, whose labor turned large areas of the New World into Edens. One of the fundamental truths of this slavery was the enormous yield of unpaid labor it supplies to those who dealt in human chattel. In 1948 the Venn Sugar Commission estimated that slaves in British Guiana had moved by hand, with their shovels, *one hundred million tons* of mud to create the system of dikes and sluices that powered the sugar plantation system (Rodney 1981:2). Why is this not taken into account, when we tot up the disappointments of freedom? No such stunning accomplishment of brute labor can be credited to Hitler's camps; his captives—above all those in the death camps—had much less time. The intentions of each of these enslavements were quite different (even though the concentration camps were used to extract labor and even though the loss of life on the plantations was staggering). This comparison may seem otiose. It is introduced to underline the point that the slaves were acculturated to their condition; millions of them were born into it. And a culture—or better, many cultures—of slavery and enslavement was hence created.

It was an odd acculturation, since its victims had few prerogatives at the outset over what happened to them (Mintz and Price 1992). Yet it was acculturation, all the same. The enslavement, transportation, seasoning, and plantation experience was, among other things, an intensely individualizing process. Victims were sold or stolen from their regions, villages, and families and heterogenized and terrorized by what happened to them afterward. So many died during the first year of enslavement that all who lived must have thought of themselves as survivors—which they in fact were. Yet, as Price and I argue, slavery required that its victims establish social bonds with others to increase their chances of surviving. The remarkable proliferation of dyadic links, for example, which came to be associated with slavery, is eloquent evidence of the importance of such ties to survival (ibid.).

Implicit in this line of argument is the destruction of the social forms that could not be transported from Africa and the retention of the cultural content that could. The radical individualization of the enslaved was accompanied by the rapid (and still poorly documented) proliferation of new kinds of social linkage: new kinds of family, of ceremonial sponsorship, of cousinhood, and of friendship. Throughout Afro-America, improvised social systems emerged over time, forged under the harshest conditions imaginable, providing the enslaved with frameworks within which to experience life patterns that they themselves were inventing and that were endowing their lives with meaning.

For the slaves, access to land for individual agricultural production, and the opportunity to establish familial continuity through land and earned wealth, must have been paramount objectives. They were objectives that freedom might make more attainable, in the view of many. In situations where land could be acquired, individual freeholders undertook to produce food and goods for their families and themselves. They commonly produced items for sale, as well. The wider social and cultural consequences of this reconstitution of peasantries are well known; historical documentation for Haiti and Jamaica is so rich that it needs no repetition here.

But outcomes such as these also speak to wider political issues. In Jamaica, the Morant Bay rebellion—which was, as Elsa Goveia used to say, more a land riot than a rebellion—was the beginning of the end of peasant hopes. In Haiti—which the late Benoît Joachim once referred to as the world's oldest experiment in neocolonialism—the destruction of the peasantry was already under way in the nineteenth century. In hispanophone islands such as Puerto Rico, U.S. plantation development largely eliminated peasantries already embattled and impoverished by isolation and suffering from a total lack of official support. From the very beginning, wherever peasant and plantation were present in the same Afro-American society, all of the subsidies, all of the seedlings, all of the irrigation, all of the transport always went to the plantation, not to the peasantry. Those peasantries were, nearly everywhere, descended from the enslaved.

So there are solid grounds for claiming that Caribbean postemancipation agrarian history is a chronicle of defeat for freed people. But that defeat is still not total, nor did it happen instantaneously. What is more, the chronicle is inspirational, because it contains within itself some access to the slaves' vision of the meaning of freedom. That such freedom has never been fully realized anywhere in the region is not the same as its never having been realized at all.

The objectives of freed people probably include nearly everywhere some version of "forty acres and a mule," though varying in detail from locale to locale. For good historical reasons that vision did not rest upon a communitarian base but upon an individual view of enterprise, even if accompanied at times by quite sophisticated ideas of collective activity or cooperative unity. The push in British Guiana to purchase plantations collectively; the use of cooperative work groups for house building, harvesting, and planting; the growth of credit institutions; and the links between kinship and coordinated work all suggest that the powerful individualism that slavery helped to create did not wholly obviate group activity. Conceptions of individualistic agrarian communities were sometimes accompanied by political concepts—as in the case of Jamaica—though this was rarely articulated. Of course, such political visions were consistently thwarted. Even in the case of Haiti, government eventually settled on an extractive relationship to the peasantry, taking what it could and giving nothing back. We are unable to specify the extent to which ideas of individual productive independence on the land may have been tied to larger political and philosophical conceptions of the good, the just, or the ideal society. Slave philosophers there were; slave political economists were numerous; political tracts by slaves, however, are few in number. After freedom, most freed people, even if they were literate, were too busy struggling to stay independent economically to do much pamphleteering.

But is it not possible to imagine that slaves, individualized by slavery but not dehumanized by it, could conceive of a distinctive agrarian way of life for themselves? Could not that way of life, though lacking some of the structures of community and ethnic membership that must have typified the societies they came from, yet be free of the awful coercion that marked the slavery experience? To be sure, no such total vision can be documented, to my knowledge; nor can we infer, either from the experience of Christophe's kingdom or from what we know of the missionary villages of Jamaica, anything to verify its reality as a point of view. Yet I would argue that, if counterfactual explorations are in order, it is unconvincing to begin with freed people as *tabulae rasae* or, as Carlyle would have it, as simpletons whose only ambitions were to eat and to lie down. The fact is that the free people faced the vengeance of those who had ruled them, a vengeance enlivened by the persisting desire to extract labor from their free bodies. That did not end with freedom, and it continuously conditioned the struggle of the freed to improve their situations. The peculiar marriage of a slave labor system with burgeoning European capitalism produced handsomely for Europe; now the hope was that the newly freed could be domesticated entirely by the social and economic system that had enslaved them. That many freed people rejected in their minds the future that was chosen for them seems likely to me. That we are unable to know what future they would have chosen for themselves does not allow us to belittle it.

New World slavery reshaped the cultures of millions of persons. The structure of those new cultures has not been convincingly conceptualized as yet, either by anthropologists or by historians. Simple Europe-Africa contrasts, as if there had been mixture but not synthesis, are too simple. The tendency to see such cultures as coffee and cream—although not quite creamy enough and with pools of undisturbed coffee underneath—is an ethnocentric (and, in this instance, unforgivably Western) failing.

There are inescapable limitations to this way of thinking through the meanings of freedom. One is obvious enough, but bears remembering: none of us has ever lived even one minute as a Caribbean slave. Ask the survivor of a death camp whether he could have imagined one minute as a death camp inhabitant before becoming one. Few of us have ever even known a Caribbean slave personally; I knew one, but he was very old at the time, and I was quite young. Furthermore, as oppressed people—overworked, illiterate, driven—slaves had few opportunities to express themselves at length, and few were able to do so on paper so that we might study their reflections. For the most part, we must infer what slaves wanted from freedom from what they did with it, and there, too, we are reading mostly aggregate evidence, about a still insufficiently considered aspect of New World slavery.

Our thinking about the outcome of emancipation has been conditioned by an acceptance of the notion that slaves were non-Western folk whose future lay in westernization. This was one thing upon which missionaries and planters were agreed. After freedom, they were equally disappointed, as free people "backslid" into peasant life and "Africanized" religion. But what if—instead of using every means to drive the free back into the toils of the system that had enslaved them in the first place—the free had been helped to become what they themselves aspired to? Such a question is subversive, even in today's world; it might open a tiny window to the dread possibility that the West might not be best.

In any event, we keep remembering that, once emancipation arrived, those who had been slaves were no longer slaves. To forget that, in the welter of the criticisms we make of the Pollyannas and the Dr. Panglosses, is to forget too much.

NOTES

I wish to thank for their help and criticisms Seymour Drescher, Michel-Rolph Trouillot, and Jacqueline Mintz. None of them can be held responsible, however, for persisting errors of fact or interpretation.

REFERENCES

Adamson, Alan. 1972. *Sugar Without Slaves*. New Haven: Yale University Press.

Carlyle, Thomas. 1853. *Occasional Discourse on the Nigger Question*. London: Thos. Bosworth.

Leyburn, James. 1941. *The Haitian People*. New Haven: Yale University Press.

Mintz, Sidney. 1961. Review of S. Elkins, *Slavery*. In *American Anthropologist* 63: 579–87.

———. 1979. Slavery and the Rise of Peasantries. In *Roots and Branches,* edited by Michael Craton, 213–42. Toronto: Pergamon.

Mintz, Sidney, and Richard Price. 1992. *The Birth of African-American Culture: An Anthropological Perspective*. Boston: Beacon.

Rodney, Walter. 1981. *A History of the Guyanese Working People, 1881–1905*. Baltimore: Johns Hopkins University Press.

Trouillot, Michel-Rolph. 1990. *Haiti: State Against Nation*. New York: Monthly Review Press.

RAYMOND T. SMITH

Race, Class, and Gender in the Transition to Freedom

I have come to the sad conclusion that SLAVERY, whether established by law, or by law abrogated, exists very extensively in this world, in and out of the West Indies; and, in fact, that you cannot abolish slavery by act of parliament, but can only abolish the *name* of it, which is very little!

— Thomas Carlyle

Slavery has not existed in the Western Hemisphere for more than a hundred years, but African Americans still suffer unique disabilities. Emancipation was a revolutionary event, completely altering the legal basis on which social relations had been constructed since the settlement of the slave colonies of the New World, and yet the core of those social relations changed hardly at all. This paradox can be understood only when it is realized that the suffering of African Americans is not caused by slavery but by the forces that reproduce the social systems established after slavery: the systems forged by the reforming zeal of abolition working on a resistant power structure and carried forward to the present.

The contributors to this volume take, or discuss, a wide range of views about the ending of slavery. Was it a tragedy? Economically unnecessary? Unfortunate, even? Did it constitute a social revolution? Did nothing change? Were the changes merely cosmetic? Was emancipation a lost opportunity, and if so who lost it? There can be no question of settling these issues. As Max Weber observes, "in the cultural sciences concept-construction depends on the setting of the problem, and the latter varies with the content of the culture itself" (Weber 1949:105). Peter Kolchin thinks that modern historians are too subjective, over-identifying with nineteenth-century advocates of one position or another instead of getting on with the job of objective history. But there is no objective history; historical interpretation is always driven by current values.[1]

The dreams of racial and cultural integration that inspired the concept of the melting pot seem curiously inappropriate as militant nationalism reappears in Europe and continues elsewhere in the world. In the United States the first black mayor of New York City has offered a replacement for the image of the melting pot; that of the "gorgeous mosaic of race and religious faith, of national origin and sexual orientation" (*New York Times,* 3 January 1990). Many Caribbean politicians have shifted from materialism to cultural nationalism as ideologies tack to catch the prevailing wind, and social theory itself, reacting, as it always does to dominant political concerns, shows a renewed interest in "pluralism" and the "primordial attachments" that Clifford Geertz identifies as "the 'givens'—or, more precisely, as culture is inevitably involved in such matters, the assumed 'givens'—of social existence: immediate contiguity and kin connection mainly, but beyond them the givenness that stems from being born into a particular religious community, speaking a particular language, or even a dialect of a language, and following particular social practices" (1963:109). But this statement contains its own paradox: the key phrase is "the assumed 'givens'—of social existence." "Primordial attachments" are not primordial; they must continually be reproduced. They are frequently invented to suit the purpose of the moment and then appear to have always existed (see Hobsbawm and Ranger 1983).

The societies that succeeded slave regimes incorporated those assumed givens of social existence in a particularly debilitating way, and here I focus on the way in which that incorporation took place. Any such discussion must begin with a conception of how slave societies themselves were articulated, and here we tread dangerous interpretive ground. More than forty years of argument has not produced agreement on the apparently simple question of whether slavery was, or was not, more harsh in Protestant northern European slave colonies than in the colonies of Catholic Spain and Portugal (if not France). All that commands agreement is that local conditions were important and that conditions of servitude varied a good deal over time. Anthropologists are generally fastidious about these particularities of time and place, but here generalization, with its attendant danger of vacuity, cannot be avoided.

Hierarchy and Equality

The meaning of freedom from slavery can be seen as the outcome of a conflict that lies at the heart of modern society—between belief in the equality of individuals and belief in the reality and significance of race and other markers of hierarchy. The dilemma is not, of course, achieving ideological consistency; it is the unequal distribution of power in class society.

The key development following emancipation was the transformation from societies in which race and servile status formed the basis of the legally constituted social hierarchy to one in which hierarchy was officially denied—the equality of all individuals was the only legal basis of social order, and class (supposedly based on achievement) was the only valid basis of social distinction. The way in which this transformation was managed, and the consequent dialectic between hierarchy and egalitarianism, is the source of variation among the different New World societies in which slavery was an important institution.

The utilitarian reformers responsible for implementing the transition to freedom in the British West Indies believed that better conditions could change the character of the ex-slaves, and, once the workers were educated to the task, the natural identity of interests of the different classes would assert itself. The socially enshrined image of Africans as innately and ineradicably inferior never disappeared entirely from the consciousness of the old elites, but the new order demanded it be changed to accommodate the possibility of a reconstructed "Christian black" (see Diane Austin-Broos's chapter). In the United States, the very term *Reconstruction* embodied the intention of radical reform, an intention that collided with deeply entrenched beliefs in Negro incapacity and inferiority to produce a century of contradiction.

By the 1850s in Jamaica, and not very long after 1865 in the United States, liberal opinion had reconciled itself to a continuing conflict between black and white. In other words, the meaning of freedom resides in the perversion of liberal democratic principles by racist ideas, by outright substitution, by a subtle infusion of racist logic into liberal ideas, or by a continuing tension between them. As Eric Foner warns, one should not view "racism as a deus ex machina that independently explains the course of events"; it is "an intrinsic part of the process of historical development, which affected and was affected by changes in the social and political order" (Foner 1988:xxvi). The varying interpretations of the postslavery era throughout the Americas all recognize the radical nature of the new order and the neutralizing of radical change by entrenched interests, but our concern is with the mechanisms through which continuity and change were effected.

If we can understand how the ideologies of liberal democracy—and, one should add, those of Marxism-Leninism — maintain regimes that embody racist, ethnic, and gender discriminations, then we may be able to appreciate the source of current unrest as well as the meaning of freedom from slavery. That source is neither primordial attachments nor a natural aversion to the other; it is the sense of injustice that flows from the perversion of social values in the struggle for power.

Recent writers about slavery and its aftermath are wary about racism. Once treated as a mere epiphenomenon, there is a growing, if vague, realization that both race and class are important elements in the conceptual structure of the societies of the Western Hemisphere (if not everywhere in the modern world), and that native concepts should be theoretically recognized. The well-known positions that racism is a mere rationalization of economic interests (Patterson 1969; Post 1978; Williams 1944), or that race is a natural phenomenon providing a basis for social categorization that will always be with us (Tocqueville 1945; Hoetink 1967), are considerably muted. In the 1980s, these extreme views were enfolded in a new focus on practice, part of a wider theoretical reorientation in the social sciences (Bourdieu 1977; Comaroff 1982; Comaroff and Comaroff 1991; Giddens 1979; Ortner 1984; Sahlins 1985; see also Genovese 1972; Hall 1980). In Bourdieu's words, "What we need to do . . . is a form of structural history that is rarely practiced, which finds in each successive state of the structure under examination both the product of previous struggles to maintain or to transform this structure and the principle, via the contradictions, the tensions, and the relations of force which constitute it, of subsequent transformations" (Wacquant 1989:37).

Much the same point was made by David Brion Davis, who wrote of the challenge of "conceptualizing contradictions" and "encompassing all variables and contradictions within a dialectical theory of class and ideology" in the manner of Eugene Genovese (1974:5). Genovese boldly declares that slavery was "by definition and in essence . . . a system of class rule," but his actual analysis of "class power in racial form" is sensitive to the hegemonic power of ideologies — including those of race (1972:3–4). Many writers declare an intention to envelop contradictions within the language of dialectics or indulge in wishful thinking about the infinite adaptability of Marxism (see Mills 1987:75–81), but actual discussions generally fall back onto economic interests, adaptation, institutional pluralism, or the world system of capitalism as the prime movers in social life — and downplay ideology. It is now important to shift attention from the accepted idea that both race and class are important variables, to the question of just what we take these variables to be.

Race

Is Racism a Rationalization of Class?

It has been widely accepted, at least since the 1930s, that consciousness of race, and racism, are merely the transposed perception of class or manipulative attempts (conscious or unconscious) to divide and rule the working class by setting sections of it against each other. This carries the implication that race consciousness is false consciousness and will cease to be significant once its class basis is unmasked or changed — allowing for cultural lag of course. Quite what happens then is not always made clear, but often there is the further implication that racial minorities will be assimilated into the dominant culture. Hoetink refers to this as "sociologistic optimism" (1967:84ff.).

Optimism aside, the position is well known; racial prejudice and discrimination originate in a particular form of labor system, either in the slave plantation system or in postslavery conditions, where the intensification of racial hostility was functional for the maintenance of class relations. To say that this is a respectable position in the social sciences is not to be sarcastic; it is my own point of departure. The chapters in this volume provide abundant evidence for the functionality of racial discrimination in maintaining class privilege after the ending of slavery. Few would share Pieter Emmer's view that racism was a negligible factor when compared with the rational demands of the economic order. The mere assumption that racism hides class interest has proven quite powerful as a device for uncovering the operation of economic and political forces in the transition from slavery to freedom. But a point is always reached where the stubborn reality of ideological forces refuses to submit to economic reductionism, and, for anthropologists and social historians in particular, the analysis of racist beliefs and practices is too important and interesting to ignore.

Does Race or Racism Determine Social Relations?

The idea that race or racism determines social relations is just as misguided as the idea that class structure underlies racism, but it is harder to characterize. Eighteenth-century writers provide a window into the taken-for-granted common sense of that period. In discussing the various classes of eighteenth-century Jamaican society, Bryan Edwards notes that free People of Colour are not all the same, for "the free Blacks, not having the . . . advantage [of some portion of Christian blood in their veins] . . . differ but little from their brethren in bonds" (1794:2:26). The assumption that race determines (or should determine) social status and the distribution of power was so pervasive at the time, and the actual distribution of wealth and privilege so apparently congruent with this assumption, that it is easy to take it to be the structuring principle of those societies. And yet, the exceptions were so many and so obvious that it seems the intensity of expression of the principle was proportionate to the frequency of the exceptions. Edward Long's most virulent racism was directed against the spreading tendency to *ignore* racial etiquette in social relations and to rear up a "race of mongrels," but even he advocated a special privileged place for Free Coloured persons: "They would then form the centre of connexion between the two extremes, producing a regular establishment of three ranks of men, dependent on each other, and rising in a proper climax of subordination, in which the Whites would hold the highest place. I can foresee no mischief that can arise from the enfranchisement of every Mulatto child" (ibid., 333).

When Elsa Goveia concluded that "the integrating factor which affects the [Leeward Islands slave] society as a whole, *is the acceptance of the inferiority of Negroes to whites*" (E. Brathwaite 1971:184), she did so in full recognition that this was a means of social control necessary to counteract egalitarian ideologies that were already in circulation. And Bryan Edwards's formulation, couched in terms of "Christian blood," contains its own ambiguity as to whether that miraculous substance, black blood, could ever be transubstantiated into the Christian type.

Acceptance of racial inferiority and superiority is not the integrating principle of modern New World societies, but Hoetink makes a powerful case for the idea that "each multiracial society is racist in the sense that membership in a socioracial group prevails over achievement in the allotment of social position. . . . An affluent black doctor in the United States is considered black first; his professional qualities and economic achievements only serve to determine his position on the socioeconomic scale within the black group" (Hoetink 1973:49). In Afro–Latin America, he argues, it may be much more difficult to assign a person to one of the many differentiated socioracial categories, but socioracial stratification still prevails over the socioeconomic. "From the moment that such a stratification is formed, racist principles of selection predominate over nonracist ones in such a manner as to preserve this strati-fication" (ibid., 50). But the true basis of his belief is revealed in his idea that racial "prejudices can be regarded genetically as instruments of the human desire to make distinctions" and "if within one society groups occur with clearly different physical characteristics, the existence of ra-cial prejudices cannot be denied" (ibid., 89). In other words, if race is an essential quality of groups and individuals, racial prejudice will be real. Like the people he is writing about, he believes that those physical differences are self-evident and much more significant than differences in stature, head shape, eye color, and hair color within any supposed racial group.

Alexis de Tocqueville also saw race differences and slavery as the great problem areas in American life. Why are they problematic? First, because slavery contradicts the principle of democracy and the spirit of the nation, but also because Americans (by which he means Anglo-Americans) regard it as abhorrent to engage in precisely the kind of ac-tivity that would, he thought, solve the problem of race relations, that is, intermarriage. Intermarriage, for Tocqueville, would not be a means of just producing closer social relations; it would result in the creation of a new, third race, thus solving a problem of nature rather than a problem of society. Tocqueville predicts a calamitous end as the im-balance of the races leads to confrontation, because physical reality is immutable and the horror of interracial marriage (which would alone alter this natural state of affairs) is unlikely to disappear. The same kind of thinking in terms of race as a physical problem underlies the think-ing of many white supremacists; for them, the inevitable outcome of equality would be miscegenation.

Hoetink's answer to sociologistic optimism is deep pessimism; it is folly to believe that exposing racial prejudices as mere myths will put an end to them. "As soon as man is able to explain that it is the force of gravity which causes objects to fall downwards, there is little point in his cherishing the hope that he will ever come across a waterfall flow-ing upwards" (1967:89). This neglects the fact that it is precisely an un-derstanding of gravity and hydraulics that enabled somebody to make the Chicago River flow backward and to make waterfalls produce light and power.

However, Hoetink is wrong to think that a view of race as a mere distortion of class must be optimistic. One can be just as pessimistic about the difficulty of changing the class structure of a society like the United States as one can be about eradicating racial prejudice or making waterfalls flow upward. There is extensive literature on this problem—class interests are not transparent.

Race, Class, and Social Practice

Writers in this volume (with a few exceptions) agree that both race and class must be considered in studying the complexities of social practice. The question is, how? Even more important, what are these entities of race, class, and the associated concept, gender? The material reality of the formations in which the socially constructed categories of race, class, and gender are embedded is not in contention, nor are the historical processes through which they are reproduced and transformed. It is the taken-for-granted systems of concepts that enter into the processes of social life that need more attention. To stress their importance is not to embrace idealism or to abandon science; it is merely to assert the social reality of concepts and to refuse to treat them as epiphenomenal and therefore of no causal significance.

Race and the "Biologizing" of Social Relations

Whenever the word *race* is used, it carries the implication of an embedded theory of physical difference, but not all theories of physical difference are theories of race, of course. Gender is built around a theory of physical difference that cuts across race. In Euro-American societies the distinctive feature of race is common substance symbolized by blood. Since this is also the distinctive feature of kinship, it is clear that the two are closely linked at the level of cultural conceptions. We are not, therefore, surprised to discover that in nineteenth-century England different status groups, virtually endogamous, were referred to as races. Racial and kinship blood is not readily visible to the naked eye (or the unnaked eye for that matter; this kind of blood defies the powers of even an electron microscope), and, therefore, external indices—such as appearance, manners (breeding as they say), and intelligence—are believed to point to this difference of substance. Socially constructed theories of physical differences are widespread in the societies we are dealing with, and I use the term *race* to indicate such theories.

The taken-for-granted nature of these conceptions of race are illustrated by the following anecdote.[2] On 12 August 1988, Senator Daniel Inouye presided over a Senate select committee hearing on an application by a group of people from North Carolina to be recognized as an Indian tribe. Looking at the applicants who had assembled in the hearing room, the casual observer would have been excused for believing that they were African Americans, but, in fact, they claimed to belong to the Lumbee tribe, whose homeland is in Robeson County, North Carolina. The Bureau of Indian Affairs of the federal government of the United States is vested with the power to determine whether any given individual is or is not an Indian. While there has been a lot of discussion about community continuity and cultural identity, the basic criterion is blood. The felt problem is how to detect the requisite presence or absence of the statutory proportion. In the 1930s, anthropologists used anthropometric instruments to make complex head and body measurements that supposedly would reveal just how Indian they were.[3] This fact of contemporary U.S. politics reveals the pervasiveness of racialist assumptions. The point is not that the society of the United States is structured around the cultural principle of racial difference but that, in an attempt to ensure equity based on the principles of liberal individualism, taken-for-granted commonsense assumptions about race are mobilized.

Although race and gender are erected on the presupposition of differences of substance (the distinctive feature of gender is not blood but genitalia), it would be a mistake to think that we can understand either a putative race or gender as a thing in itself. A race is an element in a system of races, and the analytical problem is to understand the social construction of that system and the way it is used in social practice.

Class

Raymond Williams, in that useful little compendium *Keywords: A Vocabulary of Culture and Society,* says that "*class* in its modern social sense, with relatively fixed names for particular classes (*lower class, middle class, upper class, working class* and so on) belongs essentially to the period between 1770 and 1840" (1976:51), when ideas of political freedom and the repudiation of hierarchy were being forged at the same time as a formally free market in industrial labor was being developed and extended. Williams argues that the increasing use of the word *class* as a name for social divisions "relates to the increasing consciousness that social position is made rather than merely inherited" (52) and to a new sense that society itself was a *system* that created specific kinds of internal division.

By the 1840s, it was becoming increasingly clear that the dislocations and mobility accompanying the development of industry were creating new rigidities in the structure of European societies. Friedrich Engels, in his *The Condition of the Working Class in England,* based on almost two years of close study of Manchester—the "classic type of modern industrial town"—confidently predicted a bloodbath as the misery of the working class caused it to rise up in righteous fury against the middle classes. "The war of the poor against the rich will be the most blood-thirsty the world has ever seen" (1958:334). At the same time, he drew a picture of England as a plural society in which "the working classes have become a race apart from the English bourgeoisie. . . . The work-ers differ from the middle classes in speech, in thoughts and ideas, in customs, morals, politics and religion. They are two quite different na-tions, as unlike as if they were differentiated by race" (ibid., 139).

In spite of such dire predictions, and the image of pluralism shared by conservative writers like Disraeli (1845), Britain managed to contain its class conflicts within a social order that Engels described as being worse than slavery because it lacked the security that bonded servitude provided. The conflicts were contained not only through economic ex-pansion, which ameliorated some of the stressful conditions of early capitalism, but also through the development of ideological structures and instruments remarkably like those in the West Indies in roughly the same period. They included the spread of state-supervised elementary education, the stabilization and elaboration of the monarchy during Vic-toria's reign, the development of an expansionist nationalism, and the creation of an "aristocracy of the working class" as industry evolved (Cannadine 1983; Corrigan and Sayer 1985:114–65; Foster 1974:203–50).

The process of state formation that followed upon the abolition of slavery in the Western Hemisphere was necessarily different from that in the great capitalist societies of Europe and North America, but it is not difficult to see the parallels as formally free markets in labor replaced slavery and created new classes of laborers, cultivators, peasants, bu-reaucrats, professionals, and so forth, to complement the diminished planter class and the revived corporate capitalists. Several essays in this volume detail the course of this process in the mid–nineteenth century and the way in which the ideology of an open class system was aban-doned in favor of explicit racial segregation or, more insidiously, was subverted by the insertion of racism into the very texture of class. Seg-regation could be, and eventually was, attacked, but the "biologizing" of social relations, of which racism is just one manifestation, has proven far more resistant to change and is perhaps an intrinsic part of the struc-ture of egalitarian individualistic social orders (Stolcke 1981:39–40; see also Dumont 1980:261–66).

Gender

Sex discrimination has often been compared to racial discrimination, but gender divisions never follow class, as race distinctions frequently do. Still, the comparison is interesting because in both cases there is a biologizing of social relations that seems to have been part of a more general trend in a European society composed of nation-states, a trend that culminated in the extreme of Germany's Third Reich.

Gender, as an analytical term, has generally been used to mean the cultural rather than the natural basis of sexual difference, what some refer to as sex-role differentiation. It would be valuable to have a parallel term for the cultural, as opposed to the natural, basis of racial difference, though that would grant to race a reality in nature that is highly questionable.[4] As an analytical term, *gender* has been largely confined to discussions where femaleness is the major issue, but this ignores the fact that gender embraces the social construction of masculinity as well as femininity and thereby neglects some of the most important sites of power (Alonso 1988:125ff.). Some Marxist discussions of gender have broken away from this narrow view, but they have generally focused on the class exploitation of female labor, thus unduly restricting the significance of gender and effectively reducing it to class.

The complexities of the relation between gender and the hierarchical societies in which slavery was institutionalized have not been extensively explored. Verena Martinez-Alier's (1974) analysis of marriage, class, and color in Cuba is one notable exception; here, she shows the intimate relationship between female honor, male sexual aggression, and the hierarchical nature of Cuban society. Wyatt-Brown's *Southern Honor* (1982) contains suggestive material on the relation between the social construction of masculinity and the southern decision to fight the Civil War, and he also brings out the importance of extensive kinship ties among all ranks of white society. As George Fredrickson has remarked, this book is a sort of white counterpart to the detailed work of Eugene Genovese on the culture of the slaves, documenting some of the cultural assumptions and community sentiments that operated beyond the boundaries of legal and political regulation.

But we still need a much more detailed examination of the relation between gender construction and social, economic, and political practice in slave societies and their successor regimes. For example, in the nineteenth century it seems to have been the case from Brazil to the United States that one meaning of freedom was the withdrawal of female labor from plantation work, a matter that has not been given the attention it deserves (see, however, Jones 1985 for an excellent discussion of these issues). Was this solicitude for women an attempt by freedmen to establish their own control over women, women's own declaration of their primary interest in domesticity, or what?

In the Caribbean, the position of women of mixed race is of great interest when considering the relation between gender and power. As is well documented, during the slavery period, women of mixed race were the preferred nonlegal partners of white men and frequently managed to establish a measure of relief from field labor for themselves and their children with access to privileged status. From these hypergamous unions (generally the very archetype of matrifocality and rarely legal, coresidential, or socially recognized), the core of a new class of Free People of Colour emerged in those territories where the shortage of whites made their recruitment into a range of intermediate positions functionally expedient. By the 1870s, in most of the British West Indies the Coloured woman had become transformed from the "kept miss" to the exemplar of conjugal respectability and the principal denouncer of the immorality of the black lower class (R. Smith 1988:101–06). And, as Diane Austin shows, the element of power that inhered in the differential status of white and racially mixed offspring was transferred to the cultural concept of the inferiority of the "outside" child of poor women and wealthy men in modern Jamaica. In other words, the cultural construction of gender is inextricably bound up with the meaning of power, and one might add, of race. As she says, "illegitimacy represents for Jamaicans a paradigmatic social subservience which was realized simultaneously between classes, cultures and races for much of Jamaica's history" (Austin 1984:156).

The Meaning of Freedom

A pervasive anger was unleashed by abolition and the Civil War in North America and nobody working in the Caribbean or Latin America needs to be reminded of the expressions of anger from Haiti in the late eighteenth century, from Jamaica in 1865, from Cuba in the late nineteenth century, and so on. But the crucial question is, what was the anger about? To say that people were angry because they were exploited or oppressed is not to say a great deal, because oppression and exploitation have been the pervasive human condition. Nor can we give an answer that will suffice for all places and all times, even within the broad area of our concern.

Michel-Rolph Trouillot has shown that in Haiti during the early days of the 1791 uprising, the rebels' representatives presented peace claims demanding freedom in a very specific way—freedom for the leaders of the rebellion, freedom from the whip, and "the right for each *slave* to cultivate his provision ground, every other day." His conclusion is that *"the acquisition of family land and the labourer's rights to the product of his labour done on such land were the terms in which freedom was first formulated"* (1980:114). Perhaps this confirms the existence of countercapitalist values mentioned by Jean Besson, but it is surely a matter of the utmost importance that emancipation, when it finally came, was part of a broader movement toward the social definition of individual rights, a movement that Pieter Emmer is wrong to ignore as being insignificant for ex-slaves ignorant of the demands of a market economy. Indeed, what makes the burden of racist or sexist oppression so unbearably onerous is precisely that it is a denial of the very principles upon which the modern state is ideologically constructed. To say that these constructions mystify the real basis of state power is a truism; the question is not even how successful they are in that mystification. The question is, what part does ideology play in social practice?

Slavery in democratic societies, such as the United States, is a contradiction, but even the most ardent proponents of freedom—such as Thomas Jefferson and George Washington—managed to express both aversion and attachment to slavery. The position was much the same in the Caribbean; neither Bryan Edwards nor Moreau de Saint-Mery allowed their radical sentiments to overwhelm their defense of slavery as the economic bedrock of the slave colonies. By 1865, slaves and ex-slaves alike must have had a surfeit of rhetoric, enough to make anybody angry, but the surprising fact is that they were so reasonable in their demands and so patently wrong in their conviction that fairness would triumph. In Jamaica the rioters at Morant Bay in 1865 did not resort to violence until they had exhausted all other forms of protest, including a petition to the queen. Even in the midst of their most militant protest they seemed to have faith in the fairmindedness of the governor—an illusion that was to be washed away in blood (Heuman 1981:190).

In his recent book on Reconstruction, Eric Foner notes that "'freedom' itself became a terrain of conflict, its substance open to different and sometimes contradictory interpretations, its content changing for whites as well as blacks in the aftermath of the Civil War" (1988:77). Foner examines a number of areas in which "the desire for independence from white control, for autonomy both as individuals and as members of a community" found expression (ibid., 78). They include freedom of movement, the reuniting and stabilization of families, the withdrawal of women from field labor, the consolidation of independent black churches and voluntary associations, the pursuit of education, an end to economic exploitation through the freedmen's ownership of their own land, and political representation. With some important differences of emphasis, these were common concerns among ex-slaves throughout the hemisphere.

Freedom of Movement, Land, and Labor Markets

The most fundamental dimension of the transformation from slavery to a capitalist order was the creation of a formally free market in labor. Without access to a free market, there can be no commodification of labor. The agitated movement of newly freed slaves, especially in the American South and Brazil, could have been a simple test of the limits of coercion, a movement away from that coercion, or a search for kin separated by the inhumanity of slave sales, but there is a deeper issue: did the ex-slaves want to participate in a transformed social economic system? No issue in the meaning of freedom is more fundamental than this. Foner says that "between the planters' need for a disciplined labor force and the freedmen's quest for autonomy, conflict was inevitable" (1988:134–35), but what was the autonomy that freedmen were seeking? Of the numerous answers given to this question, each reflects a particular theoretical perspective but rarely provides information on the culture of the slaves themselves.

Peter Kolchin's nicely balanced discussion of the factors involved in the transformation of the American South after emancipation does not resolve the matter; in some senses, it creates more problems than it solves. To say that there is irony in the fact that freedmen almost everywhere decried the new dispensation as not sufficiently free, while at the same time they demonstrated an unexpected attachment to many of the old ways does not answer the question of what freedom meant to them. Increasing black social stratification based on new economic opportunities is shown to coexist with an apparent reluctance to abandon customary ways, including a resistance to punctuality, frugality, restraint, and Victorian sexual morality. In other words, Kolchin seems to reproduce the very dichotomy of explanation that separates, he says, the tragic from the transformative vision of southern Reconstruction history and, in the process, slants some of the comparative evidence. For example, to say flatly that Jamaican freedmen withdrew from the plantation economy ignores a controversy that has produced a complex literature of its own. The issues are dealt with by Jean Besson.

Besson's position is that the Afro-Caribbean villages established after the full emancipation of 1838 were not simply a flight from the estates (or a withdrawal from the plantation economy), but rather the material embodiment of a long tradition of resistance to slavery through the development of Creole institutions of kinship, community, and land tenure. In her chapter in this volume, Besson's central point is that slaves "desired personal liberty and . . . land of their own" (Farley 1954) and that the slaves sought to establish autonomy and community, often based on customary and legal rights to land. In this regard, slaves were no different from other settlers.

Gavin Wright makes the point that there was no large-scale agriculture in America other than the slave plantation for the simple reason that free labor would not work on plantations, preferring independent farm ownership. "Perhaps farmers valued independence for its own sake, but they also valued the economic security which landownership provided, and they also enjoyed the earnings of the land and the prospect of realizing large capital gains from an increase in land values" (1976: 321). Why should we think that blacks were any different from whites in this regard? Resistance to the plantation was, at least in part, an expression of this universally noted preference, and the main justification for slavery was the simple fact that, in areas of available land, free labor would always choose independent farming. Michel-Rolph Trouillot's material on Haiti and Dominica makes crystal clear the different attitudes toward plantation agriculture of the mixed-race elites and the ex-slave workers; the former had ambitions to becoming planters themselves, while the latter were reluctant to engage in plantation labor even if it was to their economic advantage. Besson—following Mintz—asserts a pan-Caribbean protopeasant adaptation within slavery, combining kinship, community, and customary rights to land in a distinct Creole way of life—which embodies some continuities from Africa that persisted through emancipation to the present day.

The question of African continuities is a perennial one in studies of

African-American social life, and Besson is properly wary of exaggerated attributions. Although the postemancipation situation in Jamaica was full of conflict over land, there is no report of deep-seated African concepts of landownership being expressed in slave claims to rights in sugarcane land. By far the majority of ex-slaves were forced by circumstances to remain on plantations as tenants-at-will after emancipation and were often forced to pay rent for the back lands they had regarded as theirs by customary tenure during slavery. Agitation against the imposition of these rents was combined with profound dissatisfaction at being prevented, on pain of eviction, from growing cash crops, such as sugar. In Guyana, where ex-slaves acquired whole sugar plantations, there were fewer restrictions on what could be grown on newly acquired lands, but other mechanisms—such as planter control of shipping— were used to restrict the ability of ex-slaves to enter cash crop markets.[5] In short, the land question was not so much a matter of the persistence of precapitalist conceptions of ownership as a matter of the continuing struggle of the planter class to control labor on its terms. In the case of the United States, it is clear that the struggle was over the control of cash crop land and labor rather than over precapitalist conceptions.

The observation that workers drawn into expanding capitalist production were resistant to the dehumanizing features of that social order is certainly not new; many of those who lived through the early development of industrial expansion in Europe wrote movingly of the human cost it entailed, and historians have documented that cost (cf. Thompson 1963, 1975; Hobsbawm 1968). Whether we label plantation production in the New World *capitalist* or not, it was certainly part and parcel of the process of European industrial expansion and used techniques of large-scale organization characteristic of industrial production. Fogel and Engerman's description of the southern U.S. plantation as a rationally managed capitalistic enterprise, staffed by workers with a positive attitude toward regulated labor (Fogel and Engerman 1974:147; Fogel 1989:162), served to counteract some of the more emotional stereotypes of lazy black workers and their demoralized social life; but the less cautious idea that they were possessed of a Protestant ethic does not accord with what we know of the complexities of the social practice of the ex-slaves.

Jean Besson, Michel-Rolph Trouillot, and others show that landownership symbolized both freedom and a sense of community, but the freed population could not escape the increasing influence of the state, whether it was colonial, in the case of most of the Caribbean (including such nominally independent territories as Haiti), or regional and federal, in the case of the United States and South America. As in Europe, a working class did not spring into being overnight; it had to be made and to make itself in resistance to state and class coercion. That class was neither a disciplined industrial proletariat nor a withdrawn and culturally autonomous peasantry; it was forced to develop within the boundaries set by the racial ideologies of the dominant class, boundaries that engendered a deep, abiding, and wholly rational sense of injustice.

One factor that seems to be generally neglected in the debate on the flight from the plantations is the ex-slave's sense of status and dignity. This is a complex matter that cannot be reduced to a simple formula, but at least part of the autonomy desired by ex-slaves was the opportunity for enhanced status. Ownership of land, or even sharecropping, was preferable to a status approximating that of slave. It is no accident that indentured laborers were referred to as slaves and looked down upon by freemen. In the 1950s, it was common for Indo-Guyanese rice-farming villagers to look down upon sugar estate residents in the same way; supporters of village cricket teams playing against sugar estate teams were known to flaunt their land title documents as a sign of contempt for opponents.

Enhanced status did not always mean abandoning estate labor, and indeed its major characteristic is precisely its relative character. In the later nineteenth century, African villagers came to constitute an aristocracy of sugar plantation labor in Guyana, proud of their superior strength and endurance in canecutting and of their skill as "shovel-men" responsible for the maintenance of drainage and irrigation works (Rodney 1981:31–59). In Jamaica in the 1960s, there were frequent complaints from midsized farms that they were unable to obtain labor, while sugar estates, paying similar wages, suffered no shortage. By that time, wage labor on large impersonal plantations was considered less demeaning than subservience to employers of roughly the same status.

Both Gavin Wright and Jay Mandle observe that, if land distribution had been carried out in the American South after the Civil War, it might have changed the racial and class basis of southern politics. A similar conclusion could be drawn for Jamaica. Was the resistance to land reform a matter of class or racism? I am unconvinced by Mandle's argument that the restoration of the plantation complex in the southern United States created the racist authoritarian regime that denied true freedom to blacks. The empirical separation of class and racism is a mistake: race was built into the very fabric of the social formation, so that if class is conceived as an empirical entity rather than an analytical category, its very embodiment was racial; in that case, one can indeed speak of the black lower class.

There is no point in quibbling over the facts of this particular matter, but it does raise the question of how historians can analyze cultural concepts that are difficult to elucidate even with extensive field research material.

The Stabilization of the Family

Kinship and the family are prime areas for the study of race, class, and gender, for it is here that all the forces that reproduce the social order converge. Consideration of kinship and the family raises the most difficult and far-reaching questions about the meaning of freedom, about the nature of African-American culture, and about the integration of the ex-slave population into the societies of the colonies and nation-states where they lived. It cannot be divorced from the discussion of land, labor, and economic issues generally, but all too often kinship is treated as a mere reflex of material factors.

Comparative consideration of the United States, the Caribbean, and South America is made difficult by the paucity of information on African-American kinship in the United States. This statement may appear exaggerated in view of the refined analysis of a considerable body of aggregate data derived from censuses and surveys, but it generally has been interpreted within limited frames of reference, often closely tied to discussions of welfare policy in the United States. Even historical studies are sometimes referred to as contributions to the ongoing policy debate. See for example the vast literature surrounding the Moynihan report (Rainwater and Yancey 1967) and the more recent controversies generated by the publication of Murray's *Losing Ground* (1984). The cardinal points are marked by the following assertions:

- The black family was hopelessly disorganized by slavery and has never recovered, though a few upwardly mobile individuals have been able to stabilize their family life and achieve the American norm.
- Black family life showed enormous resilience during and after slavery, was stable, nuclear, and essentially the same as so-called normal family life among other groups.
- Deviations from normal family life among African Americans are due to the adaptations forced upon people by poverty, unemployment, and social isolation.

- Deviations from normal family life among African Americans are caused by the demoralizing effect of dependency produced by welfare benefits, which destroy incentives for work and respectable independence.

Most of these arguments (except the last) have been widely applied to African-American kinship throughout the hemisphere — it has been generally assumed that there is a "normal" nuclear family pattern, from which deviations have been forced by circumstances of one kind or another. The literature is extensive and need not be reviewed yet again (cf. R. T. Smith 1988; Patterson 1982; Martinez-Alier 1974; Stolcke 1987), but it is increasingly evident that these materialist arguments neglect the ideological elements that shape kinship relations as well as interpret them.

Since at least the late eighteenth century it has been common to assume that African slaves had no family life. Adam Smith, in *The Wealth of Nations*, declares that "among our slaves in the West Indies there is no such thing as a lasting union. The female slaves are all prostitutes, and suffer no degradation by it" (1976:451). Adam Smith's view is echoed in recent work by Orlando Patterson (1969:159–74; 1982:139–43), although there is no evidence that slaves regarded their own familial relations in these terms. Careful demographic research shows that the majority of slave households looked like "simple family households, most of them nuclear units" (Higman 1976:168).

But as Elizabeth Fox-Genovese says, "The ways in which various authors want the story to end impinges on every effort to write it" (1988: 49). Slaves had families all right, and they were even influenced, eventually, by the models of stable, nuclear families held out by missionaries and by European norms, but they were shaped mainly by the forces of class, race, and gender hierarchies. As I have shown elsewhere, West Indian Creole society developed its own complex kinship system, which established a hierarchy of marriage forms in which free men married status equals and contracted nonlegal unions with women of inferior status (R. T. Smith 1987).

Superimposed upon the formal equality of free legal marital partners was the pervasive gender hierarchy that treated all women as jural minors. In the North American slave states, African Americans were embedded in a social matrix that was different from that of the Caribbean colonies, being perhaps closer to that of Brazil. As Fox-Genovese (1988) argues, the key concept for understanding the productive and social relations of the southern slave states is the household. Whether the households were of small or yeomen farmers using limited amounts of slave labor alongside family members or the households of large plantations relying on a large complement of slave labor with a complex internal division of labor, their patriarchal nature is stressed. Unlike the West Indies, where plantations were organized more on factory principles, the southern plantation was an *oikos* (this term is used to indicate the precapitalist nature of the household economy), under the patriarchal domination of a white man. This is not the place to review Fox-Genovese's complex discussion of *haciendas,* the domestic mode of production, or the precise nature of the southern social formation, but her emphases suggest the solution to some stubborn problems of kinship interpretation.

If the domestic units of slaves were encompassed by the household relations of the plantation as a whole, then the model of legal Christian marriage would, here, as in the Catholic world, be an immediate one and would be frequently achieved during the slave period. This would explain two aspects of behavior at emancipation that are often remarked upon by scholars of the period: (1) the agitated geographic movement of slaves as they attempted to redefine their position within a society where the whole structure of the household as *oikos* was destroyed, and (2) the apparent rush to marry. In the first case, the movement would indicate a desire to remove oneself from the household; the second would be conceived as the necessary basis for establishing a new household in the full socioeconomic and legal sense. This would also explain why sexual relations between white and black are frequently construed as rape, since there is no place within the structure of such units for contracting nonlegal coresidential, or even visiting, unions, whereas in the Caribbean they were an intrinsic and widely recognized part of the system. Although demography is an important predisposing element here, we are dealing with a fully constituted social and cultural system in which relations are defined in this way.

In the West Indies, slaves had already established a high degree of autonomy of domestic life, complete with an economic base in the form of provision grounds and a complex system of extended family organization. The "total institution" aspect of plantation organization was certainly a measure of its oppression, wherever it was found, but the evidence assembled by writers such as Higman (1984) and Besson shows that slave community life had a marked effect on family structure. One could hardly say for the West Indies that "slaves can more appropriately be regarded as members of the household of their master—defined as the plantation or farm—than as primarily members of distinct slave households" (Fox-Genovese 1988:95).

If emancipation meant the transformation of slaves into citizens, it also involved the creation of new modes of interference in the most intimate recesses of their private and domestic life. No longer subject to the continual invasions of the slave order, freedmen now were subjected to the ministrations of the clergy and the magistrate. Fox-Genovese has pointed out that Afro-American slaves "were not free to ground their particular vision of the proper relations between women and men in their own institutions" (1988:373), and, therefore, the most important meaning of freedom for slaves in the American South was the ability to "ground the relations between women and men in institutions, without which no people could hope to determine its destiny, shape its young, and define its own virtues" (ibid., 396).

Unfortunately, those institutions reflected the hierarchical system that pervaded southern society and that inhibited southern white women from embracing ideas of gender equality that were beginning to permeate northern society. The withdrawal of women from field labor placed them in a clearly subordinate position within households dominated by men, a domination reinforced by the coercive influence of those forces that Austin-Broos summarizes in the shaping of the Christian black. The struggles of African Americans to restructure the expression of Christian values in conformity with their own experience was deeply influenced by the denial of the equality and Christian brotherhood that was the promise of emancipation.

More is at stake than the influence of the Christian message and church doctrine; the proliferation of state organs and institutions that served to maintain the class relations already established under slavery is often neglected in discussions of kinship and gender relations. In a pioneering study of legal practice and its effect on kinship in Antigua, Lazarus-Black has shown how the individualizing effects of the law in relation to property and labor were offset by a new emphasis on familial control and familial responsibility in the field of poor laws and social legislation. As she says, "The history of kinship law in Antigua leads one inescapably to the conclusion that lawmakers used kinship statutes to structure an organization of domination which directly served and legitimized class relations" (1990:332).

The parallel between the contradiction of bourgeois egalitarianism and a continuing racism on the one hand, and that egalitarianism plus the subordination of women in bourgeois law on the other, is remarkable.

In both cases, the premise of individualistic egalitarianism is denied by reference to biology.

Women and Field Labor

The withdrawal of women from field labor at emancipation is more remarked upon by historians of the United States than by commentators on the ending of Caribbean slavery and is clearly related to the dramatic increase in the marriage rate in many southern states. However, there is ample evidence that the practice itself was widespread in the Caribbean. For example, a British Guiana planter testifying before the 1848 select committee on sugar remarked on the unpredictability of ex-slave labor and then continued: "Every woman on the estate then [during slavery] worked in the field, now the case is altered; and as they get rich they keep their wives at home to take care of their houses, or look after the children, who used all to be reared in the nursery of the estate; and for that reason at least half the female labourers have to be taken from the field and from the estate and applied to other purposes" (Adamson 1972:40).

What is not mentioned here, of course, is the female labor diverted to provision grounds, to collecting firewood, and to caring for large numbers of children. Also, it would be a great mistake to think that all women withdrew their labor from the estates; the wage rates for British Guiana sugar estates for 1844 show specific rates for women for the tasks of weeding, "threshing young canes," fetching megasse, and feeding canes to mill, and in each case the rates were 20 to 25 percent below those for males (Young 1958:221–22). In the United States, emancipation intensified the gender hierarchy among African Americans in many subtle ways; freedmen were officially regarded as heads of households, signed labor contracts for the whole family, and were enfranchised, while freedwomen were not. And, as in the Caribbean, women were paid less than men for the same work on plantations (Foner 1988:87).

If freedom held out to African-American women the promise of taking their place as keepers of the home as a haven in a heartless world, of—in other words—adopting the prevailing models of bourgeois American and European society, that promise has never been fulfilled. The triple handicap of devalued class, race, and gender status, combined with the economic necessity to labor, ensured that women could only exceptionally take their place on the pedestal of domestic adoration. Their central place in African-American kinship was earned—or forced upon them—not as wives, but as mothers and grandmothers. Men might seek to enhance their masculine honor by requiring their wives to stay at home rather than to work out for wages, and women perhaps wished to emulate the domestic status of white women, but white families, and the families of middle-class persons of all races, lacked domestic servants for only a short time in the immediate aftermath of emancipation. Free black women picked cotton, loaded cane, weeded farms, loaded banana boats, broke rocks for surfacing roads, and engaged in myriad dirty, strenuous, backbreaking jobs in order to earn the money to keep their families together. If freedom meant the dignity of domestic harmony and a husband's devotion, few ex-slave women achieved that freedom. At best, freedom meant for them "not a release from back-breaking labor, but rather the opportunity to labor on behalf of their own families and kin within the protected spheres of household and community" (Jones 1985:78).

Religion and Voluntary Associations

Clifford Geertz has remarked that "anthropology, or at least interpretive anthropology, is a science whose progress is marked less by a perfection of consensus than by a refinement of debate. What gets better is the precision with which we vex each other"(1973:29). Religion is the terrain on which social scientists have chosen to vex each other the most in arguments over whether Catholic slavery was more benign than Protestant, and whether ex-slaves really practiced the same Christianity as whites or developed their own religious institutions. The first argument does not concern us, though the Catholic church in Latin America and the French colonies provided a continuity of religious participation and experience that was absent elsewhere. In the British Caribbean, Christianity came with a rush and was an intrinsic part of the struggle for freedom itself, making somewhat less surprising the fact that a people long denied human stature should so quickly embrace the religion of their oppressors. Or did they?

From Philip Curtin's dramatic assertion that in Jamaica in 1862 "the Great Revival had turned African" (1955:171), to M. G. Smith's less equivocal declaration that folk and elite practice different religious institutions, to Herskovits's elaborate demonstrations of the survived cultural focus of Africans in their religious beliefs and practices, we have long been urged to find an African core in the Christianity of African Americans, as well as in various syncretic cults and practices. The day is long past when scholars could seriously assert that African slaves were stripped of their culture in the passage to the New World, and the repeated invocation of the opposition between Frazier and Herskovits on this question merely gets in the way of serious study. Diane Austin-Broos quotes Derek Walcott's acute observation that "the subject African . . . understood too quickly the Christian rituals of a whipped, tortured and murdered redeemer. . . . [No] race is converted against its will." But, equally, that understanding was tempered by cultural meanings rooted in the life of the slave and ex-slave communities, meanings that were specifically African American and embraced a wide range of beliefs and practices that were not abandoned, whatever the missionaries instructed. But the central moral problems of the freedmen's lives were addressed in terms of Christianity, which to Austin-Broos is the structuring element that Jamaicans continually reinterpreted.

Within that process of reinterpretation, the realities of class and racial discriminations were bound to find expression, in the Caribbean as well as in North and South America. In the United States, disillusionment with white professions of the brotherhood of man came early and by 1865 the foundations for a segregated Christianity were firmly in place. No such simple solution existed elsewhere in the hemisphere (although the Jamaica Native Baptists came close to constituting a similar pattern), and after the first wave of missionary influence was diluted by the hardships of the postemancipation economic regime, there was an upsurge of new (or revived) forms of religiosity. Austin-Broos's discussion of the ideological underpinnings of the missionaries' attempts to reconstruct the ex-slaves in the image of the Christian black, and to substitute for the old concepts of innate depravity an environmental theory of the debilitating effects of slavery itself, is important for extending our understanding of the dynamics of postemancipation society.[6]

The analytic problem would be an easy one if such a thing as a plural society existed, but in reality we are faced with the complex interpretive activities of African-American freedmen as they struggled within and against the stereotype of the Christian black. No single or simple outcome would prevail. In Guyana, African villagers partitioned their religious and ritual activities, effecting almost no syncretism in doctrine or liturgy (R. Smith 1976), while in Jamaica, Haiti, and Brazil there was a rich process of syncretism. Furthermore, the doctrines and imagery of Christianity and Enlightenment philosophy have both been incorporated in more explicitly formulated political ideologies, of which Garveyism is a prime example. Philip Potter notes the lack of attention paid to the religious element in Garvey's thought and makes good that

omission, showing very clearly that his ideas of racial separation and
back-to-Africa migration were born of disillusionment with the white
understanding of Christian doctrine, but not with the values it enshrined
(1988).

With religious expression, as with other institutional forms, the shaping force was the configuration of class and racial practice developed
in the aftermath of slavery. Indeed, it is central to Austin-Broos's analysis of Christianity in postemancipation Jamaica that the enterprise of
proselytization formed itself around the image of a concrete social environment quite separate from the plantation, in which the ex-slave must
become "a viable, independent economic unit within a cash economy"
and the exemplary practitioner of a way of life in which mission model
family life based on Christian marriage is dominant. As she shows, that
image has persisted, and even found expression, in small sections of
the rural and urban lower middle class, but the historical experience
of the vast majority of Jamaicans has been quite distant from the missionary model, a model that was outmoded almost as soon as it was
constructed. And integral to that experience were the hierarchies of race
and class that contradicted the missionary image of the environment
that would nurture the Christian black, an experience that called forth
the alternate forms of religiosity—revivalism, Pentecostalism, and Rastafarianism—each embodying some aspect of the environment in which
it developed.

Education and Social Mobility

One of the continuing paradoxes of African-American life throughout the hemisphere is the coexistence of the high value attached to education and the low levels of educational achievement. Education is the
machine in which the contradictions of legal equality, racial hierarchy,
and cultural hegemony were blended to produce the distinctive features
of postslavery regimes.

In the Protestant Caribbean, education was an intrinsic part of the
missionary effort to Christianize slaves and came to be seen as an essential part of the state of civilization. In the United States, while white
missionaries were equally responsible for the early establishment of
schools for free blacks, it appears that by the early nineteenth century
the free black community itself had assumed responsibility for education in many areas (Holt 1977:52). After the Civil War, sending children
to school went with keeping one's wife at home as the mark of freedom

and status. In 1860, over 90 percent of the black population of the American South was illiterate (Foner 1988:96), and the same condition prevailed in the preemancipation Caribbean.

Education itself came to be symbolic of freedom, and adults as well as children flocked to classes wherever they were available. The free villages founded after emancipation in the West Indies were invariably built around a church and a school, and Foner reports that in the American South the availability of schooling for their children was often the first requirement before freedmen would accept employment (ibid., 96). In South Carolina, the free black and mulatto elite took primary responsibility for educating the ex-slave population (Holt 1977:52–55). Despite the thirst for learning and the rapid expansion of schooling, the harsh reality was that freed black women and children were obliged to work and had to forgo education. Especially among small farmers and sharecroppers, the need for family labor precluded aspirations of that kind (Foner 1988:86).

Political Representation

If the abolition of slavery implied full citizenship, equality, and individual rights for the freedmen, then in many places they were well placed to enter politics as a force for social change. There is considerable literature on Reconstruction politics in the American South but relatively little on the Caribbean. Gad Heuman's work on the role of the Free Coloured in Jamaica makes for a fascinating comparison with Thomas Holt's analysis of postemancipation politics in South Carolina (Heuman 1981; Holt 1977). Both show the crucial role of the mulatto population in political representation, raising once again the issue of the conjoining of race and class and the forging of an ideology of transformation. Holt remarks that the Coloured population of Jamaica never assumed the degree of identification with, and leadership of, the freed slaves that the mulattoes of South Carolina did, although he is careful to note that the American mulattoes never gave up their sense of brown superiority over blacks. Clearly, the brown, mulatto, Coloured, or whatever one wants to call the mixed African-European population, owed its very existence to the continuing strength of the ideology of race, and they were the first to fuse the concepts of color, class, and culture into the potent symbols of education. And it was through education and command of culture that they paved the way for eventual control of the state in those places where that was possible.

Trouillot compares the fate of the free mulattoes in Haiti and Dominica, islands where they attained a proportionate strength that was unique. He shows that in both cases the mulattoes identified with the whites, hoping to share a privileged position as against the emancipated slaves. In Haiti, this illusion was rudely shattered by the execution of the mulatto leaders Ogé and Chavannes, but even then the reluctance of the *gens de couleur* to identify with the slaves showed the strength of the racial hierarchy, even after the whites were driven from the island. Trouillot argues that it is as wrong to reduce the historical developments in Haiti to a matter of color alone as it is to treat color as mere epiphenomenon. He says that we are dealing with a metaevent, which encapsulates an opposition of class and color in addition to personal oppositions.

However, his analysis focuses on the economic and political mechanisms through which the mulatto *anciens libres* secured their position. Unable to compel the ex-slaves to return to work on the plantations, they turned the state into a machine that would suck off the peasant surplus, mainly through the imposition of import and export duties that taxed both the consumption needs and the export crops of the peasants. In the British sugar producing colonies, planter-controlled legislatures similarly extracted revenues from the ex-slaves through import duties on consumer goods, but they refrained from taxing their own export products. In Haiti, the governing elites formed an alliance with foreign merchants, to whom they transferred government revenues through state expenditures on consumer goods or through private consumption of luxuries. These transfers, according to Trouillot, led to the progressive impoverishment of the nation. In countries such as Guyana, the ex-slaves who had, by the 1840s, become small farmers and part-time plantation laborers were able to form an alliance with import merchants resentful of planter-dominated legislatures that used import taxes to finance the importation of cheap Indian labor. This process struck at the prosperity of African laborers, whose wages were depressed, and of the merchant class, whose prime customers were thereby impoverished. By the end of the nineteenth century many, if not most, of those merchants were Portuguese, Chinese, or Coloured, thus forming an interesting contrast to Haiti and demonstrating the importance of the class factor.

The question of racism and ideology we started with has here come full circle.

Conclusion

The essays in this collection make abundantly clear the mechanisms by which contradictions were incorporated into the new social orders that replaced slave regimes in the Western Hemisphere. As I note at the beginning, the situations were highly diverse and local conditions extremely important, but a common feature was the creation of status systems combining race and class distinctions in potent ways. Often referred to as the color-class system, and represented by complex pyramidal diagrams (cf. Braithwaite 1953:47–53; Davis, Gardner, and Gardner 1941:10; Henriques 1953:36, 42), this system is far too complex to be conveyed in that way. Indeed, such diagrams—like M. G. Smith's attempt to diagram the "active" and "inactive" margins between the social segments of his imagined "plural society" (1955:60)—betray the positivist conception of society as an aggregate of classifiable individuals, each with his or her array of relevant characteristics.

The system I refer to is a system of cultural categories combined into a complex of normally unexamined assumptions that proportion themselves to conform to the contours of specific social circumstances without, however, being determined by those circumstances. In a conference paper not included in this volume, Diane Austin-Broos discusses the relative importance of race and class in Jamaica, a discussion that opens with the observation that "race is an idiom of class" and that there is "no simple racial principle which underlies the society" (1988:1). Objecting to the idea that the racial concepts of the dominant group are capable of racializing the structure of the whole society, and more especially to the idea that a system of racial concepts forged in the colonial past is in any way viable in a greatly altered present, she asserts that the logic of race as a contemporary issue must "proceed from another milieu" (ibid., 4). That milieu is "class as a malleable phenomenon amenable to different modes of historical interpretation" (ibid., 5).

One can see the source of her unease with theories that proceed from the assumption that race is an ineradicable physical presence on which social constructions are built, and even with the idea that race is a system of concepts "separate from class and as real cause or consciousness a component of Jamaican history" (Austin-Broos 1988:5). But the interpretive problem is clearly posed by her assertion that race is "an element in Jamaica's history negotiated through the political economy of the region" and that "although race is always a socially constructed phenomenon this does not mean that race is simply ideational or confined to the cognitive realm" (ibid., 5 nɪ). While this poses the problem, it hardly solves it because it confuses the nature of reality and experience with the analytic methods that are necessary to interpret it. Austin-Broos seems to think that class as an empirical phenomenon can be apprehended directly, whereas I am arguing that it is impossible to capture the complex phenomenon of the color-class system without analytically proceeding as if its components were separable. In practice, she does just that when she describes various ways of "mythologizing class," which include the idea of disorganization proceeding from a slavery past and the idea of genetic inferiority in the form of "a slave mind," which "allows a genetic component to reside within a notion of class." She continues:

Both these major forms of mythologizing class involve notions of heritable identity anchored in slavery. They constitute together a consciousness of class that supports rather than undermines a concurrent regime of race, for differential class experience is explained by genealogical reference and this experience is frequently glossed in colour terms. . . . The relation between consciousness of race and class is nevertheless an intimate one in which class, that eminently environmental phenomenon is to a degree assimilated to notions of genetic inheritance. . . . The overall discourse is one of heritable identity in which race and class both play as separable but thoroughly intertwined conceptions. (Ibid., 8)

Precisely. The differential weighting of these analytically distinguished factors (though informants are also perfectly capable of distinguishing them) both reflects and influences the course of social action. And one can readily agree that this consciousness, or more accurately *habitus* (Bourdieu 1977), is not a mere continuity from the past but something that has to be reproduced in the present from which it draws its meaning. The abolition of slavery held out promises that perhaps could not be kept, as Emmer argues, but for all the changes and variations in the configuration of class relations, a stubborn residue of racism had remained in that "overall discourse of heritable identity" to which Austin-Broos refers.

The locus of the meaning of freedom has now shifted from the plantation areas of the New World to the cities, to those areas often referred to as the ghetto, much to the distress and annoyance of those who live there. In view of the marked improvement in the class position of many urban black people, it has become increasingly difficult to attribute lack of achievement to race (not that this has deterred people from trying). But even my colleague William J. Wilson, who has argued extensively that the battle against racial discrimination is no longer the crucial issue in fighting urban poverty, acknowledges that "historic racism" has resulted in the undue proportion of blacks in "impoverished urban ghettos" even though the problems are now primarily economic (Wilson 1988).

All the evidence that Wilson adduces in support of his position is highly relevant. It is certainly true that massive restructuring of the economy has produced pockets of persistent poverty in the inner cities of many industrialized countries, including the United States (and, one might add, many nonindustrialized countries such as Jamaica), and that there is a close relation between these economic conditions and the social disorganization one finds there, including crime, teenage pregnancy, educational inadequacy, welfare dependency, and so on. But even the most ardent proponents of the idea that race is just an idiom of social class have to acknowledge the powerful symbolism of the equation of poverty and social dislocation with race. In the United States, it is necessary to issue periodic reminders that the center of gravity of poverty is in the mainly white rural areas and not in the inner cities, but that does not alter the dominant image.

It is not argued here that concepts of race cause class to be structured in the way it is in the United States, or anywhere else; once we have a careful analysis of cultural concepts, whether pertaining to racial categories or class, we have a better chance of understanding their respective interactions in the practice of social life. Unlike Hoetink, I believe that racial hierarchies can be demolished and socially constructed racial categorizations can be dissolved, but ignoring them or insisting that they are really class systems will not achieve that end. One is reminded of Aimé Césaire's letter of resignation from the Communist party in which he says, "we coloured men . . . have consciously grasped . . . the notion of our peculiar uniqueness. . . . The peculiarity of 'our place in the world' isn't to be confused with anybody else's. The peculiarity of our problems aren't to be reduced to subordinate forms of other problems" (Katznelson 1976:7).

NOTES

1. In his now classic study of postemancipation Jamaican society, *Two Jamaicas*, Philip Curtin notes that for him the experience of Jamaica in the nineteenth century was brought into focus by the experience of African decolonization in the twentieth (1955: preface).

2. I am grateful to Professor Raymond D. Fogelson, an expert witness before the committee, for this information.

3. See Blu (1980) for a full account of this fascinating case.

4. It is significant that the plural society theory as adumbrated by M. G. Smith starts from the assumption that races or "racial stocks" are in fact distinguishable entities and that it is from that physical base ("phenotypical" and "genealogical") that social distinctions depart (M. Smith 1955:51–57).

5. In his chapter Trouillot notes similar mechanisms in Dominica.

6. Austin-Broos acknowledges the influence of Russell (1983) on this discussion.

REFERENCES

Adamson, Alan H. 1972. *Sugar Without Slaves: The Political Economy of British Guiana, 1838–1904.* New Haven: Yale University Press.

Alonso, Ana. 1988. Gender, Ethnicity, and the Constitution of Subjects: Accommodation, Resistance, and Revolution on the Chihuahuan Frontier. Ph.D. diss., University of Chicago.

Austin, Diane J. 1984. *Urban Life in Kingston, Jamaica: The Culture and Class Ideology of Two Neighborhoods.* New York: Gordon and Breach.

Austin-Broos, Diane J. 1988. Class and Race in Jamaica. Paper prepared for the Conference on the Meaning of Freedom, University of Pittsburgh, August.

Blu, Karen I. 1980. *The Lumbee Problem: the Making of an American Indian People.* Cambridge: Cambridge University Press.

Bourdieu, Pierre. 1977. *Outline of a Theory of Practice.* Translated by Richard Nice. Cambridge: Cambridge University Press.

Brathwaite, Edward. 1971. *The Development of Creole Society in Jamaica 1770–1820.* Oxford: Clarendon Press.

Braithwaite, Lloyd. 1953. Social Stratification in Trinidad. *Social and Economic Studies* 2:5–175.

Cannadine, David. 1983. The Context, Performance and Meaning of Ritual: The British Monarchy and "The Invention of Tradition," c. 1820–1977. In *The Invention of Tradition,* edited by Eric Hobsbawm and Terence Ranger, 101–64. Cambridge: Cambridge University Press.

Comaroff, John L. 1982. Dialectical Systems, History and Anthropology. *Journal of South African Studies* 8:143–72.

Comaroff, Jean, and John Comaroff. 1991. *Of Revelation and Revolution: Christianity, Colonialism, and Consciousness in South Africa.* Vol. 1. Chicago: University of Chicago Press.

Corrigan, Philip, and Derek Sayer. 1985. *The Great Arch: English State Formation as Cultural Revolution.* Oxford: Basil Blackwell.

Curtin, Philip D. 1955. *Two Jamaicas: The Role of Ideas in a Tropical Colony 1830–1865.* Cambridge: Harvard University Press.

Davis, Allison, Burleigh B. Gardner, and Mary R. Gardner. 1941. *Deep South: A Social Anthropological Study of Caste and Class.* Chicago: University of Chicago Press.

Davis, David Brion. 1974. Slavery and the Post–World War II Historians. In *Slavery, Colonialism, and Racism,* edited by Sidney W. Mintz, 1–16. New York: Norton.

Disraeli, Benjamin. 1954 (1845). *Sybil, or the Two Nations.* London: Penguin Books.

Dumont, Louis. 1980. *Homo Hierarchicus: The Caste System and Its Implications.* Translated by Mark Sainsbury, Louis Dumont, and Basia Gulati. Chicago: University of Chicago Press.

Edwards, Bryan. 1793–1794. *The History, Civil and Commercial, of the British Colonies in the West Indies.* 2 vols. London: John Stockdale.

Engels, Friedrich. 1958 (1845). *The Condition of the Working Class in England.* Stanford: Stanford University Press.

Farley, Rawle. 1954. The Rise of the Peasantry in British Guiana. *Social and Economic Studies* 2:76–103.

Fogel, Robert William. 1989. *Without Consent or Contract: The Rise and Fall of American Slavery.* New York: Norton.

Fogel, Robert William and Stanley L. Engermann. 1974. *Time on the Cross: The Economics of American Negro Slavery.* 2 vols. Boston: Little, Brown.

Foner, Eric. 1988. *Reconstruction: America's Unfinished Revolution 1863–1877.* New York: Harper and Row.

Foster, John. 1974. *Class Struggle and the Industrial Revolution: Early Industrial Capitalism in Three English Towns.* London: Methuen.

Fox-Genovese, Elizabeth. 1988. *Within the Plantation Household: Black and White Women of the Old South.* Chapel Hill: University of North Carolina Press.

Geertz, Clifford. 1963. The Integrative Revolution: Primordial Sentiments and Civil Politics in the New States. In *Old Societies and New States: The Quest for Modernity in Asia and Africa,* edited by Clifford Geertz, 105–57. New York: Free Press.

———. 1973. *The Interpretation of Cultures.* New York: Basic Books.

Genovese, Eugene D. 1972. *Roll Jordan Roll: The World the Slaves Made.* New York: Pantheon Books.

Giddens, Anthony. 1979. *Central Problems in Social Theory.* Berkeley and Los Angeles: University of California Press.

Hall, Stuart. 1980. Race, Articulation, and Societies Structured in Dominance. In *Sociological Theories: Race and Colonialism.* Paris: UNESCO Press.

Henriques, Fernando. 1953. *Family and Colour in Jamaica.* London: Eyre and Spottiswoode.

Heuman, Gad. 1981. *Between Black and White: Race, Politics, and the Free Coloreds in Jamaica, 1792–1865.* Westport: Greenwood.

Higman, B. W. 1976. *Slave Population and Economy in Jamaica, 1807–1834.* Cambridge: Cambridge University Press.

———. 1984. *Slave Populations of the British Caribbean 1807–1834.* Baltimore: Johns Hopkins University Press.

Hobsbawm, Eric. 1968. *Industry and Empire.* Vol. 3 of *The Pelican Economic History of Britain: From 1750 to the Present Day.* Harmondsworth: Penguin Books.

Hobsbawm, Eric, and Terence Ranger, eds. 1983. *The Invention of Tradition.* Cambridge: Cambridge University Press.

Hoetink, H. 1967. *The Two Variants in Caribbean Race Relations: A Contribution to the Sociology of Segmented Societies.* London: Oxford University Press.

———. 1973. *Slavery and Race Relations in the Americas: An inquiry into Their Nature and Nexus.* New York: Harper and Row.

Holt, Thomas. 1977. *Black Over White: Negro Political Leadership in South Carolina During Reconstruction.* Urbana: University of Illinois Press.

Jones, Jacqueline. 1985. *Labor of Love, Labor of Sorrow: Black Women, Work and the Family, from Slavery to the Present.* New York: Basic Books.

Katznelson, Ira. 1976. *Black Men, White Cities: Race, Politics, and Migration in the United States, 1900–1930, and Britain, 1948–1968.* Chicago: University of Chicago Press.

Lazarus-Black, Mindie. 1990. Legitimate Acts and Illegitimate Encounters: The Development of Family Ideology and Structure in Antigua and Barbuda, West Indies. Ph.D. diss., University of Chicago.

Long, Edward. 1774 (1972). *The History of Jamaica.* 3 vols. London: T. Lowndes in Fleet Street (New York: Arno Press).

Mandle, Jay R. 1978. *The Roots of Black Poverty: The Southern Plantation Economy After the Civil War.* Durham: Duke University Press.

Martinez-Alier, Verena. 1974. *Marriage, Class, and Colour in Nineteenth Century Cuba: A Study of Racial Attitudes and Sexual Values in a Slave Society.* London: Cambridge University Press.

Mills, Charles W. 1987. Race and Class: Conflicting or Reconcilable Paradigms? *Social and Economic Studies* 36:69–108.

Mintz, Sidney W., ed. 1974. *Slavery, Colonialism and Racism.* New York: Norton.

Murray, Charles. 1984. *Losing Ground: American Social Policy, 1950–1980.* New York: Basic Books.

Ortner, Sherry B. 1984. Theory in Anthropology Since the Sixties. *Comparative Studies in Society and History* 26:126–66.

Patterson, Orlando. 1969. *The Sociology of Slavery.* Rutherford: Fairleigh Dickenson University Press.

———. 1982. Persistence, Continuity, and Change in the Jamaican Working-Class Family. *Journal of Family History* 7:135–61.

Post, Ken. 1978. *Arise Ye Starvelings: The Jamaican Labour Rebellion of 1938 and Its Aftermath.* The Hague: Martinus Nijhoff.

Potter, Philip. 1988. The Religious Thought of Marcus Garvey. In *Garvey: His Work and Impact,* edited by Rupert Lewis and Patrick Bryan, 145–63. Mona: University of the West Indies, Institute of Social and Economic Research.

Rainwater, Lee, and William L. Yancey, eds. 1967. *The Moynihan Report and the Politics of Controversy.* Cambridge, Mass.: MIT Press.

Rodney, Walter. 1981. *A History of the Guyanese Working People, 1881–1905.* Baltimore: Johns Hopkins University Press.

Russell, Horace O. 1983. The Emergence of the Christian Black: The Making of a Stereotype. *Jamaica Journal* 16:51–58.

Sahlins, Marshall. 1985. *Islands of History.* Chicago: University of Chicago Press.

Smith, Adam. 1976 (1776). *An Inquiry into the Causes of the Wealth of Nations.* Chicago: University of Chicago Press.

Smith, Michael G. 1955. *A Framework for Caribbean Studies.* Mona: University College of the West Indies, ExtraMural Department.

Smith, Raymond T. 1976. Religion in the Formation of West Indian Society. In *The African Diaspora: Interpretive Essays,* edited by Martin L. Kilson and Robert I. Rotberg, 312–41. Cambridge: Harvard University Press.

———. 1987. Hierarchy and the Dual Marriage System in West Indian Society. In *Gender and Kinship: Essays Toward a Unified Analysis,* edited by Jane Collier and Sylvia J. Yanagisako, 163–96. Stanford: Stanford University Press.

———. 1988. *Kinship and Class in the West Indies: A Genealogical Study of Jamaica and Guyana.* Cambridge: Cambridge University Press.

Stolcke, Verena. 1981. Women's Labours: The Naturalization of Social Inequality and Women's Subordination. In *Of Marriage and the Market: Women's Subordination in International Perspective,* edited by K. Young, C. Wolkowitz, and R. McCullagh, 30–48. London: CSE Books.

———. 1987. The Slavery Period and its Influence on Household Structure and the Family: Jamaica, Cuba and Brazil. Paper prepared for the Seminar on Changing Family Structure and Life Courses in LDCs, Honolulu, January.

———. 1989. New Reproductive Technologies: The Old Quest for Fatherhood. *Reproductive and Genetic Engineering* 1:5–19.

Thompson, E. P. 1963. *The Making of the English Working Class.* New York: Pantheon Books.

———. 1975. *Whigs and Hunters: The Origin of the Black Act.* New York: Pantheon Books.

Tocqueville, Alexis de. 1945. *Democracy in America.* 2 vols. Translated by Henry Reeve, revised by F. Bowen, and edited by P. Bradley. New York: Knopf. (First published in 1835.)

Truillot, Michel-Rolph. 1980. Review of *Peasants and Poverty, a Study of Haiti,* by Mats Lundahl. *Journal of Peasant Studies,* 8:112–16.

Wacquant, Loïc J. D. 1989. Towards a Reflexive Sociology: A Workshop With Pierre Bourdieu. *Sociological Theory* 7:26–63.

Weber, Max. 1949. *The Methodology of the Social Sciences.* Translated and edited by Edward A. Shils and Henry A. Finch. Glencoe: Free Press.

Williams, Eric. 1944. *Capitalism and Slavery.* Chapel Hill: University of North Carolina Press.

Williams, Raymond. 1976. *Keywords: A Vocabulary of Culture and Society.* New York: Oxford University Press.

Wilson, William J. 1988. *The Truly Disadvantaged: The Inner City, the Underclass, and Public Policy.* Chicago: University of Chicago Press.

Wright, Gavin. 1976. Prosperity, Progress, and American Slavery. In *Reckoning with Slavery,* edited by Paul A. David et al., 302–36. New York: Oxford University Press.

Wyatt-Brown, Bertram. 1982. *Southern Honor: Ethics and Behavior in the Old South.* New York: Oxford University Press.

Young, Allan. 1958. *The Approaches to Local Self-Government in British Guiana.* London: Longmans, Green.

PETER KOLCHIN

The Tragic Era?
Interpreting Southern
Reconstruction in Comparative
Perspective

Despite sweeping changes in interpreting the post–Civil War South, the Tragic Era remains the most persistent theme in Reconstruction historiography. Of course, historians have long since abandoned the once-prevalent view that after the war the already suffering South was "literally put to the torture" by a hideous alliance of venal carpetbaggers, degraded scalawags, and ignorant freedmen who humiliated the virtuous southern people by placing the "bottom rail" on the top (Bowers 1929:vi; Dunning 1907; Fleming 1905; Coulter 1947). But most present-day historians still share the view that something went disastrously wrong in the postwar South. Indeed, themes of hardship, disappointment, failure, and missed opportunities pervade the recent literature on the post-emancipation South. Apparently, the aftermath of slavery produced no real winners, only diverse groups of losers.

For southern whites, the trauma of military defeat and emancipation was compounded by the humiliation of having to submit to hated Reconstruction governments imposed by conquering Yankees. Both rich and poor suffered. "Almost overnight, Southern planters crossed from the world of slave labor to that of compensated labor, from substantial wealth and ease to relative poverty and drudgery, from political dominance to crippled influence," explains James L. Roark in his sensitive and revealing study, *Masters Without Slaves*. Their postwar world was one of struggle, hardship, bitterness, and the need to adjust to radically new conditions. "Most adjusted," Roark concludes, "merely enough to make their way, rarely enough to make real peace" (1977:196, 208).

Poorer whites, too, evidently had trouble adjusting to changed conditions. A growing number of scholars, including Steven Hahn, Lacy K. Ford, and Eric Foner, have turned their attention to the hardships faced by up-country whites, whose supposedly sturdy independence was undermined by the postwar spread of commercial agriculture. Although Reconstruction first seemed to offer new hope to many yeoman farmers, that hope quickly faded as new railroad construction "brought market relations into the upcountry," higher taxes increased the need for cash (and hence spurred commercial farming), and the crop-lien system trapped indebted farmers into producing more and more cotton at lower and lower prices. "Increasingly, upcountry farmers fell into new forms of dependency," writes Foner; "by 1880, one third of the white farmers in the cotton states were tenants renting either for cash or a share of the crop, and a region self-sufficient before the Civil War was no longer able to feed itself" (1988:394; also see Hahn 1983; Ford 1984).

If southern whites suffered hardship and disappointment, the plight of northern whites who went south after the war, according to current scholarship, was dismal. Teachers and missionaries were ostracized, reviled as "nigger lovers," and subjected to physical violence (Jones 1980; Richardson 1986). So too were politicians, the much-abused carpetbaggers, who were eventually forced to concede defeat and abandon their hopes to bring republican government — with or without a capital R — to the South (Trelease 1971; Rable 1984; Perman 1984; Foner 1988; Current 1988). Even those with more prosaic goals experienced failure. Thousands of young, well-educated northern professionals moved south in the wake of the war to try their hands at planting, hoping at once to make money, demonstrate the superiority of the free-labor system, and help uplift the former slaves. Despite their high hopes, however, they were stymied by unexpected obstacles. Free black laborers proved to be "lazy" and "ungrateful," and complained about low pay. Local whites resented the Yankee planters' contempt for southern backwardness as well as their desire to promote bourgeois values. Cotton prices — and hence profits — did not hold up as expected. And the Reconstruction governments that many of the new planters supported (and some served in) collapsed. "With the failure of their dreams," writes Lawrence N. Powell, "most Yankees drifted back to the free states" (1980:151).

But it is among historians of the postwar black experience that the tragic theme is most in evidence. Of course, scholars recognize that with emancipation came concrete benefits, benefits that permitted the freedmen to exercise substantially more authority over their lives than they did as slaves. Most modern experts agree, however, that the central failure of Reconstruction was the failure to provide the ex-slaves with real freedom and equality. Thus, Eric Foner concludes the most recent synthetic history of the postwar years, appropriately titled *Reconstruction: America's Unfinished Revolution,* with the blunt assertion that "whether measured by the dreams inspired by emancipation or the more limited goals of securing blacks' rights as citizens and free laborers . . . Reconstruction can only be judged a failure" (1988:603).

If historians see Reconstruction as a tragic failure, they do not always entirely agree about the precise nature of that failure. Some stress the failure to maintain Republican Reconstruction governments that would promote the rights and interests of the freedmen (Tunnell 1984). Others, however, point to the unwillingness of those very governments to protect the freedmen by combating white terrorism and pursuing egalitarian economic policies. Thus, according to Leon F. Litwack, although it was "established to ease the ex-slaves' transition to freedom, the Freedmen's Bureau ultimately facilitated the restoration of black labor to the control of those who had previously owned them" (1979:386). Numerous historians see the absence of land redistribution as a key cause of the freedmen's continuing dependence (Ransom and Sutch 1977:13; Wiener 1978:6; Mandle 1978:16–17).

A major focus of scholars has been the postwar continuation — despite early hopes that the overthrow of slavery would usher in an era of progress and prosperity — of black (and southern) poverty. Scholars offer varying explanations for this continued poverty. For many social historians, the key failure was the inability or unwillingness to revolutionize the South's hierarchical and authoritarian social structure. "The South's characteristic poverty and political oppression arose out of the . . . Prussian Road," writes Jonathan Wiener, "with its dominant planter class and its labor-repressive system of agricultural production" (Wiener 1978: 72–73). Crandall A. Shifflett agrees that continuing "class rule" was responsible for the persistence of poverty in Louisa County, Virginia: "The social structure remained essentially unchanged," he asserts. "Only the labor system had changed. . . . The story of Louisa is one of a missing revolution" (Shifflett 1982:64, 65, 103).

Most economic historians place the emphasis more on various institutional shortcomings. Roger L. Ransom and Richard Sutch, for example, argue that "the lack of progress in the postemancipation era was the consequence of flawed economic institutions" — primarily the usurious credit system that emerged throughout most of the rural South — while Gavin Wright sees the South's "separate regional labor market" as the main cause of economic stagnation (Ransom and Sutch 1977:2; Wright 1986:7). The central theme remains, however, the failure of the free-labor system to live up to the hopes of either its Republican spokesmen or the freedmen themselves. Whatever the cause, things went dreadfully wrong in the postwar South.

There is obviously much that rings true about this interpretation. There *was* much tragedy in the wake of civil war and emancipation; the works I cite chronicle with considerable sensitivity widespread frustration, bitterness, violence, and material suffering. Still, at the risk of challenging what appears to be a universally shared assumption, I propose to reexamine the tragic theme, exploring both its basis and its utility as a way of conceptualizing the postwar South. Although my focus in this chapter is on the southern United States, I take a broad comparative approach, putting southern developments in the context of those of other postemancipation societies. Doing so, I believe, raises serious questions, not about whether there was widespread hardship in the South, but about whether this hardship is the appropriate theme around which to organize our interpretation of postwar southern history. In short, I maintain that the concept of the Tragic Era has outlived its usefulness.

Although rarely spelled out, two kinds of implicit comparative judgments lie at the heart of the tragic theme. One of these involves an external comparison between what happened in the postwar South and what happened in other postemancipation societies. The other involves an internal comparison, evaluating the postwar South in light of previous or future southern developments, whether actual or desired. In other words, these implicit judgments involve an understanding of what could have been and what should have been. Both deserve our attention.

Let us begin with what could have been. As early as 1866, Radical Republican congressman Thaddeus Stevens contrasted the landless emancipation in the United States with the supposedly more farsighted emancipation of the Russian serfs begun in 1861. He praised Tsar Alexander II as a "wise man" who "compelled their masters to give them homesteads upon the very soil which they had tilled" and concluded that "the experiment has been a perfect success" (Foner 1983:8). Despite the frequent assumption that emancipation was handled more successfully elsewhere than in the United States, however, the birth of freedom was troubled everywhere. The land that the former serfs received in Russia hardly constituted a gift, for according to the extraordinarily complicated terms of the legislation that accompanied the emancipation decree of 1861, the peasants were required to pay for their land allotments — and in effect for their freedom — with interest at highly inflated prices over forty-nine years. Nor did the abolition of serfdom produce the miraculous social consequences that some expected: during the half century after emancipation, Russia not only remained poor, but in terms of such basic indices as per capita income and infant mortality, it actually fell further behind the economically advanced nations of Western Europe and the United States (Emmons 1968a, 1968b; Zaionchkovskii 1968; Druzhinin 1978; Shanin 1986; Gatrell 1986:30–40).

In the Americas, too, the sequel to bondage was marked by hardship. In Haiti, where establishment of an independent black republic in 1804 signaled the one example of a successful slave rebellion in the modern world, the population gradually fell into impoverished autarky with the almost total collapse of the plantation system and sugar production. By the twentieth century, the land that was once the pride of France's American empire had become the poorest country in the New World, its inhabitants suffering from despotic rule, massive unemployment, malnutrition, and illiteracy. Truly, the Haitian freedmen's struggle for the land amounted to a "Pyrrhic victory" (Foner 1983:12; James 1963; Lacerte 1978; Moya Pons 1985:181–84, 195–96, 206).

If Haiti stood as a bitter disappointment to those who expected a felicitous future for blacks freed from white oppression, the aftermath of emancipation also appeared bleak in countries that remained under colonial domination. In the British West Indies, as in Haiti and other sugar-producing Caribbean countries, freedmen withdrew from the plantation economy wherever they could, seeking to establish themselves as independent peasant proprietors; with the exception of Cuba, where capitalistic relations had replaced slave labor on most large sugar estates before the completion of the gradual emancipation process in 1886, sugar production declined virtually everywhere following emancipation. In some colonies, such as Trinidad and British Guiana, the plantation economy eventually reemerged on the basis of newly imported, quasi-forced Asian labor. In others, such as Jamaica, the withdrawal of black labor dealt a devastating blow to the plantation economy; Jamaica did not regain its 1832 level of per capita income until 1930 (Scott 1985: xii–xiii; Klein and Engerman 1985:262; Green 1976; Engerman 1982: 196–203, 1986:333–37; Foner 1983:8–38).

Nor were conditions better in independent countries where political power was in the hands of white elites. Brazilian blacks quickly fell from national attention after emancipation was completed in 1888 and were largely ignored even by most of the abolitionists who had struggled for so long on their behalf. As Robert Brent Toplin notes, "political power remained in the hands of the great *fazendeiros,"* while "an extraordinarily disproportionate number of Negroes were locked in the culture of poverty." In much of the country, as on the coffee-growing estates of São Paulo, former slaves found themselves marginalized and replaced by immigrant laborers, mostly from Italy (Andrews 1988; Fernandes 1974; Toplin 1971:257, 264).

Although the birth of freedom was difficult everywhere, comparison suggests that in some respects conditions for freedmen were better in the southern United States than elsewhere. The unique vehicle of emancipation in the southern United States—civil war—produced a uniquely radical effort to reconstruct slave society along democratic lines; because they were defeated traitors, southern slaveholders played a much smaller role in helping define the new social order than did landowners in Jamaica, Brazil, Cuba, or Russia. As Rebecca Scott points out, in Cuba "the government made no effort to influence and mediate the integration of former slaves into the new society comparable to the efforts of the Freedmen's Bureau or the legislation that accompanied Reconstruction in the United States." Indeed, among societies undergoing emancipation, only Russia experienced—for very different reasons—a "reconstruction" effort at all similar to that undertaken in the United States, a point to which I shall return shortly (Scott 1985:285; Foner 1983:39–73; Pressly 1989:27–30). By today's standards, of course, much of the Reconstruction legislation seems woefully inadequate; new facilities available to blacks, for example, were typically segregated, either legally or informally. As Howard N. Rabinowitz perceptively reminds us, however, in most cases segregation replaced not integration but exclusion; for ex-slaves, segregated schools were far preferable to no schools at all (Rabinowitz 1976, 1978).

Economically, too, the postemancipation South fared relatively well when judged in comparative terms. The South remained substantially poorer than the North, but despite the prolonged agricultural depression of the 1870s to 1890s—which (as in Russia) played a major role in dashing reformers' expectations that free labor would produce a flourishing agricultural economy—emancipation did not herald the decline of commercial agriculture, as it did in most of the Caribbean. Indeed, production of cotton for market expanded to include a significant number of up-country whites who had been isolated from the market before the war. Equally important, with the abolition of slavery, as many free-labor advocates had predicted, the South experienced rapid industrial development: from 1869 to 1899 the real value added by manufacturing grew at an annual rate of 7.8 percent in the ex-Confederate states, versus 5.8 percent in the United States as a whole (Wright 1986:61; Ransom and Sutch 1977:41–44).

Although many southern blacks were mired in poverty and some became trapped in debt peonage, there can be little doubt that material conditions among the freedmen as a whole were better in the southern United States than in most other postemancipation societies; certainly the South experienced nothing like the poverty and hunger of rural Haiti or Russia. Furthermore, the political repression that followed the overthrow of southern Reconstruction governments masks continuing gains among blacks in institution building, literacy, and landownership. In the same book in which he argues that "the story of Louisa [County, Virginia] is one of a missing revolution," Shifflett mentions in passing that the number of black landowners there surged from 27 in 1870 to 1,314 in 1900, by which date 88 percent of black heads of households owned land (Shifflett 1982:65, 53). Although this elevated figure was atypical of the South as a whole—sharecropping emerged as the dominant form of agricultural relations in the Cotton South—black landownership continued to expand, even as political repression increased. By 1900, as Claude F. Oubre points out, "25.2 percent of the black farmers owned their own farms" in the South, and even in the deep South 19.1 percent did; in Virginia, the proportion of black farm owners was 59.2 percent (1978:178–80).

The point of all this is not to argue that conditions in the postwar South were rosy. They weren't. But they were not uniquely bad, and in some respects they were not as bleak as those in other countries following emancipation. Wherever slavery and serfdom were abolished, they were replaced, not by equality, prosperity, and democracy, but by dependence, poverty, and repression (Kloosterboer 1960; Emmer 1986). That this was so suggests that something more was going on than the failure of specific policies.

A similar conclusion emerges from an examination of the second implicit comparative judgment at the root of the tragic theme: comparison of what was with what should have been. Every moral judgment of past behavior carries with it an implicit preferred alternative. During the first half of the twentieth century, most historians viewed the Republican authors of Reconstruction as harsh or vindictive; the assumption behind these judgments was that a proper policy should have been lenient, based on forgiveness of the rebels. More recently, most scholars have decisively rejected this approach, correctly noting the subjective nature of terms such as *leniency* and *harshness:* a policy that was lenient for ex-Confederates was usually harsh for ex-slaves.

The implicit—and sometimes explicit—moral judgment at the root of most current works is very different. Arguing that Republicans did not provide "real" freedom or equality for the ex-slaves implies that they should have done more. Historians differ, of course, over precisely what should have been done, and as scholars supposedly more concerned with explaining the past than offering prescriptions for the future, they rarely spell out their goals in detail. It is not hard, however, to piece together the implicit collective recipe for a successful Reconstruction that underlies most recent scholarship; not all historians offer exactly the same ingredients, but the recipe's flavor varies only slightly. Most now imply that a proper Reconstruction policy should have included, as a minimum, protection of the freedmen's civil and political rights and a labor policy designed to promote less repressive relations between landowner and laborer. Many historians go much further, suggesting that Republicans should have insisted on full racial integration of schools, promoted land confiscation and redistribution, and, indeed, fostered a true democracy—a social structure without great inequality and an economic system without exploitation.

Historians have not, of course, manufactured their judgments out of thin air; each of these versions of failure and tragedy was originally enunciated by some group of Reconstruction protagonists who, for differing reasons, were disillusioned about the course of events. For decades, most historians uncritically swallowed the rhetoric of former Confederates, accepting their definition of reality; according to this outlook, refusal immediately to forgive the leaders of one of history's bloodiest rebellions constituted extreme vindictiveness and tyranny. More recently, historians have rejected this judgment and have instead accepted the perspective and goals of either the Republican reformers or the former slaves.

Thus it is hardly surprising that Claude Bowers's descriptions of radical vindictiveness, southern white suffering, and the deficiencies of the black character sound remarkably like numerous writings and speeches of southern whites and northern Democrats in the 1860s and 1870s. "We are not unfriendly to the negro," declared a convention of white South Carolinians in a typical broadside on 21 September 1867, but "we protest against this subversion of the great social law, whereby an ignorant and depraved race is placed in power and influence above the virtuous, the educated and the refined" (Fleming 1966:1:425–26). Similarly, current Reconstruction scholarship often reads very much like Radical rhetoric of the 1860s. "We have turned, or are about to turn, loose four million slaves without a hut to shelter them or a cent in their pockets," Thaddeus Stevens told Congress on 18 December 1865. "This Congress is bound to provide for them until they can take care of themselves. . . . If we fail in this great duty now, when we have the power, we shall deserve and receive the execration of history and of all future ages" (ibid., 149). In their shifting versions of Reconstruction historiography, scholars have largely accepted at face value—and appropriated—differing moral judgments first articulated by the subjects of their historical study. The one constant has been perception of tragedy, although the nature of that tragedy has changed.

It is perfectly acceptable, of course, for historians to feel empathy for those about whom they write; indeed, such empathy is often a natural by-product of the effort to understand the outlook of past figures that is essential to historical inquiry. I would suggest, however, that in writing from the perspective of different groups of Reconstruction contemporaries, historians have too often crossed the line between sympathizing with the views of their subjects and adopting those views. (This misstep is most common among historians studying groups enjoying current political popularity, especially the freedmen; by contrast, James Roark manages to write sympathetically about the plight of the planters without becoming their spokesman.) In the process, scholars have lost much of the special perspective that comes from historical hindsight, embracing instead judgments based upon subjective considerations.

Each interpretation of tragedy articulated by contemporaries and adopted by later historians, for example, could be replaced by an opposite interpretation, based on a different implicit comparison. When former slaveowners (and historians who identified with them) described events as tragic, they were implicitly comparing their current condition with what had previously existed; they resented the loss of their slaveholding prerogatives as well as the loss of their slaveholding Confederacy. By other standards, however, they could be judged unbelievably fortunate, for where else in history have defeated rebels been treated so leniently as were ex-Confederates following the American Civil War? When former slaves (and historians who identified with them) described events as tragic, their comparison was not with the past but with a goal or ideal; they deplored the failure to provide full equality, whether in terms of political power, landownership, educational opportunity, or race relations. Compared to their previous status, however, the changed position of the freedmen seemed nothing short of miraculous; who could have predicted in 1859 that within a decade not only would slavery be abolished, but former slaves would be going to school, voting, and serving on juries?

If it is understandable that planters and freedmen focused on what they had lost or what they had failed to achieve, for historians to take the perceptions of those historical actors at face value entails an unfortunate surrender of historical perspective. No matter how laudable we may judge the goals of civil rights, integration, and land distribution, to organize an interpretation of postemancipation southern history around failure to achieve these goals and conclude that their absence is synonymous with tragedy seems naive, to say the least. The very question, What went wrong? which underlies so many interpretations of the postwar South, implies a Panglossian view of the world, in which it is assumed that things usually go right and that the existence of less than idyllic conditions needs to be explained, a view usually foreign to historians not contaminated by excessive doses of neoclassical economics. For "flawed economic institutions," "class rule," and exploitation were not aberrations with which the South somehow became saddled and whose presence we must explain; they are the stuff of history. Of course class rule and exploitation continued in the postwar South (as they did in the postwar North); one wonders what one might expect to find in their stead. The nonarrival of the millennium disappointed post–Civil War southerners, but it hardly justifies the conclusion that disaster was everywhere.

An examination of contemporary perceptions of tragedy and failure in other postemancipation societies underscores both the prevalence and the subjective nature of such perceptions. Given the difficulties associated with the transition from forced to free labor, it is hardly surprising that disappointment and perception of trouble were widespread. In Brazil, the government made little effort to ease the plight of the newly freed blacks, and even abolitionists quickly turned their attention to other matters. The resulting disappointment was apparently responsible for the emergence of considerable promonarchist sentiment among the former slaves following the overthrow of the emperor and the establishment of a republic in 1889, one year after the completion of emancipation (Chalhoub 1988:1–6).

The aftermath of emancipation in the British West Indies was equally distressing to the freedmen (who frequently manifested their displea-

sure with the new order the same way they had with the old—in flight)
and to both pro- and antislavery spokesmen. Southern defenders of
slavery in the 1840s and 1850s pointed to the islands as proof of abolition's folly, suggesting that in the wake of the freed blacks' refusal to
work without the compulsion of the lash—and the ensuing decline of
once-flourishing sugar economies—only a madman could favor emancipation of the southern slaves. British abolitionists were also troubled
by what they saw as laziness on the part of the ex-slaves and bemoaned
the failure of emancipation to transform the character of the free blacks.
As David Brion Davis notes, "The abolitionists, for all their rhetoric
about the debilitating effects of bondage, could not conceal their disappointment or hide their fear that blacks were somehow predisposed
to the cardinal sin of idleness" (Davis 1984:226; Eltis 1987:25–27).

But it was in postemancipation Russia, more than anywhere else outside the United States, that perceptions of things gone wrong were most
pervasive. There, as in the southern United States, almost everyone
seemed a loser in the last third of the nineteenth century. Noblemen
pointed to their loss of status—and land—in a new world, which did
not take their prerogatives seriously. Many peasants believed that the
real freedom they had been promised was being withheld from them.
Subscribing to what Soviet historians term "naive monarchism," that
is, the conviction that the tsar was really on their side but was prevented
from acting in their behalf by greedy noblemen and corrupt officials,
the serfs expressed disbelief—and outrage—when they learned the terms
of the emancipation settlement. The disorders that spread across the
countryside during the spring and summer of 1861 gradually subsided,
but peasants continued to harbor a sullen resentment at the betrayal
they had supposedly suffered.

Reformers and government bureaucrats shared in the general sense
of disillusionment, as peasants persisted in defying the logic of mod-
ernizers and the rural economy seemed mired in ignorance, inefficiency,
and corruption. By the 1870s and 1880s there was widespread perception of a new crisis, although observers differed over whether it was
primarily one of agricultural production, village organization, or rural
administration. As in the decades before emancipation, commission after
commission was established to study the "peasant question," an issue
supposedly resolved in 1861: somehow, things seemed to have gone ter-
ribly wrong (Emmons 1968a; Zaionchkovskii 1968; Field 1976:1–29,
208–15; Druzhinin 1978; Becker 1985; Macey 1987; Pearson 1989).

On one level, the ubiquitous sense of things gone wrong reflected hard times that, in fact, existed everywhere during the transition to free labor. On another level, however, the situation was a good deal more complex. In addition to actual material conditions, people's hopes and expectations can play an important part in shaping their perception of events; dashed expectations can produce feelings of unhappiness every bit as real as those generated by poverty, discrimination, and political repression. I suggest that such dashed expectations operated with particular force in the U.S. South — as they did in Russia — not because conditions there were objectively worse than elsewhere, but because emancipation there aroused such enormous hopes for social regeneration. In order to understand how this process worked, one must turn to a second major theme in Reconstruction historiography: transformation.

The view that emancipation and the ensuing Reconstruction represented a turning point in southern — and indeed American — history is emerging as a central theme among many historians. This position is not, of course, entirely new: it was first articulated by Reconstruction contemporaries and found renewed support both in Charles and Mary Beard's interpretation of the Civil War as a "second American Revolution" and in C. Vann Woodward's pioneering exploration of change in the post–Civil War era (Beard and Beard 1927:2:51–121; Woodward 1951). Now, after a generation more impressed by historical continuity than discontinuity (both in general and with reference to the postwar South), many scholars — including in some cases those committed to the tragic view of Reconstruction — are resurrecting the notion that the postwar years witnessed a "fundamental and revolutionary transformation of the South" (Woodman 1985:99; Hahn 1990).

According to this view, emancipation was both central to the transition within the United States to a free-labor (or capitalist) system and part of a worldwide process; the overthrow of slavery thus represented a turning point in American political, economic, and social history, ushering in the beginning of the modern era. Unlike the Beards, however, who stressed the destruction of the slaveholding aristocracy as essential to the ascendancy of northeastern capitalists but who said little about southern blacks, present-day scholars are especially interested in the impact of the Civil War, emancipation, and Reconstruction on the *South* and pay particular attention to the lives of the freedmen. "Like a massive earthquake, the Civil War and the destruction of slavery permanently altered the landscape of Southern life," writes Eric Foner, who notes that "the term 'revolution' has reappeared in the most recent literature as a way of describing the Civil War and Reconstruction" (1988:11, xxiv).

This theme of revolution or transformation is not without problems. The economic viability of slavery — both southern and Caribbean — raises questions about whether modernization in fact required abolition (e.g., Fogel and Engerman 1974:86–106, 191–209, 247–57; Goldin 1976; Engerman 1986:326–33; Drescher 1987; Eltis 1987:4–25). Equally important, one must distinguish carefully between the revolutionary causes and revolutionary consequences of emancipation; the existence of one is not dependent on the existence of the other. Similarly, one must distinguish between a revolution in southern society and one in American society as a whole. These problems — which are serious but not, I think, insurmountable — will receive my attention elsewhere.

Suffice it to say here, much of what we have learned about the postemancipation South points to the existence of a fundamental social transformation. An important element in this process was the political environment in which it occurred: the defeat of the slaveholding Confederacy and the political ascendancy of Republican reformers committed to a thoroughgoing restructuring of southern society meant that the changes stemming from abolition would be unusually sweeping compared to those occurring in most other societies undergoing transition from coerced to free labor. As both defenders and critics of the old order recognized, the destruction of a social system based on extra-economic compulsion and the emergence of a free-labor economy not only in itself constituted a fundamental break with the past, but also — in conjunction with Republican political hegemony — produced numerous attendant changes in economy, polity, ideology, race relations, and patterns of life. In short, political Reconstruction shaped, and gave special force to, the transformation resulting from emancipation.

An outline of some of the key elements in the postemancipation transformation in the lives of southern blacks indicates the revolutionary nature of the Reconstruction era. In general, the freedmen's behavior in the immediate postwar years was shaped by what they had not been allowed to do as slaves; following their release from thralldom, southern blacks strove to render their condition as far removed from slavery as possible. Thus, many freed blacks left their homes, either temporarily or permanently, in order to test and prove their freedom, and widespread black migration remained a notable feature of the postbellum black South. Freedmen defended their families, seeking reunion with loved ones forcibly separated under slavery, vigorously resisting the apprenticing of their children to former owners, and often promoting a new housewife status for women who had previously labored in the fields.

Rural blacks strove, usually unsuccessfully, to acquire land of their own, and, barring that, expressed a clear preference for sharecropping over wage labor, because the former seemed to provide them with greater independence than the latter. In most of the Cotton South, this preference usually led to a progression from share wages to various share-renting arrangements, accompanied by a rapid breakup of the slave quarters and abandonment of driver-supervised gang labor (Ransom and Sutch 1977:81–99; Shlomowitz 1979; Jaynes 1986:280–301). Other developments of significance include the education of black children, in which black teachers played an increasingly prominent role; the secession of freedmen from the white Protestant churches and the formation of independent black churches; the emergence of a new black leadership class; political participation in local and state government; a substantial decrease in the number of hours worked by agricultural laborers; the passage of legislation at both state and national levels protecting civil and political rights regardless of race; and a decline in black deference that led many whites to label freedmen "uppity." Underlying all of these developments was the freedmen's effort to achieve as much independence for themselves as possible (Kolchin 1972; Litwack 1979).

Although transformation went hand in hand with emancipation wherever abolition occurred, the particular constellation of political forces that produced "Radical" Reconstruction set the United States off from other New World societies and guaranteed that changes in the South would be especially far-reaching. The absence of any sweeping government-sponsored efforts to remake society elsewhere in the Americas—that is, the absence of any real equivalent to American Reconstruction—served to limit the revolutionary nature of the postemancipation changes there.

Only in Russia was emancipation part and parcel of something approaching an American-style effort to restructure the social order. There, as in the southern United States, the former bondsmen remained at the center of national political attention, as the government struggled with what continued to be known as the peasant question. There, too, emancipation was accompanied by a series of sweeping measures known as the Great Reforms, measures designed to modernize the army, the judiciary, and the political system and to bring Russia into the nineteenth century. There, as well, these reforms aroused extraordinary hopes among diverse groups, who foresaw the dawning of a bright new era (e.g., Pearson 1989; Emmons and Vucinich, 1982; Zakharova 1989; Druzhinin 1978; Emmons 1968b).

It is not surprising, then, to find the same kind of emphasis on revolutionary transformation among historians of Russia as exists among historians of the American South. As L. G. Zakharova puts it, emancipation and the ensuing reforms constituted "a most important event, a 'watershed,' a 'turning point'" in Russian history (1989:3). If Soviet historians typically argue that emancipation was associated with "transition from a feudal to a capitalist formation" (Druzhinin 1978:3), many Western scholars also stress the radical changes that saw "Russia's transition from a society based on estate privilege to one based on the legal equality of individuals" (Becker 1985:154). Whether they use the terms *democratization, modernization, social transformation,* or *transition to capitalism,* historians of Russia, like those of the U.S. South, typically see emancipation as part of a revolutionary process that fundamentally altered the social order.

At first glance, tragedy and transformation would seem to be contradictory themes. To the extent that Reconstruction was part of a basic social transformation, it is difficult to argue that it represented failure or missed opportunity. Indeed, the notion that emancipation and Reconstruction constituted a turning point in southern history provides still one more reason to question whether the Tragic Era interpretation is a useful way for historians to conceptualize the postwar years.

I suggest, however, that for those who lived through the Civil War and Reconstruction there was an integral connection between transformation and tragedy, a connection highlighted by a similar relationship between social revolution and perceived misfortune in Russia. During his travels through Russia in the 1870s, British journalist Sir Donald MacKenzie Wallace was struck by the negative view of emancipation's consequence that prevailed among educated Russians. "Very soon," he observed, "I came to perceive that my authorities were . . . evidently suffering from shattered illusions. They had expected that the Emancipation would produce instantaneously a wonderful improvement in the life and character of the rural population, and that the peasant would become at once a sober, industrious, model agriculturist. These expectations were not realized" (1961:338–39). Frenchman Anatole Leroy-Beaulieu made the same point when, drawing an analogy with the French Revolution, he noted that Russian emancipation was a "revolution" that "was a great success; yet, to many of those who took part in the work, it proved disappointing." As with the French Revolution, the disappointment was to be explained by "the excessive hopes raised. . . . Not less than the ignorant serf, the politician and the literary man, private speculation and public opinion, had built up illusions. The cultivated Russians had conjured up a vision of an Eden very nearly as fanciful as the Eldorado of the peasant's dreams: of a free Russia, all new, all different from the Russia of serfdom" (1969:1:450–51).

Shattered illusions . . . expectations not realized . . . excessive hopes raised—these observations about Russia provide a clue to understanding the disillusionment that prevailed in the postemancipation U.S. South. Could it be that the perception of things gone wrong, rather than indicating an absence of significant changes, was at least in part a function of dashed hopes raised by those very changes? I believe so. In other words, because so many people thought they were witnessing a revolutionary restructuring of the social order, any outcome short of the most ideal was likely to seem unsatisfactory.

Emancipation generated an extraordinary range of regrets, fears, hopes, and expectations. To former slaveowners, loss of previous prerogatives loomed so large in the postwar period that virtually any settlement would have appeared tragic. Although some planters professed in retrospect to welcome emancipation, insisting that they were better off without their troublesome property, such sour grapes protestations only thinly masked feelings of outrage, humiliation, and anxiety; the twin losses of their slaves and their war left former masters bitter and hostile. Small wonder, then, that in their minds the Reconstruction drive to force additional changes on the South would, by definition, constitute a tragedy.

What is more remarkable (and significant) is that the effort to transform the South created a sense of things gone wrong among the Civil War's winners, as well. To understand how this happened, it is necessary to emphasize the extraordinary—indeed, the revolutionary—expectations that emancipation and Reconstruction generated. These expectations were not only grandiose but diverse; abolitionists, free-labor spokesmen, Radical Republicans, freedmen, and many nonslaveholding southern whites all looked forward to a transformation of the South, but they had very different ideas about what that transformation should entail.

Former slaves typically sought to maximize their autonomy, whether this meant working their own land or defending their own customs; in doing so, ironically, they often demonstrated an attachment to established ways, even as they derided the new dispensation as not being sufficiently free. For example, despite the efforts of northern white missionaries to "convert" the freedmen, their Christianity remained largely that of the slave community. In their drive for autonomy and independence, southern freedmen showed the same concerns as those of other newly emancipated peoples around the world: those concerns were evident in the withdrawal of Jamaican freedmen from the plantation economy and in the continued adherence of Russian peasants to the "customary law" of the village commune, despite the strenuous efforts of reformers to rationalize village life (e.g., Mironov 1985; Frank 1987).

If the principal goal of the freedmen was increased autonomy, that of their allies—Republican reformers in and out of government—was more likely to be increased efficiency. They looked to the free-labor system to produce almost instant prosperity throughout the South, turning a benighted land into a garden of Eden; "the wilderness shall vanish, the church and school house will appear; . . . the whole land will revive under the magic touch of free labor," one Radical Republican declared with typical exuberance in 1866 (Foner 1988:235). They also looked to that system to work a miraculous transformation in the character of the former slaves, turning them into hardworking, sober, industrious, and productive workers. Northern missionaries who went south were generally believers in greater rights for blacks and toiled tirelessly on their behalf; those missionaries also typically sought to instill in the freedmen the bourgeois values of sobriety, punctuality, initiative, and self-discipline.

The resulting revolutionary dynamic was virtually bound to produce frustration and feelings of betrayal, for despite profound changes in southern society, expectations were so elevated that they could not possibly be met. This was especially so because these expectations were so diverse: no change could at the same time satisfy groups with such disparate values, perceptions, and interests as those groups that made up the Reconstruction coalitions. In short, the sense of tragedy that pervaded the postwar South was in part a function of the far-reaching effort undertaken to transform society.

Let me return, in conclusion, to the question of Reconstruction as a tragic era. This enduring historical image is a result, as we have seen, of historians' appropriating the views of Reconstruction protagonists themselves. I believe that this appropriation is a mistake (although it is easy to see how it occurred) and that it is time to move on to new ways of conceptualizing Reconstruction. Although diverse groups of people who lived through Reconstruction experienced intense feelings of disillusionment, these feelings do not add up to a tragic era. As historians, we must be careful, even as we seek to understand the subjective views of those we study, not to take those views entirely at face value, or to let them totally shape our judgments of the past. After all, we have the advantage of hindsight.

NOTE

I would like to thank Stanley L. Engerman, Drew G. Faust, William A. Green, Howard N. Rabinowitz, and Raymond Wolters for helpful comments on a previous version of this chapter.

REFERENCES

Andrews, George Reid. 1988. Black and White Workers: São Paulo, Brazil, 1888–1928. *Hispanic American Historical Review* 68:491–524.

Beard, Charles A., and Mary R. Beard. 1927. *The Rise of American Civilization.* 2 vols. New York: Macmillan.

Becker, Seymour. 1985. *Nobility and Privilege in Late Imperial Russia.* Dekalb: Northern Illinois University Press.

Bowers, Claude G. 1929. *The Tragic Era: The Revolution After Lincoln.* Cambridge: Houghton Mifflin.

Chalhoub, Sidney. 1988. Slaves, Freedmen and the Politics of Freedom in Brazil: The Experience of Blacks in the City of Rio. Paper prepared for the Conference on the Meaning of Freedom, University of Pittsburgh, August.

Coulter, E. Merton. 1947. *The South During Reconstruction, 1865–1877.* Baton Rouge: Louisiana State University Press.

Current, Richard Nelson. 1988. *Those Terrible Carpetbaggers.* New York: Oxford University Press.

Davis, David Brion. 1984. *Slavery and Human Progress.* New York: Oxford University Press.

Drescher, Seymour. 1987. *Capitalism and Antislavery: British Mobilization in Comparative Perspective.* New York: Oxford University Press.

Druzhinin, N. M. 1978. *Russkaia derevnia na perelome: 1861–1880 gg.* Moscow: Izdatel'stvo "Nauka."

Dunning, William A. 1907. *Reconstruction: Political and Economic, 1865–1877.* New York: Harper Brothers.

Eltis, David. 1987. *Economic Growth and the Ending of the Transatlantic Slave Trade.* New York: Oxford University Press.

Emmer, P. C., ed. 1986. *Colonialism and Migration: Indentured Labour Before and After Slavery.* Dordrecht, Netherlands: Martinus Nijhoff.

Emmons, Terence. 1968a. The Peasant and Emancipation. In *The Peasant in Nineteenth-Century Russia,* edited by Wayne S. Vucinich, 41–71. Stanford: Stanford University Press.

———. 1968b. *The Russian Landed Gentry and the Peasant Emancipation of 1861.* Cambridge: Cambridge University Press.

Emmons, Terence, and Wayne S. Vucinich, eds. 1982. *The Zemstvo in Russia: An Experiment in Local Self-Government.* Cambridge: Cambridge University Press.

Engerman, Stanley L. 1982. Economic Adjustments to Emancipation in the United States and British West Indies. *Journal of Interdisciplinary History* 13:191–220.

———. 1986. Slavery and Emancipation in Comparative Perspective: A Look at Some Recent Debates. *Journal of Economic History* 46:317–39.

Fernandes, Florestan. 1974. Beyond Poverty: The Negro and the Mulatto in Brazil. In *Slavery and Race Relations in Latin America,* edited by Robert Brent Toplin, 277–97. Westport, Conn.: Greenwood.

Field, Daniel. 1976. *Rebels in the Name of the Tsar.* Boston: Houghton Mifflin.

Fleming, Walter L., ed. 1966 (1906). *Documentary History of Reconstruction: Political, Military, Social, Religious, Economic, and Industrial, 1865 to 1906.* 2 vols. New York: McGraw Hill.

Fogel, Robert William, and Stanley L. Engerman. 1974. *Time on the Cross: The Economics of American Negro Slavery.* Boston: Little, Brown.

Foner, Eric. 1983. *Nothing but Freedom: Emancipation and Its Legacy.* Baton Rouge: Louisiana State University Press.

———. 1988. *Reconstruction: America's Unfinished Revolution, 1863–1877.* New York: Harper and Row.

Ford, Lacy K. 1984. Rednecks and Merchants: Economic Development and Social Tensions in the South Carolina Upcountry, 1865–1900. *Journal of American History* 71:294–318.

Frank, Stephen P. 1987. Popular Justice, Community and Culture among the Russian Peasantry, 1870–1900. *Russian Review* 46:239–65.

Gatrell, Peter. 1986. *The Tsarist Economy, 1850–1917.* London: B. T. Batsford.

Goldin, Claudia Dale. 1976. *Urban Slavery in the American South, 1820–1860: A Quantitative History.* Chicago: University of Chicago Press.

Green, William A. 1976. *British Slave Emancipation: The Sugar Colonies and the Great Experiment, 1830–1865.* London: Oxford University Press.

Hahn, Steven. 1983. *The Roots of Southern Populism: Yeoman Farmers and the Transformation of the Georgia Upcountry, 1850–1890.* New York: Oxford University Press.

———. 1990. Emancipation and the Development of Capitalist Agriculture: The South in Comparative Perspective. In *What Made the South Different?* edited by Kees Gispen, 71–88. Jackson: University Press of Mississippi.

James, C. L. R. 1963. *The Black Jacobins.* 2d ed. New York: Vintage Books.

Jaynes, Gerald D. 1986. *Branches Without Roots: Genesis of the Black Working Class in the American South, 1862–1882.* New York: Oxford University Press.

Jones, Jacqueline. 1980. *Soldiers of Light and Love: Northern Teachers and Georgia Blacks, 1865–1873.* Chapel Hill: University of North Carolina Press.

Klein, Herbert S., and Stanley L. Engerman. 1985. The Transition from Slave to
Free Labor: Notes on a Comparative Economic Model. In *Between Slavery and
Free Labor,* edited by M. M. Fraginals, Frank Moya Pons, and Stanley Enger-
man, 259–69. Baltimore: Johns Hopkins University Press.

Kloosterboer, W. 1960. *Involuntary Labour Since the Abolition of Slavery: A Survey of Compulsory Labour Throughout the World.* Leiden: E. J. Brill.

Kolchin, Peter. 1972. *First Freedom: The Responses of Alabama's Blacks to Emancipation and Reconstruction.* Westport, Conn.: Greenwood.

Lacerte, Robert K. 1978. The Evolution of Land and Labor in the Haitian Revolution, 1791–1820. *The Americas* 34:449–59.

Leroy-Beaulieu, Anatole. 1969. *The Emperor of the Tsars and the Russians,* translated from the 3d French edition (1893), by Z. A. Ragozin. 3 vols. New York:
AMS Press.

Litwack, Leon F. 1979. *Been in the Storm So Long: The Aftermath of Slavery.* New
York: Knopf.

Macey, David A. J. 1987. *Government and Peasant in Russia, 1861–1906: The Pre-
history of the Stolypin Reforms.* Dekalb: Northern Illinois University Press.

Mandle, Jay R. 1978. *The Roots of Black Poverty: The Southern Plantation Economy After the Civil War.* Durham: Duke University Press.

Mironov, Boris. 1985. The Russian Peasant Commune After the Reforms of the 1860s.
Slavic Review 44:438–67.

Moya Pons, Frank. 1985. The Land Question in Haiti and Santo Domingo: The
Sociopolitical Context of the Transition from Slavery to Free Labor, 1801–1843.
In *Between Slavery and Free Labor,* edited by M. M. Fraginals, Frank Moya
Pons, and Stanley Engerman, 181–214. Baltimore: Johns Hopkins University Press.

Oubre, Claude F. 1978. *Forty Acres and a Mule: The Freedmen's Bureau and Black
Landownership.* Baton Rouge: Louisiana State University Press.

Pearson, Thomas S. 1989. *Russian Officialdom in Crisis: Autocracy and Local Self-
Government, 1861–1890.* Cambridge: Cambridge University Press.

Perman, Michael. 1984. *The Road to Redemption: Southern Politics, 1869–1879.*
Chapel Hill: University of North Carolina Press.

Powell, Lawrence N. 1980. *New Masters: Northern Planters During the Civil War
and Reconstruction.* New Haven: Yale University Press.

Pressly, Thomas J. 1989. Reconstruction in the Southern United States: A Comparative Perspective. *Magazine of History* 4:14–34.

Rabinowitz, Howard N. 1976. From Exclusion to Segregation: Southern Race Relations, 1865–1890. *Journal of American History* 63:325–50.

———. 1978. *Race Relations in the Urban South, 1865–1890.* New York: Oxford
University Press.

Rable, George C. 1984. *But There Was No Peace: The Role of Violence in the Politics of Reconstruction.* Athens: University of Georgia Press.

Ransom, Roger L., and Richard Sutch. 1977. *One Kind of Freedom: The Economic
Consequences of Emancipation.* Cambridge: Cambridge University Press.

Richardson, Joe M. 1986. *Christian Reconstruction: The American Missionary Association and Southern Blacks, 1861–1890.* Athens: University of Georgia Press.

Roark, James L. 1977. *Masters Without Slaves: Southern Planters in the Civil War
and Reconstruction.* New York: Norton.

Scott, Rebecca J. 1985. *Slave Emancipation in Cuba: The Transition to Free Labor, 1860–1899*. Princeton: Princeton University Press.

Shanin, Teodor. 1986. *Russia as a "Developing Society": The Roots of Otherness: Russia's Turn of the Century*. Vol. 1. New Haven: Yale University Press.

Shifflett, Crandall A. 1982. *Patronage and Poverty in the Tobacco South: Louisa County, Virginia, 1860–1900*. Knoxville: University of Tennessee Press.

Shlomowitz, Ralph. 1979. The Origins of Southern Sharecropping. *Agricultural History* 53:557–75.

Toplin, Robert Brent. 1971. *The Abolition of Slavery in Brazil*. New York: Atheneum.

Trelease, Allen W. 1971. *White Terror: The Ku Klux Klan Conspiracy and Southern Reconstruction*. New York: Harper and Row.

Tunnell, Ted. 1984. *Crucible of Reconstruction: War, Radicalism, and Race in Louisiana, 1862–1877*. Baton Rouge: Louisiana State University Press.

Wallace, Donald MacKenzie. 1961. *Russia on the Eve of War and Revolution*. Edited by Cyril E. Black. New York: Random House.

Wiener, Jonathan. 1978. *Social Origins of the New South: Alabama, 1860–1885*. Baton Rouge: Louisiana State University Press.

Woodman, Harold D. 1985. The Reconstruction of the Cotton Plantation in the New South. In *Essays on the Postbellum Southern Economy*, edited by Thavolia Glymph and John J. Kushma, 95–119. College Station: Texas A&M University Press.

Woodward, C. Vann. 1951. *Origins of the New South, 1877–1913*. Baton Rouge: Louisiana State University Press.

Wright, Gavin. 1986. *Old South, New South: Revolutions in the Southern Economy Since the Civil War*. New York: Basic Books.

Zaionchkovskii, P. A. 1968. *Otmena krepostnogo prava v Rossii*, 3d ed. Moscow: Prosveshchenie.

Zakharova, L. G. 1989. Samoderzhavie, biurokratiia i reformy 60-kh godov xix v. v Rossii. *Voprosy istorii*, no. 10:3–24.

Select Bibliography
Notes on Contributors
Index

SELECT BIBLIOGRAPHY

This bibliography is intended to provide the researcher with a Cook's tour of those books published during the past decade that provide significant signposts for research in the 1990s. These books are a sample of themes and research protocols dealing with life history, ethnohistories, and macrohistories of region or nation or global constructs of the era under consideration. In all cases, these works may be profitably utilized in continuing research into late slavery, emancipation, free labor, racism, and the sundry issues of comparison and analysis that these topics promise and demand.

The Abolition of Slavery in the Americas: The United States, the Caribbean, Brazil, and Mexico. Itinerio (special issue) 12:2 (1988).

Albert, Bill, and Adrian Graves, eds. *Crisis and Change in the International Sugar Economy, 1900–1914*. Norwich, 1984.

Anderson, E., and A. Moss. *The Facts of Reconstruction: Essays in Honor of John Hope Franklin*. Baton Rouge, 1991.

Anderson, James. *The Education of Blacks in the South, 1860–1935*. Chapel Hill, 1988.

Andrews, George Reid. *Blacks and Whites in São Paulo, Brazil, 1888–1988*. Madison, 1991.

Archer, Leonie J. *Slavery and Other Forms of Unfree Labor*. New York, 1988.

Barney, William. *The Passage of the Republic: An Interdisciplinary History of Nineteenth-Century America*. Lexington, 1987.

Benedict, Marion, and Burton Benedict. *Men, Women, and Money in Seychelles*. Berkeley, 1982.

Bennett, Norman. *Arab Versus European: Diplomacy and War in Nineteenth-Century East Africa*. New York, 1986.

Bergad, Laird W. *Coffee and the Growth of Agrarian Capitalism in Nineteenth-Century Puerto Rico*. Princeton, 1983.

———. *Cuban Rural Society in the Nineteenth Century: The Social and Economic History of Monoculture in Matanzas*. Princeton, 1990.

Besson, Jean, and Janet Momsen, eds. *Land and Development in the Caribbean*. New York, 1987.

Betnel, Elisabeth. *Promiseland: A Century of Life in a Negro Community*. Philadelphia, 1981.

Blackburn, Robin. *The Overthrow of Colonial Slavery, 1776–1848*. New York, 1988.

Blight, David. *Frederick Douglass' Civil War: Keeping Faith in Jubilee*. Baton Rouge, 1989.

Bolland, O. Nigel. *Colonialism and Resistance in Belize: Essays in Historical Sociology*. Belize, 1988.

Boles, John. *Black Southerners, 1614–1869*. Lexington, 1984.

Bremen, Jan. *Taming the Coolie Beast: Plantation Society and the Colonial Order in Southeast Asia*. London, 1989.

Brereton, Bridget. *A History of Modern Trinidad*. London, 1981.

————. *Social Life in the Caribbean, 1838–1938*. Kingston, 1985.

Carter, Dan T. *When the War Was Over: The Failure of Self-Reconstruction in the South, 1865–1867*. Baton Rouge, 1985.

Cell, John. *The Highest Stage of White Supremacy: The Origins of Segregation in South Africa and the American South*. Cambridge, 1982.

Changing Sugar Technology and the Labour Nexus: The Caribbean, 1750–1900. *New West Indian Guide* (special issue). 1989.

Cohen, Robin. *The New Helots: Migrants in the International Division of Labor*. Aldershot, 1987.

Cohen, William. *At Freedom's Edge: Black Mobility and the Southern Quest for Racial Control, 1861–1915*. Baton Rouge, 1991.

Cooper, Frederick. *From Slaves to Squatters: Plantation Labor and Agriculture in Zanzibar and Coastal Kenya, 1840–1925*. New Haven, 1980.

Cox, Lawanda. *Lincoln and Black Freedom: A Study in Presidential Leadership*. Columbia, 1981.

Cross, Malcolm, and Heuman Gad, eds. *Labour in the Caribbean: From Emancipation to Independence*. New York, 1988.

Currie-McDaniel, Ruth. *Carpetbagger of Conscience: A Biography of John Emory Bryant*. Athens, 1987.

Curtin, Phillip. *The Rise and Fall of the Plantation Complex: Essays in Atlantic History*. Cambridge, 1990.

Davis, David Brion. *Slavery and Human Progress*. New York, 1984.

De Vertinel, A. *The Years of Revolt: Trinidad, 1880–1888*. Port of Spain, 1984.

Devlin, George A. *South Carolina and Black Migration: Bound for the Promised Land*. New York, 1990.

Drescher, Seymour. *Capitalism and Antislavery: British Mobilization in Comparative Perspective*. London, New York, 1986.

Eltis, David. *Economic Growth and the Ending of the Transatlantic Slave Trade*. New York, 1987.

Emmer, P. C., ed. *Colonialism and Migration: Indentured Labor Before and After Slavery*. Dordrecht, 1986.

Ennew, Judith. *Debt Bondage: A Survey*. London, 1981.

Fields, Barbara. *Slavery and Freedom on the Middle Ground: Maryland During the Nineteenth Century*. New Haven, 1985.

Flynn, Charles Jr. *White Land, Black Labor: Caste and Class in Nineteenth-Century Georgia*. Baton Rouge, 1983.

Fogel, Robert William. *Without Consent or Contract: The Rise and Fall of American Slavery*. 4 vols. New York, 1989–.

Fogel, Robert William, and Stanley Engerman. *Time on the Cross: The Economics of American Negro Slavery*. Rev. ed. New York, 1989.

Foner, Eric. *Nothing But Freedom: Emancipation and Its Legacy*. Baton Rouge, 1983.

————. *Reconstruction: America's Unfinished Revolution, 1863–1877*. New York, 1988.

Fox-Genovese, Elizabeth, and Eugene Genovese. *The Fruits of Merchant Capital: Slavery and Bourgeois Property in the Rise and Expansion of Capitalism.* New York, 1983.

Fraginals, Manuel Moreno, Frank Moya Pons, and Stanley Engerman. *Between Slavery and Free Labor: The Spanish-Speaking Caribbean in the Nineteenth Century.* Baltimore, 1985.

Frederikson, George. *White Supremacy: A Comparative Study in American and South African History.* New York, 1981.

———. *The Arrogance of Race: Historical Perspectives on Slavery, Racism, and Social Inequality.* Middletown, 1988.

Galloway, J. H. *The Sugar Cane Industry: An Historical Geography from Its Origins to 1914.* Cambridge, 1989.

Glymph, Thavolia, ed. *Essays on the Post Bellum Southern Economy.* College Station, 1985.

Greenberg, Stanley. *Race and State in Capitalist Development: Comparative Perspectives.* New Haven, 1980.

Hahn, Steven. *The Roots of Southern Populism: Yeoman Farmers and the Transformation of Georgia's Upper Piedmont, 1850–1880.* New York, 1983.

Haley, John. *Charles N. Hunter and Race Relations in North Carolina.* Chapel Hill, 1987.

Harms, Robert. *River of Wealth, River of Sorrow: The Central Zaire Basin in the Era of the Slave and Ivory Trade, 1500–1891.* New Haven, 1981.

Hayward, Jack, ed. *Out of Slavery: Abolition and After.* London, 1985.

Heuman, Gad. *Between Black and White: Race, Politics, and the Free Coloreds in Jamaica.* Westport, 1981.

Hine, Darlene, ed. *The State of Afro-American History: Past, Present, and Future.* Baton Rouge, 1986.

Hoetink, H. *The Dominican People, 1850–1900: Notes for an Historical Sociology.* Baltimore, 1982.

Hoffman, Charles, and Tess Hoffman. *North by South: The Two Lives of Richard James Arnold.* Athens, 1988.

Holloway, Thomas. *Immigrants on the Land: Coffee and Society in São Paulo, 1886–1936.* Chapel Hill, 1980.

Holt, Thomas C. *The Problem of Freedom: Race, Labor and Politics in Jamaica and Britain, 1832–1938.* Baltimore, 1992.

Huggins, Martha. *From Slavery to Vagrancy in Brazil: Crime and Social Control in the Third World.* New Brunswick, 1985.

Jaynes, Gerald David. *Branches Without Roots: Genesis of the Black Working Class in the American South, 1862–1882.* New York, 1986.

Jones, Jacqueline. *Soldiers of Light and Love: Northern Teachers and Georgia Blacks, 1865–1873.* Chapel Hill, 1980.

———. *Labor of Love, Labor of Sorrow: Black Women, Work, and the Family from Slavery to the Present.* New York, 1985.

Kahn, Joel, and Joseph L. Lobera, eds. *The Anthropology of Pre-Capitalist Societies.* New York, 1981.

Klein, Herbert S. *African Slavery in Latin America and the Caribbean.* New York, 1986.

Knight, Franklin, and Colin Palmer, eds. *The Modern Caribbean*. Chapel Hill, 1989.

Kolchin, Peter. *Unfree Labor: American Slavery and Russian Serfdom*. Cambridge, 1987.

Kottak, Conrad. *The Past in the Present: History, Ecology, and Cultural Variation in Highland Madagascar*. Ann Arbor, 1980.

Kousser, J. Morgan, and James McPherson, eds. *Region, Race, and Reconstruction: Essays in Honor of C. Vann Woodward*. New York, 1982.

Levy, Claude. *Emancipation, Sugar, and Federalism: Barbados and the West Indies, 1833–1876*. Gainesville, 1980.

Lewis, Gordon. *Main Currents in Caribbean Thought: The Historical Evolution of Caribbean Society in Its Ideological Aspects, 1492–1900*. Baltimore, 1983.

Litwack, Leon, and August Meir, eds. *Black Leaders of the Nineteenth Century*. Urbana, 1987.

Lobdell, Richard. *Economic Structure and Demographic Performance in Jamaica, 1891–1935*. New York, 1987.

Lovejoy, Paul, ed. *Africans in Bondage*. Madison, 1986.

McLewin, Philip. *Power and Economic Change: The Response to Emancipation in Jamaica and British Guiana, 1840–1865*. New York, 1987.

McMillen, Neil. *Dark Journey: Black Mississippians in the Age of Jim Crow*. Urbana, 1989.

McPherson, James. *Ordeal by Fire: The Civil War and Reconstruction*. New York, 1982.

———. *Battle Cry of Freedom: The Civil War Era*. New York, 1988.

———. *Abraham Lincoln and the Second American Revolution*. New York, 1991.

Magazine of History 4 (Winter, 1989). Special issue on Reconstruction.

Magid, Alvin. *Urban Nationalism: A Study of Political Development in Trinidad*. Gainesville, 1988.

Manning, Patrick. *Slavery, Colonialism and Economic Growth in Dahomey, 1640–1960*. Cambridge, 1982.

Martin, Waldo. *The Mind of Frederick Douglass*. Chapel Hill, 1984.

Meier, August, and Elliott Rudwick, eds. *Black History and the Historical Profession, 1915–1980*. Urbana, 1986.

Miers, Susanne, and Richard Roberts, eds. *The End of Slavery in Africa*. Madison, 1988.

Miles, Robert. *Capitalism and Unfree Labor: Anomaly or Necessity?* New York, 1987.

Miller, Randall, and John D. Smith, eds. *Dictionary of Afro-American Slavery*. New York, 1988.

Mintz, Sydney. *Sweetness and Power: The Place of Sugar in Modern History*. New York, 1985.

———. *Caribbean Transformations*. New York, 1989.

Moore, Brian. *Race, Power, and Social Segmentation in Colonial Society: Guyana After Slavery, 1838–1891*. New York, 1987.

Mörner, Magnus. *The Andean Past: Land Societies and Conflict*. New York, 1985.

Morton, Fred. *Children of Ham: Freed Slaves and Fugitive Slaves on the Kenya Coast, 1873–1907*. Boulder, 1990.

Nash, Gary B., and Jean R. Soderlund. *Freedom by Degrees: Emancipation in Pennsylvania and Its Aftermath*. New York, 1991.

Oakes, James. *Slavery and Freedom: An Interpretation of the Old South*. New York, 1990.

Paquette, Robert L. *Sugar Is Made with Blood: The Conspiracy of La Escalera and the Conflict Between Empires Over Slavery in Cuba*. Middletown, 1988.

Parish, Peter. *Slavery: History and the Historians*. New York, 1989.

Perman, Michael. *Emancipation and Reconstruction, 1862–1870*. Arlington Heights, 1987.

Perez, Louis. *Cuba Between Empires, 1878–1902*. Pittsburgh, 1983.

———. *Lords of the Mountain: Social Banditry and Peasant Protest in Cuba, 1878–1918*. Pittsburgh, 1989.

Plant, Roger. *Sugar and Modern Slavery: A Tale of Two Countries*. London, 1987.

Prakash, Gyan. *Bonded Histories: Geneologies of Labor Servitude in Colonial India*. Cambridge, 1990.

Rabinowitz, Howard, ed. *Southern Black Leadership of the Reconstruction Era*. Urbana, 1982.

Rable, George. *But There Was No Peace: The Role of Violence in the Politics of Reconstruction*. Athens, 1984.

Rachlett, Peter. *Black Labor in Richmond, 1865–1890*. Urbana, Ill., 1984.

Rameriz, Francisco, ed. *Rethinking the Nineteenth Century: Contradictions and Movements*. New York, 1988.

Ransom, Roger. *Conflict and Compromise: The Political Economy of Slavery, Emancipation, and the American Civil War*. Cambridge, 1989.

Richardson, Bonham. *Caribbean Migrants, Environment, and Human Survival on St. Kitts and Nevis*. Knoxville, 1983.

Richardson, David, ed. *Abolition and Its Aftermath: The Historical Context, 1790–1916*. London, 1985.

Roberts, Richard. *Warriors, Merchants, and Slaves: The State and the Economy in the Middle Niger Valley, 1700–1914*. Palo Alto, 1987.

Robinson, Cedric. *Black Marxism: The Making of the Black Radical Tradition*. New York, 1983.

Rodney, Walter. *A History of the Guyanese Working People*. Baltimore, 1981.

Roseberry, William. *Coffee and Capitalism in the Venezuelan Andes*. Austin, 1983.

———. *Anthropologies and Histories: Essays in Culture, History, and Political Economy*. New Brunswick, 1989.

Samarin, William. *The Black Man's Burden: African Colonial Labor on the Congo and Ubangi Rivers, 1880–1900*. Boulder, 1989.

Saunders, Kay, ed. *Indentured Labor in the British Empire, 1834–1920*. London, 1984.

Sawyer, Roger. *Slavery in the Twentieth Century*. New York, 1986.

Saxton, Alexander. *The Rise and Fall of the White Republic*. New York, 1990.

Schuler, Monica. *'Alas, Alas Kongo': A Social History of Indentured African Immigration to Jamaica, 1841–1865*. Baltimore, 1980.

Shlomowitz, Ralph. "The Transition from Slave to Freeman: Labor Arrangements in Southern Agriculture, 1865–1870." Ph.D. diss., University of Chicago, 1978.

Scott, Rebecca. *Slave Emancipation in Cuba: The Transition to Free Labor, 1860–1899*. Princeton, 1985.

Scott, Rebecca J., S. Drescher, et al. *The Abolition of Slavery and the Aftermath of Emancipation in Brazil*. Durham, 1988.

Singh, Kelvin. *Bloodstained Tombs: The Muharren Massacre, 1884*. London, 1988.

Shifflett, Crandell. *Patronage and Poverty in the Tobacco South: Louisa County, Virginia, 1860–1900*. Knoxville, 1982.

Smith, John P. *An Old Creed for the New South: Pro-Slavery Ideology and Historiography, 1865–1918*. Athens, 1985.

Smith, Keithyn, and Ferando Smith. *To Shoot Hard Labor: The Life and Times of Samuel Smith, an Antiguan Workingman, 1877–1982*. Toronto, 1986.

Smith, R. T. *Kinship and Class in the West Indies: A Genealogical Study of Jamaica and Guyana*. Cambridge, 1988.

Spitzer, Leo. *Lives in Between: Assimilation and Marginality in Austria, Brazil, and West Africa, 1780–1945*. Cambridge, 1989.

Stein, Stanley J. *Vassouras, A Brazilian Coffee County, 1850–1890: The Roles of Planter and Slave in a Plantation Society*. Rev. ed. Princeton, 1985.

Stolcke, Verena. *Coffee Planters, Workers, and Wives: Class Conflict and Gender Relations on São Paulo Plantations, 1850–1980*. New York, 1988.

Stoler, Ann Laura. *Capitalism and Confrontation in Sumatra's Plantation Belt*. New Haven, 1985.

Sutton, Paul, ed. *Dual Legacies in the Contemporary Caribbean: Continuing Aspects of British and French Dominion*. London, 1985.

Taussig, Michael. *The Devil and Commodity Fetishism in Latin America*. Chapel Hill, 1980.

Toplin, Robert. *Freedom and Prejudice: The Legacy of Slavery in the United States and Brazil*. Westport, 1981.

Trouillot, Michel-Rolph. *Peasants and Capital: Dominica in the World Economy*. Baltimore, 1988.

———. *Haiti, State Against Nation: The Origins and Legacy of Duvalierism*. New York, 1990.

Troutman, David. *Crime in Trinidad: Conflict and Control in a Plantation Society, 1838–1900*. Knoxville, 1987.

Tunnell, Ted. *Crucible of Reconstruction: War, Radicalism, and Race in Louisiana, 1862–1877*. Baton Rouge, 1984.

Tyrell, Alex. *Joseph Sturge and the Moral Radical Party in Early Victorian Britain*. London, 1987.

Viotti da Costa, Emilia. *The Brazilian Empire: Myths and Histories*. Chicago, 1985.

Walker, Clarence. *A Rock in a Weary Land: The African Methodist Episcopal Church During Civil War and Reconstruction*. Baton Rouge, 1982.

Wallenstein, Peter. *From Slave South to New South: Public Policy in Nineteenth-Century Georgia*. Chapel Hill, 1987.

Walvin, James. *England, Slaves and Freedom, 1776–1838*. London, 1986.

Ward, J. R. *Poverty and Progress in the Caribbean, 1800–1960*. London, 1981.

Watts, David. *The West Indies: Patterns of Development, Culture and Environmental Change Since 1492*. Cambridge, 1987.

Wayne, Michael. *The Reshaping of Plantation Society: The Natchez District, 1860–1880.* Baton Rouge, 1983.

Wolf, Eric. *Europe and the People Without History.* Berkeley, 1982.

Wright, Gavin. *Old South, New South: Revolutions in the Southern Economy Since the Civil War.* New York, 1986.

NOTES ON CONTRIBUTORS

DIANE AUSTIN-BROOS is Associate Professor of Anthropology at the University of Sydney. Her publishing and research interests span the Caribbean and Australia. She has written an ethnography, *Urban Life in Kingston, Jamaica* (1984), and has recently published a number of articles on Jamaican pentecostalism.

JEAN BESSON is Senior Lecturer in Anthropology, Department of Anthropology and Community Studies, Goldsmiths' College, University of London. She has conducted extensive fieldwork in Jamaican rural communities and published widely on Caribbean peasantries and Caribbean oral history. She is co-editor of *Land and Development in the Caribbean* (1987), and editor of *Caribbean Reflections* (1989).

O. NIGEL BOLLAND, Professor of Sociology at Colgate University, has carried out extensive archival research on issues of colonialism and development in Belize, and on the transition from slavery to wage labor in the British Caribbean. His publications include *Belize: A New Nation in Central America* (1986) and *Colonialism and Resistance in Belize: Essays in Historical Sociology* (1988).

SEYMOUR DRESCHER is University Professor of History at the University of Pittsburgh. The author of a number of studies of Alexis de Tocqueville, his more recent research has focused on slavery and abolition in comparative perspective. His publications in this field include *Econocide: British Slavery in the Era of Abolition* (1977), *Capitalism and Antislavery: British Mobilization in Comparative Perspective* (1986), and *The Abolition of Slavery and the Aftermath of Emancipation in Brazil* (1988, with Rebecca Scott et al.).

PIETER C. EMMER is Professor of the History of European Expansion at the University of Leiden. His publications in English include the edited volumes *Reappraisals in Overseas History* (1979, with H. L. Wesseling) and *Colonialism and Migration: Indentured Labour Before and After Slavery* (1986).

STANLEY L. ENGERMAN is John H. Munro Professor of Economics and Professor of History at the University of Rochester and a Research Associate of the National Bureau of Economic Research. Among his many publications are: *Time on the Cross: The Economics of American Negro Slavery* (1974, with R. W. Fogel), *Between Slavery and Free Labor: The Spanish-Speaking Caribbean in the Nineteenth Century* (1985, co-edited with M. Moreno Fraginals and F. Moya Pons), and *The Atlantic Slave Trade* (1991, co-edited with J. E. Inikore).

PETER KOLCHIN is Professor of History at the University of Delaware. He is the author of *First Freedom: The Responses of Alabama's Blacks to Emancipation and Reconstruction* (1972) and of *Unfree Labor: American Slavery and Russian Serfdom* (1987), which won the Bancroft Prize in American History for 1988.

FRANK MCGLYNN is Associate Professor of Anthropology, University of Pittsburgh at Greensburg. He is the editor of *Health Care in Central America and the Caribbean* (1985), and co-editor of *Anthropological Approaches to Political Behavior* (1991, with Arthur Tuden). His research interests are in ethnohistory and the Caribbean.

JAY R. MANDLE is W. Bradford Wiley Professor of Economics at Colgate University. He is the author of *Not Slave, Not Free: The African American Economic Experience Since the Civil War* (1992) as well as numerous articles concerned with Caribbean economic history and development.

SIDNEY W. MINTZ is the William L. Straus, Jr., Professor of Anthropology at the Johns Hopkins University. He has carried out fieldwork in Puerto Rico, Jamaica, and Haiti. He is a co-author of *The People of Puerto Rico* (1956), and the author of *Worker in the Cane* (1960), *Caribbean Transformations* (1972), *Sweetness and Power* (1985), and *The Birth of Afro-American Culture* (1992, with R. Price).

RAYMOND T. SMITH is Professor of Anthropology at the University of Chicago. He has carried out field research in Guyana, Ghana, Jamaica, and Chicago, and is the author of various works including *Kinship and Class in the West Indies* (1988), and editor of *Kinship, Ideology, and Practice in Latin America* (1984).

MICHEL-ROLPH TROUILLOT is Professor of Anthropology at the Johns Hopkins University. Haitian-born, he has written a study of the beginnings of the Haitian Revolution, the first book-length monograph written in Haitian creole; *Peasants and Capital: Dominica in the World Economy* (1988); and *Haiti – State Against Nation: The Origins and Legacy of Duvalierism* (1990).

GAVIN WRIGHT is Professor of Economics at Stanford University. He is a specialist in American economic history and has published two books on the economy of the U.S. South: *The Political Economy of the Cotton South* (1978) and *Old South, New South: Revolutions in the Southern Economy since the Civil War* (1986). His current research interest is the historical origins of U.S. economic preeminence.

SUBJECT INDEX

Abolition, 3–5; and European expansion, 26; meaning of, 24; planters' view of, 25
Abolition Act (1833), 117–18
Abolitionists: free labor and, 62–63; hopes of, 23, 24–25, 33–34; and meaning of freedom, 143; and nature of blacks, 301; view of planters by, 29–30
Advance and truck systems, 123–24, 197–98
Affranchis, 148
Africa: Christianity in, 226–27; emancipation in, 26; immigration from, 132–33; influence of, 221–33, 250–51, 252, 271–72, 279–81
American Revolution, 24
Anciens libres, 160–65, 283. *See also* Mulattoes; Coloreds
Anglican Church, 136
Anglican Church Union, 229
Antigua, wage-rent system in, 120–21
Anti-Slavery Society, 118
Apprenticeship, 35, 51, 117–19, 148, 157, 245; in British Caribbean, 128; in Dutch Caribbean, 37; and own-account activities, 125–26
Ashanti, kinship system of, 200–01, 203
Asia, European expansion in, 26–27

Bahamas, 198, 207
Bailey decision (1912), 104
Baptists: declining influence of, 233–34; and free villages, 192–93, 226; and wage labor, 227
Baptist War (1831), 229
Barbados, 138, 248; free communities in, 196–97; prison costs in, 131; wage-rent system in, 121
Barbuda, 198, 204–07
Beaumont, Joseph (chief justice), 135
Belize, 123–24, 197–98; credit, 131

Bentinck Committee (1848), 119
"Biologizing," of social status, 264–65, 266–67
Black Codes, 90
Blacks: and autonomy, 142–43; and credit, 104; employment opportunities of, 74–75, 78–83; landownership by, 163; in Republican Party, 90. *See also* Freedmen
Boyer, Jean-Pierre (general), 162
Brazil: agriculture in, 56; coffee production in, 40–41, 88–89, 91; education in, 38; emancipation in, 295–96, 300
British Caribbean, 132–37; apprenticeship in, 128; credit and truck systems in, 123–24; freedom in, 143; labor in, 119–20, 127–28, 140; property rights in, 125; racism and imperialism in, 138; squatting in, 126–27; strikes in, 130; tax burden in, 131. *See also* Caribbean; Christianity; names of individual countries
British Guiana: emancipation in, 253–54, 295; free communities in, 193; landownership in, 127; masters and servants acts in, 131; peasantization in, 129; prison costs in, 131; slavery in, 252; strikes in, 129; sugar industry in, 248–49; tax increases in, 132
British West Indies: desire for land in, 187; emancipation in, 295, 300–02; intestacy in, 199–200; proto-peasantry in, 188–89, 190–91; provision grounds in, 185–86; sugar production in, 188
Brown Privilege Bill (Dominica), 156
Burial grounds, 203

Capitalism, 18, 115–17, 272
Caribbean: economic decline in, 42–43; education in, 38; emancipation in, 10, 70–71, 250; indentured labor

327

Trinidad, free communities in, 193–94, 295

U.S. Census Bureau, 78, 79, 80
U.S. South, 8, 32, 38, 59, 69, 282; agriculture in, 90–91; blacks in, 65–66, 72, 73 (table 1); coercion in, 81–82; development in, 93–96; education in, 107, 281–82, 304; kinship in, 274–75; landownership in, 93–96, 272, 297, 304; production declines in, 54–55; Reconstruction in, 89–93; segregation in, 106–08; sharecropping in, 9, 55, 61, 71, 73; small farms in, 94–95; Tragic Era in, 16–17, 291–308
U.S. North, 80–82

Venn Sugar Commission, 252
Volunteer Force (British Guiana), 135

Wage labor, 97–98, 124–25, 168, 227, 273; and capitalism, 115–17; in Jamaica, 234–35
Wage rent system, 120–22
Welfare, 7–8, 32, 36–37, 61, 67n5
Whites: and coloreds, 151, 154, 159; in Jamaica, 229; in U.S., 63, 73, 91–92, 107, 291–92
Women: and autonomy, 142–43; in labor force, 61, 236–37, 267–68, 278–79; and Pentecostalism, 237–40; in slave society, 275–78

Mexico Through Russian Eyes, 1806–1940
William Harrison Richardson

OTHER NATIONAL STUDIES
Black Labor on a White Canal: Panama, 1904–1981
Michael L. Conniff

The Catholic Church and Politics in Nicaragua and Costa Rica
Philip J. Williams

The Origins of the Peruvian Labor Movement, 1883–1919
Peter Blanchard

The Overthrow of Allende and the Politics of Chile, 1964–1976
Paul E. Sigmund

Peru and the International Monetary Fund
Thomas Scheetz

Primary Medical Care in Chile: Accessibility Under Military Rule
Joseph L. Scarpaci

Rebirth of the Paraguayan Republic: The First Colorado Era, 1878–1904
Harris G. Warren

Restructuring Domination: Industrialists and the State in Ecuador
Catherine M. Conaghan

A Revolution Aborted: The Lessons of Grenada
Jorge Heine, Editor

SOCIAL SECURITY
Ascent to Bankruptcy: Financing Social Security in Latin America
Carmelo Mesa-Lago

The Politics of Social Security in Brazil
James M. Malloy

Social Security in Latin America: Pressure Groups, Stratification, and Inequality
Carmelo Mesa-Lago

OTHER STUDIES
Adventurers and Proletarians: The Story of Migrants in Latin America
Magnus Mörner, with the collaboration of Harold Sims

Authoritarianism and Corporatism in Latin America
James M. Malloy, Editor

Authoritarians and Democrats: Regime Transition in Latin America
James M. Malloy and Mitchell A. Seligson, Editors

The Catholic Church and Politics in Nicaragua and Costa Rica
Philip J. Williams

Female and Male in Latin America: Essays
Ann Pescatello, Editor

Latin American Debt and the Adjustment Crisis
Rosemary Thorp and Laurence Whitehead, Editors

Perspectives on the Agro-Export Economy in Central America
Wim Pelupessy, Editor